# SCOTLAND

## FODOR'S TRAVEL GUIDES

are compiled, researched, and edited by an international team of travel writers, field correspondents, and editors. The series, which now almost covers the globe, was founded by Eugene Fodor in 1936.

### OFFICES
New York & London

**Fodor's Scotland:**

Area Editor: LESLIE GARDINER
Editorial Contributors: JOHN MAYOR, IRA MAYER, DAVID TENNANT
Editor: RICHARD MOORE
Assistant Editor: THOMAS CUSSANS
Maps: C. W. BACON, BRIAN STIMPSON
Drawings: LORRAINE CALAORA
Photographs: SCOTTISH TOURIST BOARD

# FODOR'S
# Scotland

Fodor's Travel Guides
New York

All the following Guides are current (most of them also in
the Hodder and Stoughton British edition.)

CURRENT FODOR'S COUNTRY AND AREA TITLES:

| | |
|---|---|
| AUSTRALIA, NEW ZEALAND AND SOUTH PACIFIC | ISRAEL |
| AUSTRIA | ITALY |
| BELGIUM AND LUXEMBOURG | JAPAN |
| | JORDAN AND HOLY LAND |
| BERMUDA | KENYA |
| BRAZIL | KOREA |
| CANADA | MEXICO |
| CARIBBEAN AND BAHAMAS | NORTH AFRICA |
| CENTRAL AMERICA | PEOPLE'S REPUBLIC OF CHINA |
| EASTERN EUROPE | |
| EGYPT | PORTUGAL |
| EUROPE | SCANDINAVIA |
| FRANCE | SCOTLAND |
| GERMANY | SOUTH AMERICA |
| GREAT BRITAIN | SOUTHEAST ASIA |
| GREECE | SOVIET UNION |
| HOLLAND | SPAIN |
| INDIA | SWITZERLAND |
| IRELAND | TURKEY |

CITY GUIDES:

| | |
|---|---|
| BEIJING, GUANGZHOU, SHANGHAI | ROME |
| CHICAGO | SAN DIEGO |
| LONDON | SAN FRANCISCO |
| LOS ANGELES | STOCKHOLM, COPENHAGEN, OSLO, HELSINKI, AND REYKJAVIK |
| MADRID | |
| MEXICO CITY AND ACAPULCO | TOKYO |
| NEW YORK CITY | WASHINGTON, D.C. |
| PARIS | |

FODOR'S BUDGET SERIES:

| | |
|---|---|
| BUDGET BRITAIN | BUDGET ITALY |
| BUDGET CANADA | BUDGET JAPAN |
| BUDGET CARIBBEAN | BUDGET MEXICO |
| BUDGET EUROPE | BUDGET SCANDINAVIA |
| BUDGET FRANCE | BUDGET SPAIN |
| BUDGET GERMANY | BUDGET TRAVEL IN AMERICA |
| BUDGET HAWAII | |

USA GUIDES:

| | |
|---|---|
| ALASKA | HAWAII |
| CAPE COD | NEW ENGLAND |
| COLORADO | PENNSYLVANIA |
| FAR WEST | SOUTH |
| FLORIDA | TEXAS |
| GRAND CANYON | USA (in one volume) |

# CONTENTS

vi CONTENTS

**SUPPLEMENTS**

# FOREWORD

It has taken us nearly fifty years to get around to adding Scotland to our series with a book all to itself. We are not entirely sure why. Scotland is a natural destination for the traveler of taste, the visitor with a well-developed sense of wonder. Not that it is entirely easy to come to realistic grips with Scotland—the country is so heavily disguised by a swirling reputation for high romance.

It is a reputation of fairly recent date, the result of a massive operation mounted by the powerful public-relations firm of Scott and Hanover—Sir Walter Scott and Queen Victoria. Scott began it by devising, virtually single-handed, a new and instantly successful appreciation of the violent and complex history of his native land. Victoria added her own infallible touch to the process by creating Balmorality and the tartanitis virus which, from her day down to the present, has infected untold millions.

We hope that we have managed in this Guide to hold a balance between fact and fantasy, while paying due respect to the fascination of the country's legends and lore—though, where Scotland is concerned, the border between reality and embroidery is sometimes hard to define.

A pair of simple, but very revealing, statistics are that Scotland is three-fifths the size of England (30,405 square miles against 50,333 square miles) but that it has a population of only just over five million—most of which is in the southern half of the country. Not only is Scotland justly known as one of the most beautiful countries on earth but, as these figures show, it also has great tracts which are virtually unpopulated. Indeed, it is still possible to discover places where, in all likelihood, yours will be the first human foot to tread. To find a country of such magnificent scenery and to be able to enjoy it in peace is increasingly rare these days.

The Scots are a friendly, welcoming people who have, by and large, managed to preserve a courtesy and warmth that may sometimes be lacking south of the border. Their understanding of the needs of tourism has noticeably sharpened over the last few years and standards of hotel accommodations and restaurant food have improved greatly. The Book-a-Bed-Ahead scheme to which we refer in *Facts at Your Fingertips* is just one of the enterprising ideas that are in full swing. It is a particularly valuable scheme, too, as it gives visitors a chance not only of staying in hotels but of trying the delights of bed-and-breakfast, of seeing how the Scots live and sampling their home fare.

While Scotland suffers the same drastic cutbacks in public transport that afflict the rest of Great Britain, it is still a country that can be explored to great advantage by bus and train—and, of course, by boat, since the coastal waters and the islands are linked by a spider's web of ferry routes. To explore this way needs a lot of planning, but if you are the kind of traveler to whom a railway timetable is more evocative than a book of poetry, then you are in for a wonderful time.

We would like to thank the many staff members of the Scottish Tourist Board who gave us invaluable help while we were compiling this book. We know that our readers will be greeted by the same enthusiasm that welcomed us when they visit one of the Board's offices.

Our chief debt, however, is to Leslie Gardiner, who has so cheerfully put his vast knowledge and sympathetic understanding of Scotland at our disposal.

All prices quoted in this Guide are based on those available to us at time of writing, late-1982. Given the volatility of current costs, it is inevitable that changes will have taken place by the time this book becomes available. We trust, therefore, that you will take prices quoted as indicators only, and will double-check to be sure of the latest figures.

We would like to stress that the hotel and restaurant listings in this Guide are *not exhaustive,* we do not profess to provide a complete listing for accommodations or for eating places. We select those we feel would interest our readers, and change that listing year by year, so as to include new establishments that we have found or exclude those we feel may not any longer be such as our readers would appreciate. We really do welcome letters, telling us of your experiences or correcting any errors that may have crept into the Guide. Such letters help us to improve our coverage, and also give us that essential "consumer's eye view," which is so helpful to all compilers of travel guides.

We would like to thank Peter McArthur and Co. of Hamilton for their considerable help in the matter of tartans.

Our addresses are:

**in the U.S.A.:** Fodor's Travel Guides, 2 Park Avenue, New York, N.Y. 10016.

**in Europe:** Fodor's Travel Guides (UK), 9-10 Market Place, London W.1.

# FACTS AT YOUR FINGERTIPS

 **SOURCES OF INFORMATION.** The principal source of information in North America on all aspects of travel, including tours and tour operators, to Scotland is the British Tourist Authority. Much of the information they are able to supply is free; all of it is to the point and well laid out. The B.T.A.'s addresses are:

**In the U.S.:** 680 Fifth Ave., New York, N.Y. 10019; 875 North Michigan Ave., Chicago, Ill. 60611; 612 South Flower St., Los Angeles, Ca. 90017; 1712 Commerce St., Dallas, Texas 75201.

**In Canada:** 151 Bloor St. West, Toronto 5, Ontario.

**In the U.K.:** 64 St. James's St., London S.W.1.

The Scottish Tourist Board also has an office in London at 5/6 Pall Mall East, London S.W.1. Their main office, however, is in Edinburgh at 23 Ravelston Terrace. While they will be happy to send out information, note that this office is *not* an information center.

Britain's nationwide network of Tourist Information Centres also covers Scotland. We list details of these centers in the Practical Information sections of our regional chapters. Most are open Monday–Friday, 9–5, with shorter hours on Saturday and Sunday and longer hours in midsummer. Some are open April to September only.

Scotland's biggest centers (called National Information Centres) are at Bannockburn, Edinburgh, Jedburgh, Prestwick Airport and Stranraer. There is also a National Information Centre at Southwaite (Cumbria) for the benefit of motorists approaching Scotland on the M6 motorway.

There are about 150 regional and local information centers sited strategically throughout the country. They bear the distinctive "i" sign and provide information about their own districts as well as operating accommodations services for their localities and, in most cases, a "book-a-bed-ahead" scheme for other districts. These centers are supported by a number of miscellaneous information offices run by organizations such as the Forestry Commission, the National Trust for Scotland and others; and by "tourist points"; kiosks or notice boards at viewpoints, picnic sites and the like.

 **TRAVEL AGENTS AND TOURS.** The range of tours to Europe is so immense, and the savings many represent over independent travel so significant, that it is well worth investigating those on offer. A reliable and efficient travel agent is a considerable advantage in this respect. Even those who prefer to travel independently may well find that at the very least a good agent is able to advise on the tangle that currently constitutes the air fares scene. But for those on a limited budget or who wish to combine a trip to Scotland with one to England, or perhaps elsewhere in Europe, or who are interested in the many special interest vacations on offer, there is little doubt that a good agent can save you time and money.

If you are uncertain about which agent to go to, the British Tourist Authority or Scottish Tourist Board will be able to point you in the right direction. Similarly, the American Society of Travel Agents, 711 Fifth Ave., New York, N.Y. 10022, and the British Association of Travel Agents, 53 Newman St., London W.1., can help.

Below we list some of the more popular and more unusual vacations available for Scotland.

**Tours from the U.S.** Most general interest tours to Scotland are part of packages concentrating on Great Britain as a whole and dividing time primarily between England, Scotland and Wales. Exceptions to the rule are the B.T.A.'s 9-day Royal Tartan and Cosmos' 7-day Windermere and The Best of Scotland. The B.T.A. tour is a medium-priced excursion that features two days and two nights in Edinburgh before taking off for the countryside. Prices begin at about $500 in the off-season.

The Cosmos tour is a 7-day trek that rolls rapidly through the countryside with tourist hotel stays in Oban, Strathpeffer, Thurso, Dornoch and Edinburgh. This is a bargain tour that hits all the highlights while utilizing accommodations that are out of the mainstream. London-to-London price is about $280 including most breakfasts and dinners.

(All prices quoted are per person, double occupancy and, as with the tours themselves, are representative of these companies' recent offerings. The same package may or may not still be available through 1983, but the firms cited have proven reliable in the past and are likely to have similar tours in the future.)

Most unique, for those who can afford the time and money, is Abercrombie & Kent International's The Castles and Palaces of Scotland. This self-driven tour (chauffeur-driven is also available at about double the price) makes its stops at mostly 15th-century castles such as Johnstounburn House in Edinburgh and Cromlix House in Fife. Land arrangements including car begin at $1,829 per person for a compact, standard transmission car; four times a year the tour is escorted by an Oxford or Cambridge graduate. Cost with escort: $3,676. Abercrombie & Kent International, Inc., 1000 Oak Brook Road, Oak Brook, Illinois 60521 (tel. 312–887 7766).

Maupintour's 8-day Edinburgh Festival tour, with its highlight on nightly entertainment, spends but five nights in that city—the remaining three in London. Land-only rate is about $1,000. Among other possibilities: Globus Gateway's 11-day tour of England, Wales and Scotland, spending about four days motorcoaching through Ayr, Inverness and Edinburgh, with fees roundtrip from London starting at about $600; Percival's 15-day British Heritage tour also spends four days in Scotland, with Glasgow, Aviemore and Edinburgh the stopovers. Land costs are about $1,100, with first class hotels all the way. All of these tours must be booked through travel agents.

For those with keen interest in golf, some tour operators will put together special itineraries. For example, Golf Group Tours, 1101 Vermont Ave. NW, Washington, D.C. 20005 (tel. 800–424 8895), will make specially designed links tours available to travel agents or groups. A typical 8-day jaunt would include 5–6 rounds of golf, with The Old Course, Turnberry and Gleneagles among the definite stops, and green and caddy fees along with the usual transportation, accommodations and meals (breakfasts and dinner). Cost of one recent such package was $985 for golfers and $795 for non-golfers, with sightseeing trips arranged for the non-golfers. The company will also tailor its tours to the specific tastes and requests of a group; a golf club, for example, wanting to play some of its more exclusive counterparts' courses.

Golf *and* fishing fans generally might wish to check the advertisements in specialty magazines—especially the classified ads—for listings of tour operators and individual guides living in Scotland but whose services can be contracted prior to your departure.

**U.S.-based tour operators** whose Great Britain packages take in Scotland include:

*American Express,* American Express Plaza, New York, N.Y. 10004.

*Barclay Travel Ltd.,* 261 Madison Ave., New York, N.Y. 10016.

*C.I.E.* (British Tourist Authority), 590 Fifth Ave., New York, N.Y. 10036.

*Cook's,* 380 Madison Ave., New York, N.Y. 10017.

*Cosmos,* P.O. Box 862, 69–15 Austin St., Forest Hills, N.Y. 11375.

*Globus-Gateway,* 105–14 Gerrard Pl., Forest Hills, N.Y. 11375.

*Maupintour,* 408 East 50th St., New York, N.Y. 10021.

**U.K.-based tour operators** offering special interest tours around Scotland include:

*Activity Travel,* 12 Raeburn Place, Edinburgh EH4 1HN. Pony-trekking, skiing, hill-walking, water sports, hang-gliding.

*Anglo-World Travel,* 30 Stafford Street, Edinburgh EH3 7BD. Bus and boat tours, Edinburgh-centered vacations.

*Anne Kennedy,* 2–3 Jamaica Mews, Edinburgh EH3 6HN. Youth and adult tours, hostel and economy accommodations, home-stay vacations.

*Capital Travel,* 146 Morrison Street, Edinburgh. Special interest and study tours, stately homes.

*Classique Luxury Coaches,* 8 Underwood Road, Paisley, Strathclyde. Vintage coach and steamer cruises, leisurely nostalgic tours.

*Core Leisure Travel,* 15 Bread Street, Edinburgh EH3 9AL. Inclusive "Discover Scotland" programs, bus tours and tailor-made vacations.

*Euro-Scot Travel,* 13 Newton Street, Kilbirnie, Strathclyde KA25 6HN. Specialized tours of distilleries, woollen and tartan mills, antiques, winter tours.

*Fairway Tours,* 9 Roseberry Place, Gullane, East Lothian EH31 2AN. Golf, shooting, fishing and sightseeing. Estate-car transport.

*Ghillie Personal Travel,* 64 Silverknowes Road East, Edinburgh EH4 5NY. Complete à la carte service by automobile or coach.

*Grampian Tours,* 27 St. John Street, Perth PH1 5SH. Bus and special interest tours, sporting, skiing, farming, heritage of Scotland.

*Highland Holidays* (Aberfeldy), Prospect House, Aberfeldy, Tayside. Hotel, guest-house, self-catering and bus tours from central Highlands.

*Ian Dickson Travel,* 50 Dundas Street, Edinburgh EH3 6JN. Industrial, study, sporting and special interests. Friendly and efficient travel agencies in several Lothian towns.

*Paton's Travel Services,* 5 Crown Street, Aberdeen. Custom-made itineraries, fishing and shooting in Grampian Region.

*Scotgame,* 28 Minto Street, Edinburgh EH9 1SB. Medium-priced shooting and deer-stalking vacations in Lowland areas.

*Sportina Travel,* 15 Napier Way, Cumbernauld, Strathclyde. Skiing, fishing, sea-angling, self-catering.

*Thomas Cook,* 9–11 Castle Street, Edinburgh EH2 3BD. Complete travel service for overseas visitors. Seven-day Highland bus tour from Edinburgh every Wednesday in summer.

*Tourist Promotion (Scotland),* 36 Castle Street, Edinburgh EH2 3BN. Luxury vacations in Scottish castles and country houses, Edinburgh Festival arrangements, cultural and genealogical tours.

*Travel Scotland,* 10 Rutland Square, Edinburgh EH1 2AE. Coach tours, shooting, deer-stalking, salmon-fishing, Hebridean cruises, self-drive or chauffeured automobiles.

**HANDICAPPED TRAVEL.** A growing number of travel agencies and societies for the disabled specialize in holidays for the handicapped. Generally their tours parallel those for the non-handicapped traveler, but at a more leisurely pace, with everything checked out in advance to eliminate all inconvenience, whether the traveler happens to be deaf, blind or in a wheelchair. For a complete list of tour operators who arrange such travel, write to the Society for the Advancement of Travel for the Handicapped, 26 Court St., Brooklyn, New York, 11242. An excellent source of information in this field is the book *Access to the World: A Travel Guide for the Handicapped,* by Louise Weiss, available from Facts on File, 460 Park Ave. S., New York, N.Y. 10016. This book covers travel by air, ship, train, bus, car and recreational vehicle; hotels and motels; travel agents and tour operators; destinations; access guides; health and medical problems; and travel organizations.

Another major source of help is the Travel Information Center, Moss Rehabilitation Hospital, 12th St. and Tabor Rd., Philadelphia, Penn. 19141. *Access Travel: Airports* is a brochure for listing design features, facilities, and services at 220 airports in 27 countries. For a copy, write to: Consumer Information Center, Pueblo, Colorado 81009. It is published by the US Dept. of Transportation. For an international directory of access guides, write to Rehabilitation International, 20 West 40th St., New York, N.Y. 10018.

In the U.K., the Royal Association for Disability and Rehabilitation (RADAR), 25 Mortimer St., London W.1. (tel. 01–637 5400), in addition to publishing its excellent handbook, *Holidays for the Physically Handicapped,* also acts as an information service. Within Scotland the best source of information is the Scottish Council on Disability, Princess House, 5 Shandwick Place, Edinburgh (tel. 031–229 8632). They produce an annually updated information list giving details of hotels, places of interest, transport facilities and the like that are suitable for the disabled. They also have a considerable number of contact addresses. Among their publications they produce an invaluable *Access to Public Conveniences* guide. The S.T.B. also produces two useful publications, *Holidays with Care* and *Guide for the Physically Handicapped.*

 **CLIMATE.** The Scottish climate has been much maligned; sometimes with justification. You can be unlucky: you may spend a summer week in Scotland and experience nothing but low cloud and drizzling rain. But, at the same time, you can be lucky: you may enjoy month-long spells of calm Mediterranean-like weather even in early spring and late fall.

Generally speaking, Scotland is three or four degrees cooler than southern England. The east is drier, and colder, than the west; Edinburgh's rainfall, for example, is comparable to Rome's, while rainfall in Glasgow is more like that in Vancouver—yet the cities are only 44 miles apart and both are at sea level.

All visitors comment on the long summer evenings, which grow longer still as you travel north. Dawn in Orkney and Shetland in June is at around 1 A.M., no more than an hour or so after sunset. The other side of this coin, though, are the very short winter days.

Scotland has few thunderstorms and little fog, except for local sea mists near coasts. But there are persistent variable winds which reach gale force even in summer. But they do at least blow away the hordes of gnats and midges (the curse of the western Highlands). On the subject of which, if you plan to visit the western Highlands, bring or buy a repellent.

The following are average temperatures for central Scotland in degrees Centigrade:

|  | Jan. | Feb. | Mar. | Apr. | May | Jun. | Jul. | Aug. | Sep. | Oct. | Nov. | Dec. |
|---|---|---|---|---|---|---|---|---|---|---|---|---|
| Daily temp. | 3 | 3 | 4.5 | 7 | 11 | 14.5 | 17 | 15.5 | 13 | 9.5 | 5 | 4 |
| Humidity | 85 | 82 | 79 | 75 | 73 | 73 | 73 | 75 | 80 | 85 | 86 | 86 |
| Days with rain | 11 | 13 | 14 | 13 | 14 | 15 | 16 | 15 | 12 | 14 | 13 | 13 |
| Sea temp. | 4.5 | 5 | 5 | 7 | 8 | 10 | 12 | 13.5 | 12.5 | 10.5 | 8 | 6 |

 **SPECIAL EVENTS.** The Scottish Tourist Board, 23 Ravelston Terrace, Edinburgh EH4 3EU, will send you on request a free calendar of *Events in Scotland* for the forthcoming year (it is usually available in November). Here we note the principal activities for each month without specifying precise dates since most of them change every year. In addition there are always one-off events—special celebrations and commemorations.

**January.** Glasgow, Ayr, Dumfries, Edinburgh and many other towns and villages: Burns Night dinners and entertainments; 25th.

Lerwick, Shetland: Up Helly Aa, ancient Viking festival; end of month.

**February.** Perth: Aberdeen-Angus Show, important cattle sales; early in month.

**March.** Perth: Ladies' World Curling Championships, the premier "roaring game" event; usually middle of month.

Glenshee: Snow Fun Week, games, competitions, apres-ski entertainment; middle of month.

Edinburgh: Edinburgh Folk Festival, an international event in city halls and clubs; end of month.

**April.** Ayr: Scottish Grand National, important horse race; usually second Saturday in month.

St. Andrews: Kate Kennedy procession, historic university pageant.

**May.** Various Borders towns: "Springtime in the Scottish Borders," series of weekend events including raft racing on Tweed, rally of agricultural steam engines, country fairs; from mid-May to mid-June.

Perth: Festival of the Arts, drama, music, painting and sculpture.

All areas: Historic Houses Festival, concerts, guided tours and lectures in various great houses; from early May to end June.

**June.** Hawick: Common Riding, historic patrolling of boundaries, general holiday in locality, first of several similar events in Borders towns; first week in month.

Selkirk: Common Riding; second week in month.

Galashiels: Braw Lads' Gathering, another form of Common Riding; end of month.

Dumfries: Guid Nychtburris, traditional festival; middle week of month.

Peebles: Beltane Festival, traditional observance of midsummer, of pagan origin; around 21st.

Kirkwall, Orkney: St. Magnus Festival, arts and music; mid-month.

Edinburgh: Royal Highland Show, principal agriculture, commerce and outdoor displays. At Ingliston showground, seven miles from city; third week in month.

Jedburgh: Jethart Callants Festival, traditional processions and entertainments; end of month.

**July.** Duns: Gala Week, civic celebrations, children's events.

Moffat: Gala Week.

Kelso: Gala Week. Also Border Union Show, large agricultural exhibition and horse racing; end of month.

Rothesay, Isle of Bute: Rothesay Fair, local festivities and games; middle of month.

**August.** Lauder: Common Riding.

Edinburgh: International Film Festival; last two weeks of month. Military Tattoo, colorful international regimental ceremonial; mid-month to early Sept. International Festival of Music, Drama and the Arts, famous annual *kulturfest;* mid-month to early Sept. Festival Fringe, a festival-within-the-festival for off-beat and avant-garde entertainments in and around the city; mid-month to early Sept.

Glamis: National Sheepdog Trials, big social occasion for farmers and shepherds; third week in month.

**September.** Arbroath: Abbey Pageant, historical drama; early in month.

Largs: Viking Festival, commemoration of battle of 1263; second week in month.

Oban: Sailing regatta; mid-month.

**October.** Various centers: Showcase, season of Scottish theater; all month.

Highland towns, in rotation annually: National Mod, Gaelic cultural assembly.

Oban: Highland Cattle Autumn Show; mid-month.

**November.** St. Andrews: International St. Andrew's Day Dinner; 30th.

**Highland Games.** The principal Highland Games and Gatherings are held in the following months, usually on Saturdays: **May,** Glasgow; **June,** Forfar, Aberdeen; **July,** Dundee, Kenmore, Inverness, Fort William, Inveraray, Strathyre; **August,** Aboyne, Brodick, Strathpeffer, Assynt, Crieff, Edinburgh, Glenfinnan, Birnam, Argyllshire (Oban), Cowal (Dunoon); **September,** Braemar.

 **WHAT TO TAKE.** Lightweight clothing is usually adequate in summer, but add a jacket, sweater or cardigan for evenings. A waterproof coat or parka (anorak) is essential. In Scotland casual clothes are *de rigueur* and you will find very few hotels or restaurants which insist on jackets and ties for men in the evenings. If you expect to attend some gala occasion (a premiere at the Edinburgh Festival for example) men should have a tuxedo, women an evening dress. Many visitors to Scotland appear to think it necessary to adopt a Scottish costume. It is not. Scots themselves do not wear tartan ties or Balmoral "bunnets" and only a diehard minority are addicted to the kilt.

Drip-dry and crease-resistant fabrics are a good bet. If you are touring, it is almost impossible to get any laundering or cleaning done, except in the most prestigious hotels.

The golden rule is to travel light; generally, try not to take more than you can carry yourself. Not only are porters more or less wholly extinct in Europe these days (and where you can find them they're very expensive anyway), the less luggage you take the easier checking in and out of hotels becomes, similarly airports (the number one nightmare of all modern travel) become much easier to get through and, if you only take one piece of luggage, the less risk there is of it being lost en route, and, in theory anyway, the less time you need to wait for it to appear when you get off the plane. It's an excellent idea also to make sure that your luggage is sturdy; there's no worse way to start or finish your vacation than by discovering that your clothes are generously distributing themselves along a station platform or, even worse, have already scattered themselves around the hold of a 747. It can also be a good idea to pack the bulk of your things in one large bag and put everything you need for overnight, or for two or three nights, in a smaller one, to obviate packing and repacking at brief stops.

 **TRAVELER'S CHECKS.** These are probably the safest and best way to carry money abroad. The best known are issued by American Express, Bank of America, Barclay's and Cook's, but there are a number of other brands as well. Most charge a small commission for issuing them. It's as well to keep a written record of the check numbers in a place other than that where you keep them, or give the numbers to a companion or friend. In the event the checks are lost or stolen this will greatly facilitate obtaining replacement checks.

**Credit Cards.** These are widely accepted in Scotland, though not in more rural areas. So keep a sharp look out for those little cards in the window, or you might find yourself in an embarrassing position. Some credit cards allow you to cash personal checks or draw cash; this can come in very handy as a back-up to your traveler's checks.

A point that should be watched with those useful pieces of plastic is the problem of the rate at which your purchase may be converted into your home currency. We have ourselves had two purchases made on the same day in the same place charged ultimately at two totally different rates of exchange. If you want to be certain of the rate at which you will pay, insist on the establishment entering the current rate onto your credit card charge at the time you sign it—this will prevent the management from holding your charge until a more favorable rate (to them) comes along, something which could cost you more dollars than you counted on. (On the other hand, should the dollar or pound be revalued upward before your charge is entered, you could gain a little.)

We would advise you, also, to check your monthly statement very carefully indeed against the counterfoils you got at the time of your purchase. It has become increasingly common for shops, hotels or restaurants to change the amounts on the original you signed, if they find they have made an error in the original bill. Sometimes, also, unscrupulous employees make this kind of change to their own advantage. The onus is on you to report the change to the credit card firm and insist on sorting the problem out.

 **TRAVEL DOCUMENTS. Passports for Americans.** Major post offices throughout the country are now authorized to process passport applications; check with your local post office for the nearest one. You may also apply in person at U.S. Passport Agency offices in various cities; addresses and phone numbers are available under governmental listings in the white or blue pages of local telephone directories. Applications are also accepted at most County Courthouses. Renewals can be handled by mail (form DSP-82) provided that your previous passport is not more than eight years old. New applicants will need:

1. A birth certificate or certified copy thereof or other proof of citizenship;
2. Two identical photographs 2 inches square, full face, black and white or color, on nonglossy paper, and taken within the past six months;
3. $35;
4. Proof of identity, such as a driver's license, employment ID card, copy of an income tax return, previous passport, governmental ID card. Social Security and credit cards are *not* acceptable.

U.S. passports are valid for 10 years and are not renewable. You should allow a month to six weeks for your application to be processed, but in an emergency, Passport Agency offices can have a passport readied within 24–48 hours, and even the postal authorities can indicate "Rush" when necessary.

If you expect to travel extensively, request a 48- or 96-page passport rather than the usual 24-page one. There is no extra charge. Record your passport's number and date and place of issue in a separate, secure place. When you have pictures taken for passports, have extra copies made, especially if you plan to travel extensively. The loss of a valid passport should be reported immediately to the local police and to the Passport Office, Dept. of State, Washington, D.C. 20524 or to the nearest U.S. consular office when abroad.

**Passports for Canadians.** Canadian citizens may obtain application forms for passports at any post office; these are to be sent to the Canadian Passport Office, Department of External Affairs, 40 Bank St., Ottawa, with a remittance of $20, two photographs, and evidence of Canadian citizenship. You may apply in person to the regional passport offices in Edmonton, Halifax, Montreal, Toronto, Vancouver or Winnipeg. Canadian passports are valid for five years and are non-renewable.

**Visas.** Americans, Canadians, citizens of EEC countries and most Commonwealth countries do not require visas to enter Scotland or any other part of the U.K. Similarly, if entering Scotland from elsewhere in the U.K., there are no immigration or customs formalities.

 **VACATION TRAVEL INSURANCE.** Generally speaking, you can insure yourself and your family, your baggage, and your travel expenses. There are policies that cover loss of life or limb and disability (unless they are the result of suicide, war, or military maneuvers) up to a limit, usually $200,000.

More recently companies such as MediCall (c/o The Siesel Company, Inc., 845 Third Avenue, New York, N.Y. 10022); Assist-Card (745 Fifth Avenue, New York, N.Y. 10022); and International Underwriters (7653 Leesburg Pike, Falls Church, Va. 22043) have begun to offer actual medical assistance to the traveler through networks of affiliated doctors. Rates vary but are relatively inexpensive ($25 for a single trip, $298 for a year.

Baggage and personal possessions can be insured up to $2,000 against loss or damage anywhere in the world. Usually covered are clothing, luggage, jewelry, cameras and recreation equipment. However, a long list of things not insured includes animals, cars and other vehicles (except bicycles), cash and securities, business and professional papers and property, artificial teeth and limbs, household effects; loss due to government seizure; and damage from war, vermin, normal wear and tear, illegal acts and nuclear contamination.

Trip cancellation insurance, up to about $5,000, covers the nonrefundable parts of your transportation and hotel expenses that you may lose from having to cancel because of death, illness, injury or complications of pregnancy either before you leave or while traveling, except in case of suicide, war, or illegal activity (smuggling, for example). Here again, "family" always includes your spouse and children, and *may* extend to siblings, in-laws and other generations.

Specific conditions, coverage and limitations vary so much from one company to another and one policy to another that it is impossible to describe them all here. Premiums vary even more. So far, travel insurance has not had the benefit of the kind of standardization-plus-comparison-shoppers' guide that occurred a few years ago in Pennsylvania for life insurance. You just have to ask one or several travel and/or insurance agents and try to find a good deal for yourself.

**TIME.** Scotland operates on Greenwich Mean Time (G.M.T.), which is five hours ahead of (later on the clock than) Eastern Standard Time. From March to October, in common with the rest of the U.K., Scotland switches to British Summer Time, which is five hours ahead of Eastern Standard Time.

**GETTING TO SCOTLAND FROM NORTH AMERICA. By air.** Air services to Scotland from North America are extensive and regular. International flights go to Prestwick Airport, Glasgow, about 30 miles from the city center. (Don't confuse it with Abbotsinch airport, eight miles from the city, which is used for domestic and European flights.) Among airlines currently flying to Scotland are Northwest Orient (from Minneapolis, Boston and Newark), Air Florida (from Miami), Air Canada (from Halifax, Toronto, Winnipeg, Calgary, Edmonton and Vancouver), CP Air (from Toronto and Vancouver) and Wardair (from Toronto, Calgary and Vancouver). If no direct flight to Scotland is available, your best bet is to fly via London (either Heathrow or Gatwick), from where there are regular flights to both Glasgow and Edinburgh, as well as to many other Scottish cities. See below for details.

Anyone venturing alone and unarmed into the maelstrom that is the current North Atlantic air fares scene is not to be envied. Following the intense, near suicidal, rivalry among airlines flying to Europe over the last few years and the sad decline of Laker, prices for 1983 will be a good bit higher than they were, say, in 1981. But at the same time, this bad news is offset by the host of special deals and discounts that have since become available. However, they are nothing if not complicated, not to say bewildering, in structure, depending on factors such as when you fly, how long you stay, how many people you fly with and so forth. Your best bet therefore is to get a reputable travel agent to explain what is available and what is best suited to your needs. Remember that there is nothing as frustrating as discovering that the person next to you on the plane has paid less for an identical seat. It may sound improbable, but it can and does happen with remarkable frequency.

**By boat.** Sad to say, there are no passenger services between North America and Scotland. The only regular sailings over the Atlantic are on the *QE2,* and even these are summer only and go to England (Southampton) rather than Scotland. At around $1,000 one way for the least expensive cabin plus the added expense of subsequently making your way to Scotland, it is a pricey way to travel.

However, you can still sail to Scotland on a freighter, though their numbers are somewhat diminished these days with the advent of bulk-carriers and container ships. This scarcity combined with the fact that most carry only 12 passengers requires that you book a very considerable time in advance. This can be as long as a year. Costs are also rather higher than even Economy class flights. But if you wish to know more about freighter trips, contact the following organizations:

Ford's Freighter Travel Guide, P.O. Box 505, 22151 Clarendon St., Woodland Hills, Ca. 91365; Freighter Travel, c/o Harian Publications, P.O. Box 404, New York, N.Y. 10019; Freighter Travel Service, 201 East 77th Street, New York, N.Y. 10021; Pearl's Freighter Tips, 175 Great Neck Rd., Great Neck, N.Y. 11021; TravLtips Freighter Travel Assn., Box 933, Farmingdale, N.Y. 11737.

**GETTING TO SCOTLAND FROM ENGLAND AND WALES. By air.** There is a virtual air bridge between London (Heathrow) and Scotland, with 10 to 12 flights daily to Glasgow and eight to Edinburgh. These are shuttle services requiring no advance booking and guaranteeing you a seat. You buy your ticket either at the desk or on the plane. Flying time is one hour. All flights are operated by British Airways. Midland Airways also have four flights a day to both Glasgow and Edinburgh. Tickets for these can be booked in advance. From Gatwick, British Caledonian have several flights daily to Glasgow and Edinburgh; these too may be booked in advance.

There are also frequent flights from London to Aberdeen and Inverness, and to Glasgow and Edinburgh from Birmingham, Manchester, Newcastle, East Midlands, Leeds/Bradford, Newcastle and Cardiff/Bristol.

**By train.** There are two main routes from England to Scotland, the east coast route from London (King's Cross) via Doncaster, York and Newcastle to Edinburgh, and the west coast route which runs from London (Euston) via Rugby, Crewe, Preston, Carlisle and Motherwell to Glasgow (Central). There are trains virtually every hour from 8 A.M. to 6 P.M. and all trains have 1st. and 2nd. class carriages plus dining or buffet cars. Journey times are between five and six hours. There are also overnight services on both routes, again with 1st. and 2nd. class carriages; these take an hour or so longer than the day time services. You can stay in your compartment till 7.30 if your train arrives earlier.

There are also a number of special services from London. The best known is the Flying Scotsman, which leaves King's Cross at 10.35 in the morning, arriving at Edinburgh at 3.10 in the afternoon, stopping only at Newcastle. Another is the Aberdonian, which leaves King's Cross at 10 and arrives at Aberdeen at 5.20. There is also a through service from Euston to Inverness, departing at 9.35 and arriving at 8.15 in the evening, calling at Birmingham, Crewe, Preston, Carlisle, Motherwell, Sterling and Perth; this is the Clansman. There is another Euston–Inverness train, the Royal Highlander, which leaves London at 9.55 P.M. and gets into Inverness at 8.55 the following morning.

A good inexpensive overnight train is that between King's Cross and Edinburgh, continuing on to Falkirk, Dundee and Aberdeen. One section also goes to Glasgow (Queen Street) from Edinburgh. There are no sleeping cars on this service.

Trains from elsewhere in England are good; there are regular services from Birmingham, Manchester, Liverpool and Bristol to Glasgow and Edinburgh. There are also overnight trains from Bristol and Birmingham with sleeping cars.

Train fares vary according to the type of ticket purchased as well as class. Many fares are under review at the time of writing (late-1982), so for details contact any British Rail Travel Centre, main line station or rail ticket agency. Ask for full information on all tickets; there can be considerable savings if you choose the right one.

Two good, all-purpose rail tickets, excellent value for anyone who plans to do a lot of rail travel in the U.K., are the All Line Railrover ticket and the Britrailpass. The former is good for 14 and 17 days respectively and costs £100 and £160 for 2nd. class and £150 and £230 for 1st. class. There are no restrictions on availability. The ticket can only be bought in the U.K. The Britrailpass, on the other hand, is available only in North America and cannot be bought by U.K. residents. It is valid for periods of 7, 14, 21 and 30 days and costs $130, $158, $195 and $230 respectively. There is also a Britrail Youth Pass (available only to those between 14 and 22). This is valid for the same periods as the main card and costs $90, $146, $168 and $208 respectively.

Note that the Eurailpass and Eurail Youth Pass are *not* valid for the U.K.

For full information on these passes (costs are subject to change) in North America apply to BritRail Travel International 630 Third Avenue, New York, N.Y. 10017; or 510 West Sixth St., Los Angeles, Calif. 90014; or 333 North Michigan Ave., Chicago, Ill. 60601; or U.K. Building, 409 Granville St., Vancouver 2, B.C. or 55 Eglinton Ave. East, Toronto 4, Ont.

**By bus.** Bus travel between England and Scotland, particularly from London, has expanded enormously of late. Standards of time-keeping and comfort have risen appreciably (videos and on-board refreshments are very much the norm these days), while fares, especially in comparison to those for trains, are low, helping to offset the principal disadvantage of bus travel, its relative slowness. Though at eight hours from London to Glasgow or Edinburgh as opposed to five plus on the train, this is considerably less of a drawback than it used to be.

A number of companies operate services to Scotland. Scottish Omnibuses have a year-round express bus service between London and Glasgow, Edinburgh and Aberdeen with stop-over and pick up points in Scotland. In summer, they have both night time and day time services. For details, contact the Scottish Coach Travel Centre, 298 Regent St., London W.1., tel. 01–580 4708 or 636 9373.

Cotters Tours also operate an express service to Glasgow and Edinburgh with on-board couriers. They also run both day and night services. Details from Cotters Tours Ltd., 1 Norris St., London S.W.1., tel. 01–930 5781.

There are regular services, also mainly to Glasgow and Edinburgh, from Manchester, Liverpool, Birmingham, Leeds, Middlesbrough and Newcastle. Most travel agents can supply details of these services, as can all bus stations in cities and main towns.

**CUSTOMS.** Entering Scotland from any other part of the U.K., you will face no customs formalities. But anyone coming from Northern Ireland may face a security check. Otherwise, there are two levels of duty free allowance for people entering the U.K.; one, for goods bought outside the EEC or for goods bought in a duty free shop within the EEC; two, for goods bought in an EEC country but not in a duty free shop.

In the first category you may import duty free: 200 cigarettes or 100 cigarillos or 50 cigars or 250 grammes of tobacco (*Note* if you live outside Europe, these allowances are doubled); plus one liter of alcoholic drinks over 22% vol. (38.8% proof) or two liters of alcoholic drinks not over 22% vol. or fortified or sparkling wine; plus two liters of still table wine; plus 50 grammes of perfume; plus nine fluid ounces of toilet water; plus other goods to the value of £28.

In the second category you may import duty free: 300 cigarettes or 150 cigarillos or 75 cigars or 400 grammes of tobacco; plus 1½ liters of alcoholic drinks over 22% vol. (38.8% proof) or three liters of alcoholic drinks not over 22% vol. or fortified or sparkling wine; plus four liters of still table wine; plus 75 grammes of perfume; plus 13 fluid ounces of toilet water; plus other goods to the value of £120 (*Note* though it is not classified as an alcoholic drink by EEC countries for Customs' purposes and is thus considered part of the "other goods" allowance, you may not import more than 50 liters of beer).

In addition, no animals or pets of any kind may be brought into the U.K. The penalties for doing so are severe and are strictly enforced; there are *no* exceptions. Similarly, fresh meats, plants and vegetables, controlled drugs and firearms and ammunition may not be brought into the U.K. There are no restrictions on the import or export of British and foreign currencies.

Anyone planning to stay in the U.K. for more than six months should contact H.M. Customs and Excise, Kent House, Upper Ground, London S.E.1 (tel. 01–928 0533) for further information.

**DUTY FREE** is not what it once was. You may not be paying tax on your bottle of whiskey or perfume, but you are certainly contributing to somebody's profits. Duty free shops are big business these days and mark ups are often around 100 to 200%. So don't be seduced by the idea that because it's duty free it's a bargain. Very often prices are not much different from your local discount store and in the case of perfume or jewelry they can be even higher.

As a general rule of thumb, duty free stores on the ground offer better value than buying in the air. Also, if you buy duty free goods on a plane, remember that the range is likely to be limited and that if you are paying in a currency different from that of the airline, their rate of exchange often bears only a passing resemblance to the official one.

**MONEY.** Britain's currency is the pound sterling, which is divided into 100 pence (100p). Notes are issued to the values of £50, £20, £10, £5 and £1 (though the £1 note will be superseded by a £1 coin in 1983). Coins are issued to the values of 50p, 20p, 10p, 5p, 1p and ½p. Scottish coins are the same as English but Scottish notes are issued by three banks: the Bank of Scotland, the Royal Bank of Scotland and the Clydesdale Bank. They have the same face values as English notes, and English notes are interchangeable with them in Scotland. However, though they are perfectly legal in England, you may find that many people, particularly in the south, are reluctant to accept them. So do not carry too many away from Scotland with you.

Banks are closed on Saturdays, Sundays and public holidays. Their weekday opening hours are 9.30 to 3.30 and most of them close for an hour at lunchtime. The larger travel agents, the more expensive hotels, the biggest multiple stores and the independent *bureaux de change* in the cities will change money for you and cash checks. But it is best to compare the rates they offer and the commissions they charge: they do vary. Banks offer the best deal. The major airports operate 24-hour banking services.

At the time of writing (late 1982) the exchange rate for the pound was $1.60. However, this will certainly change during 1983, probably unpredictably, and it is as well to watch rates carefully to get the best value for your dollar.

**HOTELS.** It used to be the case that Scottish hotels were considered either rather better or much worse than their English counterparts; the good ones were very good, and the bad ones very bad. But these distinctions have mostly been ironed out nowadays. The really grand, rather aggressively Scottish hotels built about 100 years ago to cater for the well-heeled deer stalker and grouse shooter now belong to national or multi-national chains such as Trusthouse Forte, Reo-Stakis, Grand Metropolitan, Holiday Inn and others. Similarly, Dutch and Belgian consortia have bought into country house hotels and deer stalking syndicates. And among other recent successful developments are conversions of lonely but elegant shooting lodges into exclusive hotels and restaurants.

The once reviled inexpensive Scottish hotel, meanwhile, is now at least the equal of anything that might be found in England. To a large extent, this is the result of the Scottish Tourist Board's encouragement of the improvement of existing hotels as opposed to the indiscriminate building of new ones. In many small towns and villages there are excellent value inns and hotels offering reasonable comfort (central heating, rooms with bath or shower and telephone and television) at competitive prices. But rural Scotland is also bed-and-breakfast land, and, as Scottish breakfasts are usually nothing if not hearty, these are pretty good value. Indeed, for anyone planning to tour Scotland they can be hard to beat, especially as most offer genuinely warm hospitality as well as home cooking and comforts. The Scottish Tourist Board's *Scotland—Where to Stay* (price £1.30) and *Where to Stay Bed and Breakfast* (price £1) together give details of more than 4,000 bed and breakfasts.

Hotels in the larger cities are generally also good. Glasgow and Edinburgh boast a number of very superior hotels as well as an extensive range of good hotels in all other prices categories. Both have active and helpful accommodations offices should you arrive without reservations (see *Facts at Your Fingertips* for both cities for details).

Bookings are generally easy to make as, in recent years, even in the height of the season—July and August—only some 80% of all available accommodations have been booked. So if you are touring around you are not likely to be stranded. (There are some exceptions, however. If you arrive in some small place to find a Highland Gathering or big golf tournament in progress, accommodations will be at a premium for miles around.) Nonetheless, it is best to make reservations in advance either through a travel agent at home or in England, or from one of the many STB booklets listing accommodations when you arrive in Scotland and have decided what your programme will be. Telephone bookings should be confirmed by letter and country hotels expect you to turn up by about 6 P.M. You can also make reservations through local Information Centres (which we list in the Practical Information sections of our regional chapters) making use of their "Book-a-Bed-Ahead" facilities. Grand Metropolitan Hotels Ltd., 119 West 57th St., N.Y. (tel. 212–757 2944), Bank Hotels Ltd, 444 Madison Ave., N.Y. (tel. 212–421 2353) and Trusthouse Forte Hotels Inc., 810 7th Ave., N.Y. (tel. 800–442 5886) can reserve accommodations for you in Scotland and for your onward trip in Britain and Europe in one of their hotels.

We have graded hotels and guest-houses solely according to the price you will pay; Deluxe, Expensive, Moderate and Inexpensive—denoted (L), (E), (M) and (I) in our regional listings. "City" means Edinburgh, Glasgow and Aberdeen.

| Category | City | Town & Country |
|---|---|---|
| (L) Single, per night | £42+ | £36+ |
| Double | £60+ | £48+ |
| **(E)** | | |
| Single | £25–£41 | £21–£35 |
| Double | £35–£59 | £33–£47 |
| **(M)** | | |
| Single | £16–£24 | £14–£20 |
| Double | £22–£34 | £19–£32 |
| **(I)** | | |
| Single | under £16 | under £14 |
| Double | under £22 | under £19 |

**Budget Tip.** The vacation scene in Scotland is changing. The Briton's traditional two-week summer vacation is giving way to shorter, more frequent breaks. Many hotels now offer three-day, midweek and off-season tourist packages at favorable inclusive rates. British Rail, the bus companies and ferry boat operators are into this business too. This is an aspect of Scottish tourism worth investigating. All British travel agents can help you seek out the bargains.

**Self-catering.** The STB publishes *Self-Catering Accommodation in Scotland,* price £1, a list of 2,000 places for do-it-yourself accommodations—furnished rooms, shepherds' and gamekeepers' cottages, chalets, caravans on fixed sites and so on. Many country cottages have been brought into tourist-renting schemes and some farmers and estate-owners have converted or custom built their own high class and low class lodges and log cabins for vacation use. As you tour Scotland you will see groups of log cabins in picturesque situations: forest or lochside refuges rented for self-catering, usually centered on a large house which is shop, laundry and social center for the vacationists.

In 1983 the well-known British firm Canvas Holidays (noted for its success in taking the hassle out of Continental camping and in launching the do-as-you-please Car Holidays Abroad) is operating some superior log cabin sites in the Lowlands, Highlands and islands through its subsidiary *Cabin Holidays,* Bull Plain, Hertford SG14 1DY, England.

If you like the idea of a "Highland home of your own," at least for a week or so, try to get advice from a local tourist office or from the STB if you cannot preview the property you have chosen. Some places are distinctly primitive and remote; while some, on the other hand, are particularly suitable for the elderly or disabled. Rates vary enormously, from £35 a week low season to £350 high season. *Scottish Highland Holiday Homes,* 26 Station Road, Inverness IV1 1LE offers mansions and shooting lodges for up to £550 per week! The *National Trust for Scotland* has a few historic apartments and houses, in town and country, available for short- or long-term renting at from £40 to £155 per week. The address is 5 Charlotte Square, Edinburgh EH2 4DU.

**University Accommodations.** Universities and colleges of education in Edinburgh, Glasgow, Aberdeen and Dundee have accommodations to rent in their students' halls of residence during vacations, usually end-June to end-September but in some cases all year round. The normal arrangement is about five single (occasionally double) rooms centered on a kitchen, bathroom and lavatory. Some halls of residence provide a full meal service, others bed and breakfast, others cooking facilities and room. Daily rates may be as low as £9.50 inclusive. Details are in the STB booklet *Scotland—Where to Stay.*

**Youth Hostels.** Youth Hostel membership cards are accepted at all British hostels and intending members may join at any hostel or, in Scotland, by contacting the Scottish Youth Hostels Association, 161 Warrender Park Road, Edinburgh EH9. Hostels are closed during the day and available for stays of one, two or three nights. Everyone has to lend a hand with cooking and cleaning— one reason why daily charges are low, ranging from £1.85–£2.45 (depending on age) at the top-category Scottish hostels to £1–£1.40 at the lowest; per person per night. The upper age-limit is 25.

For information and membership applications in North America, write to American Youth Hostels Inc., 1332 Eye Street N.W., 8th Floor, Washington D.C. 20005; or Canadian Youth Hostels Association, National Office, 333 River Road, Vanier City, Ottawa, Ont.

**Camping.** The Camping Club of Great Britain has a major site on the A1 at Barns Ness (tel. Dunbar 63536), about 25 miles north of Berwick-on-Tweed. The Caravan Club also has sites on or near this highway, strategically placed for first arrivals in Scotland, at Gosford Park (tel. Aberlady 487) and Yellowcraigs (tel. Dirleton 217). Information about Scotland's other sites may be obtained here or from the Warden, Caravan Site, Muirhouse, Edinburgh (tel.

336 6874). Campers and caravanners are well catered for by the local authorities all over Scotland, especially in the Loch Lomond and Clyde coast areas: local telephone directories give addresses and numbers of sites. Outside the official sites, few landowners will object if you ask permission to park a caravan or pitch a tent; except that is, in the deer-stalking country of the Highlands and on the grouse moors, where even the sight of an automobile parked a few yards off the main road reduces ghillies and gamekeepers to apoplexy.

 **RESTAURANTS.** Scotland is more of a home-cooking, home-baking country than most. Ideas of café society or family meals in restaurants are alien to the Scots. In Glasgow and Edinburgh there are one or two expensive old-established restaurants where you may eat a gourmet meal and dance in the evenings; in Aberdeen one or two expensive new ones where you may even see a floor show. But apart from these (which are not really expensive by, say, London standards) the best restaurants are of a relatively modest standard and are usually attached to the grand hotels in town and country.

In recent years many of Scotland's multitudinous pubs (around 260 in Glasgow's central square mile alone!) have smartened themselves up and diversified into basket-meal, bar-lunch, shepherd's-supper and similar services. Such meals are generally inexpensive, with generous portions: a good bet for the passing traveler. Scottish pubs, however, tend to be small, crowded and noisy with conversation.

In cities and towns the department stores and bakery shops often have their own cafés and restaurants (not always allowed to supply alcohol) and, while the food may be generally unimaginative, the places themselves are clean and cheap. High streets (main streets) abound with snackeries and coffee bars: some good, some quite disgusting. Country villages go in a lot for old-fashioned tea-rooms with waitress service: usually very good value.

Non-Scottish restaurants are on the increase. In Glasgow and Edinburgh, Italian restaurants, French bistros, American-style hamburger joints, Indian and Pakistani restaurants, spaghetti houses and other Continental-flavored establishments from Norwegian to Turkish threaten to overwhelm the stuffy, solid native equivalents. Even in the lonely places of the far north you will see "tandoori" and "to go" signs. Scots, rather surprisingly, have become enthusiastic patrons of such exotic eating-houses.

Lunchtime in certain country towns, especially in the twinset country (see "Borders" chapter), is 12.00 to 1.00 P.M. If you arrive for lunch around one o'clock you may find the restaurants closed and the shops and banks open again. The normal lunch period, however, is 12.30–2.30. The evening meal in many provincial establishments is "high tea"–a substantial feast of one hot dish and masses of cakes, scones, shortbreads, oatcakes, bread and butter and jam, served with tea only around 5.30–6.30. In more sophisticated hotels and restaurants the international dinner hour, 8 P.M. onward, is observed.

You will come across restaurants which offer "A Taste of Scotland"—traditional dishes with peculiar names, often cooked and served in traditional pots and pans. The Taste of Scotland scheme, initiated by the STB, enables the Scots to play their favorite game of bewildering strangers with outlandish words.

The restaurants listed at the end of each of our Regional chapters—and they are only a selection, not necessarily the best or worst in the Region—are categorized (L), (E), (M) and (I) according to the prices they charge for a full meal for *two* persons, including a bottle of wine, VAT and service charges.

(L) £50+; (E) £30–£50; (M) £18–£30; (I) under £18

At an unpretentious main street department-store or roadside cafe you will pay about £3 per head for lunch, at a selfservice snack bar or restaurant rather less. Motorway cafes have a poor reputation in Britain but those along the Scottish motorways are new and for the present generally tidy and good value for money.

House wine in a restaurant will cost you around 40p a glass, a pint of beer up to 75p, whisky, gin or vodka 65p–75p. Coffee for two adds about £1 to your bill. Water is supplied free on request: iced water is almost unheard-of. Post-prandial liqueurs from 80p.

 **DRINKING.** The Scot's staple drink is tea, but coffee (of variable quality) is always available. In another sense the staple drink is whisky (note spelling—only the Irish variety is called "whiskey"); but it is worth remembering that some towns of the central belt built their prosperity on brewing and that Scots ale and lager is sold all over Britain. "Hawf and hawf "—a dram of whisky and a half-pint of beer—is the Glasgow tipple, a somewhat lethal one. Many pubs, formerly ultra-dour and men-only, now sell wine by the glass. We deal more fully with whisky in our Grampian Region chapter.

Once more tightly controlled than anywhere else in Britain, drinking in Scotland is quite promiscuous. Long after English pubs have closed for the afternoon the tills are ringing merrily in Scotland. Subject to a local licensing authority's approval, rarely withheld, the publican may sell liquor from 11 A.M. to 11 P.M.

The nearest things to liquor stores in Scotland are the "licensed grocers." They too, like the wine merchants, may sell bottles all day long.

 **TIPPING.** The Scots themselves are not over-generous tippers and most have no great expectations of tips. The barber, the waitress, even the taxi-driver will normally regard your tip as a pleasant bonus—a very different situation from that which seems to involve so much aggression and ill-feeling in England and other countries. But there are now, of course, a good many non-Scots in the hotels and restaurant business to which the general Scottish attitude does not apply.

After a meal ask, or see from your bill, whether a charge has been made for Service as well as for VAT (Value Added Tax). If it has not, a tip of not less than 10% is appropriate.

 **MUSEUMS, HOUSES, AND GARDENS.** In the Practical Information sections at the end of each regional chapter you will find details of museums, galleries, houses, castles and gardens in each area. Check opening times if possible: they do occasionally vary.

A comprehensive catalogue of museums and galleries all over Scotland is published annually by the *Scottish Tourist Board*. It is called *Museums & Galleries* and costs £1.70 by post from the STB or £1.50 from information offices, bookshops and stationers.

Many historic Scottish castles and houses—not to mention islands, stretches of coastline, gardens, cottages and waterfalls—are in the care of the National Trust for Scotland. An annual membership fee of £7.50 (£12 for a family), with reductions for the young or the elderly, entitles you to visit most properties free. Application forms from the NTS at 5, Charlotte Square, Edinburgh EH2 4DU. But entrance charges to houses and museums in Scotland are so small, and often non-existent, that the membership is of value only to the most dedicated stately-homes buffs.

A most agreeable organization called Scotland's Gardens Scheme operates from 26 Castle Terrace, Edinburgh EH1 2EL. Through its activities several hundred gardens, from the most elaborate and formal to the most quaint and wild, are periodically open to the public. A nominal admission charge covers owners' expenses and leaves a little over for charity. Teas are usually provided and tours of the house or some village-fête-like entertainment offered. The booklet *Scotland's Gardens* is available from the above address, price 60p or 90p including postage in the U.K., with details of openings for the current year. Opening times are also published week by week in the following Scottish newspapers: *Glasgow Herald, Scotsman, Edinburgh Evening News, Dundee Courier* and *Aberdeen Press & Journal.* They normally appear on Fridays, since most gardens open on Saturdays or Sundays. Where gardens are open in the locality you happen to be in, you will see yellow posters in shop windows, advertising the fact.

 **LANGUAGE.** "Much," said Doctor Johnson (who else?), "much may be made of a Scotchman *if he be caught young.*" Some middle-class and professional Scots take this remark to heart and send their sons, rarely their daughters, to English boarding schools or to those boarding schools in Scotland—Fettes, Loretto, Glenalmond—which are modelled on English lines. They, when they grow up, are Scots who speak with English accents.

The vast majority of Scots speak English with regional accents, lilting or harsh, sometimes impenetrable, attractive or irritating according to the listener's taste. If your ear is attuned to southern English speech you may find it a problem to switch to the wavelength of the Borderer or the Glaswegian. If the Scots who live nearest to England murder the language like that, what can we expect from the Highlanders? But as you journey north, accents grow smoother. Around Inverness the natives speak a clear soft English, purer than you will hear anywhere else in the British Isles. It was a language imposed on them by the English of 200-odd years ago, when the tongue was more refined.

English is understood all over Scotland but in the northwest Highlands and some of the islands the common speech is Gaelic, a variant of the old languages of Ireland and Wales. Gaelic speakers diminish year by year—there are fewer than 100,000 now—in spite of the strenuous propagandizing of language societies. Its structure is archaic and rigid, not adaptable to modern times. Critics point out that Scottish Gaelic has no written literature nor a book of grammar universally accepted and that Gaelic speakers from different districts find it hard to understand each other.

 **SHOPPING.** Shops are usually open 9–5 or 9–5.30; in country districts from 8.30; in Highland villages whenever the shopkeeper feels like it. Most shops close one afternoon per week, either Tuesday, Wednesday or Thursday; large stores in cities close on Saturdays after lunchtime. Every Scottish town has a "local" holiday on Monday two or three times a year and a "trades holiday" (which affects some shops) for two weeks in midsummer: the dates vary from place to place. On January 1 and 2 the Scots recuperate from Hogmanay (New Year) and these are blank days in the calendar for virtually everyone.

The best buys in Britain in general are antiques, craft items, woollen goods, china, men's shoes, books, confectionery and toys. In Scotland, many visitors go for tweeds, Border knitwear, Shetland and Fair Isle woollens, tartan rugs and materials, Edinburgh crystal, Caithness glass, Celtic silver and pebble jewelry. The Scottish Highlands bristle with old "bothies" (farm buildings) which have been turned into small craft workshops where visitors are welcome—but not pressured—to buy attractive hand-made items of bone, silver, wood, pottery, leather and glass. Hand-made chocolates, often with whisky or Drambuie fillings, and the traditional "petticoat tail" shortbread in tin boxes are popular; so too, at a more mundane level, are boiled sweets in jars from particular localities—Berwick cockles, Jethart snails, Edinburgh rock and suchlike crunchy items. Dundee cake, a rich fruit mixture with almonds on top, and Dundee marmalades and heather honeys are among the other eatables which visitors take home from Scotland.

On most purchases VAT (Value Added Tax) at 15% is charged. Under retail export schemes, this charge may be refunded. Unfortunately, not all Scottish shops operate the scheme, but those which specialize in souvenir and peculiarly Scottish goods—kiltmakers, bagpipe makers and so on—will be familiar with the routine. If you have difficulty, and if the saving on the concession is worth your while, contact the VAT Office, H.M. Customs & Excise, 44 York Place, Edinburgh EH1 (tel. 556 2433).

**Clothing Sizes.** Although you may see several charts with comparative U.S.–British sizings, in our experience these are not truly standardized. Best take along a tape measure, or rely on the shop assistant's assessment (in the first place) of your sizing. Always try on a garment before purchasing: an apparently correct sizing may prove to have arm-holes too wide or too narrow, sleeves too long or too short.

**MAIL.** British postage rates are: Inland (including islands and all Ireland), 12½p slow rate and 16p fast (for letters and postcards up to 60g.); ordinary postage plus £1.50 for special delivery. To Europe: 19½p for letters and postcards up to 20g.; Air Mail stickers are not required. To the U.S. and Canada: 26p for Air Mail letters up to 10g, 14p per 10g. thereafter; 24p for postcards; 24p for aerogrammes, on flimsy paper, obtainable at post offices.

**Telegrams.** You can send a telegram overseas from post offices or by telephone. If the latter, dial 100. Have plenty of small change to put in the slot if you do this from a public call box. There are no inland telegrams but you may send a telemessage (dial 100) which is delivered next day.

**TELEPHONES.** Public call boxes are plentiful and easy to spot: they are bright red as a rule. Coinboxes take 5p and 10p coins and a directory, dialing instructions and list of code numbers are ready to hand. In some isolated places without call boxes you will see a blue sign on a shopfront: "You may telephone from here." Minimum cost for any call is 5p; if you speak for several minutes or to a number outside the area you will need several 5p and 10p pieces.

Calls made before 9 A.M. and after 6 P.M. and at weekends and public holidays are significantly cheaper than others. Similarly, calls made to places within a 35-mile radius are significantly cheaper than those made over longer distances. IDD (International Direct Dialling) also varies in cost according to distance and time of day. You may dial direct from Scotland to more than 30 U.S. cities and 14 Canadian ones, the rate being 50p–65p per minute. Country codes and international prefixes are listed in telephone directories.

For general enquiries dial 191; for directory enquiries dial 192 (be prepared for a long wait); for international enquiries dial 100.

The telephone numbers that we quote in this Guide must all be prefixed with the code for the city, town or village mentioned in the address if you are calling from outside that locality. You do not need to use the code if you are calling from the same locality. The North British hotel in Edinburgh, for example, has the number 556 2414, and that is what you dial if you are calling from anywhere in Edinburgh. If you call from outside the city, you should dial 031 556 2414, 031 being the code for Edinburgh.

You are warned not to make long-distance phone calls from your hotel room without checking very carefully what the cost will be. Hotels frequently add *several hundred percent* to such calls. This is an international practice, not one confined to Britain. It is worthwhile utilizing your telephone credit card for these calls to avoid the massive hotel surcharge and certain U.S. cards are valid in Europe for this purpose.

**PHOTOGRAPHY.** American and Continental color films are obtainable in Britain. Most types can be processed in the country in about three days at more or less any time of year. Charges can be quite high.

Don't leave already exposed film in your pockets or in any hand luggage while passing through airport X-ray machines. The process can sometimes fog the film and you may find a whole trip's photographs ruined. It is worth investing in a product called Filmashield, a lead-laminated pouch. It stores flat when not in use and holds quite a lot of film or, indeed, your camera with half-used film in it. It is available in many countries.

**SPORT.** For further information on sports in Scotland, see the sports chapter on page XX. Deer-stalking and shooting can be arranged on the spot by most Highland hotels or in advance by some of the tour operators and handling agents mentioned earlier in this section. We have included a summary of the golf scene in the regional Practical Information sections. Further details, including lists of golf-vacation operators and hotels, are available from the Scottish Tourist Board's booklet *Scotland: Home of Golf,* price 75p by post. No special license is required for fishing Scotland's rivers, lochs and sea-coast—all you need is a local permit from a neighborhood hotel, tackle shop or angling club. We have summarized this sport too in our Practical Information sections for each region, and the STB's booklets *Scotland for Fishing* (80p by post) and *Scotland for Sea Angling* (75p by post) give full details, including hotels which cater specifically for anglers.

The various winter sports developments in Scotland are described in the STB's free booklet *Winter Sports in Scotland:* best pick up the latest edition when you arrive; this is a rapidly changing scene. Wherever you come to a sizeable and reasonably accessible loch you will find water sports—sailing, canoeing, water-skiing and the like—going on under the control of some local hotel group. Details are in the STB's free booklet *Adventure and Special Interest Holidays* —which also offers way-out pursuits like gem-collecting, carriage-driving, parachuting, powerboat handling and caber-tossing and, for the really energetic, learning Gaelic!

All the booklets mentioned above are normally available in Scottish bookshops, newsstands and hotel kiosks, from information centers or by mail from the Scottish Tourist Board, 23 Ravelston Terrace, Edinburgh EH4 3EU. Note: prices quoted include postage for U.K. and Republic of Ireland only.

**TRAVELING IN SCOTLAND BY CAR.** If you bring your own car you must also bring the vehicle's registration documents and a nationality plaque or sticker.

Driving your own or hired car you must have a current driving license or International Driving Permit. Then you may drive in Britain for 12 months, after which you will have to pass a test and obtain a British driving license.

Membership of a recognized automobile club in your own country gives you access to certain facilities in the major automobile clubs of Britain. The Royal Automobile Club (RAC) has blue signs and vans and offices at 83 Pall Mall, London SW1 and in several English cities; and at 242 West George Street, Glasgow G2; 17 Rutland Square, Edinburgh EH1; and the Port Office, Stranraer in Scotland. The Automobile Association (AA) has yellow signs and vans and offices at Fanum House, Basingstoke, Hampshire and in several English cities; and at 20 Melville Street, Edinburgh EH3; Blythswood Square, Glasgow G2; and the Port Office, Stranraer in Scotland. Both organizations offer literature, roadside help and get-you-home services. Foreign visitors and non-members will find the RAC helpful; the AA is strictly member-oriented.

There is also in Scotland a Royal Scottish Automobile Club (11 Blythswood Square, Glasgow G2), a social and motor-sporting organization.

**Car Rental.** Our Practical Information sections give details of places where you may rent an automobile. Many visitors to Scotland arrive in vehicles they have rented in England and the major car-rental firms allow you to pick up a vehicle in the south and leave it in a Scottish city, or vice versa.

To rent a medium-sized automobile in Scotland costs up to £20 per day in high season—including insurance but not gas. Some firms insist on payment in advance; some will not rent to those under 21 or over 70.

**Rules of the Road.** Drive on the left, overtake on the right. Maximum permitted speeds are 70 m.p.h. on motorways, 60 on ordinary roads, 40 or 30 in built-up areas in and around towns. Traffic signs are similar to those in use all over Europe. In the centers of many towns parking is allowed only in metered spaces where you pay about 10p an hour by day, nothing at night. Where a single continuous line is painted parallel to the sidewalk, parking is restricted to the hours shown on adjacent time-plates. A double yellow line or zigzag markings indicate that parking is prohibited at all times. Most towns have off-street parking lots. Edinburgh is notoriously poorly-equipped with parking areas; Glasgow, on the other hand, is very good.

**Gasoline.** Prices vary slightly from area to area, but, thanks to the proximity of refineries, central Scotland tends to have less expensive petrol than elsewhere in Britain. The price fluctuates but around £1.70–£1.80 per imperial gallon (4.5 liters or 1.2 American gallons; there are five British, or Imperial, gallons to six U.S. gallons) is what you will probably pay in 1983.

**Maps.** From the Scottish Tourist Board, 23 Ravelston Terrace, Edinburgh EH4 3EU and its offices and information centers at home and abroad you may obtain a good *Touring Map of Scotland,* price £1.20 by post in U.K.; or the *Enjoy Scotland Pack* of useful material, including the map, price £2.30. This map is scaled 5 miles to the inch. Among more detailed maps (1½ miles to the inch) are the Ordnance Survey's Scottish series and town plans and Bartholomew's National maps, available at most booksellers.

**TRAVELING IN SCOTLAND BY BUS.** There is a very extensive bus network throughout the country. Main routes and many suburban and short distance services are operated by the state-owned Scottish Bus Group with its various subsidiary companies such as Walter Alexander, S.M.T., Central S.M.T., Highland, Western Scottish and Eastern Scottish.

Express services link main cities and towns; for example, Glasgow to Edinburgh, Inverness, Aberdeen, Perth, Skye, Ayr, Dumfries and Carlisle, and of course similar services from Edinburgh. From Inverness there are routes to Aberdeen, Wick, Thurso and Fort William.

Full details of all these services can be had from most bus stations or the Travel Centre, Buchanan Bus Station, Glasgow G2 3NP tel. (041) 332 9644; and Eastern Scottish, St. Andrew's Square Bus Station, Edinburgh, tel. (031) 556 2515.

In addition, Glasgow operates its own extensive city and suburban bus services in close collaboration with the rail and Underground network. Edinburgh also has its own bus network. And there are many private companies operating services, usually as a back up to the main networks.

Bus tours are operated by the Scottish Bus Group, as well as by a number of private companies. Among the latter are Silver Fox Coaches of Edinburgh; Cotters Tours Ltd. (Glasgow); Parks of Hamilton; Doigs Tours (Greenock) Ltd.; McIntyre's Coach Tours (Aberdeen). Details of these services and others on similar lines are available from travel agents.

There is no general runabout ticket for bus travel in Scotland. But each company issues its own in conjunction with the local tourist authority. These are based on cities or towns or resorts. Costs vary but range from around £2.50 for a day ticket to around £14 for a family ticket for a week, with unlimited travel within a fixed zone. Details from bus stations and local tourist offices.

 **TRAVELING IN SCOTLAND BY TRAIN.** Scotland has a good rail network extending all the way to Thurso and Wick, the most northerly stations in the British Isles. Services are generally reliable and fast. They radiate mostly from Glasgow and Edinburgh, between which there is a half-hourly shuttle taking some 45 minutes. Glasgow has two main stations, Central (for all services from England and southwest Scotland) and Queen Street (for services to Edinburgh, Aberdeen and the north). The city also has an extensive electrified suburban system and an Underground (subway) which serves the city center. Edinburgh has only one station, Waverley.

Although many routes in Scotland run through extremely attractive countryside, several are outstanding. The best are from Glasgow (Queen Street) to Oban via Loch Lomond; to Fort William and Mallaig via Rannoch (ferry connection to Skye); from Edinburgh to Inverness via the Forth Bridge and Perth; from Inverness to Kyle of Lochalsh and to Wick; and from Inverness to Aberdeen.

Some lines in Scotland—all suburban services and lines north and west of Inverness—are one class only. Otherwise, 1st. and 2nd. class predominate. Long distances services carry buffet and refreshment cars. There are also sleeper services between Inverness and Glasgow and Edinburgh.

A runabout Freedom of Scotland rail ticket is available for seven and 14 days, costing £30 and £44 respectively. It is issued for 2nd. class travel only. It also gives free travel on the ferries on the Firth of Clyde and on the ferry from Kyle of Lochalsh to Skye. It is available from all stations and ticket agencies in Scotland and from British Rail Travel Centres throughout the U.K. There are no regional runabout tickets. For details of the All Line Railrover ticket, which

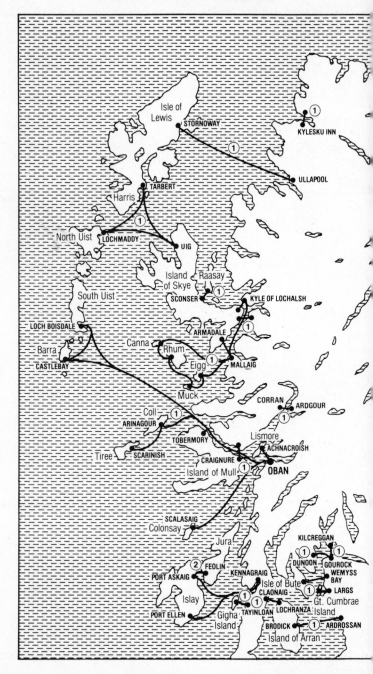

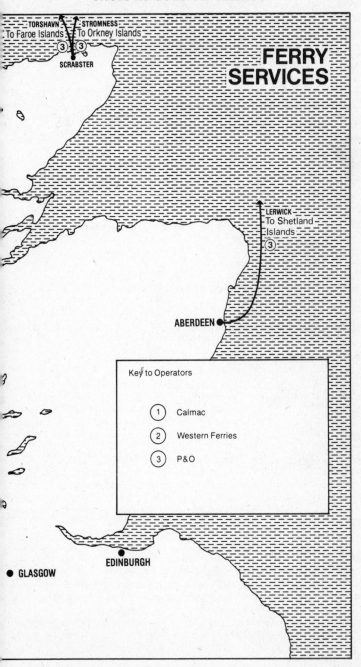

TORSHAVN
To Faroe Islands
STROMNESS
To Orkney Islands
③ ③
SCRABSTER

FERRY
SERVICES

LERWICK
To Shetland
Islands
③

ABERDEEN ●

Key to Operators

① Calmac

② Western Ferries

③ P&O

EDINBURGH ●

● GLASGOW

is also good for Scotland, see page XX. For details of Travelpass '83, see page XX.

**Preserved Steam Railways.** *Strathspey Railway,* Boat of Garten, Highland Region. About 6 miles from Aviemore off the A95, this is part of the former Highland Railway's Aviemore to Forres branch. It is five miles long and there are trains, mainly steam operated, on weekends from May to September and daily in July and August. For up to the minute information telephone the Station, Boat of Garten, (047 983) 692.

*Lochty Private Railway,* Lochty, near Crail, Fife. On the B940 between Cupar and Crail, about 7 miles from the latter. Owned by a local farmer, it is 1½ miles long. Operates most Sunday afternoons from June to September with steam engines.

*Scottish Railway Preservation Society,* Wallace Street, Falkirk, Stirlingshire. Museum and workshop for restoration of railway vehicles etc. Also organizes many railway outings. Write for details.

**TRAVELING IN SCOTLAND BY AIR.** Although a small country, Scotland nonetheless has a significant internal air network, made necessary in part by the rugged nature of the terrain and the multitude of islands. British Airways, Loganair (Glasgow Airport, Paisley, Renfrewshire, tel. 041–889 3181), Air Ecosse (Dyce Airport, Aberdeen, tel. 0224–724782), Inter-City Airlines (Dyce Airport, Aberdeen, tel. 0224–723090), Air Orkney (Kirkwall Airport, Orkney, tel. 0856–4607), and Burnthills Aviation—helicopters only— (Glasgow Airport, tel. 041–887 7733), are the principal carriers.

Services to the islands, especially Orkney and the Shetlands, are regular and rapid.

**TRAVELING IN SCOTLAND BY FERRY.** With so many islands, plus the great Firth of Clyde waterway, ferry services in Scotland are of paramount importance. Most of these are now vehicle ferries, although a number of the smaller ones are passenger only. All vehicle ferries also carry foot passengers.

The main operator is Caledonian MacBrayne Ltd., Ferry Terminal, Gourock, Renfrewshire, tel. 0475–33755. They are a state-owned company, known generally as Caley-Mac. Their services extend from the Firth of Clyde, where they operate an extremely extensive network, right up to the northeast of Scotland and all of the Hebrides. Western Ferries, 16 Woodside Crescent, Glasgow, tel. 041–332 9766, also operate ferries on the Clyde.

The Orkney Islands are linked to the mainland by car ferry from Scrabster (near Thurso) to Stromness (on the main island of Orkney, called Mainland). This is operated by P & O Ferries, Jamieson's Quay, PO Box 5, Aberdeen, tel. 0224–572615. The ferry runs daily with an extra service from June to September. The Shetlands are linked to the mainland by car ferry from Aberdeen to Lerwick; three sailings weekly in each direction. The main ferry on this route, the *St. Clair,* has cabin accommodations. This service operated by P & O, too.

There is also a series of inter-island ferries between the Shetlands and the Orkneys. Details of these are given in the comprehensive guide, *Getting Around the Highlands and Islands;* see below for details.

**TRAVELPASS '83.** One of the most useful runabout tickets in the British Isles is the Travelpass '83, issued by the Highlands and Islands Development Board. This covers travel by train, bus and ferry within the entire region and also includes ferries to Orkney and of course all the ferries to the Outer Hebrides. In area it stretches from the Firth of Clyde to the Orkneys and Barra to Aviemore. In addition to the normal buses it also includes the Post Buses operated by the Post Office in remoter areas. Only a few local bus services are outside the scheme. And you can use the pass to travel by train (2nd. class) or bus from Glasgow or Edinburgh into the Highland region.

Issued for 8 or 12 days consecutive travel it costs respectively in March, April and October, £47 and £56; for May, June and September, £55 and £65; and for July and August, £68 and £83.

For full information on this worthwhile pass see your travel agent or contact Highlands & Islands Travelpass, Pickfords Travel, 25 Queensgate, Inverness, tel. 0463 32134.

All holders of the Travelpass receive a free copy of the comprehensive guide-timetable *Getting Around the Highlands and Islands* which covers the entire transport system within the region by plane, train, bus and ferry. The guide can also be purchased (£1.45 including postage) from Travelguide, Information Services, H.I.D.B., Golspie, Sutherland, Scotland. It is also on sale (cost £1) at many bookshops and tourist information centers in Scotland. The 1983 edition is due to be published in late April.

 **CUSTOMS ON RETURNING HOME.** If you propose to take on your holiday any *foreign-made* articles, such as cameras, binoculars, expensive timepieces and the like, it is wise to put with your travel documents the receipt from the retailer or some other evidence that the item was bought in your home country. If you bought the article on a previous holiday abroad and have already paid duty on it, carry with you the receipt for this. Otherwise, on returning home, you may be charged duty (for British residents, Value Added Tax as well). In other words, unless you can prove prior possession, foreign-made articles are dutiable *each time* they enter the U.S. The details below are correct as we go to press. It would be wise to check in case of change.

**U.S. Residents.** You may bring in $400 worth of foreign merchandise as gifts or for personal use without having to pay duty, provided you have been out of the country more than 48 hours and provided you have not claimed a similar exemption within the previous 30 days. Every member of a family is entitled to the same exemption, regardless of age, and the exemptions can be pooled.

The $400 figure is based on the fair retail value of the goods in the country where acquired. Included for travelers over the age of 21 are one liter of alcohol, 100 cigars (non-Cuban) and 200 cigarettes. Any amount in excess of those limits will be taxed at the port of entry, and may additionally be taxed in the traveler's home state. Only one bottle of perfume trademarked in the U.S. may be brought in. Unlimited amounts of goods from certain specially designated "developing" countries may also be brought in duty-free; check with U.S. Customs Service, Washington D.C. 20229. Write to the same address for information regarding importation of automobiles and/or motorcycles. You may not bring home meats, fruits, plants, soil or other agricultural items.

Gifts valued at under $50 may be mailed to friends or relatives at home, but not more than one per day (of receipt) to any one addressee. These gifts must not include perfumes costing more than $5, tobacco or liquor.

If you are traveling with such foreign made articles as cameras, watches or binoculars that were purchased at home, it is best either to carry the receipt for them with you or to register them with U.S. Customs prior to departing. This will save much time (and potentially aggravation) upon your return.

Military personnel returning from abroad should check with the nearest American Embassy for special regulations pertaining to them.

**Canadian Residents.** In addition to personal effects, the following articles may be brought in duty free: a maximum of 50 cigars, 200 cigarettes, 2 pounds of tobacco and 40 ounces of liquor, provided these are declared in writing to customs on arrival and accompany the traveler in hand or checked-through baggage. These are included in the basic exemption of $150 a year. Personal gifts should be mailed as "Unsolicited Gift—Value Under $15". Canadian customs regulations are strictly enforced; you are recommended to check what your allowances are and to make sure you have kept receipts for whatever you have bought abroad. For details ask for the Canada Customs brochure, *I Declare*.

# THE
# SCOTTISH
# SCENE

# PRESENTING THE SCOTS

## *A Race Apart*

In some old collection of phonographs, you may well turn up *Roamin' in the Gloamin'* or *I Love a Lassie* or one of the other comic songs of Harry Lauder, a star of the music halls of the 1920s. With his garish kilt, short crooked walking stick, rich rolling "r's" and "pawky" (cheerfully impudent) humor, chiefly based on the alleged meanness of the Scots, he impressed the Scottish character on the world. But it was, needless to say, a false impression and one the Scots have been trying to stamp out ever since.

So, how then do you characterize the Scots? Temperamentally, they are a mass of contradictions. They have been likened, not to a Scotch egg, but to a soft-boiled egg: a dour hard shell, a mushy middle. The Scot laughs and weeps with almost Latin facility, but to strangers he is reserved, non-committal, in no hurry to make an impression. Historically, fortitude and resilience are his hallmarks; and there are streaks of both resignation and pitiless ferocity in his make up, warring with sentimentality and love of family. Very Scottish was the instant reaction of an old lady of Edinburgh 200 years ago, when news arrived of the defeat in Mysore in India and of the Scottish soldiers being fettered in irons, two by two: "God help the puir chiel that's chained tae oor Davie."

The Scots are in general suspicious of the go-getter. Whizz kid is a term of contempt. But they are by no means plodders, though it is true to say that they are determined and thorough, respecting success only when it has been a few hundred years in the making. Praise of some bright ambitious youngster is quenched with the sneer: "Him? Ah kent (knew) his faither."

Yet this is the nation which built commerce throughout the British Empire and opened wild territories and was responsible for much of mankind's scientific and technological advancement, a nation boastful about things it is not too good at, shame-facedly modest about genuine achievements. From a hand-out about the Edinburgh school of medicine:

"If one excepts a few discoveries such as that of 'fixed air' by Black, of the diverse functions of the nerve-roots by Bell, of the anaesthetic properties of chloroform by Simpson, of the invention of certain powerful drugs by Christison and of the importance of antiseptic procedures by Lister, the influence of Edinburgh medicine has been of a steady constructive rather than a revolutionary type."

A further paradox is that, while Scotland always does badly compared with the rest of Europe when the crime, poverty, poor health and drunkeness statistics appear, Scotland is a land where old values are cherished, where honesty and plain dealing are the rule, where more children are brought up according to old-fashioned moral precepts than elsewhere. In country districts one still sees the effects of religious teachings and frugal habits: "porridge and the Shorter Catechism."

Among things which strike most newcomers to Scotland are: the generosity of the Scots; the narrowness of their minds; their obsession with respectability; their satisfaction with themselves and their desire to stay as they are; and above all their passionate love of Scotland.

The qualities which unite the English and Scots are more important than those which divide them. And when we travel through Scotland we may never meet a native who fits the descriptions we have outlined here: so diverse is mankind, even in a small, tightly-knit land. Glaswegians will tell us the Edinburghers are hardly Scots at all; Edinburghers will point out that if every Irishman in Glasgow walked out with a Jew under his arm there would be no one left; we shall observe that Highlanders look on Lowlanders as Sassenachs, no better than the English ... Maybe it is best to come to Scotland without any preconceived ideas at all, but to take the Scots as you find them.

## Education, Law and the Church

Obstinate refusal to go along with English ideas has led the nation to be accused of a head-in-the-sand attitude to progress. But the Scots have their own ideas of progress and they jealously guard the few institutions which remain unique to them.

Educationally, Scotland has a proud record. It is her boast that she had four universities—St. Andrews, Aberdeen, Glasgow and Edinburgh—when England had only two: Oxford and Cambridge. The "lad o' pairts" (parts, i.e. talents), the poor child of a feckless father and a fiercely self-sacrificing mother, sternly tutored by the village "dominie" (schoolmaster) and turned loose at the age of 13 with so firm a base of learning that he rose to the very top of his profession . . . this type of lad is a phenomenon of Scottish social history. The sacrifices that boys made as a matter of course to further their education are an old Scottish tradition. "Meal Monday," the mid-semester holiday at a Scottish university, is a survival of the long weekend that used to be granted to enable students to return to their distant homes—on foot—and replenish the sack of "meal" (oatmeal) which was their only subsistence.

As to university education, a reformer has written that nothing shows so clearly the Scots' passion for learning than the willingness of students to crowd into medieval lecture-rooms to listen to inaudible, inarticulate—but erudite—professors.

It is a British cliché that an English education teaches you to think and a Scottish education stuffs your head with information. The average Scot does appear to be better informed than his English neighbor and to discuss facts rather than ideas. Scots pride themselves on their international outlook and on being better linguists than the English. The Scots get on well with foreigners and they offer strangers a kindly welcome and a civility which is not often found in the modern world.

As the Scots have their own traditions in education, so is their legal system distinct from that of England's. Indeed, when you see your first policeman sporting a "diced" (checkered) cap, you know you have arrived in Scotland. It is a visible sign that there are two legal systems in the United Kingdom.

For the most part, however, you will notice few practical differences except in terminology. The barrister in England becomes an advocate in Scotland. Law-office name-plates designate their occupants "S.S.C." (Solicitor to the Supreme Court) or "W.S." (Writer to the Signet); cases for prosecution go before the "procurator fiscal" and are tried by the "sheriff" or "sheriff-substitute." The terms are different in England; and procedures are slightly different too, for Scotland is one of the few countries which still bases its legal system on the old Roman law.

Crimes with picturesque names from ancient times remain on the statute-book without precise equivalents in England: "hamesucken," for example, which means assaulting a person within his/her own home. In criminal cases Scotland adds to "Guilty" or "Not Guilty" a third verdict: "Not Proven." This, say the cynics, signifies "Don't do it again."

The Presbyterian Church of Scotland—the "Kirk"—is entirely independent of the Church of England. Up to the 20th century it was a power in the land and did much to shape Scottish character. There are still those who can remember when the minister visited houses like an inquisitor and put members of the families through their catechism, punishing or reprimanding those who were not word-perfect. On Sunday mornings the elders patrolled the streets, ordering people into church and rebuking those who sat in their gardens or stared idly out of the windows.

Religion in Scotland, as elsewhere, has lost much of its grip. But the Kirk remains influential in rural districts, where Kirk officials are pillars of local society. Ministers and their wives are seen in all their somber glory in Edinburgh in the springtime, when the General Assembly of the Kirk takes place and, for a week or more, Scottish newspapers devote several pages every day to their deliberations.

The Episcopalian Church of Scotland has bishops, as its name implies (unlike the Kirk, where the ministers are all equal) and a more colorful ritual. It approximates to a Church of England north of the Border. Episcopalianism is considered genteel and has been described rather sourly by the Aberdeenshire novelist Lewis Grassic Gibbon as "more a matter of social status than theological conviction . . . a grateful bourgeois acknowledgment of anglicisation."

Of the various nonconformist offshoots of the established Kirk, the Free Kirk of Scotland is the largest. It remains faithful to the monolithic unity of its forefathers, promoting the grim discipline that John Knox promoted long ago. The Free Kirk is strong in the Highlands and western isles and is responsible for the absence in those parts of buses and trains on Sundays, for all the shops being shut and for a general atmosphere of a people cowering under the wrath of God.

Among the fishing communities of the west, and more especially of the north-east around Buckie and Macduff (Grampian Region), evangelical movements such as the Close Brethren and Jehovah's Witnesses have made impressive inroads.

Outside religion, Scotland on the whole is mercifully free of that class-consciousness and social elitism which so often amuses or disgusts foreign residents in England. But her turbulent history has left Scotland a legacy of sectarian bigotry, comparable to that of Northern Ireland, which England grew out of centuries ago. Scotland's large minority population of Roman Catholics is still to some extent under-privileged. Catholics tend to stick together, Protestants to mix only with Protestants. Even the two most famous soccer teams in Scotland—Rangers and Celtic—are notorious for their sectarian bias.

## Scots and Scotch

A word, finally, is needed on the vexed subject of nomenclature. A "scotchman" is a nautical device for "scotching" or clamping a running rope. It is not a native of Scotland. Though you may find some rather more conservative people refer to themselves as "Scotchmen" and consider themselves "Scotch", most prefer "Scot" or "Scotsman", and call themselves "Scottish" or "Scots."

There are exceptions to this rule. Certain internationally known Scottish products are "Scotch." There is Scotch whisky, Scotch wool, Scotch tweed, Scotch mist (persistent drizzling rain). The flip of the strings at the start of a phrase of martial music, a trade mark of the old Scottish fiddlers, is called the Scotch snap. A modern addition to the list is Scotch tape. A snack food of a hard-boiled egg wrapped in sausage is a Scotch egg.

You may include the Scots in the broader term British. But they dislike the word Brits. And nothing infuriates them more than being called English. Nonetheless there are a lot of Anglo-Scots; that is, people of Scottish birth who live in England or the off-spring of marriages between Scottish and English people. But they are not to be confused with Sassenachs, a word applied jokily or disdainfully to all the English and which is the Gaelic word for Saxon. But at the same time, English people who live in Scotland remain English to their dying day, and their children after them. Similarly, the description of North Britain for Scotland, which crept in during Victorian times, has now crept out again. It survives only in the names of a few North British hotels. Scots feel that it denies their national identity and there are some who, on receiving a letter with "N.B." or "North Britain" in the address, will cross it out and return the envelope to the sender.

# SCOTTISH HISTORY

## *The Rulers of the North*

The preoccupation with genealogy that most Scots share has led some Scottish historians to trace links between the earliest Scots and the ancient civilizations of the Mediterranean. Thus "Gael" has been linked with Gaythelos, a mythical Greek warrior, and connections have been sought between "Scot" and Scota, daughter of an Egyptian pharaoh. Sadly, however, these antecedants have no very strong basis in fact. But on the other hand it is known, from monuments and artefacts dating from the Neolithic period (about 6,000 years ago), that numbers of short, dark immigrants from the Mediterranean did establish themselves in Scotland.

But they were, as might be imagined, very much in a minority among the other early settlers in Scotland. A very much larger body of peoples came from what is now Germany, while at the same time there were interminglings with ancient Britons from the south, with Irish from the west and with Norsemen from Scandinavia. In fact, Scotland was overrun by turbulent hordes from all quarters. Some liked it there and stayed on.

## The Romans in Scotland

A more precise history begins with the arrival of the Romans in Scotland in A.D. 80, pushing north from Hadrian's Wall with the idea of consolidating absolutely the Empire's northwestern frontier. And at Mons Granpius in A.D. 84 the Roman general Agricola destroyed the Scottish tribes in what, in point of numbers involved, was the largest battle ever fought on British soil. The defeated leader of the tribes is credited with a quote which has rung down the ages: "They make a desert and call it peace."

Agricola built a number of forts in his newly conquered territories, while his successor, the Emperor Antoninus Pius, piled up further barriers of stone and turf (the Antonine Wall) across the narrowest point of Scotland, from Bo'ness on the Firth of Forth to Old Kilpatrick on the Firth of Clyde. But as an outpost of Empire it proved difficult to hold and after 40 years the Romans abandoned it, retreating to the security of the more massive Hadrian's Wall. Until they left Britain altogether, they were content to make brief punitive raids into the northern provinces. Apart from a few still impressive fragments of the Antonine Wall, which survive in the care of the National Trust for Scotland, and one or two picturesque legends (such as, that Pontius Pilate, son of a Roman centurion and a Scots girl, was born at Fortingall, Tayside Region), the Romans have left scarcely a mark on Scotland.

## The Four Tribes

The curtain had hardly risen on Scottish history when it fell again. The Dark Ages—darker than most—saw disparate bands of violent peoples fighting, combining, splitting up and coming together again until, about A.D. 600, four recognizable tribal divisions emerged. They were the Picts, of unknown origin, in the north; the Scots, of Irish origin, in the west; the Britons, kinfolk of the Welsh, in the southwest; and the Angles, first of many Sassenach invaders, in the southeast. The Angles spoke low German and Saxon English, the Scots and Britons Gaelic dialects, and the Picts an aboriginal patois all their own. Very gradually, external pressures from England, a larger and more sophisticated country, from the seaborne invasions of the Norsemen, and, as much as anything else, from the growth of Christianity, molded these groups into something like a nation. (The painfully slow spread of Christianity, during this darkest of Dark Ages, received important impulses with the building by Ninian of his chapel at Whithorn (Dumfries and Galloway) around A.D. 400, Mungo preaching on the banks of the Clyde in A.D. 550 and the establishment in A.D. 563 by Columba, disciple of St. Patrick himself, of a community of monks and missionaries on the island of Iona.)

## Enter Macbeth

The Declaration of Arbroath, which the Scots sent to the Pope in 1320, boasted the continuous reign in Scotland of 113 kings and queens of "royal stock, the line unbroken by a single foreigner." The bulk of them, however, (about 100) were shadowy figures, and monarchs of limited authority only. One such, for example, was Kenneth II, who, so it is said, adopted the thistle as the national emblem of Scotland after a Danish invader trod on one and let out a yell, thereby giving the alarm which saved the Scots at the battle of Luncarty near Perth. Unfortunately, there is no clear evidence that the battle took place, while the thistle did not appear as Scotland's emblem until many years later.

Kenneth MacAlpin, a chieftain of the Scots and Picts, is sometimes called the first king of Scotland (843). But strict genealogies begin only with Malcolm II (1005–1034), who recovered the southeastern territories from the English, received the southwest by inheritance and handed a more or less united land to his successor Duncan. The warring lines of the Atholls and Morays tore Scotland apart again, however, shortly afterwards. It was during this period, for example, that Duncan of Atholl was slain by Macbeth of Moray—an incident which, centuries later, was to provide Shakespeare with the idea for his play. Malcolm III, called "Canmore" (Great Head), ultimately secured victory for the house of Atholl in 1057, though his successors had to deal with Moray rebellions for another 200 years.

However, even then ambitious earls, claiming absolute sovereignty over certain districts, and Norwegian monarchs, who retained possession of their Scottish colonies, frequently ensured that these Scottish kings of the 11th and 12th centuries were rulers in name only. (The Hebridean islands did not become Scottish until 1263, Orkney and Shetland not until 1472; and constitutionalists say that Norway is entitled to buy these islands back whenever she cares to.)

In their troubles, the Scottish monarchs turned increasingly to England for help. Royal marriages with English princesses and pacts with the Norman rulers of England brought Scotland some domestic stability, but at the cost of making her a client state of England.

## The "Sair Sanct"

"Sair Sanct" means "sore saint" or "sore saintly"—an expression applied ruefully to King David I, who almost bankrupted the kingdom by the building of great abbeys. Both before and after he became king he busied himself erecting tourist attractions of the future, notably the four graceful sisters of Tweedside: the abbeys of Jedburgh (1118), Kelso (1128), Melrose (1136) and Dryburgh (1150).

This "most courtly king," as an English chronicler called him, was brought up in the care of William the Conqueror and was eager to give his rough countrymen some Norman polish. For a start, he offered tax concessions to lairds who "agreed to dwell in a more civil manner, and be attired with more refinement, and be more particular about their food." He persuaded Norman friends of his youth to live in Scotland and set the natives an example. Some of the best-known Scottish family names—Seton, Fraser, Lamont, Lindsay and others—have stemmed from the "Norman invasion" which David encouraged.

David, in periodic bouts of warfare, nonetheless managed to keep Scotland reasonably unified: he was a man of his time, cunning and cruel as well as courtly. But after his death, the feuding and fighting between the rival factions increased. At the wedding of King Alexander III and Jolande de Dreux in Jedburgh Abbey a ghostly figure appeared, prophesying the sorrows of Scotland. To many, it must have seemed like a statement of the obvious.

## Freedom Fighters

By the latter part of the 13th century, Scotland came more closely under the control of England, specifically in the person of the ambitious and successful Edward I, the "Hammer of the Scots." The death of Alexander III in 1286 (he and his horse fell over a cliff at Kinghorn one dark night—some say they were pushed) gave Edward a wonderful opportunity to bind Scotland's fortunes to his own. He promptly betrothed his son to Alexander's granddaughter and successor, a small child called Margaret, envisaging a union of the crowns in due course. This plan, however, failed when the little girl died on the way home from the Norwegian court where she had been brought up.

But Edward was presented with another opportunity of bringing his northern neighbor under control when he was appointed to arbitrate among the new claimants to the Scottish throne, no fewer than 13 of them. Quite properly he nominated John Balliol—having first obtained Balliol's promise to acknowledge his overlordship. In 1296, dissatisfied with Balliol's performance as a puppet, he threw him out and took over the government of Scotland himself.

But Scotland's affairs went no more smoothly than they had done before. The patriot William Wallace, a private citizen, organized a rabble into an army and gained surprising victories over the English forces in central Scotland. The stirring battle-hymn of Robert Burns, *Scots wha hae wi' Wallace bled,* an unofficial national anthem to this day, expresses the pride and passionate love of country which Scotland found under Wallace.

In 1305, William Wallace was hunted down and executed for breaking an oath of allegiance he had never sworn. The subsequent turmoil threw up another freedom fighter in the person of Robert Bruce. (He was sometimes known as Robert *the* Bruce, or simply as The Bruce.)

How Bruce learned patience and perseverance from a spider while he was in hiding in a cave on Rathlin Island (Northern Ireland) is a story every Scottish child is told. Whatever the truth of it, he certainly survived many defeats and disgraces before writing some of the most glorious pages of Scottish history. Luckily for him, the "Hammer of the Scots" had been succeeded by an ineffectual son, Edward II, in 1307.

In 1314, a date ever-memorable to true Scots, Bruce snatched Edinburgh Castle from Edward II and then vanquished the English army as it marched to the relief of its beleaguered comrades in Stirling Castle. The fight immortalized the field of Bannockburn, a place which is ready to sink today under the weight of its commemorative statuary; and a name which is still hurled defiantly at the "auld enemy"—England— whenever the two nations meet in sporting encounters.

## "It Cam' wi' a Lass"

Robert the Bruce lived to see Scotland's nationhood confirmed by the Treaty of Northampton (1328) but, like his old antagonist Edward I, he produced a weak and vacillating son, David II. And during his long reign Scotland almost fell again under English domination.

The crown then passed through Bruce's daughter Marjory to her son, another Robert. Marjory had married Walter the Steward—the Stewardship of Scotland being one of the ancient high offices of state— and thus the name Steward, or Stewart, became the name of Scotland's royal dynasty. Later on, through French influence, the spelling was altered to Stuart.

The Stuarts ushered in an eventful and mainly unhappy era. Nearly every one of them—11 kings, three queens and two "pretenders" (claimants to the throne)—met bloody or miserable ends, fighting the English, unruly barons and obstinate churchmen.

James I, for years a prisoner in England, was brutally murdered at Perth; James II was killed when one of his cannon exploded at Roxburgh Castle; James III died by an assassin's hand after losing the battle of Sauchieburn; James IV fell at the battle of Flodden (Northumbria), along with the flower of Scottish chivalry; James V, vanquished at Solway Moss on the Border, died of a broken heart in Falkland Palace. Hearing, as he expired, that his Queen had given birth to a daughter in Linlithgow Palace he muttered: "It cam' wi' a lass and it'll gang (go) wi' a lass"—"it" being the House of Stuart; the two lasses being Marjory Bruce who began the dynasty and the newborn princess with whom, James supposed, it would come to an end.

## The Monstrous Regiment of Women

Things did not turn out like that. The baby Mary, succeeding to the throne within a few days of her birth, revived Stuart hopes and Scottish fortunes. To protect her in her extreme youth an arrangement called the "auld alliance" was made use of: a mutual assistance pact between France and Scotland, two nations with little in common but their hatred and fear of England and love of good wine. Adhered to by the Scots with sentimental fervor and by the French with cynical opportunism, the "auld alliance" crops up at various turning-points of history down to our own times.

So Mary went to France for safety. At 16 she married the sickly Dauphin (crown prince). Her French mother ruled Scotland on behalf of the French king until Mary, now a bewitching widow of 18, returned to take over her realm. She and her mother were two of the ladies the Protestant agitator John Knox had in mind when he thundered against the "monstrous regiment (regime) of women."

Mary was universally acknowledged Queen of Scots. Thanks to a complex Anglo-Scottish family tree, she also had a better title to the throne of England than her cousin Elizabeth, the incumbent. But she was a Roman Catholic. In Scotland the Reformation was in full swing, in England it had already been accomplished. Both nations declared for a Protestant royal family. Mary faced the irreconcilable tasks of placating Queen Elizabeth, whom she had hopes of succeeding, and of restoring Catholicism to Britain. After five years her patience gave out and in 1565 she made a foolish marriage to Lord Darnley, another cousin, and allegedly another Catholic.

Disaster followed. Her Italian secretary David Rizzio was stabbed to death in her presence; Darnley her husband was booby-trapped and blown up in his lodging at Kirk o' Field near Edinburgh. (Tradition has it that Mary went off and played a round of golf at Seton (Lothian) when she heard the news—which showed a sense of priorities that some Scots would approve of.) Piling folly on folly she next married the uncouth Earl of Bothwell who was supposed to have arranged Darnley's murder and was reputed to be a practitioner of the Black Arts.

Abandoned by him and driven from Scotland, she became Elizabeth's prisoner. For the next 20 years she was moved from castle to castle in England, a captive of state whose life depended entirely on political whims. In 1587 Queen Elizabeth finally signed the death warrant and the Queen of Scots, lovely still though racked with rheumatism from damp apartments, was beheaded for treason. She had spent nearly half her life in prison.

Almost as much romantic ink has been spilled over Mary Queen of Scots as over that other fascinating leader of lost causes, her great-great-great-grandson Bonnie Prince Charlie. She was a sharp and wilful schemer, even when handicapped in prison, she was a Catholic and half a foreigner, her private life did not bear looking into . . . despite all that she is Scotland's heroine and she can still bring out the latent chivalry of a nation notorious for its sturdy chauvinism, stern Protestantism and respect for moral values.

## A Counterblaste

Mary's son, another James, is depicted as a shambling, perverted, feeble-minded prince, so cowardly that when he had to tap a shoulder with a sword to bestow the accolade of knighthood his trembling hand almost decapitated the recipient. His talents inclined him to doggerel verse and tracts. (Among the latter, his *Counterblaste to Tobacco* is often quoted.) But during his mother's long imprisonment he had opportunities to study the ways of courtiers and churchmen. He played off Catholics against Protestants and he governed Scotland more successfully from a distance of 400 miles in London than his royal predecessors on the spot had managed to do.

When Elizabeth of England died childless in 1603 the prize which had eluded his mother fell into his lap. He became James I of England. He was already James VI of Scotland and in the table of succession he is styled "James VI and I."

As King of England, Scotland and Ireland, James's power and prestige were greatly increased. His method of "ruling by the pen" seemed to work. Unusually for a Stuart he never fought a battle, never allowed the Kirk (the Scottish Presbyterian Church) to dictate to him—and died peacefully in his bed.

### The End of an "Auld Sang"

Arrogance, obstinacy, extravagance, ingratitude and a firm belief in the divine right of kings were implanted in all the later Stuarts. Both England and Scotland suffered from their clumsy handling of economic problems and in addition they brought to England the bitterness of religious conflict with which Scotland was all too familiar.

In Scotland these were the years of the Solemn League and Covenant (1643) which called for a Presbyterian nation and a Presbyterian monarch; and of the Killing Times (1666 onwards) when the pendulum swung against Presbyterianism and the Covenanters, goaded into rebellion, were pursued and hacked to death wherever they could be found. Readers of Sir Walter Scott will remember "Old Mortality," the aged wanderer who went from place to place tidying up the Covenanters' neglected graves.

When in 1688 England forced the Catholic James II and VII to abdicate, no one north of the Border raised a hand to save the last Stuart king. The Protestants were now firmly on top. It was decreed that no Roman Catholic should henceforth sit on the English or Scottish throne—and none has ever done so. Joint sovereigns were brought over from Holland to share the vacant crown; one of them, Mary, was a Stuart and their successor, Anne, who came to the throne in 1702, was the last of the Stuarts.

During Anne's reign, men and nations had time to let the dust settle and to contemplate their fortunes and their relationships. There came the realization that a mere union of crowns suited neither Scotland nor England: it had to be a full political partnership or nothing. The result was an Act of Union of 1707 by which the two nations became one united kingdom. Scotland insisted on retaining her own Kirk and her own legal system; and was promised a full share in the benefits of England's foreign trade and colonial exploitations.

At the last session of the Scottish Parliament in Edinburgh in 1707, when the Honours of Scotland (crown, scepter and sword of state) were carried out for the last time, Lord Chancellor Seafield pronounced an epitaph on seven centuries of nationhood: "There's the end of an auld sang."

### Charlie was their Darling

Historical novelists have mined glittering seams from the triumphs and troubles of the Stuarts, but the richest nuggets have been found in the adventures of two who never quite made it to the throne: the Jacobite pretenders of the early-18th century. ("Jacobite" signifies a follower of Jacobus, the Latin for James.)

Many people both in Scotland and England regarded the Hanoverian successors of Queen Anne (George I, the first of the Hanoverians, came to the throne in 1714) as usurpers. James, offspring of James II and VII, based his claim to the throne on his status as the senior surviving Stuart. His assets were the sympathy of Catholics everywhere; a general discontent in Scotland at the first effects of the Union; and, as always, France's eagerness to stir up trouble.

The Old Pretender, however, was not a very inspiring personality and his campaign of the Fifteen (1715) petered out after a few half-hearted skirmishes.

The Forty-five (1745) was a different matter. The Young Pretender, otherwise Prince Charles Edward or Bonnie Prince Charlie or the Young Chevalier—Jacobites gave him various affectionate names—enthusiastically embraced his father's cause.

He owed his chance to the French, who were again at war with Britain and seeking a diversion. Bonnie Prince Charlie landed on Eris-kay in the Outer Hebrides, crossed to the mainland and set up his standard at Glenfinnan in August 1745. His youth (he was only 24), his courageous energy, his charm and vivacity (he was a mixture of Scot, Italian and Pole) attracted the Highland chiefs and their clans to his banner in satisfactory numbers: they were mostly Catholics and not averse to the idea of a little Lowland foray.

Marching south the small army took Edinburgh by surprise, in-stalled the Prince at Holyroodhouse and proclaimed his father King James III and VIII. Government forces rallied, but the Jacobites brushed them aside. The rebel army marched rapidly towards London, gathering supporters as it went. Why it turned back at Derby, 140 miles from the capital, and whether it was wise to do so, are questions which right-wing romantics still debate.

Hanoverian troops under the Duke of Cumberland, who was also 24 years old, started in pursuit. The Jacobites retreated steadily north, growing increasingly demoralized. Large numbers deserted, pleading pressure of work at home: the spring sowing season was coming on. The government troops caught up with the rebels on Culloden Moor near Inverness.

As a tactician the Prince was no match for cold ruthless professionals like the Duke of Cumberland and Major James Wolfe (afterwards Wolfe of Quebec). In 40 minutes at Culloden 9,000 Hanoverians routed 5,000 Jacobites and left 1,000 dead on the moor.

The Prince escaped. For the next five months he was a fugitive in the western Highlands and islands, during which time a young lady from South Uist protected him—and so the Flora Macdonald legend was born. Eventually a French ship took him away from Borrodale, from the spot where he had landed the previous year.

Driven from Paris under the terms of an Anglo-French peace treaty, the Young Pretender set up house in Rome. Faithful Scottish followers bore stoically with his petulance and drunken rages until his death in 1788. Back in Scotland, Jacobite sympathizers suffered harsh reprisals and the myth of the "King over the water" was born, lairds symbolical-ly passing their glasses over the water jug whenever they were required

to drink the King's health. (Some still do.) Wits in Georgian England
recited the Jacobite toast:

"God bless the King—I mean the Faith's Defender.
God bless (no harm in blessing) the Pretender.
But which the former is, and which the latter—
God bless us all! That's quite another matter."

## Learning to Live Together

Rebellions apart, it took time for the Scots and English to settle into
harness. Old scars were slow to heal, old antipathies persisted. In the
Border counties pleas for "one nation" are stifled to this day by memories of centuries of viciousness and vendetta on both sides.

The Scots resented their neighbors' patronizing condescension, the
assumption that a Scot was an inferior kind of Englishman. The
English mocked the apparent poverty of Scotland and the readiness
with which those super-patriotic porridge-eaters migrated to the south.
When a London alderman complained to Doctor Johnson that "poor
old England is lost" the sage answered that the tragedy was "the Scots
have found it."

## Scottish Genius

After the Union of 1707 Scotland's history was carried forward not
by kings and queens but by pioneers in the arts and sciences. There had
already been a few who had shown the world what Scotland could do.
John Napier of Edinburgh (1550–1617) had invented logarithms and
if that ingenious method of multiplying large numbers by simple addition was one day to be taken over by the computer and digital calcula-
tor it is worth remembering that the same mathematician also devised
a set of rods ("Napier's bones") that anticipated modern calculating
machines.

Among the Scots who helped organize the finances of Europe and
laid the foundations of the national reputation for shrewdness in insurance and investment was William Patterson (1658–1719). He proposed,
and afterwards directed, the Bank of England.

We shall deal with some outstanding writers and poets in a separate
chapter, *Literature and the Arts.*

Until the Act of Union much of Scotland had remained medieval.
Foreigners regarded the north as a barbarous, introverted land where
a traveler might easily get himself eaten by cannibals. The Union
changed all that. It lifted the Highlands into the 18th century, improved communications and opened horizons of opportunity to the
inhabitants. Astonishingly quickly the tide of enlightenment turned
and flowed the other way, from Scotland to England. One phenomenon
was the way Scottish doctors monopolized the health scene in England.
Many had interests in the Highland distilleries and recommended
whisky as medicine: thus the popularity of a drink formerly unknown
south of the Border was spread.

From the beginning of the industrial revolution Scots were marching
into the Hall of Fame in numbers out of all proportion to the popula-

tion. David Hume (1711–1776) and Adam Smith (1723–1790) pro-
pounded theories of philosophy and economics that launched those
sciences on their modern paths. James Hutton (1726–1797) wrote the
seminal treatise for present-day geology, *Theory of the Earth.* John
Hunter (1728–1793) pioneered modern surgery. Robert Adam of Kirkcaldy (1728–1792) was responsible for the neo-classical "Adam style"
which gave much of England and Scotland their dignified Georgian
architecture and urban planning.

James Watt of Greenock (1736–1819) devised the principles of steam
propulsion while walking on Glasgow Green—not, as legend has it, by
watching his mother's kettle boil. Watt is entitled to be called the
Father of Industry, for without steampower the industrial revolution
could not have proceeded. Among Scottish contemporaries who enabled mankind to profit from his inventions were David Dale (1739–
1806), cotton-mill builder and philanthropist; Henry Bell (1767–1830),
"hero of 1,000 blunders and one success," who designed and operated
commercially the first steamship in Europe; Thomas Telford (1757–
1834), "Colossus of Roads," who built the first highways, bridges and
canals in various parts of the world; John Loudon Macadam (1756–
1836), who gave his name to the ideal road-surfacing material; Robert
Stevenson (1772–1850), lighthouse engineer and inventor of the lantern
reflector. . . .

The list grows tedious. Suffice it to say that a few everyday items the
19th century owed to innovative Scots were the vacuum flask, the
raincoat or macintosh, the first reaping and threshing machines, the
coal-gas lamp, shale oil, pneumatic rubber tyres, the steam hammer,
the bicycle and the telephone!

## New Times in the Glens

Up to 1801 the population of Scotland had remained fairly stable at
around 1½ millions. In the next 100 years it rose to more than 4½
millions. Industry moved to the towns and small elegant cities like
Glasgow became the smoky workshops of the world. Most people were
employed in the heavy industries of coal-mining, engineering, iron
smelting and shipbuilding; or in the domestic industries of brewing,
milling, paper-making, tanning and wagon-building, to which the Scots
and their climate were well suited. Country craftsmen, weavers and
woodworkers migrated to the urban fringes of central Scotland's towns;
and the villages, wholly agricultural once again, reverted to a mean,
monotonous existence.

The demand for labor brought Irish workers into the west of Scotland. Highland families too were tempted to move to Glasgow to look
for a better life which, on the whole, they did not find. Pressure from
their landlords forced many Highland folk out of their ancestral crofts
(farm cottages). The discovery that mutton and wool yielded better
profits and needed fewer workers than beef and dairy produce precipi-
tated the infamous Clearances when large numbers of western Highlanders and islanders were evicted to make room for sheep pastures.
The 1800s were years of mass emigrations to America, the West Indies,
New Zealand and Australia. On paper the numbers involved were not

enormous: but the Clearances emptied the glens and broke down clan loyalties, destroying a way of life—something the Duke of Cumberland's redcoats after Culloden had tried in vain to do.

Emigration was a blessing for some young people. Scotland's superior education system was producing "lads o' pairts" (i.e. lads of talents) so fast that one small country could not accommodate their skills and thousands went off to seek careers in the United States and the British colonial possessions; a few, like the African explorers Mungo Park and David Livingstone, blazing trails where no white man had been before.

## Scots in the New World

Thomas Edison, Samuel Morse, Edgar Allan Poe, Washington Irving, Robert E. Lee, Presidents Jefferson, Monroe, Jackson, Grant and Polk, Patrick Henry and James McNeil Whistler all claimed Scottish ancestry. Allan Pinkerton of the detective agency was born in Glasgow, John Paul Jones, founder of the U.S. Navy, came from the Solway shore. Samuel Wilson, whose parents sailed to America from Greenock on the Clyde, has been officially recognized as the original Uncle Sam.

The Scots John Macdonald and Alexander Mackenzie were Canada's first and second Prime Ministers. That country's Fraser and Mackenzie rivers are named for Scottish pioneers, as is her leading university, McGill.

Perhaps the most famous American Scot was Andrew Carnegie, steel baron and multimillionaire, who started work as a bobbin boy in a Pittsburgh mill. When he was a baby in Dunfermline (Fife) his parents sold everything they had to raise the fare for the passage to New York.

Scots went in droves into the British armed forces and into administration and commerce in India. Before long every man of influence was Mac-something. "Did you meet Jones while you were out there?" an old India hand asks another—"No, no, I only mixed with the top people." The expatriates came home as nabobs and many of Scotland's beautiful country houses and mock-Gothic castles were built on "Indian money."

Sir John Moore the general who was killed at Corunna (1809) and immortalized in the poem by Charles Wolfe was a Scot; so was Sir Ralph Abercrombie who achieved the first successes against Napoleon's "invincibles." Robert Douglas and Patrick Gordon built the armies of the King of Sweden and the Czar of Russia and another Scottish soldier of fortune, Samuel Greig, created the Russian Navy.

A patriotic historian, Agnes Mure Mackenzie, has claimed that in 40 years after 1797 the island of Skye (population 3,500) gave the British Army "21 generals, 48 colonels, 600 majors, captains and subalterns; and to the Civil Service in the same period one governor-general, four colonial governors, a Chief Baron of England and a high court judge." There is a hint here of another maxim that Scots live by: look after your friends and relations and help them up the ladder.

To complete the military tale, Britain's senior commanders of World War I, Earl Haig and Sir Ian Hamilton, were both Scots. Scottish-born sailors and airmen of World War II included Admiral Viscount Cunningham and Air Marshals Lords Tedder and Dowding. The inventors of the Lee-Enfield and Ross rifles (and, they say, the Bowie knife) were dyed-in-the-wool Scots. America's General MacArthur descended from a west-Highland family.

## Tartanitis

England had railways 10 years before Scotland (1825) but when they arrived north of the Border they proliferated swiftly and pushed on the work of opening up the Highlands that the military road-builder General Wade had begun 100 years earlier. Simultaneously the poems and novels of Sir Walter Scott whetted tourists' appetites. Jules Verne, Mendelssohn, Paganini, Chopin, Ruskin, Shelley, Wordsworth, Keats, Hans Andersen, Bret Harte, Washington Irving and Harriet Beecher Stowe were only a few of the celebrities who came to see if "Caledonia stern and wild" really existed.

It was Queen Victoria who had confirmed Scotland's role as a prestige tourist destination. Urged on by her consort Prince Albert, she attended Highland Gatherings and stayed at ducal castles. Very soon she acquired a small castle of her own, Balmoral, enlarged it and bought up the countryside round about. (The price for Ballochbuie forest was a length of tartan cloth, from which circumstance it is known as "the bonniest plaid in Scotland.")

The Queen spent her summer holidays at Balmoral. Tartanitis, a rare disease before her time, became a national epidemic. Kilts and sashes, stags' antlers and the targes (shields) and claymores (swords) of the warrior clans chimed in with the fussy decor of the period in many a suburban home; and a curiously romanticized vision of Scotland took shape. Queen Victoria and her playboy son, afterwards Edward VII, made summer travel in Scotland fashionable and set examples in deer-stalking, salmon-fishing, grouse-shooting and pony-trekking which their subjects eagerly copied.

## The Twentieth Century

Scotland's recent history is, generally speaking, the history of the United Kingdom of which she remains of course an integral part. In science and technology Scots continued to shine. Without going into a very long list of names, we might just look at the field of telecommunications. Along with the name of Alexander Graham Bell (first practical telephone) stand the names of Lord Kelvin (first Atlantic cable), John Logie Baird (first practical television), Sir Robert Watson Watt (radar) and James Clerk-Maxwell (electro-magnetic theories which put Einstein and Marconi, as they said, "on the right track").

Scots have shown a peculiar aptitude for politics. Keir Hardie of Bellshill near Glasgow founded the Labour party and is regarded as Britain's first socialist. The first working man to become a member of the British Cabinet (John Burns) and the first British Marxist (John Maclean) were Scots. Since the beginning of this century six British Prime Ministers have been Scots: A.J. Balfour, Henry Campbell-Bannerman, Bonar Law, Ramsay Macdonald, Harold Macmillan and Lord Home.

Politically the nation has held her own with England. In 1745 the office of Scottish Secretary was abolished "in the interests of national unity" and until 1885 Scotland was merely North Britain. Not until 1928 was a Scottish Office established in Scotland with departments to administer the country from Edinburgh. About the same time the Scottish Secretary became a senior minister in the Westminster government and his prestige, cares and duties have increased ever since.

Industrially Scotland has known good times and bad. Venerable industries have declined. The great Clydebank shipyards which turned out the *Queen Mary* and *Queen Elizabeth* are now in public ownership or converted to other uses. Scotland once produced 43 different makes of automobile; the Depression of 1931 swept them all away and today she has none. Rightly or wrongly, Scots tend to blame England for their industrial troubles; and the Scottish labor unions are among the most left-wing and militant in the British Isles.

Numerous industrial and commercial operations with good Scottish names are controlled by English giants. The "dawn raiders" from the south have had more success with takeovers than their freebooting ancestors who operated when Robert the Bruce was a boy. It involves some swallowing of national pride, but it has given Scotland a high technology and a better communications system than almost any country in Europe.

## The Oil Bonanza

In 1970 British Petroleum struck oil under the sea in an area known as The Forties, about 100 miles east of Aberdeen. Thus began the most significant industrial development in Scotland of the century.

Britain's new-found oil and natural gas reserves lie in a straggling line about 100 miles off the Scottish coast, approximately from the Firth of Tay to Shetland; most therefore comes within what might loosely be called Scotland's territorial waters. Visions of a race of tartan sheikhs have evaporated, but the British economy has received a boost and there is a separate spin-off for Scotland in the well-paid jobs available in rig, platform and module construction and repair, in specialist shipbuilding, transportation and pipe-laying, in technical services and in the processing of the crude product at Grangemouth. Although the jobless total for Great Britain is high, almost full employment has come to some eastern Scottish cities and towns which, as they report, are "up to their necks in oil."

Scotland's traditional commodities have proved successful in the consumer society. Whisky distillers have created a world-wide demand. Textiles, especially the Border woollens and Shetland knitwear and Harris tweeds (now largely under multinational control) attract buyers from overseas. Scottish enterprise, self-confidence and inventiveness are still evident, though home-based companies complain of a lack of investment capital.

## Shotgun Marriage

How is the Union, that shotgun marriage of 1707, getting along? Whenever polls are taken, about 90% of the English are satisfied with the way things are, about 50% of Scots would prefer some kind of Home Rule; 20% want complete independence and a separate seat at the United Nations.

The Scottish National Party was born out of the Great Depression of the 1930s and achieved its greatest strength to date in the late 1960s and early 1970s. At one period it had a dozen members of Parliament at Westminster out of a grand total of 635. The Party has since declined to a point where the two main parties, Conservative and Labour, can afford to ignore it. It has been split by ideological in-fighting, but remains respectable, vociferous and a perpetual talking-point with young Scots.

Complete independence for Scotland, such as is enjoyed by the Republic of Ireland, is probably an impossible dream. Statisticians say that Scotland would lose by it—that England disburses considerable aid to Scotland and that Scotland's *per capita* contributions to the cost of running Britain are smaller than England's. But all admit that a true basis of comparison is hard to arrive at.

Meantime, the closer the two nations are bound together the more stridently Scotland proclaims her individuality. What Robert Louis Stevenson wrote 100 years ago will probably apply 100 years from now:

"There is nothing more provoking than the great gulf which is set between England and Scotland. Here are two peoples almost identical in blood, the same in language and religion; and yet a few years of quarrelsome isolation (in comparison with the great historical cycles) have so separated their thoughts and ways that not unions, nor mutual dangers, nor steamers, nor railways, nor yet the king's horses and the king's men seem able to obliterate the distinction."

Within the framework of the United Kingdom, national politics in Scotland incline to the left of center. It is often said that the Scottish vote puts the Socialists in power at Westminster. The industrial towns of Fife and the central belt are traditionally Labour, the rural Lowlands and Grampian traditionally Conservative. In the far north and the northwestern isles, voters are traditionally Liberal but there has been recent support for the Scottish Nationalists.

The Scottish Conservatives hold their garden fêtes and the Scottish National Party its memorial services for patriots dead and gone . . . and the ordinary citizen goes amiably to both. In this matter, as in much else down the ages, things have turned out better for Scotland than might have been expected. The members she sends to the British Parliament and to the European Parliament have a powerful voice. By maintaining a voting presence in the councils of her neighbors and at the same time keeping alive the cry of "Freedom for Scotland" she probably enjoys the best of both worlds.

And diehard Jacobites (of whom a few survive) have the consolation of knowing that, although the Stuarts had their chance and threw it away, the Queen of Great Britain and her family today are in a direct

line of descent from the "Merry Monarch" Charles II, and from Mary
Queen of Scots, and indeed from Walter the Steward himself.


# A MINI-HISTORY OF SCOTLAND

| *Reigning Monarch* | *Dates* | *Events* |
|---|---|---|
| | A.D. 80 | Romans arrive in Scotland |
| | 392 | Ninian founds the first Christian church on Isle of Whithorn |
| | c.400 | End of Roman occupation |
| | c.500 | First "Scots" arrive from Ireland |
| | 563 | St. Columba on Iona |
| | 685 | Pictish army defeats invading Angles at Nectansmere |

**Houses of Alpin, Atholl and Moray**

Kenneth MacAlpin, 843–58, first "king" of Scots and Picts
Numerous short-lived "kings," drawn from descendants of MacAlpin. His great-great-grandson was:

| | | |
|---|---|---|
| Kenneth II, 971–95 | 990 | Supposed battle of Luncarty, Scots against Danes, adoption of thistle as national emblem |
| Constantine III, 995–97 | | |
| Kenneth III, 997–1005 | | |
| Malcolm II, 1005–34 | 1018 | Battle of Carham. Lothian annexed to Scotland |
| Duncan I, 1034–40 | | |
| Macbeth, 1040–57 | | |
| Lulach, 1057–58 | 1057 | England abandoned northern Northumbria to the Scots. The kingdom of Alba ("Alba" is still the Gaelic word for Scotland) took shape. King Malcolm III, by the time he murdered Lulach, had already begun to mold the old Scottish, Pictish and Anglian kingdoms into one, and to bring the tribes under one head and one law |

# SCOTTISH HISTORY

| Reigning Monarch | Dates | Events |
|---|---|---|
| Malcolm III, 1057–93, called Canmore (Great Head) | 1093 | Death of saintly Margaret, wife of Malcolm Canmore and founder of modern Edinburgh |
| Donald, 1093–4, displaced by Duncan | 1093–1200 | Kingdom torn by internal strife and threatened by Norse invasions |
| Duncan II, 1094–5 | | |
| Donald (restored) 1095–7 | | |
| Edgar, 1097–1107 | | |
| Alexander I, 1107–1124 | | |
| David I, 1124–53, the Sair Sanct | 1118–50 | Building of abbeys at Holyrood, Melrose, Kelso, Dryburgh and Jedburgh |
| Malcolm IV, 1153–65, called The Maiden | | |
| William, 1165–1214, called The Lion | 1174 | Scotland becomes a vassal state of England |
| Alexander II, 1214–49 | | |
| Alexander III, 1249–86 | 1263 | Battle of Largs. Scotland acquires the Hebrides from Norway |
| Margaret, 1286–92, called Maid of Norway | | |
| John Balliol, 1292–1306 | 1297 | Patriots under William Wallace defeat the English at Stirling Bridge |
| | 1305 | Wallace captured and executed |
| Robert I, 1306–29, called The Bruce | 1314 | Battle of Bannockburn |
| | 1328 | Treaty of Northampton, by which Scotland achieves her independence |
| David II, 1329–71 | 1368 | Edinburgh Castle rebuilt, takes on its present shape |

## House of Stuart

| | | |
|---|---|---|
| Robert II, 1371–90 | 14th–15th centuries | The MacDonalds, Lords of the Isles, and the "Black" Douglases wage war on the crown |
| Robert III, 1390–1406 | 1388 | Battle of Otterburn. "Black" Douglas repels the English |
| | 1396 | Battle of the Clans at Perth |
| James I, 1406–37 | 1411 | St. Andrews University founded |
| James II, 1437–60 | 1451 | Glasgow University founded |
| | 1472 | Scotland acquires Orkney and Shetland |
| James III, 1460–88 | 1482 | Scots lords hang the King's favorites from Lauder bridge |
| | 1488 | Battle of Sauchieburn. King slain |
| James IV, 1488–1513 | 1494 | Aberdeen University founded |
| | 1513 | Battle of Flodden. King slain |
| James V, 1513–42 | 1542 | Battle of Solway Moss |
| Mary, 1542–67, called Queen of Scots | 1544 | Edinburgh burned by invading English |
| | 1560 | Reformation of the Church. Roman Catholicism abolished |

| *Reigning Monarch* | *Dates* | *Events* |
|---|---|---|
| James VI, 1567–1625 | 1582 | Edinburgh University founded |
| | 1587 | Mary Queen of Scots beheaded |
| | 1603 | Union of Crowns. James VI of Scotland becomes James I of England |
| Charles I, 1625–49. | 1643 | Solemn League and Covenant, making Presbyterianism compulsory in Scotland |
| (Interregnum, 1649–60) | 1650 | Cromwell's victory over Scottish royalists at Dunbar. Cromwell rules England and Scotland as Lord Protector. |
| | 1658 | First stage-coach from Edinburgh to London |
| Charles II, 1660–85 | 1660–88 | Episcopacy re-established. The Killing Times. Presbyterian Covenanters brutally persecuted |
| James II and VII, 1685–88 | | |
| William III (1689–1702) and | 1689 | Battle of Killiecrankie. |
|   Mary II (1689–1694), a joint monarchy | 1692 | Massacre of Glencoe |
| Anne, 1702–14 | 1707 | Union of Parliaments, by which Scotland and England become one nation |

**House of Hanover**

| | | |
|---|---|---|
| George I, 1714–27 | 1715 | First Jacobite rebellion. The Old Pretender defeated at Sheriffmuir |
| | 1736 | Birth of James Watt |
| George II, 1727–60 | 1745 | Second Jacobite rebellion |
| | 1746 | The Young Pretender defeated at Culloden. Wearing of the kilt forbidden |
| | 1759 | Birth of Robert Burns |
| George III, 1760–1820 | 1771 | Birth of Sir Walter Scott |
| | 1782 | Wearing of the kilt permitted |
| | 1788 | Death of Bonnie Prince Charlie |
| George IV, 1820–30 | c.1820 | Beginning of Highland Clearances |
| William IV, 1830–37 | | |
| Victoria, 1837–1901 | 1842 | Edinburgh–Glasgow railroad opened |
| | 1846 | Edinburgh–London railroad opened |
| | 1854 | Construction of Balmoral Castle, the Queen's Highland home |

**House of Saxe-Coburg-Gotha**

Edward VII, 1901–10

**House of Windsor**

| | | |
|---|---|---|
| George V, 1910–36 | 1914–18 | World War I |
| | 1928 | Scottish Office established as Government department in Edinburgh |

| Reigning Monarch | Dates | Events |
|---|---|---|
| Edward VIII, 1936, abdicated | | |
| George VI, 1936–52 | 1938 | St. Andrew's House opened in Edinburgh as center of Scottish administration |
| | 1939–45 | World War II |
| Elizabeth II, 1952 | 1970 | Exploitation of North Sea oil begins off Scottish coasts |
| | 1973 | Britain becomes a member of EEC or Common Market |
| | 1975 | Local government counties reorganized as Regions |

# LITERATURE AND THE ARTS

## *Originality and Vigor*

The English-reading world meets Scottish literature at an early age. Every child knows *Treasure Island* by Robert Louis Stevenson, scribbled on a sick-bed at Braemar. And every child makes the acquaintance of *Peter Pan,* the creation of Sir J.M. Barrie, while few are not familiar with *Robinson Crusoe:* the real-life hero, not the author, was a Scot named Alexander Selkirk from Largo.

In a literary tradition remarkable for its richness and diversity, two giants stand out: Robert Burns the poet and Sir Walter Scott the poet and novelist.

Not many outside Scotland appreciate the depth of affection that Scotland has for Robert Burns (1759–1796). To his fellow-countrymen he is more than a great lyric bard; he is the champion of the under-dog, the lover of noble causes, the hater of pomposity and cant, the prophet of social justice. "A man's a man for a' that"—such homely phrases have exalted the Scottish character and the Scottish tongue. His love-songs warm the coldest Presbyterian hearts. His own mixed-up love life and sordid end evoke a curious sympathy in the "unco' guid," as Burns called the ultra-respectable pillars of society of his time. The man in the street still quotes Burns—which is more than can be said, south of the Border, of Shakespeare. Burns societies and federations abound all over the globe. Burns Night, 25th January, is an anniversary of some importance in Scotland.

Walter Scott (1771–1832) was an Edinburgh lawyer with aristocratic pretensions, an assiduous collector of old ballads and tales, an expert on rhyming couplets and later a novelist universally acclaimed. His long narrative poems included *The Lay of the Last Minstrel, Marmion, The Lady of the Lake* and *The Lord of the Isles.* The most widely-read of a long string of historical novels were *Waverley, Ivanhoe, The Talisman, Redgauntlet, The Heart of Midlothian* and *Old Mortality.* Told seriously and thoroughly documented, his works lifted fiction high above the Gothick romances of his contemporaries. Not many readers these days get through Scott without skipping pages, but when he was alive his popularity was tremendous and he has been described as Scottish tourism's best-ever propagandist.

### Scotland's First Poet

Thomas of Ercildoune (c.1225–c.1300) was the sort of semi-mythical character whom Scott delighted in. Ercildoune is modern Earlston and Thomas was that "True Thomas" or "Thomas the Rhymer" who spent seven years in Elfland with the Fairy Queen. Whatever the truth of that, a few of Thomas's ballads and rhyming prophecies have survived and he is to be considered Scotland's earliest poet.

Over the next 200 years, the only outstanding names are those of the court poets William Dunbar (c.1465–c.1513), whose *Lament for the Makaris* (*makar* meaning poet) is well-known; and Sir David Lindsay (c.1490–c.1555), whose sprawling verse-drama *Ane Satire of the Thrie Estates* is a valuable critique of administrative systems under the Stuarts.

During that same period anonymous ballads of poignant simplicity became a vital element in Scottish literature. Most verse anthologies contain samples of them, and schoolchildren learn them by heart: *Otterburn, The Twa Sisters, Lord Randal, Tam Lin, Sir Patrick Spens* and scores besides.

Scottish literature dealt with everyday themes before that of most of Europe; the country's writers were expressing the life and character of ordinary people when most of Europe thought it proper to write and read only about lords and ladies. Allan Ramsay (1684–1758) wrote ballads and songs of rustic life; Robert Fergusson (1750–1774) gave liberal sentiments lusty voice and inspired Burns; Tobias Smollett (1721–1771) depicted the young Scot seeking his fortune abroad in novels such as *Roderick Random, Humphrey Clinker* and *Peregrine Pickle;* and James Boswell (1740–1795), companion and biographer of Dr. Samuel Johnson, established himself as one of the greatest diarists of all time.

### The Golden Age

Then came the golden age of Scottish literature, represented by Burns and Scott and James Hogg (1770–1835). Hogg's poetry did not enjoy great popularity after his death, but during his life-time his writings and table-talk were thought much of. Recently, Scotland has rediscovered the "Ettrick Shepherd" as he was called—he was a friend and neighbor of Sir Walter Scott—and his tortured apology for a life oppressed with fears of Hell, *Confessions of a Justified Sinner,* is more appreciated today than when it was written.

In the era of Burns, Scott, Hogg and many lesser lights, Edinburgh became a hotbed of poetic talents and a metropolis of the printing, publishing and bookselling trades. Several long-running magazines were started, some of international repute. The brothers William (1800 –1883) and Robert (1802–1871) Chambers of Peebles set up their first small shop in Edinburgh, taking it in turns to sleep under the counter at night to save the expense of a nightwatchman. From that address came *Chambers' Journal* and eventually an issue of reference books, of which *Chambers' Encyclopaedia* is perhaps the most prestigious today. William Blackwood (1776–1834) launched *Blackwood's Magazine,* a conservative institution in Britain and the Empire for nearly 170 years. Francis Jeffrey (1773–1850), at the opposite extreme of the political spectrum, founded the influential *Edinburgh Review.*

From a tiny room in the Old Town of Edinburgh in 1771 the *Encyclopaedia Britannica* was issued. The first work of its kind, the model for encyclopedias the world over, it was written almost single-handed by the journalist James Tytler (c.1742–1806) on a washer-woman's upturned tub.

### "Kailyard"

In the shadow which Burns and Scott had cast before them, a generation of regional writers appeared, facetiously christened the "Kailyard" (cabbage-patch) school for their parochialism and use of impenetrable local dialects. Head and shoulders above the rest stands John Galt (1779–1839), author of delightful tales about country life in Ayrshire in *Annals of the Parish, The Provost* and other works. The best-known of latter-day kailyard novelists is Lewis Grassic Gibbon (1901–1935), author of a trilogy of stories set in rural Aberdeenshire, *The Scots Quair:* rather a high-flown title—*Quair* means book—but perhaps the nearest thing Scotland has known to the *roman fleuve* or saga.

Kailyard is not an adjective to be applied to William McGonagall (1830–1902) of Dundee, though more derisory terms have been heaped on him. McGonagall, the clown of Scottish literature, applied poor rhymes, worse meter and over-florid metaphor to grand subjects with a bathos that amounted almost to genius. He is a cult figure in some circles as the only truly memorable bad poet.

### Monoliths of Scholarship

The survey of Scottish literature must cover a few of the works of immense scholarship which became standard text-books of the sciences and philosophy. Before the 1800s there had been David Hume's *Concerning Human Understanding* (1748) and Adam Smith's *The Wealth of Nations* (1776).

Thomas Carlyle (1795–1881), born at Ecclefechan, dominated literary scholarship in the 19th century. His rugged, powerful style in *Sartor Resartus* and the monumental *French Revolution* led Walt Whitman to say of him that "no man else will bequeath to the future more significant hints of our stormy era, its fierce paradoxes, its din." Carlyle's wife Jane (1801–1866), a native of Haddington, was almost as notable in her day. Her letters and critical essays reveal her to be one of the most accomplished women of the century.

The Scottish genius for laborious and painstaking research is exemplified in Hugh Miller (1802–1856), a stonemason from Cromarty and a self-taught journalist and geologist. *Old Red Sandstone* and *Testimony of the Rocks,* like the works of Hume, Adam Smith and Carlyle, are more than treatises on themes of narrow specialism: they are masterpieces of literature.

## Long John Silver and Sherlock Holmes

Son and grandson of two famous Scottish engineers, Robert Louis Stevenson (1850–1894) wrote his memorable *Treasure Island* and *Kidnapped* as serials for boys' magazines while contemplating more serious works. With *Travels with a Donkey* and *An Inland Voyage* the owner of the second best-known set of initials in literature (R.L.S.) produced two short classics of travel writing. He was a genuine poet and his short stories of life in the Pacific islands where he lived for some years and died young are the finest any Scottish writer has written. And in his parable of the schizoid personality, *Dr. Jekyll and Mr. Hyde,* he demonstrated a psychological perception that would have interested his contemporary Sigmund Freud.

The same preoccupation with the darker forces existing within man is found in a number of Stevenson's short stories with a supernatural, or related, theme. Indeed, in their apparent predilection for morbidity and melancholy there is often more than a hint of that other master of fictional horror, Edgar Allan Poe, who of course had claims of his own to Scottish ancestry.

R.L.S. is not as popular in Scotland as he might be (he spoke slightingly of Sir Walter Scott), but his work shows an acute sense of Scottish life and history and he is one of the most stylish writers the English language has known.

Something of Stevenson's mastery of the craft appears also in Sir Arthur Conan Doyle (1859–1930), another Scot with a creative imagination and first class control over suspense and drama. His incomparable Sherlock Holmes stories ensure Doyle's immortality, but he wrote many other tales and a few novels on quite different subjects.

## Modern Literature

The first half of the 20th century produced no British playwright more successful than Sir J.M. Barrie (1860–1937). Born very poor, his many successes ensured that he died extremely rich. As with Conan Doyle and Sherlock Holmes, his name will always be linked to one great work: *Peter Pan,* the perennial juvenile. His other great money-spinners—*Dear Brutus, What Every Woman Knows, Quality Street, The Admirable Crichton* and others—are considered lightweight for the modern theater. Though dismissed sometimes as cloyingly whimsical, they are marvelously constructed and infused with sure touches of humor which completely conquered the London theaters of Barrie's day.

James Bridie (1888–1957), a playwright who has achieved less success than he deserved, is best remembered for *Tobias and the Angel.* There are signs of a resurgence of interest in Bridie; he has become a favorite of the Pitlochry Theatre in the Hills. Another author half-forgotten but recently revived—thanks to television—is Neil Munro (1864–1930). He wrote the romantic tale *John Splendid* but was most at home in the humorous *Para Handy Tales,* the adventures of the men who manned the puffers (small coasting vessels) of the Clyde.

Among 20th-century poets Edwin Muir (1887–1959) is better remembered as an essayist, critic and first translator of Kafka than for his rather turgid poetry. Poetry—perhaps one should say verse—is very much alive in Scotland today. It has marched along with nationalism and tends to be polemical, stridently self-conscious and marred for the non-Scot by a preference for "Lallans" or "braid Scots" (broad Scots) instead of English. But Hugh MacDiarmid (1892–1979) will probably go down in history as the best Scots poet since Burns. Of the living poets, Norman MacCaig (b. 1910) is the best of a mediocre bunch.

20th-century prose writers of stature are Compton Mackenzie (1883–1972)—in his time the Grand Old Man of Scottish letters—and Eric Linklater (1899–1974), author of *Private Angelo, Don Juan in America* and other novels.


## Art and Architecture

Scotland has never been supreme in the visual arts, but she has produced four good painters and two great architects. Allan Ramsay (1713–1784), not to be confused with his father the poet, painted many portraits while active in London literary life. Sir Henry Raeburn (1756–1823) did many more—600-odd, it is said—and was knighted by King George IV. Alexander Nasmyth (1758–1840) is regarded as the father of the Scottish landscape school, although his best-known picture is a portrait of Robert Burns.

As Sir Walter Scott preserved the old life of Scotland on paper, so Sir David Wilkie (1785–1841) recorded it on canvas. *Pitlessie Fair, The Penny Wedding* and *John Knox Preaching* are examples of the homely scenes and historical reconstructions he specialized in. His work is comparable in sentiment and subject matter to the many pictures of Highland life, which did so much to promote the 19th-century popular image of Scotland, produced by his English near-contemporary Sir Edwin Landseer.

In architecture Robert Adam (1728–1792) of Kirkcaldy continued the impressive work of his father William and was assisted by his brother John. He originated the stately and rather fanciful Gothick and, later, the palatial neo-classical styles of most of Scotland's elegant

# CLAN TARTANS

**Hunting MacPherson**

**MacDonald**

**MacBain**

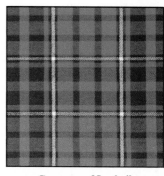

**Cameron of Locheil**

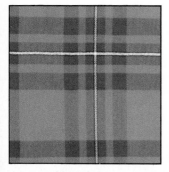

**MacGregor**

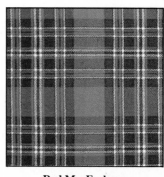

**Red MacFarlane**

# CLAN TARTANS

**Old Stewart**

**Hunting Stewart**

**Royal Stewart**

**Red Ross**

**Red Robertson**

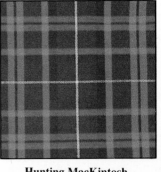

**Hunting MacKintosh**

# CLAN TARTANS

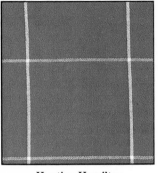

**Hunting Hamilton**

**MacArthur**

**MacKay**

**Douglas**

**Campbell**

**Black Watch**

# CLAN TARTANS

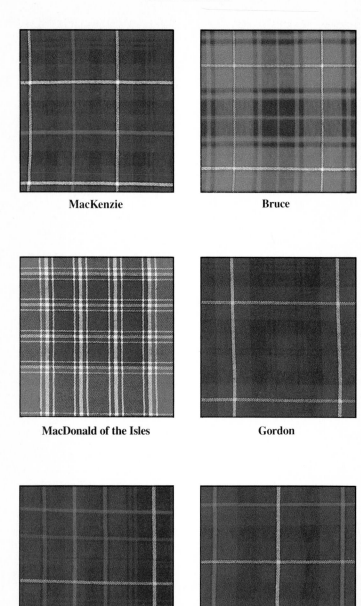

MacKenzie

Bruce

MacDonald of the Isles

Gordon

Hunting Macinnes

Hunting MacLeod

18th-century buildings, streets and squares. The best examples of the Adam style in Scotland are Edinburgh's Charlotte Square and Mellerstain House. But his success was equally great in England, especially London.

Charles Rennie Mackintosh (1868–1928), like Robert Adam before him, designed not only buildings but the furniture and fittings to go in them as well. Mackintosh was not well known at his death, least of all in Scotland, but he is now acclaimed as a phenomenon of innovative design, painting and architecture; and his deceptively stark furniture, which used to be broken up for firewood, commands extraordinary prices.

## Music

Though the bagpipe is by no means the exclusive property of Scotland—in fact, it is one of the most ancient instruments in the world and species of bagpipe existed throughout the Ancient World—its elegiac wail is popularly identified with Scotland and the instrument remains an enduring symbol of the country. Not surprisingly therefore, the bagpipe, accompanied as often as not by a fiddle or two, is at the heart of Scottish music, especially the folk tunes that comprise the bulk of what one might call Scottish national music.

Everyone knows a few traditional Scottish songs—*Annie Laurie, Auld Lang Syne, The Braes of Yarrow, Auld Robin Gray, The Bonnie Earl o' Moray* and the rest—but musicians distinguish between deliberately-composed sentimental songs and the airs and ballads which sprang from a genuine folk tradition. Somewhere between the two categories lie the haunting melodies to which the songs of Allan Ramsay and Robert Burns were set. Great composers like Haydn, J.C. Bach and Beethoven did not disdain to use them in concertos and variations.

The Scots love music and the list of foreign virtuosi who visited Edinburgh and Glasgow in the 18th and 19th centuries is a long one. But native classical compositions, with one or two exceptions—Hamish MacCunn's (1868–1916) overture *Land of the Mountain and the Flood,* for example—have made little impact abroad. Nor are many Scots-born performers internationally known. Apart from Frederick Lamond (1868–1948) the pianist, Mary Garden (1877–1967) the operatic diva and Joseph Hyslop (1887–1977) the tenor, it is hard to name one.

Of recent composers the following names appear regularly on the programs of Scottish concerts: Francis George Scott (1880–1958), noted for song settings of poems by Burns and MacDiarmid; Ian Whyte (1901–1960), composer of opera and ballet scores and some chamber music; Robin Orr (b. 1909) and Thea Musgrave (b. 1928), composers of operas on Scottish historical themes; and Cedric Thorpe Davie (b. 1913), best known for his music for films and plays.

Sir Alexander Gibson (b. 1926) ranks with the best living conductors; his entrepreneurial talents also helped the Scottish National Orchestra and Scottish Opera get off the ground.

## Seeing and Hearing

The National Galleries of Scotland, the National Gallery of Modern Art, the National Portrait Gallery and the National Museums of Scotland are all located in Edinburgh. There are also superb picture galleries in Glasgow, including—at last!—a home for the famous Burrell Collection which, under the terms of its bequest, had to be housed in a pollution-free atmosphere. Aberdeen, Dundee and Perth also have excellent picture galleries.

The National Library of Scotland is in Edinburgh and the famous Mitchell Library in Glasgow. Thanks to benefactions by Andrew Carnegie, the 19th-century American steel tycoon, many small Scottish towns have remarkably large and well-stocked public libraries.

There are major touring theater companies in Glasgow, Edinburgh and Aberdeen and repertory theaters in Glasgow, Edinburgh, St. Andrews, Dundee and Perth; and a summer season at the Pitlochry theater. The MacRobert Arts Centre at Stirling University offers variegated and avant-garde fare in concerts, operas, drama, films and art exhibitions.

Scottish Opera is young but already well-known at home and abroad and Scottish Theatre Ballet is establishing itself as the national dance company. The Scottish National and Scottish Symphony orchestras give regular concerts in the principal cities and towns. The Scottish Arts Council promotes and supports local artistic activities throughout Scotland and also provides about 12 annual touring exhibitions of painting, sculpture and crafts. The Council's program sums up the situation in Scottish arts and crafts when it says that "those who come in search of the past will be agreeably surprised by the vitality of the present."

# CLANS AND TARTANS

## *Gaeldom's Savage Splendor*

The word "clan" means children. That definition is the key to the social organization of the Scottish Highlands—not the Lowlands—in history and legend.

The clan system is archaic. It goes back to an era when savage tribes gave up their restless wanderings and chose places to settle down in. A clan chief was revered by his followers as the lineal descendant of him "who first raised smoke and boiled water in that place"—the first landholder, the sacred embodiment of the race. But all the clansfolk, rich and poor, bore that patriarch's name and regarded themselves equally as his children.

This explains the extreme loyalty and docility of the clans towards their chiefs down the generations. It also explains the pride and arrogance which early travelers in the Highlands found so ludicrous in gangs of cattle-thieves who looked to them like the dregs of humanity.

There are about 90 clans, some old and some fairly new, and between them they cover every square inch of the Highlands and islands, excluding Orkney and Shetland. Their territorial boundaries were not always clearly defined: some clans mingled freely with others, some progressively enlarged their holdings and others lost the ground they claimed. Territorial boundaries have no significance at all today and the only survivors with any claim to the land are one or two great chiefs who still live on their ancestral acres. But the descendant of a clansman, wherever in the world he may be, regards the glen or island of his forebears as his native heath.

## Lords of the Isles

Clan origins may be rooted in Norse and Celtic legends but their actual histories go back not much farther than the 13th and 14th centuries, when their names and deeds were first recorded. The Clan MacDonald is considered to be the oldest. The first MacDonald was, as his name implies, "son of Donald" and Donald was the grandson of a Norse adventurer named Somerled who flourished around 1100.

Donald's descendants took over much of the western Highlands and for centuries boasted the title of Lords of the Isles. Offshoots formed separate clans: MacDonalds of Sleat, MacDonells of Glengarry, Mac-Dougalls and others. Many clans were interrelated. Some preserve venerable alliances, some are hereditary enemies. Not long ago a Mr. Campbell refused to have his son taught by a teacher named Mac-Donald. The hostility dated from the Glencoe massacre of 1692, when the clan chiefs got mixed up in national politics.

Causes of widespread strife were the Jacobite rebellions of 1715 and 1745. Most clans were pro-Jacobite because of their Catholicism and because, as the clansmen regarded the chief as their father, so the chiefs regarded the royal Stuart as *their* father. It was the natural order of the system. To this day you may hear arguments between those whose ancestors were "out" in the Forty-five and those whose ancestors stayed at home.

## Names and Titles

If you bear a name which appears in the official table of the clans you are probably a member of that clan, though your family came from Glasgow in the Lowlands, or even from England or Ireland. Emigration and soldiering dispersed the clans into some far places.

Certain proud Highland names, by the way, described characteristics not at all flattering. Campbell was "crooked mouth," Cameron meant "bent nose" and Kennedy "ugly head."

Highlanders emphasize the exclusive nature of their culture by giving the word "the" a special dignity. "Do you speak Gaelic?" is wrong; "Do you have the Gaelic?" is correct. Similarly, "Do you wear a kilt?" is wrong; "Do you wear the kilt?" is correct.

"The" is part of the majestic style of the chief and he is so described in the telephone book although, through the vicissitudes of time, he may be a secondhand automobile salesman in the United States or a bank clerk in England. (By the old custom, chiefs descend in both male and female lines.) So the chief of the Mackintosh clan is "The Mackintosh." What is more, since he lives on an estate of the same name, he is "The Mackintosh of Mackintosh." In olden times he would have been styled "The Mackintosh of that Ilk." One or two reactionary chiefs still cling to "of that Ilk."

At clan gatherings and banquets a few high-and-mighty chiefs glory in sonorous Gaelic designations. MacGregor of Macgregor's followers call him "An t-Ailpeanach," "The Alpin," which recalls the Dark-Age chieftain who fathered the first kings of Scotland. The Duke of Argyll rejoices in the name of "MacCailein-Mhor," "Great Son of the Whelp," a name long associated with the Clan Campbell of which he is the head.

## Shirt and Boots

If your Scottish family name is not in the list of clans it may be among the "septs." Septs were either collateral branches of the clan or groups of survivors from clans wiped out in battle or shipwreck who had attached themselves to the clan. The latter were known as "broken men."

The septs embrace a variety of names not obviously Scottish, which is a stroke of luck for the people who make and sell clan insignia. If your name is Brown you have a choice of the Lamont or MacMillan tartans. The Clarks claim kinship with the Camerons, the Cooks with the Stuarts. Lewises may wear the MacLeod colors, Millers the Mac-Farlane, Thomsons the Campbell and Wrights the Macintyre. Some Highland dress outfitters stock the Smith tartan.

The best authorities say we must not wear the tartan unless we belong to the clan. "To do so invites scorn and derision," says the book of rules. Not surprisingly, this is not a view shared by the manufacturers and retailers of all the paraphernalia of clannery. But in any case to insist on the prohibition in Scotland today is to be excessively punctilious. Tartan is not copyright.

If some pedantic person asks what right you have to the old Highland dress, remind them that the old Highland dress was shirt and boots—and not always boots. Kilt and sporran, badges, bonnets, brooches, buttons, belts and buckles are relatively modern mysteries. The clan societies themselves—the protocol departments of the clans—dispute the authenticity of the regalia.

## Invention of the Tartan

Kilts and tartans were not confined to the Highland Scots. Tribal folk the world over discovered that a sort of loose skirt was practical and healthy for climbing hills and wading through streams. We may suppose that colored strands were woven into the drab wool for camouflage, or for decoration, or to help with identifying drowned or mangled bodies: a sort of family stitch.

The colored strands ran vertically or horizontally through the cloth, or both, and thus the checkered tartan pattern emerged. Exclusive to the clan, it helped to tell friend from foe. Some tartans were bold and plain: the Menzies is simply white on red. Some were kaleidoscopic: the Ogilvie is red, white, dark blue, light blue, black, brown, gray, orange and yellow.

Each clan had a crest, usually the head of a wild animal associated with its own glen or island; and a slogan or war-cry, frequently the

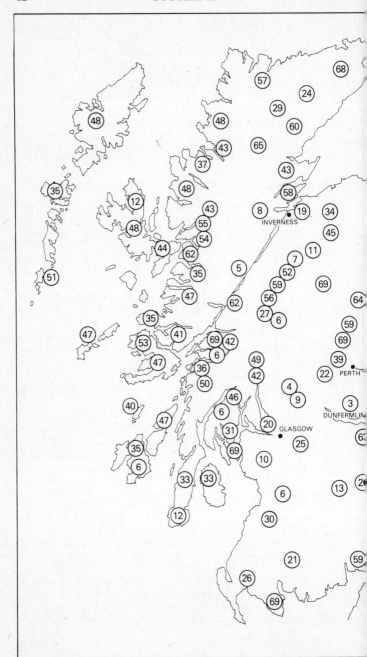

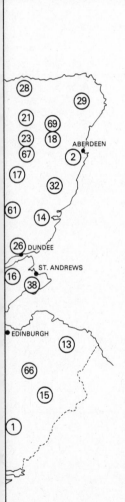

## THE PRINCIPAL HIGHLAND CLANS AND LOWLAND FAMILIES OF SCOTLAND

| | | | |
|---|---|---|---|
| 1 | Armstrong | 37 | MacDonnell |
| 2 | Barclay | 38 | MacDuff |
| 3 | Bruce | 39 | MacFarlane |
| 4 | Buchanan | 40 | MacFee |
| 5 | Cameron | 41 | MacGillivray |
| 6 | Campbell | 42 | MacGregor |
| 7 | Chattan | 43 | MacKenzie |
| 8 | Chisholm | 44 | MacKinnon |
| 9 | Colquhoun | 45 | MacKintosh |
| 10 | Cunningham | 46 | MacLachlan |
| 11 | Davidson | 47 | MacLean |
| 12 | Donald | 48 | MacLeod |
| 13 | Douglas | 49 | MacNab |
| 14 | Duncan | 50 | MacNaughton |
| 15 | Elliot | 51 | MacNeil |
| 16 | Erskine | 52 | MacPherson |
| 17 | Farquharson | 53 | MacQuarrie |
| 18 | Forbes | 54 | MacRae |
| 19 | Fraser | 55 | Matheson |
| 20 | Galbraith | 56 | Menzies |
| 21 | Gordon | 57 | Morgan or |
| 22 | Graham | | Mackay |
| 23 | Grant | 58 | Munro |
| 24 | Gunn | 59 | Murray |
| 25 | Hamilton | 60 | Murray or |
| 26 | Hay | | Sutherland |
| 27 | Henderson | 61 | Ogilvie |
| 28 | Innes | 62 | Ranald |
| 29 | Keith | 63 | Ramsay |
| 30 | Kennedy | 64 | Robertson |
| 31 | Lamont | 65 | Ross |
| 32 | Lindsay | 66 | Scott |
| 33 | MacAlister | 67 | Shaw |
| 34 | MacBean | 68 | Sinclair |
| 35 | MacDonald | 69 | Stewart |
| 36 | MacDougall | | |

name of some mountain or river or perhaps a mythical hero dear to the clan; and also a badge, a wild flower or piece of evergreen from the same locality. The Gordons' badge was rock ivy, the Mackenzies' holly, the Fergussons' foxglove and so on.

From such plants the women of the clan concocted dyes and to that extent the colors of the tartans could be traced to the botany of the district. Old tartans, now to be seen only in the clan museums, are beautifully soft and harmonious; while some modern tartans, done with aniline dyes, can look disagreeably vivid.

## The Kilt Forbidden

The Highland dress moved out of the shirt-and-boots era about 1600, when the men of the 40-odd clans then in existence adopted the plaid. It was a one-piece garment, half wrapped round the waist and the other half thrown over the shoulder. It was clothing by day and a blanket at night. Women wore the kirtle (pleated) skirt, with long stockings, and sometimes a tartan shawl over their heads.

After the debacle of the Forty-five the clans were forbidden to wear the tartan. The order was rescinded after 36 years, but it had by then begun the process of degeneration among the clans: chief into landlord, warrior into peasant. The first modern kilts were seen about that time in the 42nd Regiment. The King granted the soldiers a somber tartan of black, dark blue and green which gave the regiment a new name: the Black Watch.

## Tartanitis and Balmorality

During Queen Victoria's reign the Highland dress blossomed out magnificently. Accessories which would have struck old Highlanders with amazement were incorporated in the outfit. Arbiters of fashion ruled that those without clan connections might wear a kilt of "hodden gray" or heather mixture. Clanless subjects of the Queen claimed the right to the Royal Stuart tartan. The all-purpose Jacobite and Caledonia tartans were invented. The Prince Consort designed a Balmoral tartan, red, black and gray, for servants and retainers at the Queen's Highland home. On the Royal Deeside route there was even a tartan train—a locomotive with Royal Stuart paintwork.

Historians, or perhaps tartan manufacturers, discovered hunting, dress and mourning tartans to add to the everyday ones. Many books were written by self-styled experts, and much contradictory advice given.

The 40-odd "original" clans are those with the commonest Highland names. A few of them are: Cameron, Campbell, Forbes, Fraser, Gordon, Graham, Murray, MacCallum, MacDonald, MacFarlane, Mac-Gregor, Mackintosh, MacLean, MacLeod, MacMillan, MacNeil, MacPherson, MacRae, Ross, Stewart or Stuart, Sutherland and others. These clans, down the ages, have built up quite a wardrobe of different tartans. If you want to wear the Stuart you have a choice of no fewer than 22 patterns!

The "new" clans, riding in on the mid-Victorian wave of tartanitis, were sometimes quite old clans which had never bothered much about tartans; or Lowland families—Kennedy, Hamilton, Hay, Scott, Johnstone, Elliot and others—getting into the act; or, as the late Duke of Montrose, an authority on Highland dress, put it, "so-called clans which came into existence how or when Heaven alone can say." They increased the number from around 40 to around 140.

From Queen Victoria's heyday to the present the number of clans has remained static; but in both civil and military life the tartans have continued to proliferate. Sir Walter Scott wore "shepherd's check"—a black and white pattern; it is now the Shepherd tartan. Not content with their 22 Stuart tartans, the royal family had special tartans woven for the Prince of Wales, later Edward VII, and Princess Beatrice (Queen Victoria's youngest child); and more recently for Princess Elizabeth (the present Queen), Princess Margaret Rose (the present Princess Margaret) and Princess Mary (the late Princess Royal). They are not exclusive designs; any kiltmaker will supply them.

Certain patriotic business houses have acquired "company" tartans. The Turnberry tartan sells well among golfers. There are Clergy and Green Clergy tartans for churchmen. During World War II, a regimental tartan was bestowed on the Royal Canadian Air Force and at the nuclear submarine base in the Holy Loch the American sailors have had woven for themselves a Polaris tartan. When the astronaut Neil Armstrong visited Langholm, the town of his forebears, there was already an Armstrong tartan available, but the local woollen mill produced a Moon tartan for him as well. Even the Scottish Tourist Board has its own specially-designed and officially-registered tartan. The purists sneer but the uncommitted acknowledge that most modern designs are beautifully patterned and far more appealing than some of the esthetically chaotic mixtures of grim and garish coloring in the old "authentic" tartans.

### Dressed to Kill

In Scotland's cities there are many outfitting shops which specialize in the Highland costume. They offer a choice of about 300 approved tartans. The kilt, of course, is only the beginning. A sporran (leather purse), knitted hose (stockings) and leather brogues (shoes) go with it; plus black or tweed jacket, tweed tie and plain shirt.

Evening dress is rather more elaborate. "Dressed to kill"—the original purpose of the free-and-easy Highland garb—has taken on new meaning. Your kilt of dress tartan is backed up with a light plaid, diamond-patterned stockings with scarlet garters and rosettes, a blue bonnet and a velvet doublet. The bonnet is adorned with clan badge, cock feather, crest and motto enclosed in a belt-and-buckle surround. The doublet has lace jabot and cuffs and its diamond-shaped buttons are set with the clan crest and perhaps semi-precious Cairngorm or Scotch topaz stones.

The dress sporran is hung with tassels and ornaments and may be faced with the head of a fox, badger, otter or some other creature appropriate to the clan; all mounted in silver. Shoe buckles, waist-belt, sword-belt and shoulder-brooch complete the essential part of the dress.

Pistol and powder-horn are obsolete now and the sword is worn only on very formal occasions; but you must have the *sgian dubh* (skeean doo) or black knife thrust down your stocking. The ensemble is best worn with an air of manly dignity.

While this peacock finery is strictly for the men, a Highland lady's evening wear is striking enough. She has a white blouse with Celtic or heraldic embroidery and a skirt of tartan silk. The silk *arisaid,* feminine version of the plaid, hangs down her back and is pinned with a brooch of antique design.

Glittering ostentation is the very essence of Highland dress. The authorities insist: "Attempts by self-conscious Lowlanders to convert the garb of the Gael into a quiet style or reduce it to the monotony of Anglo-Saxon evening clothes are contemptible and an affront to the nation."

## Paying the Piper

Before we get swept away by this sartorial splendor, let us look at the price-tag. A plain outfit—jacket, kilt, sporran and hose made to measure—costs from $400; brogues another $80. The full dress outfit, with all trappings and trimmings, will be upwards of $800. It is possible to pay a great deal more than that.

Now we are all dressed up—and nowhere to go. Apart from Highland Balls, Highland Gatherings, clan society functions and the like, there are not many opportunities to wear full Highland dress. By day, in a Highland village, you might see three or four people in the costume of their ancestors—it could be precisely that, the indestructible kilt and sporran that grandfather handed down. In the cities, a few kilts get an airing at weddings or at the Kirk on Sundays. Pipe bands and the military are the outfitters' best customers. Scots still thrill to the swing of the kilt and the skirl of the pipes as a Highland regiment goes by. But for most people clan devotion is an affair of the heart, not a matter of dressing up. Financially the garb of old Gael is beyond the reach of ordinary folk and for every enthusiast you see being measured for a Montrose doublet or Prince Charlie coatee there will be two or three going in for the "quiet style"; the dinner jacket or trews (trousers) in the most restrained tartan the catalog has to offer.

# FOOD AND DRINK

## *A Farmhouse Cuisine*

If you have spent time in England, Wales or Ireland before coming to Scotland you will not find much about the Scottish cuisine which is excitingly different. This is especially so if you eat and drink in grand hotels and gourmet restaurants: they offer the same sort of international fare as their equivalents all over Europe.

But there are differences. Porridge, shortbread, haggis, malt whisky, Scotch broth, finnan haddie . . . a moment's reflection calls to mind several important items which are exclusively Scottish.

Scotland is more of a home-cooking, home-baking country than most. History and geography shaped her cuisine. She was for centuries a peasant, parochial land, a region of villages and towns rather than cities. Smalltown society thrived on neighborly visits—which meant tea parties, sewing bees and the like. They introduced the competitive element into the baking of bread, scones, biscuits, baps (soft round rolls), bannocks (griddle cakes), malt loaves, shortbreads, gingerbreads, pancakes, oatcakes and other flour-and-sugar-based concoctions. Hence the old nickname for Scotland: the "Land o' Cakes."

Her agriculture produced oats, barley and potatoes. Dr. Johnson's *Dictionary* tells us that oats are "a grain which in England is given to horses, but in Scotland supports the people"—hence porridge, the dish which supplied the roughage in a frugal diet. Many Scots still prefer porridge to packaged cornflakes at breakfast, and traditionalists season it with salt. Others, and most visitors, make it more palatable by adding cream, sugar, syrup or nutmeg.

Oatmeal is also an ingredient in some meat and fish dishes and in desserts. Scots maintain that a herring rolled in oatmeal provides all the nourishment and vitamins the human body needs: the perfectly-balanced meal.

So much for oats. As to barley, the rippling fields of grain which add such color to Lowland landscapes are nearly all destined for the maltings, to make whisky. When Robert Burns wrote of whisky he used expressions like "John Barleycorn" and the "barley bree." ("Bree" is brew or broth.)

Potatoes still loom large in Scottish diets, and Scotch seed potatoes are exported all over Europe. "Come awa' in tae your tatties," a mother tells her child—"tatties" being potatoes and potatoes meaning lunch. You may find the same kind of double meaning when, for example, your landlady goes to the butcher for her "beef"—which covers all kinds of meat—and uses the word "meat" to describe all kinds of food.

Potatoes in Scotland are the bed on which various dishes lie. Strangers imagine the Scots eat haggis six days a week, but the typical everyday dish in an ordinary household is "mince and tatties"—ground beef and mashed potatoes.

## The French Connection

If you have occasion to go to the butcher yourself, note that while the cuts are much the same as elsewhere the names are sometimes different. A leg of pork or lamb is a "gigot" (pronounced "jigget"). The best steak is "fillet" *(filet de boeuf)*. At dinner your fillet or gigot will appear on an "ashet" (an oval dish, from the French *assiette*). These expressions, hardly comprehended outside Scotland, pay a tribute to the nation which, in the days of Mary Queen of Scots, first introduced the Scots to the refinements of gastronomy. Wine, too, has a long history as a bond between the two countries—with many famous cellars deep beneath Scottish castles nursing rare French vintages.

## Soups

Cold winters and a simple life made the Scots a nation of soup-drinkers. Gardening in the domestic plot is a tradition, as in England, but where the English gardener grows flowers his Scottish counterpart tends to cultivate useful vegetables and sometimes herbs. Cabbages, leeks, beans and peas enrich the soups of Scotland. The national soup is Scotch broth, a thin peppery soup with a mutton base to which onions, leeks, grated carrots and pearl barley are added. More venerable, and a favorite with hoteliers, is cock-a-leekie, made from chicken broth and numerous vegetables. In hotels and restaurants a whole range of consommés and bisques of fish, seafood, pheasant, ptarmigan and wild duck is developing.

### Fish

Despite complaints that the European Economic Community has condemned Scotland's fishing industry to a slow death, some of the world's best saltwater fish is landed daily at Scottish ports, to make its way to most towns and cities within a few hours.

In Scottish fish shops the most popular items are haddock, cod and mackerel, which are sold fresh or smoked. The well-known native specialties, finnan haddie (haddock) and Arbroath smokies (smoked haddock) are readily available, as are the Loch Fyne kippers (kippered herring) which many Scots enjoy—and many hotels offer—for breakfast. These days the herring are fewer than formerly, but if you like fresh fish the herring rolled in oatmeal is worth seeking.

Among freshwater fish, salmon and salmon trout appear on most restaurant menus as grilled steaks or cold with mayonnaise or (the fashion of the 1980s) *en croûte*. Trout farms flourish in many districts and the grilled brown trout is a common item on the menu. Scampi have become another popular dish: at city take-out restaurants and pub lunches scampi-and-chips threaten to supplant the traditional fish-and-chips.

Considering their availability in Scottish waters, lobster, crab and scallops are not always easy to get hold of except in the more expensive restaurants and the larger coastal fishmongers. Oysters, once common, are now a rarity but in specialist seafood restaurants you may be offered Musselburgh pie, beefsteak and oysters in a pie-dish, a gastronomic treat. Eels abound in Scottish rivers, but people are suspicious of them (they are, after all, rather bony). It may be said that the Scots are down-to-earth and conservative about their fish recipes; but that the quality and freshness of the fish you will eat are beyond reproach.

### Meats

They used to say that Scotland had the best meat and the worst butchers. It is probably true of the meat, no longer true of the butchers.

When you observe how greatly in Scotland the sheep outnumber the people, you would suppose that mutton and lamb were the staple meat diet. So it used to be, but nowadays the Scots prefer beef (but not veal) and pork. The Aberdeen-Angus steak is in a class by itself. At railway buffets you may buy it in a bread sandwich, like a hamburger. Best ground beef is the filling for a variety of pies, bridies (with suet and onions in pastry) and casseroles and it may be served as a snack meal in the form of collops or Scotch egg (hot or cold boiled-egg wrapped in mince). The cuts are familiar to all, but New World descriptions such as T-bone and tenderloin are not used.

At breakfast or high tea (see below) the Scots are fond of grilled bacon or grilled sausage with fried potatoes and perhaps mushrooms. The traditional Scottish sausage, by the way, which you may still be offered, is a flat disc of sausage-meat, pork or beef, sliced on a machine; several times the diameter of the English "banger" which is steadily replacing it.

### The Mysterious Haggis

Subject of much facetious comment abroad, haggis may be bought at the butcher's or, if you want to send it home, in a sealed can at some superior grocery stores. You are not likely to come across it at table unless you ask for it, or unless it happens to be Burns Night, January 25. Some visitors are a little nervous about haggis because it contains all the bits of a sheep that cooks usually throw away and because it is stitched up in the stomach bag of a sheep (or should be: these days they often use plastic bags). But a good haggis is hot and savory, nourishing and distinctively flavored; excellent when accompanied by the traditional "tatties" and "bashed neeps" (mashed swede or turnip)—and even better when it has a generous portion of "gravy" poured over it, for that is a coy term for a glass of whisky.

### Game

Scots keep up the old custom of shooting for the pot and various game birds, notably pheasant, partridge and grouse, give the housewife room for culinary maneuver in their seasons. In and out of season you will find the birds on restaurant menus, either roasted or incorporated in game pies and pâtés. Hare and venison are also treated according to well-tried recipes. The latter, with its classy overtones of royal stag-hunts and the like, is now the raw material with which many a hotel and restaurant chef makes a declaration of his abilities—with the aid of vegetables, red wine, redcurrant preserve, rosemary, thyme and garlic.

### Desserts

Some Scots pretend to regard puddings and sweets as a decadent English habit. How then do they get their sugar intake, which World Health Organization statistics show to be the highest of all the nations? The answer is in the many kinds of bakemeats to which the "Land o' Cakes" has long been addicted. You see them in all their glory, not in smart hotels and fashionable restaurants but in humble teashops and in family-run hotels and guest-houses where early-evening "high tea" is served instead of mid-evening dinner. (Some establishments serve both.) At high tea you will sit down to one hot dish, perhaps fish or a mixed grill, and will follow it with masses of cakes and scones, not forgetting the peculiarly Scottish "black bun" (pastry top and bottom, currants, candied peel, apples, nuts, cloves and ginger inside) and a pot or two of strong tea to help them down.

Despite the diehards, a dessert course in Scotland may be the most imaginative part of the meal. Here cream and oatmeal again come into their own. Scottish honey (exceptionally sweet) and whisky-based liqueurs are involved. The plebeian "aipple tairt" is there too, along with elaborate confections of raspberries, strawberries, blackcurrants and cherries to remind you that much of Lowland Scotland is given over

to the growing of soft fruits and the preserving of jams and marmalades.

The diehard, ignoring all that, rounds off his meal with cheese and
biscuits. In restaurant and supermarket, French and English cheese are
always on hand, as are numerous so-called regional Scottish cheeses.
Apart from the unpretentious Scotch cheddar, only two native cheeses
are recognized by gourmets: the Dunlop (another kind of cheddar) and
the Orkney (soft and fatty, made from rich milk and rennet).

## The "Taste of Scotland"

The Scottish Tourist Board promotes a "Taste of Scotland" campaign: you will see the little brass "stockpot" motif outside participat-
ing restaurants. This enables the Scots to play their favorite game of
bewildering strangers with outlandish words. We may know that "partan" is Scots for crab, and therefore guess that "partan bree" is crab
soup. But what are we to make of cloutie dumpling, stoved howtowdie
and cranachan ? (They are respectively a fruit-and-spice boiled pudding, a chicken casserole and a dessert of toasted oatmeal, raspberries,
cream and Drambuie.)

Well, some French *cartes* are equally incomprehensible and in Scotland there is usually a translation on the menu and we can console
ourselves with the thought that Robert Burns himself would have been
baffled by some of these obscure dialect words.

## Drinking

The Scot's staple drink is tea, but coffee of variable quality is always
available. In another sense the staple drink is whisky (note spelling—
only the Irish stuff is "whiskey") but brewing as well as distilling
brought prosperity to many Scottish towns and Scots ale and lager are
sold all over Britain. "Hawf and hawf," a dram of whisky and a
half-pint of beer, is the Glasgow tipple, a somewhat lethal one.

Scottish entrepreneurs, two centuries ago, formed English tastes in
port and sherry—drinks the Scots themselves have never been crazy
about. There are old traditions of wine-drinking, particularly claret,
but ordinary Scots hold that there is something slightly effeminate
about wine; nonetheless many pubs sell wine by the glass.

All pubs and hotel bars, as you might expect, serve an immense
variety of whiskies. In some areas, notably Grampian and the western
isles, locally-produced "malts" of a more refined and longer-matured
character are preferred to ordinary "blended" whiskies. We deal more
fully with this subject in our Grampian chapter.

Once more tightly controlled than elsewhere, drinking in Scotland
is now quite promiscuous. Long after English pubs have closed for the
afternoon, Scottish tills are still merrily ringing. Subject to local licensing approval, the publican may sell liquor from 11 A.M. to 11 P.M. daily.

There are no liquor stores in Scotland. The nearest equivalent is the
licensed grocer's, found in the main streets of all towns and many
villages. Either there or at a supermarket you may buy drinks, both
alcoholic and non-alcoholic, from a wide selection.

## Where to Eat and Drink

Ideas of cafe society or family outings to restaurants are alien to the Scots. In Glasgow, Edinburgh and Aberdeen there are a few expensive restaurants where you may eat a gourmet meal and dance in the evenings; perhaps even see a floor show; but nothing on the scale of London for sophistication or price.

Department stores and bakery shops in cities and towns often have their own restaurants and cafeterias, not always permitted to sell alcohol, and while the food may be run-of-the-mill the places themselves are clean and cheap. High streets abound with cafes and coffee-bars: some good, some quite disgusting. Country places often go in for old-fashioned tea rooms with waitress service; generally good value.

Non-Scottish restaurants proliferate. In Glasgow and Edinburgh the home-grown establishment is hard to find among the Italian restaurants, French bistros, American-style hamburger joints, Indian and Pakistani restaurants, spaghetti houses and eating places of flavors as unlikely as Turkish and Norwegian. Even in the lonely Highlands the signs "tandoori" and "to go" are not unknown. Such places generally stay open later than Scottish restaurants and the Scots have become enthusiastic patrons of them.

## Don't Be Late for Lunch!

Lunchtime in certain country towns, the Borders in particular, is 12–1. If you arrive around one o'clock you may find the restaurants closed and the shops and banks open again. The normal lunch period in large towns, however, is 12.30–2.30.

Cafes and department store restaurants serve teas from about 3.30 to 5.30. The "high tea" is served around 5.30 to 6.30—useful if you have other plans for the evening. In the larger hotels and restaurants the international dinner hour, 8 P.M. onwards, is observed.

It is worth noting that many of Scotland's multitudinous pubs have smartened themselves up, no longer look askance at unaccompanied ladies and have diversified into basket-meal, bar-lunch, shepherd's-supper and similar amenities. Such meals are generally inexpensive and a good bet for the passing traveler. Scottish pubs however do tend to be small, crowded and noisy with conversation.

# SPORTS IN SCOTLAND

## *Pleasures and Pastimes*

It has been argued that golf came to Scotland from Holland. But all the historical evidence points to Scotland being the cradle, if not the birthplace, of the game. Citizens of St. Andrews were playing golf on the town links (public land) as far back as the 15th century; and bishops of St. Andrews were encouraging them at it in spite of laws which prohibited the game. The Stuart kings wanted their subjects to practice archery instead.

In 1754 the first association of players, the Gentlemen Golfers of Edinburgh, moved to the breezy links of St. Andrews, which in due course (1834) became the Royal & Ancient Golf Club. Maximizing the available space, golfers played nine holes out and the same nine holes back. Thus the number of holes on a golf course was fixed for all time.

The Old Course at St. Andrews coped with further congestion when a huge influx of people turned up, anxious to learn the new game. The peculiar "double greens" were devised. Exclusive to St. Andrews, they have been mystifying strangers ever since.

As time went by the manufacture and export of golf balls became the principal industry of that corner of Fife, the Royal & Ancient became the game's ruling body (as it still is) and year after year the Open Championship to determine the world's best golfer was held on the Old Course.

Scotland is now a land-mass entirely surrounded by golf courses; and packed with them too. The Gleneagles hotel boasts three 18-hole courses of its own. Every town and village has its course and its club. Celebrated courses—Carnoustie, Muirfield, Royal Troon, Turnberry and others—attract international championships in their turn.

Golf in Scotland is quite a plebeian game, whereas in England it is a distinctly middle-class pastime. A round on a Scottish municipal course costs very little and the Scottish clubs, apart from a few pretentious places modeled on the English fashion, demand only modest subscriptions.

## Snow Business

In the field of winter sports Scotland moved late into the arena. Highland folk remember the time when an Englishman coming off the train at Aviemore with his skis was asked: "What are those planks for?"

Within a couple of decades Aviemore has blossomed into a major winter-sports center, along with other villages at the foot of the Cairngorms. But it is not alone. Other popular ski centers have arisen at Glenshee and Glencoe, though accommodations are limited and likely to remain so. Up-and-coming winter-sports developments include Ben Lawers, the Lecht near Tomintoul, Ben Wyvis near Strathpeffer and Green Lowther north of Dumfries.

Compared with the well-known Swiss and Austrian centers the ski resorts of Scotland suffer from cloudy weather, high winds and difficulty in keeping access roads snow-free; but when conditions are right the skiing in Scotland is said to be first class. The season varies in length because the climate is unpredictable. It can begin as early as November, but the experts prefer February and March.

## The Roaring Game

The winter game is curling, a uniquely Scottish invention, now exported to other countries, particularly Canada and Switzerland. Curling has increased in popularity of late and a number of towns have indoor rinks, so the "roaring game"—so-called from the humming of the stones in motion—may be played all the year round. But ideally it is an outdoor spectacle. About once in ten years sustained frosty weather produces thick ice on big shallow lochs and then a Grand Match takes place, North of Scotland against South. Hundreds of players and thousands of curling stones—polished, one-handled ovals of granite—occupy the ice; and the fun is more important than the result. The big mass-curling venues are Loch Leven near Kinross and the Lake of Menteith near Aberfoyle.

A winter game confined to the Highlands, and to two sharply-defined areas of the Highlands at that, is shinty. To the uninitiated it looks like a mixture of football and hockey, a brutal conflict between two teams of young men whose principal qualifications are brawn and energy. But devotees insist that shinty has its finer points.

Insignificant villages like Newtonmore and Kingussie are the Giants and Dodgers of this game. It will be a lasting experience if, while

traveling on Speyside in early spring, you happen on those villages
when they are battling it out for the annual trophy, the Cammanachd
Cup.

## "Fitba' Daft"

Association football (known as football in Scotland, never soccer)
and rugby football (never rugger) are the mass spectator games. Cricket
has never established itself as the religion it is to so many in England;
in any case the football season starts in August and goes on until the
following June, and Scotsmen talk football all the year round.

The professional game, which Scotland claims to have invented,
rouses extraordinary passions and displays aspects of national tempera-
ment which other nations smile at: excessive elation in victory, black
depression in defeat; and a strident partisanship which has to be heard
to be believed. Moralists say the Scots lost religion and found football.
The uninterested—women, mostly—say that Scotsmen are "fitba'
daft"—football crazy.

## Licensed to Kill

Fish, game and deer, the three ingredients of Scotland's renowned
field-sports tradition, are carefully controlled; and of course you cannot
own or use a gun without a license. Fishing, shooting and deer-stalking
are expensive hobbies. Since World War II there has been a sad falling-
off in the numbers of shooting tenancies and angling "beats" on which
impecunious Highland lairds so heavily depended for an income. The
parties you see on the moors these days are either the laird and a few
friends or else a syndicate of businessmen, frequently Germans or
Belgians, on a costly sporting vacation package.

Most rivers and lochs teem with salmon and trout, but the poacher
risks a stiff fine. In the Border country, along the Tweed, they used to
say that a man would be hanged for taking a salmon but not for killing
his mother-in-law. Occasionally you may hear of a stretch of water
where the fishing is free to all: one such is the "town water" of Peebles.
Angling is popular, however, and some country bus services seem to
be designed more to get the fisherman to his beat than to get shoppers
and commuters into town.

From the time when Queen Victoria and her Scotophile consort
Prince Albert began spending their summers at Balmoral, the Highlands became a sporting Mecca for the princes, potentates and politicians who went north to visit her. In late Victorian and Edwardian days
vast quantities of deer, game birds and assorted wildlife were slaughtered. The annual massacre of the fauna does not go on to the same
extent now, but dates like the "Glorious Twelfth"—August 12, when
grouse-shooting begins—are still hallowed. Highland estates have arrangements with New York restaurants, the beaters and the guns are
out at dawn that day, the first few brace of grouse are rushed to the
nearest airport and charter jets fly them across the Atlantic. They are
on the menu for lunch. Some Scots consider this stunt the height of

vulgarity; the gourmet does not look at grouse until it has been hung for a week or two.

Fox-hunting in Scotland is chiefly confined to the southern country-side and to the winter and early spring. It is a more democratic pursuit in Scotland than in England but as a feature of rural life it is declining. The tide of Scottish opinion generally seems to be running against blood sports.

## Gathering of the Clans

If you look good in the kilt, here is your big chance: the Highland Games, more properly called Highland Gatherings, which add such brilliance and color to the Scottish summer. But beware of getting too deeply involved. The Games have become commercialized and the rates charged for meals and accommodations at the venues betray a rapacity one does not usually associate with Highland hospitality. So-called Highland Games also take place on a professional basis in the cities and mining towns of the central belt, where the Highland tradition is much diluted.

Long ago a Highland Gathering was simply an assembly of clansfolk, called by the chief in some convenient valley or glen. It was his opportunity to inspect their weapons, advise them about their affairs and confirm their loyalties; and for them to meet old friends and exchange family gossip. The young men whiled away the time with races, feats of strength and vigorous dancing. The girls, not allowed to participate, egged them on.

In course of time friendly neighborhood clans joined in and the games were put on a more systematic footing. Typical activities, displays of manhood with the raw materials most readily available, were tugs-o'-war, hammer throwing, shot putting, caber-tossing and mountain racing.

Most events at a Highland Gathering have some story behind them. Sword-dancing goes back to King Malcolm who in 1054 slew a chief of Macbeth and, crossing the swords of victor and vanquished on the ground, danced a victory jig over them. The steps and posture of the Highland fling—arms raised and fingers pointed, like antlers—are said to imitate the movements of a rutting stag. Mountain racing—up to the summit and back—was included in the program of the first Braemar Gathering at King Malcolm Canmore's request because of complaints that the royal messengers were too slow. The lore and legends of the Gatherings are as picturesque and confused as the Gatherings themselves where for long periods, you feel, only the Master of Ceremonies knows what is going on.

The most important Gatherings in the calendar are held annually in August and September at Aboyne and Ballater, Crieff, Glenfinnan, Dunoon, the Cowal Gathering, and Braemar. Braemar attracts the biggest crowds. Queen Victoria first patronized this Gathering in 1848 and royalty has attended every year since that date.

# EXPLORING SCOTLAND

# SCOTIA'S DARLING SEAT

## *Edinburgh*

Aeons ago, a glacier started moving eastwards through what is now Lowland Scotland, scouring out a valley which became the Firth of Forth, hitting and flowing over the cones of volcanoes from an earlier era. One hard cone resisted. The glacier parted and flowed round it, leaving a diminishing trail of rubble behind. Thus, in the formation which geologists call crag and tail, the Castle rock and mile-long slope of the future Old Town of Edinburgh came into being.

The rock was one of the first inhabited places in Scotland, inhabited by the predecessors of those mixed and mysterious people we call the Picts. The Romans avoided the rock. They made for the river-ports of Cramond and Inveresk, six miles east and west respectively. After their departure, Edinburgh's history as a capital city began. Celtic chieftains made the rock their fortress. They knew it as Dun-Edin, a name which some have connected with the 7th-century Anglican king Edwin. But Dun-Edin probably means "the dun (fort) on the slope." In due course the Angles replaced the Celts and in the 10th century they were themselves replaced by the Scots. By that time Dun-Edin's name had been translated into Anglo-Saxon—Edinburgh.

St. Ninian is supposed to have preached Christianity there in the 5th century and St. Columba in the 6th (Inchcolm in the Firth of Forth is the "isle of Columba"). St. Cuthbert, a monk from Melrose, founded the first Christian church in the 7th century, perhaps on the spot where the cathedral church of St. Giles was afterwards built.

The saintly Margaret, consort of King Malcolm Canmore, lived and died (1093) on the Castle rock. She is credited with having introduced a little culture to the uncouth Scots. Her son David founded Holyrood Abbey a mile away at the foot of the slope and a small burgh called the Canongate grew up around it. From the Castle rock to Canongate and the palace of Holyroodhouse there now runs a sequence of streets called the Royal Mile.

By 1500 Edinburgh was a true capital city and proud of it. In 1596, when King James VI, faced with a riot, threatened to move palace and parliament to Linlithgow, the citizens capitulated at once. King James was shortly afterwards to forsake Edinburgh for London, where he became the first king of England and Scotland. With him some of Edinburgh's tawdry, noisy, insanitary and often violent glory departed. She was stripped of more pomp and ceremony 100 years later, when the Union with England required the disbanding of the old Scots parliament.

## "Gardy-loo!"

Up to the middle of the 17th century Edinburgh had the appearance of a medieval city. Confined to the Royal Mile—a narrow street, but a spacious boulevard compared with the suffocating "wynds" and closes, alleyways and passageways, which sloped off it—and to the huddled tenements round the Castle at one end and the Canongate at the other, its citizens lived in what visitors from England and France considered dangerously overcrowded squalor. Nobles and peasantry rubbed shoulders. Fur-robed merchants and beggarly hucksters shared the same "turnpike" (spiral) stairs in the warrens of the buildings. At night the citizens emptied their chamber pots into the street and the cry of *"Gardez-l'eau!"* or "Gardy-loo!" ("Beware water") would be followed by a noxious discharge from a fourth or fifth floor. The Royal Mile's inhabitants multiplied so fast that there was no space for shops and the tradesmen operated from little wooden stalls which they closed up at night, like traveling showmen. "Luckenbooth" (locked booth) is a word you may come across in Edinburgh today.

When the harbor of Leith, two miles from Edinburgh, developed as a port for wines, fruits and spices from the Continent, the city's trade was greatly increased and the magistrates reserved certain areas for particular commodities. You can still walk through the Grassmarket, Fleshmarket Close and Fishmarket Close. Growing rich, the merchants took over and extended some of the tall tenements in the Royal Mile: for example Gladstone's Land in the Lawnmarket ("Land" means property and "Lawn" means linen), where the ceilings are painted with motifs of fruits-and-vegetables, the wares on which a 17th-century Mr. Gladstone founded his fortune.

In 1563, during the reign of Mary Queen of Scots, Edinburgh had established the first civic university in Scotland (those already in existence, Glasgow, Aberdeen and St. Andrews, had been founded by the church). Stone houses, dour little versions of French baronial châteaux, had made their appearance. The capital was a mixture of French fashions and grinding poverty, solemn churchmen and irreverent urchins. But in the 1600s the Kirk laid its reforming hand on Edinburgh. Plays, pageants and processions were banned, the raucous frivolity of the streets was eclipsed and people took to heavy drinking in taverns—which is the chief relaxation of some Edinburghers to this day. The cathedral of St. Giles on the Royal Mile became the High Kirk of Edinburgh.

King Charles II's restoration in 1660 promised a return to the good old merry-making days; and Charles put work in hand to make the Palace of Holyroodhouse a glittering royal residence. But his reign in Scotland was clouded by religious squabbles as the Presbyterian Covenanters reasserted their authority.

## The Highest Buildings in the World

An 18th-century traveler to Edinburgh said its buildings were the highest in the world and that each stairway led to the rooms of 20 or 30 families. The city had expanded more upwards than outwards. It was still dark and dangerous at night. There was no water supply apart from one or two public wells.

A few fine buildings had appeared: George Heriot's Hospital (he was the royal jeweler and his hospital was a school for boys, as it still is); and a new Parliament Hall. The 1707 Union took national politics out of Edinburgh but the lawyers and bankers came into their own and Scottish literature and philosophy began to flourish. Edinburgh was approaching a golden age of the spirit, not courtly but aggressively cultural.

## The New Town

Edinburgh's smart set lived in the Cowgate south of the Castle rock, the suburb through which cattle had been let out to graze (200 years later the Cowgate was a slum). When a speculative builder put up George Square, which is now occupied by University buildings, fastidious citizens were quick to move there out of an Old Town susceptible to fire and plague. In 1762 an enterprising Lord Provost (in Scotland, a city mayor) started draining the swampland north of the Castle rock and over the next 40 years the New Town of Edinburgh took shape on rising ground beyond it.

The New Town, designed by a 27-year-old architect named James Craig and built with local stone, was one of the first examples of large-scale town planning in Britain. It had a gridiron pattern with squares at each end, and all the buildings in the Georgian style, severe and elegant.

Street names complimented the royal House of Hanover. The main thoroughfare was George Street. Parallel with it ran Queen Street and Princes Street, named for His Majesty's wife and son. Between them were the narrower Rose Street and Thistle Street, for the emblems of England and Scotland. The two national patron saints, St. Andrew and St. George, gave their names to the flanking squares. (To avoid confu-

# EXPLORING SCOTLAND

82

THE ROYAL MILE

Edinburgh Castle · Assembly Hall · RAMSEY LANE · ESPLANADE · CASTLEHILL · Cannonball House · Tolbooth Church · JOHNSTONE TERR. · Gladstones · James' Land · Court · LAWNMARKET · Brodie's Close · Lady Stair's Close · Bank of Scotland · BANK ST · ST GILES ST · GEORGE IV BR. · Parliament House · City Chambers · St Giles' Cathedral · HIGH · Tron Church · COCKBURN ST · NORTH BRIDGE · SOUTH BRI · Wax Museum

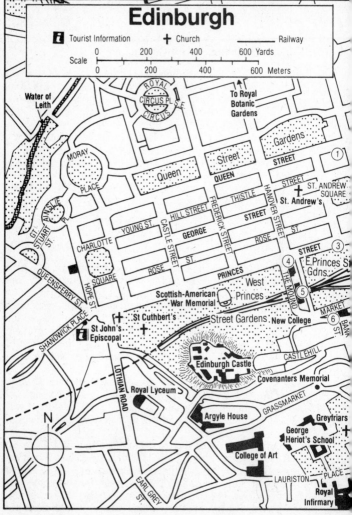

# Edinburgh

**i** Tourist Information  **+** Church  —— Railway

Scale

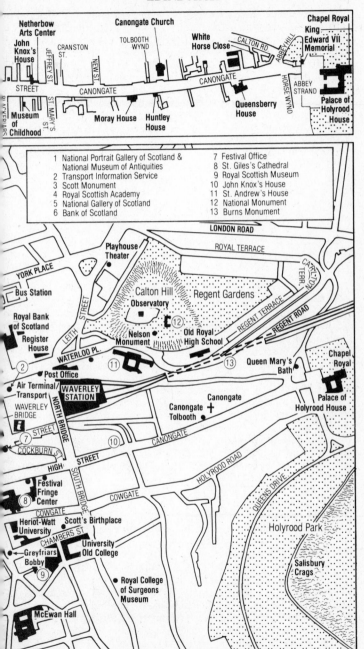

Netherbow Arts Center
John Knox's House
CRANSTON ST.
JEFFREY ST.
Canongate Church
TOLBOOTH WYND
White Horse Close
CALTON RD.
Chapel Royal
King Edward VII Memorial
ABBEY HILL
NEW ST.
STREET
CANONGATE
CANONGATE
HORSE WYND
ABBEY STRAND
Palace of Holyrood House
Museum of Childhood
ST. MARY'S ST.
Moray House
Huntley House
Queensberry House

1 National Portrait Gallery of Scotland & National Museum of Antiquities
2 Transport Information Service
3 Scott Monument
4 Royal Scottish Academy
5 National Gallery of Scotland
6 Bank of Scotland
7 Festival Office
8 St. Giles's Cathedral
9 Royal Scottish Museum
10 John Knox's House
11 St. Andrew's House
12 National Monument
13 Burns Monument

LONDON ROAD
ROYAL TERRACE
Playhouse Theater
YORK PLACE
Bus Station
Royal Bank of Scotland
Register House
LEITH
STREET
Calton Hill
Observatory
Regent Gardens
CARLTON TERR.
Nelson Monument
Old Royal High School
REGENT TERRACE
REGENT ROAD
WATERLOO PL.
11
2
Post Office
Air Terminal-Transport
WAVERLEY STATION
13
Queen Mary's Bath
Chapel Royal
WAVERLEY BRIDGE
NORTH BRIDGE
Canongate Tolbooth
Canongate
Palace of Holyrood House
STREET
7
COCKBURN ST.
HIGH
10
SOUTH BRIDGE
CANONGATE
STREET
HOLYROOD ROAD
QUEENS DRIVE
Festival Fringe Center
8
COWGATE
COWGATE
Heriot-Watt University
Scott's Birthplace
CHAMBERS ST.
Greyfriars Bobby
9
University Old College
Holyrood Park
Royal College of Surgeons Museum
Salisbury Crags
McEwan Hall

sion with George Square, St. George's afterwards became Charlotte Square, another respectful nod in the direction of King George's consort.) The chief crosstown avenue was Hanover Street, named for the ruling dynasty, side by side with Frederick Street (the King's second son) and St. David's Street (the "sair sanct" King of Scots).

A North Bridge connected the Old Town with the New, and the rubbish from the building operations was heaped up to form an "Earthen Mound", now The Mound, between Castle rock and Princes Street. The architect Robert Adam, then at the height of his powers, was involved in the designs but he died before he had had time to complete more than one street frontage in Charlotte Square.

The Old Town and the New Town represented two extremes of urban planning and social organization. Their juxtaposition and their magnificent natural situation, stepping down from the Castle on its rock to their footstool at the port of Leith, prompt many Scots to nominate Edinburgh the most beautiful city in the world.

Nowadays the New Town is as busy and congested as the Old, but it was not always so. At first the town council had to bribe traders to take shops in the New Town; and if you bought a house in Princes Street you could claim exemption from all city taxes!

## A Piece of Nova Scotia

Edinburgh is a small city, there are around 500,000 inhabitants, with a dense concentration of tourist sights at its center. If you walk the Royal Mile, conscientiously studying them, you will need two or three days; but you will then have learned a great deal about the place they used to call the Athens of the North; a title that arose not as a result of its neo-classical splendor but because of its literary and academic life.

A bus will take you close to the Castle esplanade, where you are faced with a stiff climb on foot through the citadel to its highest point, 443 feet above sea level. Since the sea is only two miles away, you have a wonderful panorama of the Firth and the country beyond. Here (you can see the apex of the crag sticking through the floor) stands tiny St. Margaret's Chapel, built about 1090 by Malcolm Canmore's pious Queen; also the Scottish National War Memorial, an elaborate shrine for the fallen of the 1914–1918 war—Scotsmen, Scotswomen, even Scottish dogs and horses.

Outside, round the Palace Yard, are the historical apartments: Crown Room, containing the Scottish regalia of crown, scepter, sword of state and various orders of chivalry, and the diminutive Parliament Hall where medieval conferences of the Three Estates (monarch, nobles and common people) were held. A United Services museum tells the story of Scottish arms on sea and land.

Lower down you come to the Half-Moon Battery whose curving ramparts give Edinburgh Castle its distinctive appearance from miles away. Mons Meg is here, a cannon from Mons in Belgium made in 1486. Hailed as the final solution to Scotland's defense problems, it was dragged about the country at vast trouble and expense and never, as far as is known, fired a shot in anger. The Battery's time gun, on the

other hand, goes off with a bang every weekday at 1, causing Edinburghers to check their watches and visitors to jump out of their skins.

The Castle's steep cobbled passageways are thronged with visitors
and soldiers of the garrison stationed here, sometimes a Highland
regiment in the kilt, sometimes a Lowland regiment in trews (tartan
trousers). You may see them changing guard or marching on the
esplanade, but between July and September that stone-flagged parade
ground in front of the citadel's drawbridge is obstructed by the scaffold-
ing of a grandstand, for this is where Edinburgh's famous military
tattoo takes place during the International Festival.

The Castle esplanade is held to be part of the North American
continent. In the 17th century when King Charles I wanted to create
baronets of Nova Scotia (New Scotland) constitutional law demanded
that the ceremony be carried out on Nova Scotian soil; for which
purpose the esplanade was declared Nova Scotian territory and the
decree was never rescinded.

## The Royal Mile

Descending Castle hill, first of the streets which make up the Royal
Mile, observe Cannonball House with the round shot embedded in it.
Tradition says it was fired by Bonnie Prince Charlie's men in 1745
when the Jacobites occupied the town but the government troops remained in the Castle.

Next comes the Lawnmarket, a corridor of antique and tartan souvenir shops among which you can penetrate to the period mansion of
Gladstone's Land (NTS) and the first of the inner courts (quadrangles)
which are a feature of old Scottish towns. Here was that mixture of rich
apartments and slum property, noble families and the mob, which
foreign travelers of bygone days marveled at. The Lawnmarket courts
housed Boswell, David Hume and Robert Burns at different times. In
Brodie's Close in the 1770s lived the infamous Deacon Brodie, pillar
of society by day and a murdering gang-leader by night. R.L. Stevenson
and W.E. Henley wrote a play about him and he may have been the
inspiration for Stevenson's *Jekyll and Hyde.*

After the Lawnmarket comes the High Street, the focus of daily life
in old Edinburgh. The Bank of Scotland, a few yards down Bank Street,
opened its doors in 1695. Where the street opens out to a square the
Old Tolbooth used to stand, the prison where the first scenes of Scott's
*Heart of Midlothian* are set. (When it was demolished in 1817, Scott
took the gates to Abbotsford.) The spot is marked with a Heart of
Midlothian set in colored stones in the roadway. Some older men spit
on it for luck as they pass.

Here too is the High Kirk of Edinburgh, the Gothic pile of St. Giles,
culminating in a stone crown 161 feet high. On the crown of St. Giles
the last stork in Scotland nested in 1416. Compared with most European cathedrals, St. Giles is small and plain, its one elaborate feature
being the modern (1911) Thistle Chapel, hung with banners of the
Knights of the Thistle, the senior Scottish order of chivalry. The
church has been here since 1385 but, having been three times Protestant and twice Roman Catholic, it has seen changes. A small brass plate

let into the stones of the square outside reads "I.K.1572"; the only indication of the grave of John Knox, before whom all Scotland trembled. But in the Albany aisle, inside the church, a bronze statue commemorates him. It was presented in 1906 by "Scots at home, in Australia, in Canada and the United States."

Knox is sometimes remembered as a bullying, pig-headed Presbyterian who loaded the Scots with the guilt and gloom which afflict some to this day. But he was not against bishops, and not opposed to dancing. The stern tyranny of Calvinism was imposed by the extremists who came after him.

A decorated stone pulpit opposite the City Chambers (seat of local government) just below St. Giles is the Mercat Cross. On royal occasions the heralds make proclamations from it with due ceremony. The cross is modern, but part of its shaft is as old as the city.

The High Street leads on to the Canongate. Almost every building has an historical tale attached to it. Careful restoration has brought back some of the street's 16th-century quaintness, when stone houses replaced wooden ones and the little "Latin quarter" of the Holyrood canons was a fashionable residential street. The first house is that of John Knox, but it is doubtful whether he owned it though he may have lodged there. It is a charming example of the domestic refinement which Mary's French followers brought to the rough northern capital. Relics of Knox are kept inside.

Under the Canongate porticos, in what within living memory were abodes of poverty and disease, you will find some of the city's best craft, antique and Highland dress shops. Passing the Canongate church and churchyard (graves of Adam Smith, Robert Fergusson the poet and "Clarinda," Burns' mistress) on the left and timber-fronted Huntly House, a municipal museum, on the right, you arrive at the foot of the Royal Mile. The gates of the Palace of Holyroodhouse are straight in front. That old stone cabin with the pyramid roof, outside the gates, is Queen Mary's bathhouse. (She used white wine as a skin-conditioner.)

### The Official Royal Residence

Holyrood Palace shows Scottish royalty's fondness for living in the midst of the people. Not for the early Stuarts the high walls and miles of parkland and the mansion invisible to common eyes: even today Holyrood has a graveyard and a brewery sitting beside it and the mainline trains between Edinburgh and London run past its windows. The royal park (called King's Park or Queen's Park according to the sex of the reigning monarch) is a public area of turf and small lochs gathered round Salisbury Crags and Arthur's Seat, a double-coned extinct volcano 823 feet high. There are footpaths to the top and a panoramic view indicator. A public road, the King's/Queen's Drive, three and a half miles long, encircles Edinburgh's inner-city mountain. You may see the Royal Company of Archers practising with their longbows. They are the Queen's Bodyguard for Scotland, a corps of elderly respected citizens whose appearance in their bizarre uniforms has been likened to generals rolled in spinach.

When the royal family is not in residence (see *Practical Information*) you can walk freely around the palace and go inside for a conducted tour. The largely redecorated apartments recall the glamor and brutality of Stuart history—especially the little supper room where, in 1566, the Queen's private secretary David Rizzio was dragged out from behind her skirts and stabbed to death. Annexed to the main quadrangle are the Chapel Royal, where several Scottish monarchs were married, and the Royal Vault where others were buried among numerous very ancient and anonymous graves.

The Chapel Royal has fragments of the Abbey of Holyrood, built in the 12th century by King David I as a thank-offering for his deliverance from a rampaging stag when this area was a hunting marsh and forest; legend says that the holy rood (cross) appeared to him as a sign from Heaven above the stag's antlers. It is a common medieval legend, also attributed to St. Hubert and St. Eustache.

From David's time onwards Holyrood was gradually adopted as a royal residence. James IV was probably the first king to live there regularly. The palace as we see it now dates from between 1671 and 1677 and was chiefly the work of Sir William Bruce in the reign of Charles II.

## The New Town

Three broad streets lead down from the Old Town to the New, two arriving at each end of Princes Street and the third, The Mound, coming in at the street's midpoint where two classical buildings house the Royal Scottish Academy and the Scottish National Gallery. You will notice as you tour Edinburgh that the museums of a special or local character are mostly found in the Old Town up and down the Royal Mile, while those which one associates with a nation's capital city are mostly sited in the New. At the east end of Princes Street you find Register House where Scottish genealogical records are kept; a little farther on, up the hill, St. Andrew's House, center of Scotland's government departments; and in Queen Street (east end) the Scottish National Portrait Gallery and the Scottish Museum of Antiquities.

When the New Town was planned, George Street was intended as the principal artery. Over the years commerce and fashion moved southward one block to Princes Street, a splendid thoroughfare, dead straight and nearly one mile long. Uniquely, it has shops on one side only, looking out over Princes Street Gardens (the swamp of pre-New Town days) to the Castle rock and Old Town skyline. A restaurant or cafe on the upper floor of a Princes Street department store is the place to be when the cavalcades and pipe bands go by. The Gardens, squirrel-haunted in spring and fall, have a secluded air despite the citizens who stroll in them, the Glasgow–Edinburgh railroad which cuts through them longitudinally and the traffic on The Mound which crosses them laterally. In summer, at a large open stage and auditorium, daily concerts and displays of Scottish country dancing are given.

What appears to be a Gothic cathedral spire chopped off and planted in the east of the Gardens is the Scott Monument; 200 feet high and 267 steps, the nation's tribute to Sir Walter.

Also in East Princes Street Gardens you will find a monument to David Livingstone, whose African meeting with H.M. Stanley is part of Scots-American history. Eastward still, on the Calton Hill opposite St. Andrew's House and close to the incomplete Parthenon lookalike known as Edinburgh's Disgrace (it was intended for a National War Memorial in 1822 but the contributions did not come in), there is a monument to Abraham Lincoln and the Scottish-American dead of the Civil War. An impressive American monument to the Scottish soldiers of World War I stands in West Princes Street Gardens, among various memorials of Scottish and foreign alliances.

Princes Street shops no longer have a distinctly Edinburgh flavor. Of the stores in which, up to a few decades ago, you could almost count on being served by a member of the family whose name had been on the signboard for generations only one survives: John Menzies, book-seller since 1833, now a magazine-and-fancy-goods emporium. The rest are chain stores, dress shops and shoe shops whose names are seen in every British town center.

In George Street, more exclusive stores are found among banks and insurance offices. The pubs and howffs of George Street's canyon-like accompaniments, Rose Street and Thistle Street, have dwindled. Coffee-bars, boutiques and cosmopolitan fast food outlets have taken their place, and in the few which remain the old clientele of drunken poets and crusaders for eccentric causes is heavily diluted with lawyers, journalists and bank tellers from offices round about.

In the middle of George Street, under the arcades of the Music Hall and Assembly Hall, you may see kilts and sporrans assembling in the evenings for a Highland Ball; the buildings are the venue for Edinburgh's most formal social occasions. At the east end of the street is St. Andrew Square and the city bus station behind it, for out-of-town and long-distance services. At the west end is Charlotte Square, round which the finest examples of Robert Adam's facades are displayed. The north side is especially admired and architects come from all over the world to study its simplicity and perfect proportions. This square was a breeding-ground of talent, too: note the number of birthplace plaques. They include Earl Haig the field-marshal, J.Y. Simpson the pioneer of anesthetics and Alexander Graham Bell the inventor of the telephone.

## On the Waterfront

Beyond the Old Town and the New, the city has plenty to offer a sightseer. The 74-acre Zoological Garden at Corstorphine ("K'stor-fin"), four miles west of the city, was one of the world's first open-planned zoos. Penguins are the specialty. The Royal Botanic Gardens (entrance in Howard Place, one and a half miles north of Princes Street) contain fine rose gardens, rock gardens and an arboretum. Inverleith House, to which the grounds formerly belonged, is now a small but highly select modern art gallery with Picassos on the walls and Henry Moore sculptures spread round the lawns. Before you leave Howard Place you may like to step into number 8, R.L. Stevenson's birthplace, and now his museum.

The port of Leith, part of the city of Edinburgh, is reached by most of the streets which run north from Princes Street, the most direct route being by way of Leith Street at the eastern end (opposite the General Post Office) and into Leith Walk. Leith is now a grain port, lined with flour mills. The most characteristic sights of maritime Edinburgh are found at Newhaven, a community with its roots in seafaring history; at the exotically-named but humdrum Portobello and Joppa, seaside suburbs; and at Granton, a deep-sea trawler base and yacht marina.

These villages form a chain of shabby suburbs along the Edinburgh waterfront where the Firth of Forth is about six miles wide. Among "those emerald isles which calmly sleep / on the blue bosom of the deep" (Scott) you may pick out Fidra far away down the Firth, Stevenson's model for *Treasure Island;* and close at hand Inchkeith, a rock, a lighthouse and not much else. On Inchkeith an early Stuart king marooned two babies with a deaf-and-dumb nurse to determine the original language of mankind. When the babies were seven years old the court philosophers agreed that they spoke "guid Ebrew." The isles of the upper Firth are described in the chapter on Fife Region.

## Voyage of Discovery

Edinburgh and its suburbs are easy places to find one's way around in and the foregoing sketches of the principal sights only skim the surface of a district which the Greek poet might have linked with his homeland when he wrote: "Prick the stones with a needle and you discover the bones of heroes." We have not described the birthplace of Sir Arthur Conan Doyle in Picardy Place or the Royal Infirmary where he learned the inference-and-deduction techniques from Dr. Joseph Bell that he gave to his fictional investigator Sherlock Holmes. We have omitted the Dean Village, the curious complex of mills and tenements beside the Water of Leith under the city's busiest streets yet apparently remote from the world; and Greyfriars Bobby, the fountain in Candlemaker Row which commemorates the fidelity of a poor man's terrier dog; and the fine schools endowed by merchants of long ago—Daniel Stewart's, George Watson's, John Watson's, James Gillespie's, Donaldson's Hospital, Fettes and others—which add their spires and cupolas to the Edinburgh silhouette; and Edinburgh University with its great dome and Old Quadrangle long outgrown and its 16-story David Hume Tower; and the large Halls gifted by millionaire brewers McEwan and Usher, one for the University and one for music; and the castle of Craigmillar whose ruined walls could tell so much of the intrigues of Mary Queen of Scots; and the stately home of Lauriston in whose gardens you may watch a croquet tournament or a country-dance display . . . the multifarious attractions of the city beyond the Old Town and the New would take days to describe, much less visit.

The tourist season reaches its climax in the Edinburgh International Festival, the most complete cultural feast in Europe of music, drama, exhibitions and dance. The Festival was inaugurated in 1947 and it would be hard to name an artistic celebrity of the latter half of the 20th century who has not appeared at it. During the three weeks of this event, late August to mid-September, the city takes on a movement and brilliance worthy of its incomparable setting. Even if you are not culturally inclined or interested in the hundreds of Fringe entertainments which accompany and sometimes steal the limelight from the main events, you cannot help being uplifted by the color and cosmopolitan bustle of a Festival day and the marvelous floodlighting of a Festival night. Even provincial Scots invade the capital in their thousands to attend the military tattoo on the Castle esplanade or watch the last-night fireworks.

### "Auld Reekie"

Finally, a word or two to explain Edinburgh's nickname: Auld Reekie. It means "Old Smoky," and was coined by a man of Fife who stood every morning on the opposite shore of the Forth and watched the fumes from 10,000 chimneys gathering into a pall above the towers and tenements of the capital. But Auld Reekie is no more. Today the city is a smoke-free zone and the old blackened buildings are gradually being sand blasted into something like their appearance when new. Nothing would more astonish a citizen of the past, time warped into the present, than the clear air and bright stonework of his native town.

# PRACTICAL INFORMATION FOR EDINBURGH

**GETTING INTO TOWN FROM THE AIRPORT.** An airport bus connects Edinburgh airport with the city bus terminal at Waverley Bridge. Buses run once every two hours and journey time is around 35 minutes. One-way fare is 80p. Taxi fare for the same trip is approximately £5.

**HOTELS.** Edinburgh has more than 300 hotels and guest houses, many very good, some not so good but nearly all an improvement on what they used to be; especially those in the lower price ranges. If you are simply looking for a night's lodging, and are motoring, you will easily find it along the approach roads to the city, at one of innumerable private houses which advertise Bed and Breakfast. You may expect to pay £6–£10 per head, rather more at Festival time.

If you arrive in central Edinburgh without a place to stay, visit the Information Bureau at Waverley Bridge (off Princes Street, close to Waverley station entrance); or telephone the City Accommodation Bureau at 226 6591. (Remember that all Edinburgh telephone numbers must be prefixed with 031 if you are calling from outside the city and its suburbs.)

*Deluxe*

**Ladbroke Dragonara,** Belford Road (tel. 332 2545). 142 rooms, all with bath. Edinburgh's smartest hotel, delightfully slotted into a ravine of the Water of Leith yet only seven minutes from West End. Several bars and restaurants, including a quick-lunch bar in old water-mill. Rooms not large, but tastefully decorated and well-equipped. A popular conference center.

## Expensive

**Caledonian,** west end of Princes Street (tel. 225 2433). 212 rooms, 204 with bath. Slightly faded grandeur from golden age of railroads undergoing a not-always-judicious facelift. Ornate and spacious interior. Like most former railroad hotels, tends to be overheated by British standards. Excellent location.

**Commodore,** Cramond Foreshore (tel. 336 1700). 49 rooms, all with bath. Open situation on seafront drive between Leith and Cramond. (Not very near bus routes.) Highly rated for meals and services. Bars crowded at weekends.

**Howard,** Great King Street (tel. 556 1393). 26 rooms, all with bath. High-class family hotel in quiet street of New Town.

**North British,** east end of Princes Street (tel. 556 2414). 193 rooms, 171 with bath. Similar to Caledonian. Sits on top of main railroad station but is well insulated. Excellent Scots cuisine in basement restaurant, the *Cleikum.*

**Prestonfield House,** Priestfield Road (tel. 667 8000). 5 rooms. Secluded situation 20 minutes from city center. Historic house in which lack of some amenities—for example, private bathrooms—must be accepted. Notable international cuisine. Peacocks on lawns. Many interesting architectural features.

**Roxburghe,** Charlotte Square (tel. 225 3921). 78 rooms, 62 with bath. Restrained elegance to match the Georgian environment. Bedrooms are especially well-furnished and service is first-class.

## Moderate

**Bruntsfield,** Bruntsfield Place (tel. 229 1393). 52 rooms, 28 with bath. Two miles from center on bus route, south side. Pleasant outlook, reasonable standard of food and service.

**Clarendon,** Grosvenor Street (tel. 337 7033). 44 rooms, 40 with bath. In quiet Georgian terrace ten minutes from West End.

**Donmaree,** Mayfield Gardens (667 3641). 18 rooms, 6 with bath. Typical of numerous town house hotels along southern approaches to Edinburgh. On main bus route. Superior Scottish cuisine.

**Ellersly House,** Ellersly Road (tel. 337 6888). 57 rooms, all with bath. High standard of service and cuisine, good big rooms, a pleasant suburban situation. Prices may increase sharply around Festival time.

**Learmonth,** Learmonth Terrace (tel. 343 2671). 62 rooms, 24 with bath. In tree-lined avenue only 5 minutes from West End. Bright and modern, lively at night. Bars, bistro and coffee lounge bring in the locals.

**Mount Royal,** Princes Street (tel. 225 7161). 156 rooms, 146 with bath. Most modern hotel in city center, above department stores, good viewpoint for pageantry. Full range of amenities, but much coming and going and a somewhat functional atmosphere.

**Oratava,** Craigmillar Park (tel. 667 9484). 54 rooms, all with bath. Modern and spacious on main south road, 3 miles from center. Excellent amenities and high-class cuisine. Very popular for weddings and other celebrations.

**Royal British,** Princes Street (tel. 556 4901). 72 rooms, 39 with bath. Old-established and reputable. Could not be more central. Traditions of personal service make up for slightly claustrophobic atmosphere.

## Inexpensive

**Abercraig,** Picardy Place (tel. 556 6257). 11 rooms, 4 with bath. East-central city; good all-round value.

**Balfour House,** Pilrig Street (tel. 554 2106). 23 rooms. Between Edinburgh and Leith. Insalubrious area, but a perfectly respectable hotel, and highly-praised for nourishing Scots cuisine.

**Gordon Bruce,** South Learmonth Gardens (tel. 332 8248). 35 rooms, 21 with bath. Good situation near West End; an exceptionally well-run hotel.

**Rothesay,** Rothesay Place (tel. 225 4125). 40 rooms, 28 with bath. A typical example of successful transformation of elegant New Town buildings. Rooms spacious and well-furnished.

**Sgian-Dhu,** Carlton Terrace (tel. 556 1761). 19 rooms, only one with bath. Quiet but fairly convenient situation among consular offices.

### Guest Houses

**Brig o' Doon Guest House,** 262 Ferry Road (tel. 552 3953). 6 rooms. Friendly atmosphere, substantial breakfasts. Not a classy district, but handy for Botanic Gardens and exit to west.

**International Guest House,** 37 Mayfield Gardens (tel. 667 2511). 7 rooms, 2 with bath. Canadian proprietor. South side of city, 15 minutes by bus from center. Clean and comfortable; cuisine so-so.

**Maranatha Guest House,** Pilrig Street (tel. 554 2106). 8 rooms. A low-priced oasis of comfort with above-average menus in a rather shabby district 1 mile from center.

### Hostels

Universities and further-education colleges offer accommodations with (usually) cafeteria-style meals during vacation periods: March to April and June to September. A single room with breakfast and evening meal will cost from £10.50 to £15.10 per day, depending on establishment and season. Double rooms (of which there are few) approximately double. Enquiries to: The Principal Warden.

**Carlyle Hall,** East Suffolk Road (tel. 667 2262). 310 rooms. On south side, 2 miles from center.

**Pollock Halls of Residence,** Park Road (tel. 667 1971). 1,508 rooms. Close to Commonwealth Swimming Pool and Queen's Park; 1 mile from center.

There are numerous Y.M.C.A. and Y.W.C.A. clubs and hostels. The principal Y.M.C.A. hostel is at 14 South St. Andrew Street, just off Princes Street (tel. 556 4303), and enquiries about membership, accommodations and social facilities should be made there. For Y.W.C.A. services, apply to Y.W.C.A. House, 7 Randolph Place (near West End, tel. 225 4379). Rates per night vary according to grading of hostel. Maximum price is £4.50.

### Self-Catering

Apartments may be rented through Frutin Travel Agency, 61 Great Junction Street, Leith (tel. 554 0632); Mackay's Agency, 30 Frederick Street (tel. 225 3539); and Northesk Self-Catering Apartments, 23 Pilrig Street (tel. 554 4205). For medium- and long-term renting, apply to City-Centre Accommodation, 15 Gayfield Square, EH1 (tel. 556 8616).

### Camping

The chief campsite for tents and caravans is at Muirhouse in the southwestern suburbs (tel. 336 6874). Tents may be hired from Purvis Equipments, 9 Portland Place, EH6 6LA (tel. 554 1331)

 **HOW TO GET ABOUT. By bus.** Bus travel in the city center costs around 15p per mile, the rate decreasing the farther you go. (Edinburgh-Glasgow, for example, is £ 2.75 for the 90-mile return journey.) Lothian Region Transport run city bus tours of from one hour to half a day, all year round, starting 9.30 from Waverley Bridge. The "Waverley Series" of half-day and whole-day tours takes in some quite faraway places; also from Waverley Bridge, just off Princes Street. City tours are from £1.50, out-of-town excursions from £4.50. You may book most trips in advance at either LRT headquarters or the Transport Information Bureau: see *Tourist Information,* in following pages.

Lothian Region Transport issue an Edinburgh Freedom Ticket, price £2.20 per head, for unlimited city bus travel for one day—buy it from either of the above addresses and validate it yourself for the day of your choice. The same organization's Tourist Card, currently priced at £5 to £10.50, provides from two to 13 days' unlimited bus travel in the city plus a half-day conducted tour, a short sightseeing tour and certain concessions at selected shops, restaurants and museums. The package also includes a map to help you plan your journeys.

Eastern Scottish, St. Andrew Square, Edinburgh EH2 (tel. 556 2126) operate a summer program of bus tours from Edinburgh throughout Scotland, lasting from four to eight days. Departures most days except Sun., May-Sept. Sample prices: Deeside, Loch Ness and Glencoe (4 days) £109; Northwest Highlands (7 days) £165. Food, accommodations and all services included.

**By car.** If you are motoring in Edinburgh, be sure to observe parking restrictions: traffic wardens are pitiless. Have plenty of small change for the meters. Driving in the city center is confusing enough for locals, let alone strangers, and many people prefer to park outside the central controlled zone and walk or take a bus into the center.

A three-hour sightseeing visit in a chauffeured automobile, including admission charges to museums, tips and parking fees costs £35-£40. City-center travel agencies can arrange it.

**By taxi.** There are taxi ranks in various parts of central Edinburgh, at the railroad and bus stations and along Princes Street. Most taxis are the black, old-fashioned, purpose-built vehicles you will be familiar with if you have been to London. Cruising taxis available for hire are those with their yellow rooftop TAXI signs illuminated. Taxis in Edinburgh are a relatively inexpensive form of transport: about 70p a mile, or 90p when you travel beyond the city limits.

 **TOURIST INFORMATION.** Edinburgh Tourist Information Center, 5 Waverley Bridge (tel. 226 6591); accommodations desk for personal callers at same address. Edinburgh Accommodation Service, 9 Cockburn Street; applications by mail only. American Consul, 3 Regent Terrace (tel. 556 8315). Citizens' Advice Bureau, 58 Dundas Street (tel. 557 1500). Lothian Region Transport, 14 Queen Street (tel. 554 4494). British Airways, 135 Princes Street (tel. 225 2525). British Caledonian Airways, 30 George Street (tel. 226 6774). British Rail, Waverley Station (tel. 556 2451).

 **MUSEUMS.** We list here the principal museums and galleries of Edinburgh. You will likely be agreeably surprised at the modest charges—most offer both free admission and free parking.

**Canongate Tolbooth,** 163 Canongate. Dates from 1591 and contains collection of clan and tartan insignia. Also mounts special exhibitions. Open Jun.–Sept., weekdays 10–6; Oct.–May, weekdays 10–5.

**City Art Centre,** 1–4 Market Street. Major exhibitions of fine and decorative arts, also Scottish portraits and landscapes. Open Jun.–Sept., weekdays 10–6; Oct.–May, weekdays 10–5.

**Huntly House,** 142 Canongate. Principal museum of city history and Edinburgh silver and glass. Open weekdays, Jun.–Sept. 10–6, Oct.–May 10–5.

**John Knox House,** 45 High Street. Early examples of stone-built town house containing Knox items and Scottish Kirk relics. Undergoing long-term restoration but partly open weekdays, Apr.–Oct., 10–5.

**Lady Stair's House,** Lawnmarket. Fascinating old tenement with relics of Burns, Scott, Stevenson. Open Jun.–Sept. 10–6, Oct.–May 10–5; weekdays only.

**Georgian House,** 7 Charlotte Square. On the Adam side of the Square. Fitted and furnished in the style of its period, 1760–1820. Open Apr.–Oct., weekdays 10–5, Sun. 2–5; Nov.–mid-Mar., Sat. 10–4.30, Sun. 2–4.30. N.T.S.

**Gladstone's Land,** Lawnmarket. 17th-century merchant's house, appropriately furnished. Open Apr.–Oct., weekdays 10–5, Sun. 2–5; Nov.–mid-Dec., Sat. 10–4.30, Sun. 2–4.30. N.T.S.

**Museum of Childhood,** 38 High Street. The social history of children, their dress, upbringing and toys through the centuries. "The noisiest museum in the world." Open weekdays, 10–6 Jun.–Sept., 10–5 Oct.–May.

**National Gallery of Scotland,** The Mound. Famous European and British artists, 1300–1900. Lunchtime concerts in summer. Open weekdays 10–5, Sun. 2–5.

**National Museum of Antiquities,** Queen Street. Archeology, medieval and modern history. Some Celtic curiosities from pre-A.D. 1000. Open weekdays 10–5, Sun. 2–5.

**National Portrait Gallery,** Queen Street (above Museum of Antiquities). Scottish portraitists and their famous and not-so-famous sitters. Open weekdays 10–5, Sun. 2–5; closed 12.30–1.30 Oct.–Mar.

**Palace of Holyroodhouse.** Official residence of Queen in Scotland. State apartments, tapestries, and portrait gallery with 100 Scottish monarchs, most looking strangely alike. Open May–Oct., weekdays 9.30–6, Sun. 11–6; Nov.–Apr., weekdays 9.30–5.15, Sun. 12.30–4.30. Occasionally closed, generally in May and early June, when royal visitors are in residence or when preparations in hand for royal visit.

**Royal Botanic Garden,** Inverleith Row. Exhibition hall for ecological displays. Open weekdays 9 to sunset, Sun. 11 to sunset.

**Royal College of Surgeons Museum,** Nicolson Street. Evolution of surgery; instruments and specimens from city's venerable medical schools. Open by appointment (tel. 031 556 6206).

**Royal Scottish Academy,** The Mound. Contemporary Scottish artists and periodical exhibitions. Open May–Jul. weekdays 10–6, Sun. 2–5.

**Royal Scottish Museum,** Chambers Street. Ideal for a wet day. All kinds of working models of industry and science. Permanent displays of silver, ceramics, primitive arts, zoology. Open weekdays 10–5, Sun. 2–5.

**Scottish Gallery of Modern Art,** Inverleith House (in Botanic Garden). Impressive collection of contemporary painters and sculptors, avant-garde and pop art (Warhol, Lichtenstein). Unfamiliar work by truly great names. Open weekdays 10–5 (or sunset); Sun. 2–5 (or sunset), in winter 1 to sunset.

 **ENTERTAINMENT AND NIGHT LIFE.** Edinburgh is not a city for those with a taste for nightlife and there is certainly no year-round program of cultural and other events that you would expect in a capital city. Indeed, with the honorable exception of Festival time, nightlife is largely confined to the pubs and clubs. However, to find out what *is* happening, collect a copy of *What's On in Edinburgh,* free every month from bars, hotels and newsstands. This details exhibitions, theater, movies, sporting and social events. The Edinburgh *Evening News* is also a helpful source of information.

## THEATER AND MUSIC

The *Royal Lyceum* theater, Grindlay Street, has two resident companies and sometimes visiting players. The *King's Theater,* in Leven Street, presents plays, ballet and opera in winter, and downmarket Scottish entertainments in summer; also amateur productions of musicals and light opera.

The *Playhouse Theater,* Greenside Place, often has big names in the rock and jazz worlds, as well as two short opera seasons in the early spring. Scottish symphony and chamber orchestras perform regularly in the *Usher Hall,* Lothian Road, and there are chamber recitals and late-night jazz at the *Queen's Hall,* Clerk Street.

Edinburgh's most prestigious theater and also the smallest is the *Traverse,* in the Lawnmarket. Its policy is to present plays that have not appeared elsewhere and to encourage younger Scottish dramatists.

## MOVIE HOUSES

The latest movies are shown at the *Dominion,* Church Hill, and *Odeon,* Clerk Street, complexes, each with three simultaneous presentations. There are half-a-dozen other movie houses in the city, among them the *Cameo* at Tollcross, which shows classics of the cinema; and the *Calton Studios,* 24 Calton Road, for minority and alternative culture works, midnight screenings Friday, Saturday nights; backstage bar.

## NIGHTCLUBS

These are few, modern and, by Edinburgh standards, costly places to spend an evening in. In fact you could dine and have a couple of drinks, dance and watch the cabaret for around £40 per head; which is cheap compared with, say, London. At the time we go to press, only one nightclub is open: *Piper's,* 23–5 Lothian Road (tel. 229 8291).

## CASINOS

These too are something of an innovation for the staid Scottish capital. The principal gambling casino is the *Regency,* 20 Great King Street (tel. 556 2828). There is also the *Casino Martell,* 7 Newington Road (tel. 667 7763). American roulette and blackjack are the games. Admission is to members only: membership is free but does not become effective until 48 hours after joining.

## DISCOS

You will find discos advertised for occasional evenings at many pubs, clubs and hotels, the music being provided by traveling discos and road shows. The principal nightly discos and dance halls are: *Adell Dance Studios,* 8 Broughton Street; *Annabel's,* 3 Semple Street; *Assembly Rooms,* 43 Constitution Street, Leith; *Bobby McGee's,* 96a Rose Street; *Coasters,* 3 Tollcross; and the *Revolva,* 8 Glencairn Crescent.

**THE EDINBURGH FESTIVAL.** In 1947 Edinburgh inaugurated a three-week season that was to become world-famous as the Edinburgh International Festival of Music, Drama and Art. That title gives only a slight idea of the immense range of entertainments and exhibitions now presented: there is music from all over the globe, performed on all variety of instruments; there are famous dance companies; celebrated theatrical groups; masterworks old and new of art, sculpture and crafts. Every year more than 20 nations give of their best in the theaters, halls, schools, churches and streets of Edinburgh.

That is the Festival. Its once-tender offspring, the Festival Fringe, comprising a handful of enthusiastic students, has grown into a giant of more than 800 events that threatens to overshadow the Festival proper. Clowns, jugglers, musicians, mystery players, cabaret stars and horse-drawn caravanners . . . strolling players of many races and types fill Edinburgh's streets at Festival time; and even if some of the shows create no memorable experience for the audiences, at least admission is inexpensive and you don't have to stand in line (and the performers are obviously enjoying themselves). Some big names in TV got their initial break at the Edinburgh Fringe.

International film festivals, jazz festivals, and the Military Tattoo on the Castle esplanade run concurrently with the official Festival. There is also very often some important international or Commonwealth event contemporaneously at Edinburgh's great athletics stadium, Meadowbank, or the Commonwealth Swimming Pool.

**Booking Details.** The Festival takes place annually during a three-week period end-August to mid-September or thereabouts. For a detailed program you can write two or three months in advance to the Festival Office, 21 Market Street, Edinburgh (tel. 226 4001). Telephone bookings may also be made (225 5756).

Details of the International Film Festival are obtainable from Filmhouse, 88 Lothian Road, Edinburgh (tel. 226 6382). The Jazz Festival office is at Beauford House, 16 Dundas Street, Edinburgh; tickets from that office or from Adam Rooms, George Street, Edinburgh. The Festival Fringe Society is in the Royal Mile Center, 170 High Street (tel. 226 5257).

Remember that if you are phoning from outside Edinburgh (beyond about a 10-mile radius) you must prefix numbers with 031.

 **SHOPPING.** In central Edinburgh, particularly along Princes Street, you will see names of large department stores familiar in London and other British cities: Marks & Spencer, Woolworth's, British Home Stores, Littlewood's, Debenham's—large emporia for nationally-known clothing, food and other consumer items.

Shops of a more Scottish character will be found in George Street and the streets which cross it at right-angles. It is in Princes Street, however, that visitors find the most typically "Edinburgh" department store in the old-established business of Jenner's (corner of St. David's Street). People shop here for the kind of gift items—tartan materials, leather goods, jewelry etc.—which are not available elsewhere. Fraser's, at the opposite end of Princes Street, is a large store of the same type, but less exclusive. Both these stores are well acquainted with the routine for exporting retail purchases.

R. & W. Forsyth, close to Jenners, is another characteristically prestigious Scottish store, as is Anderson's in Shandwick Place (West End, a continuation of Princes Street). Both these stores specialize in quality woollens, knitwear, tailoring for men and women and clan regalia.

Antique shops are dotted about. Those of the Royal Mile and its neighborhood do good business in the tourist season, but in and around the Hanover Street–Thistle Street–Queen Street intersections there are more discriminating and expensive antiques businesses. Souvenirs proliferate on Princes Street and down the Royal Mile, and in the Canongate and Lawnmarket (at opposite ends of the High Street) you will see kiltmakers, bagpipe makers and other traditional Highland industries. The leading name in Highland dress and accessories is Geoffrey (Highland Crafts), 57–9 High Street (near John Knox's House).

The greatest concentration of art and craft shops is also in the Royal Mile, though they are scattered across both Old Town and New. A very good Royal Mile location is the Scottish Craft Centre, 140 Canongate, which has a cross-section of crafts for sale, pots, weaving, glass and carving. Worth taking in as you stroll towards Holyrood House. Galleries with occasional exhibitions are attached to some of them. The Bruntsfield district, south of Tollcross, is also good for attractive and superior shops handling craftwork, quality furniture, glassware etc. Notable among them is KES Mosaics at 43 Bruntsfield Place.

 **DINING OUT.** As befits a capital city and tourist metropolis, the range of restaurants in Edinburgh is very wide. Prices at all levels are more moderate than in, say, London or Dublin, but you may not feel you have had value for money since the standards of cooking and service too often betray that puritanical Scottish conviction that enjoying yourself is a sin. It is hard to find an acceptable cup of coffee in Edinburgh. Many Continental restaurants have appeared in recent years—Italian, French, Danish, Turkish and others—but few of them would attract a regular clientele in their own countries. Most discerning visitors say that the Indian and Chinese restaurants offer the best choice and the best value—they are the least expensive too, but are usually sited in unappealing environments.

### Deluxe

**Prestonfield House,** Priestfield Road (tel. 667 8000). Excellent dining surrounded by family portraits and old silver. Open on Sunday with a limited menu. (See under Hotels)

### Expensive

**Albyn,** 77 Queen Street (tel. 225 4677). Staid and tranquil.

**Consort,** 136 George Street (tel. 225 6254). Adjunct of Roxburghe hotel. Pleasing layout, tends to be crowded and hot at lunchtime.

**Cosmo's,** 58 Castle Street (tel. 226 6743). One of the better Italian restaurants. Good for pheasant, guinea and other fowl.

**Denzler's,** 80 Queen Street (tel. 226 5467). Swiss-owned, immaculate and fastidious. Interesting wine list.

**Handsel,** 22 Stafford Street (tel. 225 5521). Scottish/French cuisine, some *flambé* specialties. Air of rather self-conscious graciousness.

**Howtowdie,** 27 Stafford Street (tel. 225 6291). As for *Handsel* on opposite side of street, but more adventurous with decor and cuisine.

**Visuvio,** 155 Lothian Road (tel. 228 2233). Sea food with exotic crab and lobster recipes by a chef trained at Caesar's Palace, Rome.

### Moderate

**Casa Espanola,** 61–65 Rose Street (tel. 225 5979). Very friendly spot for good Spanish fare at reasonable prices.

**Le Caveau,** 136 Dundas Street (tel. 556 5707). Used to be a wine merchant's and now has a good wine bar, but food only so-so.

**Cousteau's,** 109 Hanover Street (tel. 226 3355). Varied menu, large à la carte selection, particularly fish. Evenings only, closed Sun.

**Engine Room,** 7/8 Queensferry Street (Lane) (tel. 225 2142). Tucked away in a smart cellar, this is a spot to relax and enjoy simple but excellent cooking.

**Get Stuffed,** 192 Rose Street (tel. 225 2208). Celebrated for heavy eating. "The best and biggest steaks in town."

**Lafayette,** 22 Brougham Place (tel. 229 0869). Small intimate French restaurant, advance booking essential.

**Luciano's,** 10 Melville Place (tel. 226 3579). A taste of Italy.

**Maridor's,** 39a Albany Street (tel. 556 0397). Swiss, German and French influences among numerous gastronomic specialties. Also serves quick snacks and bar lunches.

**Nimmo's,** 101 Shandwick Place (tel. 229 6119). Reasonably-priced traditional fare at lunchtime, Continental dishes in evening, lavish sweets. Wine bar popular with young.

**Osman's,** 123 Corstorphine Road (tel. 337 5010). Grills, steaks, fish.

**Palumbo,** 40 Bruntsfield Place (tel. 229 5025). Rather small and sometimes crowded. Traditional Scottish and Spanish cuisine.

**Snobs,** 1 Deanbank Lane (tel. 332 0003). Imaginative variations on basic Scottish and cosmopolitan cuisine.

**Vito's,** 55 Frederick Street (tel. 225 5052). Neat basketwork decor. Classic Italian dishes, good but pricey wine list.

*Inexpensive*

**Bastille,** 36 Broughton Street (tel. 337 2602). Good-quality French cuisine.

**Bruno's,** 8–12 Morrison Street (tel. 229 4648). Mainly Italian dishes; discreet atmosphere, and good steaks in upstairs *Barn* restaurant, which stays open late.

**Cairngorm,** 47 Hanover Street (tel. 226 3082). One of numerous restaurants, mainly self-service, operated by Crawford's, the principal Edinburgh bakers.

**Chan Richard Tong Sang,** 12 Cadzow Place (tel. 661 3369). Mandarin Chinese restaurant.

**Dario's,** 87 Lothian Road (tel. 229 9625). Pizza and spaghetti house, bar service until 4 A.M.

**Henderson's,** 94 Hanover Street (tel. 225 3400). Prestigious salad table and wine cellar, much patronized by students.

**Istanbul Kebab,** 96 Dalry Road (tel. 337 9774). Turkish decor, charcoal-cooked kebabs, Turkish wines.

**Mayflower,** 5 Dundee Street (tel. 229 5414). Chop suey house.

**New York Steam Packet,** 31 North Rose Street Lane (tel. 225 4663). Cheerful, lively at night; convivial atmosphere, more than a hamburger joint.

**Punjab,** 45 St. Patrick Square (tel. 667 4432). Traditional Indian and Tandoori dishes.

**Shish Mahal,** 6 Brougham Street (tel. 229 1000). Typical Indo-Pakistani-type restaurant, popular with young.

**Skipper's,** 1a Dock Place, Leith (tel. 554 1018). Enterprizing small bistro, imaginative seafood cuisine. Rather out of the way, but large clientele obviously finds journey worthwhile.

 **PUBS.** Edinburgh pubs are a study in themselves. In the eastern and northern districts of the city you will find some grim, inhospitable-looking places which proclaim that drinking, for the Scot, is no laughing matter. In the central and western districts many pubs have deliberately improved their old "spit-and-sawdust" images and in their lounge bars (as opposed to the public bars) you may find atmospheric revivals of the warm, oak-paneled, leather-chaired "howffs" of a more leisurely age. Pubs frequented by students are often highly-rated for their evening musical entertainments. At lunchtime a snack or bar lunch service is usual. On Saturday nights most city pubs are noisy and crowded and respectable citizens tend to avoid them. Out of 400-odd city pubs we give a brief sampling:

**Abbotsford,** 3 Rose Street. Rendezvous of media people. A full restaurant service.

**Allan Ramsay Tavern,** 119 High Street. Has historic relics and associations with the 18th-century drinking clubs.

**Bannerman's,** 53–7 Niddry Street. Old-fashioned decor, log fires.

**Bird in the Hand,** Burdiehouse Road. Old-world tavern on southern outskirts. Serves light meals midday and evening.

**Chumley's,** 72 Rose Street Lane North. Favorite of serious beer drinkers in the heart of publand.

**Deacon Brodie's,** 435 Lawnmarket. Quaint and labyrinthine; attracts more tourists than locals.

**McGuffie's,** 15 Market Street. Another old landmark close to Waverley station and underneath a stolid, no-nonsense eating house, the *Doric* restaurant.

**Nicky Tam's,** Victoria Street. Highly spoken of by beer-drinking students and aged whisky-bibbers.

**Peacock,** Lindsay Road, Newhaven. A famous 17th-century waterfront "howff" in the northern suburbs. Restaurant adjoining.

**Raffles,** St. Stephen's Street. Clientele of young to middle-aged drinkers, attracted by wide range of beers including Budweiser, Schlitz and Cours.

**Scott's,** 202 Rose Street. Another old tavern in a street full of them, this bar has long been under the direction of a stern and dictatorial proprietress and is noted for its refinement and respectability.

**White Cockade,** 55 Rose Street. Another long-established "howff" in Edinburgh's publand, once the haunt of poets and litterateurs.

**White Horse** 266 Canongate. Small, usually overcrowded, but steeped in history. Dr. Johnson stayed here on first arrival in Edinburgh.

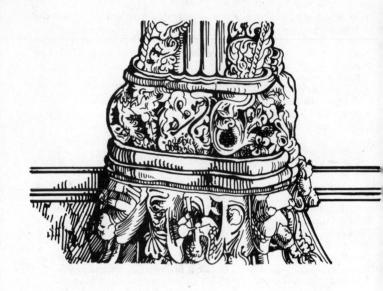

# SCOTLAND'S HOME COUNTIES

## *Lothian*

Taking the analogy of England's Home Counties, the counties immediately around London, the Lothian Region may be considered the Home Counties of Scotland. It is spread about the skirts of the capital city, Edinburgh, and consists of West Lothian (historically called Linlithgowshire from its principal town); East Lothian (Haddingtonshire); and Midlothian, which includes Edinburgh itself, a name familiar from Scott's novel *The Heart of Midlothian.*

The Region provides rich pickings for the historian. For 1,000 years Edinburgh has been Scotland's metropolis, even at periods when its castle was in English hands. How the stormy history of the Scots has been concentrated round this old gray citadel above the Firth of Forth may be seen from the battlefields and scarred fortresses strewn over the neighborhood.

In more peaceable times Lothian Region became a good address for aristocrats and rich merchants with interests in the political and commercial life of the capital. Hence the fine mansions in the countryside, the deer parks, the landscaping of gardens after the French fashion; and Lothian's fame as a seedplot of Lowland gentility.

Then, at the end of the 18th century, came the Industrial Revolution, the discovery of coalfields and the transformation of the upper Forth into a manufacturing base. Coalmines smudged many square miles of what was once idyllic scenery. Gentle streams in fairy glens—so the old writings describe them—ran foul with industrial waste. Rural mansions became colliery offices or the headquarters of papermaking companies.

However, it would be wrong to give the impression that Lothian Region is all satanic mills and smoke. Most of East Lothian is purely rural, the sort of place retired admirals live. Similarly, West Lothian and Midlothian have their black spots but a good deal of attractive country as well. And everywhere there is history, often more vivid when you stumble on it in council housing estates. As to smoke, it has been abolished. Today, tighter regulations and the decline of heavy industries have brought cleaner skies back to the workshops and playgrounds of Scotland's Home Counties. Anglers report that salmon and seatrout are once more making their way up Lothian streams which, within living memory, ran foul with industrial waste. And if you hear from your Lothian acquaintances the age-old valedictory "Lang may your lum (chimney) reek," that is a purely symbolic way of wishing you health.

The word Lothian may have something to do with lowland. The Region has no great hills to boast of. Upland areas of East Lothian reach 1,730 feet at the Lammer Law on the edge of Borders Region. Midlothian's Pentland Hills rise to 1,840 feet, which puts a breath of mountain air at the disposal of Edinburgh's suburbs. West Lothian has two clumps of hills of about 1,000 feet. But most of the Region is a coastal plain along the Forth as that river widens in its firth or seachannel. The Forth is three miles wide at the western end of the Region, 25 miles wide at the eastern end.

It is also suggested that Lothian may mean "land of Lud"—the shadowy Dark-Age king whose name crops up here and there all over Britain; at Ludgate Hill in London, for instance. A stone coffin unearthed in 1861 at the foot of Traprain Law near Haddington was thought to contain Lud's bones.

## Lothian Horizons

The obvious base for touring the Lothian countryside is Edinburgh. If you stand on an Edinburgh eminence—the castle ramparts, Arthur's Seat, Corstorphine hill—you can plan a few Lothian excursions without the aid of a map. If you leave Edinburgh by air from Turnhouse airport, eight miles from the city center on the Glasgow road, you will have a bird's-eye view of the landmarks along the Firth of Forth, including the famous rail and road bridges across the Narrows at Queensferry. If you go out by rail it will be either towards Glasgow via the Princes Street Gardens and West Lothian or towards Berwick-on-Tweed, past Holyroodhouse and the East Lothian barley fields.

The main roads exit to the west (A8, A9) for the motorways to Glasgow, Stirling and Perth; to the south (A701, A7 or A68) for the Borders Region and England; and to the east (A1) along the coast by the Great North Road to Berwick-on-Tweed. This last road was landscaped by Robert Stevenson, grandfather of R.L.S., and as you gaze back from it you see the hills closing over the city like curtains on a stage set with an improbably romantic backcloth.

West Lothian (A8, A9) starts with agriculture but grows industrialized as you progress westwards. Long ago it was the most thickly populated part of Scotland after Edinburgh herself. Even before the discovery of coal there was a considerable seaborne trade between the small Forth harbors and the Baltic countries. That trade and the coal industry have declined and you might get the impression that West Lothian consists mainly of disused mines and unsightly bings (cinder mounds). But the area has some pleasant hills and woodlands too.

## Queen's Ferry and Roman Wall

Five miles from Edinburgh on the A90 to South Queensferry it is worth while turning right to visit the village of Cramond at the mouth of a glen where the Romans built a port and fished for oysters. If you felt energetic you could walk back to Granton along the seafront road (4 miles) or cross the River Almond and follow the path by the shore, through Dalmeny woods, to South Queensferry (5 miles).

At Cramond Brig (now on the M90) James V went a-wooing in disguise and was set upon by murderers. A farmworker, Jock Howieson, went to his aid, dressed his wounds and received as a reward the neighboring lands of Braehead, the condition being that whenever the monarch passed that way Jock and his descendants should offer a basin, a towel and clean water. The Howiesons have held Braehead from that day (about 1530) to this and several British monarchs in the present century have stopped to receive the tribute and wash their hands.

The woods and policies of Dalmeny House border the M90 motorway. Trees were planted by princes and statesmen and are marked with plaques, most of them dated between 1890 and 1910 when the owner, the Earl of Rosebery, was prominent in British politics. The house is not remarkable but the park is famous for its drifts of snowdrops in early spring. Where Dalmeny park ends, South Queensferry begins, but the Rosebery's feudal village is Dalmeny (B9035), two miles inland. It is what used to be known as a model village, while its church has been described as the finest piece of Norman architecture in Scotland.

For South Queensferry, leave the M90 and continue on the A90. The burgh, wedged between hill and shore, has numerous 17th-century buildings whose grim high walls, tiny windows and turnpike stairs remind you of some corners of old Edinburgh. It also has some modern architectural monstrosities. The burgh takes its name from Margaret, Malcolm Canmore's Queen, who crossed at this point on her pilgrimages to Dunfermline Abbey. But the place has been a ferry port from the dawn of transport history.

You no longer wait hours or days for a fair wind across the Narrows of the Forth, as old-time travelers did. You have a choice of two bridges, each, in its time, the wonder of the civil engineering world.

The Forth Rail bridge, nine miles from Edinburgh's Waverley station, was designed by Benjamin Baker (who also built a tunnel under the Hudson River in New York) and opened in 1890. It is one-and-a-half miles long. Permission to walk across is sometimes granted to parties of railroad buffs by British Rail's traffic superintendent in Edinburgh. You really do need to walk to appreciate its massive size. A full-sized train could run inside its main tubular struts. It takes three years and 50 tons of paint to paint the bridge—"painting the Forth Bridge" is a household expression all over Britain, meaning no sooner have you finished a job than it is time to start again.

The Forth Road bridge, two miles upstream, was completed in 1964 to carry the M90 Edinburgh–Perth motorway. A walkway is provided for those who want to cross on foot. It was Scotland's first long-span suspension bridge, embodying many revolutionary features; but as a spectacle it is overshadowed by the bold cantilevers of the old Rail bridge.

West of South Queensferry (A904), the road skirts Hopetoun House, a large Adam mansion, seat of the Marquesses of Linlithgow. A detour (B903) drops down to the shore again at the odd-looking castle of Blackness, like a battleship thrusting its ram bow into the Forth. Next you descend steeply into Bo'ness, properly Borrowstounness, a once-important port, now rather neglected. In the grounds of its Kinneil estate you can see traces of the Antonine Wall as the Romans called it, Graham's Dyke (or Grimsdyke) to the locals. The Wall started here and marched across Scotland to Old Kilpatrick on the Firth of Clyde. From Bo'ness the A706 road will take you the four miles to Linlithgow, chief town of West Lothian.

## Palace of the Stuarts

Linlithgow was once a four-square and stern palace with mean huts clustered round it, but it announces itself most stridently these days with the startling metal sculpture of its parish church spire, said to represent a crown of thorns. From the edge of Linlithgow Loch which stretches alongside the town you have a good view of the Palace in the main street. The entrance is by drawbridge and archway. The principal features are the Lyon Hall, 100 feet long; the little room in which Mary Queen of Scots was born; the dungeons, torture chamber and secret stairway; and a 16th-century fountain in the courtyard, of which the fountain in front of Holyroodhouse is a copy. The Stuart kings were fond of this palace and, as Scottish palaces went, it must once have been a handsome residence; but while troops were garrisoned there after the 1745 rebellion its interior glories were destroyed by fire.

Linlithgow commands a rural landscape. The unclassified roads and lanes south over the Riccarton Hills might be Border roads—but in West Lothian industry is always present. Those breezy routes end at Bathgate with its British Leyland truck and tractor plant and at Livingston, a new town begun in 1965 and settled by workers in light industries, most of them from Glasgow. It is a far cry sociologically from the cosy old burgh towns to the new "deserts wi' windaes (windows)" as a Scottish comic calls them.

Returning from Linlithgow to Edinburgh by the more direct A9 route (17 miles), you may detour again in the direction of the A904 to visit The Binns, an early 17th-century mansion uncharacteristically defenseless in design. Yet its creator, Sir Tam Dalyell ("Dee-ell"), was a general who recruited a famous regiment of cavalry, the Scots Greys, on that spot in 1681. In 1944, The Binns was taken into the care of the National Trust for Scotland, the first of many that the NTS was to acquire.

West Lothian has country parks—large public areas of woodland paths and picnic places—at Almondell and Calderwood (A71). The principal archeological site is on the Bathgate Hills (off B792), where you may inspect Bronze Age (2000 B.C.) stone circles and burial cairns.

### Midlothian

Quite a lot of Edinburgh's own county consists of the Pentland Hills where no roads go. Trains and automobiles heading for the southwest and Carlisle travel under the Pentland ridges (A70, A701, A702). The A70, which ends up on the west coast at Ayr, starts with an up-hill-and-down-dale section affectionately known as the "Lang Whang" or long bootlace. The Midlothian districts served by most other routes are either overrun by Edinburgh's suburbs or dedicated to coal-mining and light industries; with pockets of scenic beauty and historic attractions.

Roslin (B7006) has a castle, a place of formidable strength in its 15th-century heyday, now an atmospheric ruin; and a chapel (usually called Rosslyn Chapel) of the same date, notable for its Prentice Pillar. In the master-builder's absence abroad his apprentice carved the exquisitely foliated column. As a warning to presumptuous trainees, the master hammered him to death, or so the story goes. At all events, the Prentice Pillar was spared. There is an old inn at Roslin where the great and famous have slept; their names are recorded on a tablet.

Beyond Dalkeith, a historic burgh which has lost all its character, the by-roads off the A7 and A68 highways wind among woods and parks and delightful villages such as Temple, Carrington and Crichton, each with its stump of castle or dignified mansion. Around Musselburgh (A1) several fine old houses cling to their pride, though time and neglect have all but "dinged them doon," as the Scots say.

### East Lothian

"Ding doon Tantallon! Mak' a brig (bridge) to the Bass!"; a country proverb, scornfully applied to one who attempts a feat beyond his capabilities. Tantallon is one of the most impressive castle ruins in Scotland. It was built in the 14th century by the Douglases, a family almost as powerful as the King himself in southern Scotland. "Three sides of rock-like wall and one of wall-like rock," was how Hugh Miller the geologist described it. The wall-like rock is a sea-cliff of the East Lothian coastline (A198).

The Bass of the proverb is the Bass Rock, one and a half miles off Tantallon, a 300-foot clump of rock whitened with the multitudes of gannet (solan geese) which crowd the ledges. It is a favorite excursion of North Berwick holidaymakers.

Off-shore rocks and crumbling seafront fortresses line the bays and headlands of East Lothian. Since the 19th century they have also supported an almost unbroken chain of seaside resorts and golf courses.

Golf and tourism owe their development to changes in the currents of the Forth (always a whimsical waterway) which brought sand sweeping in, silting up medieval harbors and creating beaches and dunes.

The chief resorts are North Berwick (A1 and A198 from Edinburgh) and Dunbar (A1). Both are small towns, the former created for golfers and commuters, the latter a fine old burgh with castle ruins and a harbor carved out of the red sandstone rock. From both places fishing boats go out after lobster, scampi and crab. In the old days Dunbar tackled bigger game. Relics of her whaling fleet are still scattered about the neighborhood in the shape of whalebone arches to garden paths and suchlike. Dunbar, incidentally, claims to have the best sunshine record in Scotland. But visitors from mild climates find this coast often cold and windy even in summer and on the hottest days a sea-fret or mist, locally called the "haar," can blot out the sun and lower the temperature by 20 degrees.

To Robert Burns in 1787 East Lothian was "the most glorious corn country I ever saw." Between coastal strip and hills is almost English-looking countryside. The fields are rich in barley and potatoes; the barley goes chiefly to make whisky and ale, the "red soil" potatoes are prized by growers all over Britain. This is the most prosperous farming country in Scotland, and the 18th-century landlords known as the Improvers were partly responsible for that. They brought the agricultural revolution to Scotland, draining and fertilizing the land, inventing or importing machinery and building groups of stone cottages for farmworkers. The landscape is therefore a patchwork of large prosperous farms and little villages which keep the communities together. Visit if you can Athelstaneford (B1347, off A1), Tynninghame ("Tinningum") (A198), Dirleton (A198) and Longniddry (A198) and the line of villages which are spaced out under the Lammermuir Hills on or near the B6355 and B6370 roads: Ormiston, Gifford, Garvald and Stenton.

A plaque opposite Gifford church commemorates a former clergyman, John Witherspoon (born 1723) who signed the American Declaration of Independence. His monument in Gifford churchyard has been renovated by the St. Andrew's Society of Philadelphia.

The strand between Tynninghame and Dunbar is part of the John Muir country park (access from A1). Muir, a local conservationist (1838-1914), emigrated to the United States and formed the Sierra Club, which set up the Yosemite and Sequoia National Parks.

In Athelstaneford's churchyard the saltire, a flag with an X-shaped cross on a blue ground, always flies. The accompanying plaque explains how King Athelstan (895-940) was inspired to victory in battle by the appearance of a white cross in the blue sky—but there are several things wrong with the legend if, as is claimed, this was the origin of the Scottish national flag. Not least is that Athelstan was a Saxon, fighting *against* the Scots. And the "X" or "decussate" cross was already associated with St. Andrew, Scotland's patron saint, who was supposed to have been martyred on it.

Devotees of war games may examine three genuine battlefields as they travel the A1 through East Lothian. Nearest to Edinburgh is Pinkie (1547) at Musselburgh, where English troops on the high ground and English warships in the Forth crushed a Scottish force and prompted the nation's leaders to send the five-year-old Mary Queen of Scots to France for safety. The next battlefield is Prestonpans (1745) near Tranent (roadside monument on A198), where Bonnie Prince Charlie's rebels overcame the government troops. The third is Dunbar (1650), where Cromwell defeated the Covenanters (roadside monument on A1 at Broxburn).

Apart from North Berwick and Dunbar, the most notable town of East Lothian is Haddington (A1), one of the best-looking burghs in Scotland and one of the most intelligently restored. A street-plan on the town house wall outlines a town trail along the banks of the River Tyne (not Newcastle's Tyne) and round a hoary flat-towered church which, as a beacon of piety in more violent times, earned the name of "Lamp of Lothian." Among several celebrated sons and daughters Haddington claims Jane Welsh Carlyle, wife of Thomas Carlyle; Samuel Smiles (1812-1904), social reformer and author of the Victorian best-seller *Self-Help;* and John Knox.

Where East Lothian's cultivated fields rise to the bare back of the Lammermuir Hills the turf and heather, selectively cropped by agile Blackface sheep (watch out for them on the unfenced roads), reflect the variegated colors of the landscape. Trout streams gush through green valleys. The moors echo to the cries of lapwing, curlew, pheasant and grouse. On the B6355 and other unclassified roads some very wild country begins within half an hour's drive of the Edinburgh conurbation.

# PRACTICAL INFORMATION FOR LOTHIAN

**HOW TO GET THERE. By air.** The main airport in Lothian is Edinburgh's Turnhouse. For details of the very frequent air services to Turnhouse, especially from London, see *Facts at Your Fingertips* page xx.

**By train.** Rail services have been much curtailed of late and more cuts are to come, but Edinburgh's Waverley station, the principal station for Lothian, is still a train spotter's mecca. There are frequent services here not only from London (see *Facts at Your Fingertips*) and many other places in England, but from the west and north of Scotland as well.

**HOTELS AND RESTAURANTS.** The environs of Edinburgh are thickly strewn with accommodations of all types, and on some routes in season it seems that every other cottage is offering bed and breakfast. Throughout the Region you will also find a considerable variety of restaurants, cafes and snack bars. Below we list some of the better places to stay and eat.

**CRAMOND** (off A90). **Restaurant.** *Cramond Inn* (M), tel. 336 2035. White-washed fishing inn on steep waterfront approach. Cramped at times, but cheerful service and sophisticated cuisine.

**DIRLETON** (A198). *Open Arms* (M), tel. 241. 7 rooms, all with bath. Light, airy atmosphere, enterprising cooking with traditional Scots dishes. Handy for golf and sightseeing on East Lothian coast.

**GIFFORD** (B6355). *Tweeddale Arms* (M), tel. 240. 8 room, 5 with bath. Ancient inn, tastefully modernized. Fishing. *Goblin Ha'* (I), tel. 244. 7 rooms. Family-run, cheerful center of life in a small, attractive village. Bar and restaurant congested at weekends.

**GULLANE** (A198). *Mallard* (M), tel. 288. 23 rooms, 5 with bath. Efficiently run. Largely golfing and sporting clientele.
**Restaurants.** *La Potiniere* (I), tel. 843214. Extremely good, French-style table d'hôte and wine. Very small dining room. Early booking essential. *Tartufo* (I), tel. 842233. Enterprising Continental cuisine, truffles with everything.

**HADDINGTON** (A1). *Brown's* (M), tel. 2254. 7 rooms, 2 with bath. Unusually classy for a small market town. Cuisine occasionally rises to superb heights.

**HUMBIE** (A6137). *Johnstounburn House* (E), tel. 696. 11 rooms, all with bath. Country house dating from 1625, appropriately furnished, set in mature lawns and gardens. Rather self-conscious touches of gracious living (e.g. classical muzak with dinner) but an undeniably impressive environment.

**NORTH BERWICK** (A198). *Marine* (E), tel. 2406. 85 rooms, all with bath. Big rooms, club armchairs, high standards of former ages maintained. Fishing.

**SOUTH QUEENSFERRY** (A90). *Hawes Inn* (M), tel. 331 1990. 6 rooms. Historic ferry inn featured in R.L. Stevenson's *Kidnapped*. Low beams, creaking floors, dwarfed by piers of Forth rail bridge. Food not bad if you like rich sauces.

**UPHALL** (A899). *Houston House* (E), tel. Broxburn 853831. 29 rooms, all with bath. Executive-class establishment on edge of West Lothian industry. Close to M8 and M9 motorways.

**WESTER HOWGATE** (A6094). **Restaurant.** *Old Howgate Inn* (I), tel. Penicuik 74244. Ancient carrier's howff, not very roomy, tries hard to live up to the reputation it acquired when restaurant was first established.

 **HOW TO GET ABOUT. By bus.** There are buses between all towns on all main routes, but country districts are not so well served though there is scarcely a village without some sort of bus or minibus service, though for the most part you are likely to have to wait a few hours for these services.

**By car.** The major car-rental firms have desks at Turnhouse airport. Elsewhere in the Region (outside Edinburgh) you may rent a self-drive automobile from Style Chauffeur Drive, Uphall, Broxburn (tel. 853553) or Fairway Tours, Roseberry Place, Gullane (tel. 842349); or from numerous garages in the country towns whose advertisements you will see in local newspapers. Unlimited-mileage rates are from £15 to £60 per day, according to size of vehicle, with off-season reductions from October to April.

There are rarely parking problems in the towns and villages of the Region, except on main streets on Saturday mornings and in coastal resorts in July and August.

**TOURIST INFORMATION.** The fullest information on the Region, and on all Regions, is supplied by the National Information Centre at Waverley Bridge, Edinburgh (tel. 031-226 6591). Regional centers at the Town House, Dunbar and Quality Street, North Berwick are open all year round; local centers at Linlithgow, Musselburgh and Pencraig (on A1 road near East Linton) open mid-May to mid-Sept. Normal hours are 9–6 weekdays, 11–6 Sundays, with extensions on some summer evenings and in some places a midday closing for one hour.

**FISHING.** Lothian has no such famous salmon river as the Tweed, but it does have many reservoirs stocked with brown and rainbow trout where you may enjoy a day in a boat for about $7 or fish from the shore for 50¢.
Reservoirs near Edinburgh include Bonaly, Gladhouse, Glencorse, Harlaw and Talla. Permits can be obtained from Lothian Water Department, 55 Buckstone Terrace, Edinburgh EH10 6XH.

The Tyne River, which flows through Haddington (A1), is good for river and sea trout. Permits from Mr. Walker, Bridge Street, East Linton (tel. 306). The following two hotels organize fishing in their own grounds to residents and non-residents: Harvesters, at East Linton (A1), and Melville Castle, Lasswade (A7).

**GOLF.** There are 23 golf courses in Edinburgh and about 40 in the rest of the Region, many of them sited among the dunes and headlands of the Firth of Forth shore. Of championship courses that periodically host the British Open and other important tournaments, Muirfield (A198 near Gullane) is the most exclusive. You will pay $17 a day and will not be allowed there without an introduction from a member or a letter from your own golf club secretary. All other courses welcome casual visitors, the only formality being payment of a fee that ranges $2.50–8 a round, $3.50–12 a day. Bar and restaurant facilities are usually available; at more exclusive places you are expected to dress semi-formally (men in jacket and tie) in the clubhouse.

**HISTORIC HOUSES AND GARDENS.** Like Borders Region, Lothian was home to many aristocratic and courtly families, and has the mansions and castles to prove it. On a more modest level the country districts bristle with the best in Scottish domestic architecture, tower houses with little cone-capped turrets and crow-stepped gables, with perhaps a "doocot" (dovecot or pigeon-house) in the garden. Gardens and lawns are features of country estates in the fertile zones of East Lothian and Midlothian. Every weekend from early spring to late fall owners open their gardens to the public and provide teas; notices in local shop windows and the Scottish press give details. The following examples are more or less permanently open.

**The Binns,** Linlithgow (off A904). Early 17th-century country house, a tasteful blend of styles. Interesting plasterwork. Historical relics. Open May–Sept., daily except Fri., 2–5.30. Park 2–7 daily.

**Dalmeny House,** South Queensferry (off A90). Large house set in fine park and containing Rothschild collection of 18th-century French furniture, tapestries, clocks etc. History of Rosebery family. Open Easter–Sept., Wed. and Sun. only, 2.30–5.30.

**Hailes Castle,** East Linton (on unclassified road near village). Old riverbank fortress with dungeons, dating from 13th and 14th centuries. Open Apr.–Sept., weekdays 9.30–7, Sun. 2–7; Oct.–Mar., weekdays 9.30–4, Sun. 2–4.

**Hopetoun House,** South Queensferry (on A904). Imposing Adam mansion buried in huge park. State rooms, family relics, stables, museum. Open May–Sept., daily, 11–5.30.

**Inveresk Lodge,** Musselburgh (on A6124). Example of the several "country villas" built by Edinburgh bourgeoisie in 17th and 18th centuries on banks of River Esk. House not open to public, but garden can be viewed at all reasonable times. N.T.S.

**Lennoxlove,** Haddington (B6369). Turreted country house, part of it dating from 15th century, in large park. Valuable paintings. Relics of Mary Queen of Scots, and of Lennox family—including "La Belle Stuart," the model for Britannia on British coinage; and of Dukes of Hamilton, who own the property. Open May–Sept., Wed., Sat., Sun., 2–5; or by appointment.

**Linlithgow Palace,** Linlithgow town center. Mixture of Gothic and Renaissance with 13th-century traces. Birthplace of Mary Queen of Scots. Open Apr.–Sept., weekdays 9.30–7, Sun. 2–7; Oct.–Mar., weekdays 9.30–4, Sun. 2–4.

 **MUSEUMS. Canal Museum,** Linlithgow. History and uses of Edinburgh–Glasgow canal. Opportunity for canal trip in replica steamboat. Open Apr.–Sept., Sat. and Sun. only, 2–5.

**Lifeboat House,** Dunbar (off A1). A working establishment with models of early lifeboats. Open May–Sept., 2–5, weekdays only.

**Mining Museum,** Morrison's Haven, Prestongrange (B1348). Old colliery powerhouse displaying history of Lothian coalmining. Working steam engines. Open daily 10–5.

**Museum of Flight,** East Fortune, North Berwick (B1347). Pioneer aircraft and space rockets on an airfield from which transatlantic airships were launched. Open 10–4, Jul. and Aug.

**Myreton Motor Museum,** Aberlady (off A198). Old vehicles and relics of road transport history. Open May–Oct., daily, 10–6; Nov.–Apr., Sat. and Sun. only, 10–5. Check if possible: curator tends to vary routine.

**Queensferry Museum,** in town council chambers, South Queensferry. History of burgh and Forth rail bridge. Open by appointment (tel. 031 331 1590).

# SONG OF THE TWEED

## Borders

The Borders Region is the heartland of minstrelsy, ballad and folk-lore, much of it arisen from murky deeds of the past. It is the homeland of Sir Walter Scott, of the tweed suit and cashmere sweater, of medieval abbeys and hints of Elfland, of the lordly Tweed and its salmon and of the descendants of the raiders and reivers (cattle thieves) who harried England.

A general term for the area is Tweeddale. The Region embraces the whole 100-mile course of the Tweed, third river of Scotland, and most of its tributaries. By mill chimneys and peel fortresses and woodland luxuriant with game birds and stately homes, in a series of fast-rushing torrents and dark serpentine pools, the rivers flow through the history of two nations.

At different times the Region has been in English hands, just as slices of northern England, when things were going well for the Scots, have been in Scottish hands. Berwick-on-Tweed ("Berrick") was six times a Scottish town and seven times an English one in the period 1200 to 1600. Nowadays the frontier of the old "debatable lands" is clearly defined—though invisible, except where the Border Fence runs over the Cheviot ("Chee-viot") hills. No customs, no checkpoints! This frontier wanders about a good deal, following hill crests and the mean-

110

# BORDERS 111

dering river Tweed; indeed Carham in England is about 15 miles due
north of Hownam in Scotland.

All the main routes from London to Edinburgh traverse the Region.
There are no commercial airports but from any point in the Borders
you can be at the check-in desks of Edinburgh or Newcastle-upon-Tyne
airports in about an hour. The eastern side of the Region is a rocky
sea-coast in which tiny fishing villages are embedded. The hinterland
of undulating pastures, woods and valleys is enclosed within three
lonely groups of hills: Cheviot (highest point 2,676 feet) to the south;
Tweedsmuir (2,700 feet) to the west; and Lammermuir (1,700 feet) to
the north.

The towns are overgrown villages. The principal centers of Hawick,
Galashiels, Melrose, Jedburgh, Selkirk and Peebles do not muster
50,000 inhabitants among them. About the same number are spread
through innumerable hamlets, so the valley slopes have quite a lived-in
look. There is a plan to open out some of the compact little towns which
cluster along the middle Tweed, to promote industry and increase the
population by 25,000. If it comes about, sheep will still outnumber
human beings by 30 to one.

Sheep and clear streams, ideal for washing wool, gave the Borders
its tweed and knitwear industries. The Scotch wool, however, is now
considered too coarse for quality products and most of the raw material
is imported.

Borderers preserve their isolation from their neighbors and are
fiercely proud of their traditions. Civic rivalries are sublimated in local
flower-shows, festivals and sporting encounters, especially rugby football. A Hawick–Selkirk clash is a Homeric struggle, but the communities sink their differences to make common cause against the rest of
Scotland and England. They think it is a disgrace if a great rugby center
like Melrose (2,000 inhabitants) or Jedburgh (4,000) fails to get players
into the international team.

## Tweedsmuir, Lyne and Manor

"From Berwick to the Bield" used to be proverbial in the Borders—
from the mouth to the source of the Tweed; in other words the length
and breadth of the land. We start at the Bield, though you won't find
it on the map. It was one of four "howffs"—inns and resting-places for
carters and carriers and their pack-donkeys—which once decorated the
desolate landscape of Tweedsmuir. Only one, the Crook Inn, midway
between Moffat and Peebles, survives.

Robert Burns and a later poet, Thomas Campbell, were habitués of
the howffs. Campbell told of his first visit to the Bield. Soon after he
had gone to bed the young girl of the house knocked on the door and,
entering, stood before him in her nightie, a candle in her hand. "Please,
sir, could ye tak' a neebor (neighbor) into your bed?"

"With all my heart," cried the gallant young poet, springing up to
make room for her.

"Thank ye, sir. It's the Moffat carrier just come in soaking wat (wet)
and we've nowhere tae put him."

Exit the lovely girl and enter a huge reeking hulk of a man.

You come on to Tweedsmuir after a winding ascent from Moffat on the A701 road to Edinburgh. Just over the summit you can walk a few yards to Tweed's Well, the river's source. It is marshy after rain. Hereabouts the infant Tweed, flowing east, is very close to the infant Clyde, flowing west. They say that on account of the hill torrents surging this way and that in heavy spate, salmon from the North Sea have been found near Glasgow, having swum across Scotland! Another tall tale suggests that Merlin's Grave near Drumelzier holds the mortal remains of the wizard from Camelot. Fragments of Arthurian legend persist around the headwaters of the Tweed. Antiquarians discount them but a pagan monolith inside Stobo church (B712) may be connected with the Druids of an earlier epoch, pre A.D. 500.

Off the A701 and on to the B712 you approach the Tweed's first town, Peebles. To the left lies Broughton village where a fine modern Scottish-baronial house, Broughton Place, opens in summer as an art gallery. An 18th-century landowner, John Murray of Broughton, spied for the Jacobites when Bonnie Prince Charlie planned his adventure and he was the Prince's private secretary throughout the rebellion of 1745. Sentimentalists execrate his memory because his evidence subsequently condemned the chief Stuart loyalists.

Before it reaches Peebles, the Tweed, already a powerful river, is swollen by two streams, Lyne Water and Manor Water, rippling down from beautiful tranquil vales. Each is worth the detour. A couple of miles up the Lyne, muse on the vanity of human ambitions at the ruins of Drochil Castle. James, Earl of Morton, all-powerful in 16th-century Scotland during the minority of King James VI, built Drochil as a luxurious home. He introduced his last batch of political victims to a new toy from France, the horrible instrument of torture known as the Maiden; a species of crude and primitive guillotine with a heavy spiked triangular blade that was dropped onto, or hammered into, the neck of the victim. But, suddenly he fell from power, was judged "art and part" in the murder of the King's father—and was himself the first to be beheaded by the grisly machine. Drochil, never inhabited, fell to ruins. The Maiden, good as new, is now in the National Museum of Antiquities in Edinburgh.

Along the Manor Water a road (unclassified) passes the Black Dwarf's cottage, where Sir Walter Scott met the misshapen eccentric who became the central character of his novel *The Black Dwarf.* The road ends after three miles at Macbeth's Castle, a heap of stones which has nothing to do with Macbeth. Excellent touring country, excellent highways and byways, plenty of accommodations and short distances between towns make motoring and sightseeing painless enough; but in this land of ancient ways and hill-paths the walker, cyclist and horse-rider have distinct advantages.

## The Old Roads

Roman and pre-Roman routes, now grassed over, intersect the Tweed at several points. The Girthgate, a pilgrims' way from Edinburgh to Melrose Abbey, is intertwined with the A68 highway from Soutra Hill southwards. The old drove road from Traquair (B709), called for some obscure reason The Paddy Slacks, threading glen and moorland to Ettrick Forest and the banks of the Yarrow Water, has been incorporated in a Border Walk of 60 miles from Galashiels to Moffat. (Note that "Water" in southern Scotland means a river, not, as in the English Lake District, a lake.)

There are Thieves' roads, Herring roads, Salt roads, Captain's roads and other picturesquely named routes of olden times up the Border valleys and over the tops into other valleys; some with their legends of medieval murder or of loot stuffed in the chinks of drystone walls and never found again.

From Cheviot to Jedburgh and the Tweed crossing near Melrose traces of forts mark Dere Street, the old Roman road.

Local tourist information offices provide leaflets on country and town walks in their localities. The Regional Council's Countryside Ranger (council offices, Newtown St. Boswells) operates a program of guided walks; historical, scenic and naturalist. From Kelso, Melrose and Peebles a special bus service runs between early July and early September to a timetable specifically devised for walkers.

## "Peebles for Pleesure"

The catchphrase, adopted as a tourist slogan, came from a native of upper Tweeddale who spent his holiday in Paris. The life of the French capital was all right in its way, he reported, "but gie me Peebles for pleesure."

The "pleesures" are not all that evident to the non-native. Unless you fish or play golf, it is a solid, rather dull town: a main street of little country shops, the Tweed racing under a 15th-century bridge, the hills and forests roundabout and the gap-toothed ruins of Border strongholds scattered above the valley. Neidpath Castle (13th-century) makes a formidable apparition as you come through the S-bends of the Tweed's ravine above the town.

Here begins the "wool run." Peebles was in the woolen business in the 1780s. The big name is Ballantyne. You can tour Ballantyne's mill in March Street and buy cashmere knitwear at their mill shop. (Mill shops all over the Borders keep ordinary shopping hours, usually 9–5 Monday to Friday, and a shorter day on Saturday.) As you travel on down the A72 road, which clings to the straights and sweeping bends of the Tweed, you soon come to more mill chimneys at Innerleithen and Walkerburn. The gaunt mid-Victorian buildings, so alien to the pastoral valley, have now settled into the landscape and begin to be valued as items of industrial archeology. Tweedvale mill at Walkerburn, still on the A72, houses both a tweed shop and the Scottish Museum of Wool Textiles.

The name "tweed" for cloth came about by accident. The original material, made up of strands of colored wool twisted together in a subtle combination of shades, was "twill" or "tweel." A London wholesaler misread the label on the samples which a Hawick firm sent him and asked for more "tweed." Seeing his chance to capitalize on the name of a river already famous through the poems and novels of Sir Walter Scott, the Hawick manufacturer didn't bother to correct him.

From Innerleithen, which once had pretensions to spa status, two charming hill routes go off, one right and one left, into the Ettrick Forest and the Moorfoot Hills respectively (both B709). They are Highland passes in miniature, well-stocked with sheep, flowery in summer. You may identify a few of the plants which used to provide dyes for the wool: yellow lichen (it produced a rich brown color), redcurrant and waterlily (chocolate brown), heather and broom (green), apple and bracken root (yellow), dandelion (magenta), bedstraw and bramble (red) . . . a wide range of natural juices, all now replaced by synthetic dyes.

## The Twinset Towns

18 miles from Peebles, the Tweedside road reaches Galashiels (locally shortened to Gala) which, along with nearby Selkirk and Melrose and the more distant town of Hawick, constitutes the tweed and twinset metropolis. The Scottish College of Textiles, established 1909, is at Gala (visitors by appointment). There are retail shops at the tweed mills in Bank Close and Huddersfield Street, Gala; at the Abbey mill, Melrose; and at the Tanneries, Mill Street and Walter Turnbull's, Dunsdale Road, in Selkirk.

Hawick, 12 miles south of the Tweed, most grim and introverted-looking of Border towns, is the important center for the classic sweater, the fully-fashioned cardigan, the plain-knit cashmere twinset . . . everything that goes with a tweed jacket or skirt, including, nowadays, the underwear and warm-ribbed tights. There are 25 knitwear firms in Hawick, including notable names like Pringle, Peter Scott, Lyle & Scott and Braemar. You will find half a dozen mill shops for individual customers and you can tour the mills at Peter Scott's, Wilson & Glenny's and Trowmill Weavers. The frequency of mill tours depends on the season and the demand. At the mill shops and local tourist information offices you will get up-to-date information.

The towns of the middle Tweed are so full of history that their everyday life may disappoint you. They are really quite provincial little burghs (pronounced "burras") with stone buildings in the Victorian Gothic style, statues of the reivers and of the two World Wars in which the Border regiments were heavily engaged, neat parks and gardens, splendid rugby football grounds, perhaps a few banners advertising the next "March Riding"—which generally takes place not in March but in midsummer because "march" in this context is a boundary or no-man's-land round the town. Mementoes of old forays impinge on the citizens' daily lives. The civic motto on Galashiels town hall is "Sour Plums." It refers to a 16th-century incident when the "braw, braw lads o' Gala Water" found some English soldiers robbing an orchard and slaughtered them to a man.

Sour plums, incidentally, or "soor plooms" in local speech, are green balls of lemon-flavored candy. Along with Berwick cockles (shell-shaped striped candy) and Jethart snails (peppermint twists from Jedburgh) they are the specialties of Borders candy shops.

All the Border towns have annual Ridings or "Gatherings"—jollifications where local patriotism explodes and the visitor feels he is in the middle of a party he has not been invited to. The celebration may be of recent origin like the Lauder Common Riding; or it may be ancient, with pagan overtones, like the Beltane Festival at Peebles. Either way it acquaints the stranger with the Borders spirit and demonstrates how much of the past still influences the present.

## The Wizard of the North

Two miles from Melrose (B6360 road) stand the gates of Abbotsford, home of Sir Walter Scott and still in the hands of female descendants, the Maxwell-Scotts. This most-visited of Scottish literary landmarks was a damp farmhouse called Clartyhole when Scott bought it in 1811. In the course of writing nearly all his Waverley novels there, Scott changed its name and turned it into a pseudo-monastic, pseudo-baronial hall. The art critic John Ruskin described Abbotsford as "the most incongruous pile that gentlemanly modernism ever devised."

It is striking but rather ignobly sited. Inside, you can see many curios and souvenirs of Scottish history which Scott, magpie-like, picked up wherever he went. Here, in 1832, he died on what his son-in-law and biographer John Gibson Lockhart describe as "a beautiful day, so warm that every window was wide open and so perfectly still that the sound most delicious to his ears, the gentle ripple of the Tweed over its pebbles, was distinctly audible as we knelt round the bed."

The neighborhood bristles with Scott memorabilia and busts. From the parking area on a bend above the Tweed (B6356), pause at the sign "Scott's View" to admire the convolutions of the Tweed—pause as the horses of his funeral cortège are said to have paused when they came to the viewpoint he loved. Leaving Galashiels by the A6091 road to Melrose, you will pass the wall-tablet which tells how the poet, brought home from Italy to die, "sprang up with a cry of delight" at that spot as his carriage came at last within sight of the Tweed. When you visit Dryburgh Abbey, a mile or so beyond Scott's View, have a look at his ornate tomb, open to the winds in a ruined chapel.

They called Scott the "wizard of the north" for his skill in weaving plots, but he was not the only one in these parts. Melrose Abbey is believed to contain the remains (unmarked) of Michael Scot, a 12th-century necromancer famous in the courts of Europe. Retiring to Scotland he was plagued by a devil who kept asking for work. To keep him out of mischief Michael told him to split the Eildon ("Eeldon") hill in three. He did it overnight and the triple peaks are there to prove it. Avid for further employment, the devil was given other seemingly impossible tasks and performed them in no time at all. Finally his master sent him to the mouth of the Tweed to spin ropes out of sand; a job on which, as far as we know, he is still working.

Here, too, under the Eildon tree at the foot of the Rhymer's Glen (close to Abbotsford), a stone marks the spot), sat Thomas of Ercildoune when the Queen of Elfland snatched him away and kept him for seven years; or so the ballad says. She returned him to the same spot as True Thomas, a poet endowed with the dubious gift of being unable to tell a lie. Students of Thomas's writings have discovered prophecies of important events like the Battle of Bannockburn and the Union of

England and Scotland; clearest of all was the destiny of the local landowning family:

"Tide, tide what may betide,
Haig shall be Haig of Bemersyde."

In 1921 a grateful nation bestowed the Bemersyde ("Beemer-") estate on the war leader Field Marshal Earl Haig and thus the prophecy was fulfilled. (He was an adopted child, only distantly related to the Bemersyde Haigs.)

## The Holy Places

Thomas the Rhymer was alive and the Haigs were newly settled on the banks of the Tweed when David King of Scots, the "sair sanct," (see *Scottish History* chapter) built four large abbeys at Melrose, Dryburgh and Kelso on the Tweed and at Jedburgh close to its tributary the Teviot ("Tee-viot"). They were meant to be colonies for monks from France and Yorkshire and perhaps David saw them as oases of sanctuary in the war-torn border lands. If so, he was mistaken. Fate decreed that for 400 years these wonderful buildings should know no peace. They were hammered down and built up again and fought over as though they were military strongpoints; and their present dilapidated appearance proclaims the turbulence of their history.

Melrose Abbey in the middle of the market town of that name was an imposing pile in its day. It is still impressive: a red sandstone shell with slender windows in the Perpendicular style and some delicate tracery and carved capitals, carefully maintained. "If thou would'st view fair Melrose aright / Go visit it in the pale moonlight," says Scott in *The Lay of the Last Minstrel,* and so many of his fans took the advice literally that a sleepless custodian begged him to rewrite the lines.

Note an enigmatic inscription on the tablet in the north aisle: "Here Lyis the Race of the House of Zair." Who or what the House of Zair was no one knows. Nor has much detail survived of the daily lives of the old Cistercian monks, except that they were acquisitive and got possession of broad farmlands in Lowland Scotland; and that when they wanted a manuscript copied they had to send for a scholar to do it. They were at Melrose from 1146 to 1544, when an English attack on the town damaged the abbey beyond repair.

Four miles out of Melrose, after descending from Scott's View (B6356), you come to Dryburgh ("Drybra") Abbey, perfect in beauty and tranquillity in a loop of the Tweed. The river is about 80 yards wide by this time, halfway from source to mouth, but shallow enough in summer for anglers in waterproof trousers to wade across. From here to Berwick-on-Tweed the salmon beats are contiguous and in the quiet reaches a good deal of poaching goes on, in and out of season.

Dryburgh's extensive ruins once housed Premonstratensian canons from Normandy. The abbey suffered from English raids until, like Melrose, it was abandoned in 1544. The style is Transitional, a mingling of rounded Romanesque and pointed Early English. The side chapel where the Haig and Scott families lie buried is lofty and pillared, detached from the main buildings. Dryburgh in its heyday must have been an epic poem in sculpted stone. It has Bemersyde park and house on one side, Dryburgh Abbey hotel hidden in woodland on the other.

Jedburgh Abbey (A68, 13 miles from Melrose), in a town center of hilly streets and chilly breezes, undercut by the swift Jed Water, dates from 1138. It was the home of Augustinian monks from France and in its first 200 years of history was destroyed and rebuilt seven times. Eventually it suffered the fate of its sister abbeys. Later on part of it became Jedburgh's parish church. The square tower still stands and the south-side windows, of unusual Transitional design, run in three tiers along the empty nave. Enough survives to confirm that the complex was justly renowned for its graceful arcades and exquisite stone carvings.

Kelso Abbey (A699, 14 miles from Melrose), tall and slim with little rounded turrets, must have looked reassuringly fortress-like when in 1128 the Benedictines from Picardy moved in. The Tweed crossing at Kelso was important to both sides in the Border wars, however, and the abbey was much knocked about by armies advancing to or retreating from each other's countries. The last monks and the townsfolk who had taken refuge with them died leaping from the turrets on to the English pikes and spears in 1545, after which the structure was reduced to its present fragmentary—but highly atmospheric—state.

The four abbeys of Tweeddale, battered and decayed as they are, represent the finest flowering of Scottish ecclesiastical architecture.


## The Lower Tweed

The Tweedside roads (A69, A698) through Kelso and Coldstream sweep with a river through parkland and game preserve and past romantic redstone gorges. Close to Kelso, where Sir Walter Scott went to school, stands the palatial mansion of Floors Castle on the "floors" or flat terraces of the Tweed bank between Kelso town and the ruins of Roxburgh ("Roxbra") Castle. Ancestral home of the Dukes of Roxburghe (note the different spelling!), it was conceived in 1718 by Sir John Vanbrugh, arch exponent of massive Baroque architecture, and afterwards given mock-Tudor touches by W.H. Playfair in the 19th century. A holly tree in the deerpark marks the place where King James II was killed in 1460 by a cannon which "brak in the shooting."

Of nearby Roxburgh Castle very little has survived. Of the once-important town of Roxburgh not a trace remains. It stood at the confluence of Teviot and Tweed; it was one of Scotland's four principal burghs with Edinburgh, Stirling and Berwick; it minted coins; it was a royal residence and the birthplace of King Alexander III . . . but diligent search reveals only a few grass-grown mounds.

Three miles above Coldstream the England-Scotland border comes down from the hills and runs beside the Tweed for the rest of its journey to the sea. Coldstream, a sleepy burgh of one long street only slightly disturbed by the traffic on the A697 road to England, is celebrated in military history. In 1659 General Monck raised a regiment of foot guards here on behalf of his exiled monarch Charles II. As the Coldstream Guards they have become a corps d'elite in the British Army.

This stretch of the Tweed is lined with dignified houses and gardens which extend to the water's edge. One estate is The Hirsel, which in the 1960s gave Britain a Prime Minister, Sir Alec Douglas Home (pronounced "Hume"). Another fine old park, noted for trees and shrubberies, is Lennel. If you are not in a hurry, stay with Scotland when the A698 for Berwick crosses into England at Coldstream bridge. Explore the network of peaceful high-hedged lanes, visit Ladykirk—a church which James IV built in gratitude for a safe passage across the Tweed before there were any bridges—and note the place-name of Upsettington, appropriate for a bitterly-contested frontierland. Your route will discover enchanting glimpses of the now-majestic river in its corridor of greenery and red rocks. You can cross again into England at the Chain bridge (officially the Union bridge) on a minor road (unclassified) which only farm tractors seem to use.

### "O, Flodden Field"

Sir Walter Scott claimed that when he stood on the Eildon hills he could see 43 places famed in ballad and war. Among them must have been Flodden in the Cheviot foothills, three miles into England from Coldstream bridge. There on an autumn evening in 1513 a Scottish army was outgeneralled and routed and its king (James IV), his son and most of his knights were slain. When Bannockburn is mentioned, says the Scottish writer Andrew Lang, the English remain calm; but Flodden has the bitterness of unavailing grief for Scots to this day. It inspired the best-known of bagpipe laments, always played at Scottish military funerals, from the song *The Flowers o' the Forest* by the 18th-century Jean Elliot of Minto House near Hawick.

A memorial on the site is dedicated "To the Brave of Both Nations." Most moving of epitaphs, perhaps, is the simple inscription on a monument in the center of Selkirk: "O, Flodden Field." Selkirk sent 100 young men to the battle and only one came home.

### Quiet Flows the Tweed

Through a flat fertile country, the Tweed, shaken free of the hills at last, flows to the sea. North and west the Borders' most rich acres are spread, sprinkled with farms and hamlets. This is the Merse, a word which may mean "marsh" or "march" (boundary). Two rough trout streams come galloping into this quiet land from the heights of Lammermuir: the Blackadder and the Whiteadder ("Whittadder"). On the Whiteadder at Abbey St. Bathans, six miles from Duns (B6355), stands the only Pictish "broch" (round tower) in southern Scotland.

Salmon are netted commercially along the last 10-mile windings of the Tweed. Between mid-February and mid-September you may see men watching the waters from ladders along the banks, and boats towing nets into midstream to trap the fish as they swim in from the North Sea. Early in the season the nets contain salmon of up to nine pounds. Later the fish may be of 20 to 25 pounds apiece. But many escape to travel the whole length of the river and provide sport for anglers even in the moorland fastnesses where our journey began.

## Bone of Contention

Berwick-on-Tweed is in England although it lies north of the Tweed and gives its name to a Scottish county, Berwickshire. Scots say the town should belong to Scotland but opinion polls among the citizens show a decided preference for remaining English. Regularly claimed and occupied by one nation or the other, Berwick in the 16th century was declared a "free burgh" and mentioned separately in Acts of Parliament: "England, Scotland, Ireland and our town of Berwick-on-Tweed." The situation lasted until 1885 and some inhabitants will tell you that they are still at war with certain nations of Europe, not having had the chance to annul the declaration since that date.

Three bridges span the Tweed estuary at Berwick: the ancient 15-arched structure built for King James VI and I about 1620; the Royal Tweed bridge of 1928 which carries the Great North Road (A1) into Scotland; and the Royal Border railroad bridge, a high viaduct of 28 arches, built in 1847 and inscribed at the Berwick station end: "The Final Act of Union."

## The Great North Road

After crossing the Tweed and negotiating the dog-legs of Berwick's claustrophobic town center, Britain's most historic highway, the A1, which runs from London to Edinburgh, enters Scotland three miles out of town. You pass in without fuss or formality; you may not even notice the roadsign which says Scotland. But a reminder of the "old unhappy far-off things," the death and destruction which it took to establish that frontier, is close at hand beside the Berwick–Duns road (A6105). On Halidon Hill in 1333 English bowmen annihilated the Scots in a set-piece battle which reversed Robert the Bruce's victory at Bannockburn 19 years earlier. The English, however, were content to retake Berwick and to leave the rest of Scotland alone.

If you are drawn to the seascapes on the A1 you may want to turn aside to inspect the fishing villages which are wedged like swallows' nests wherever the outfall of a torrent splits the cliffs. Burnmouth is typical, a precipitous half-mile from the main road. Eyemouth comes next, a major Scottish fishing port. Its river, the Eye Water, is canalized with quays and boatyards like a Mediterranean harbor. In bygone days this was the smugglers' haven and it is said that more people lived under the rocks than on top of them. (If you go looking for the caverns, beware rising tides.)

The fisheries museum at Eyemouth, opened in 1981, commemorates the centenary of a terrible disaster. Struck by a sudden squall, the Eyemouth fishing fleet was wrecked within sight of watchers on the shore and half Eyemouth's children were left fatherless.

St. Abb's Head, important to all who voyage into the Firth of Forth, takes its name from Ebba, an obscure 7th-century Christian, daughter of the first king of Northumbria. It beetles over St. Abb's, another minuscule fishing village, and is in the care of the National Trust for Scotland as a "site of special scientific interest." Many uncommon types of seabird breed on it. Close up, the lighthouse, with one of the most powerful beams in Britain, turns out to be rather a stumpy little tower, planted against a 250-foot cliff top. The keeper's cottage, on the headland itself, is higher than the lantern. Spray has reached its windows. St. Abb's Head in a northeasterly gale is an awesome place to be.

A cliff path but no road goes on three miles to Fast Castle. The building grew out of a clump of stack rocks with a perilous high shelf to the mainland. Once impregnable, it has now surrendered to wind and weather and for an idea of what it was once like you must go to Scott's *Bride of Lammermoor,* the story Donizetti used for his opera *Lucia di Lammermoor.*

The last seagirt outpost before the coastal route passes into Lothian Region is Cove—toy breakwater, toy cottages, a toy boat or two. Until recently, a tunnel through the rock was its only link with the village of Cockburnspath ("Cobunspath" or "Copath") on the A1 above. Now a stony track goes dizzily down. Round the corner, by contrast, at Pease Bay there is a huge caravan park.

Local diesel trains and expresses from London to Edinburgh follow the A1, running a few miles inland north of Eyemouth to cross a shoulder of Lammermuir. By road or rail it is about an hour from Berwick-on-Tweed to Edinburgh.

### "Jethart's Here!"

If you come to Scotland by train you are bound to arrive by way of Berwick in the east or Carlisle in the west. By road you have a choice of a dozen routes. Apart from the A1 there are firstclass main roads over Tweedsmuir (A701, Moffat to Edinburgh); through the knitwear towns (A7, Carlisle to Edinburgh); and from Coldstream (A697) and Jedburgh (A68). These last two roads combine near Lauder and continue to Edinburgh as the A68.

The A68 has much to recommend it. If you are heading for Edinburgh from the south, it is 30 miles shorter than the A1. It offers a dramatic introduction to Scotland at the summit of Carter Bar on the lonely Cheviots. It crosses the once-famous hunting chase of Jedforest —of which only one tree remains, the tottering Capon Oak near the roadside one mile south of Jedburgh; and it allows you to see something of Jedburgh itself, an archetypal Borders town.

In the Border wars Jedburgh was noted for stout hearts and thick staves—the Jethart staffs, wielded by brawny townsfolk to the battlecry of "Jethart's here!" Proverbial also in Scotland was "Jethart justice," a sort of lynch law which consisted in hanging the prisoner first and trying him afterwards.

In 1566 Mary Queen of Scots stayed for a month at the grim fortified dwelling called Queen Mary's House, and scandalized the citizens by riding to Hermitage Castle and back in one day—a round trip of some 50 miles—to comfort her sick lover the Earl of Bothwell. Relics of the Queen are shown in the house. In the Canongate, Blackhills Close and Abbey Close are some tall narrow buildings, exotic to English eyes, which at different periods gave lodging to Robert Burns, Bonnie Prince Charlie and the poet Wordsworth and his sister.

## Queen of the Gypsies

12 miles southeast of Jedburgh and eight from Kelso lies a remote village with two claims to notoriety. It is the northern terminus of the Pennine Way, the 250-mile footpath along the backbone of England that originates in Derbyshire's Peak District and which descends with the Border Fence to within a few hundred yards of the village; and it is the capital of Scotland's gypsies.

The gypsy clan called Faas were at Kirk Yetholm for centuries. Ordinary travelers learned not to go near the place. You can still see the Gypsy Palace (a humble cottage) and a street called Gypsy Row. Here the Romany kings and queens were crowned and held court until 1883 the last "Queen," Esther Faa Blyth, died. The place is quiet and respectable today but it retains the air of a lawless frontier outpost, a long way from nowhere.

## Lauderdale

Leaving Jedburgh by the A68 for Edinburgh, having maybe browsed and booked your accommodations ahead at the Scottish Tourist Board's large information center, your next landmark is the Tweed crossing at Leaderfoot, a network of bridges including a many-arched high railroad viaduct, now disused. The old Roman road, Dere Street, came this way from Corstopitum (Corbridge) on Hadrian's Wall and went on to Cramond on the Firth of Forth. The camps and stations of the route have been well excavated and most of the finds are in Edinburgh's Museum of Antiquities. But it is worth while going a mile down the Melrose road from Leaderfoot to see the block of stone at Newstead marked "Trimontium"—"of three peaks," the legionaries' name for the Eildon hills.

The next village as you continue north on the A68 into Lauderdale, valley of the Leader, is Earlston, birthplace of Thomas the Rhymer. Then comes Lauder, nominally a royal burgh, actually a village where nothing much seems to have happened since King James III's lords hanged his favorites from the river bridge in 1482. After Lauder you climb to a saddle of the Lammermuir hills at 1,200 feet and descent into Lothian Region.

## The Moorland Trails

Given time and clear weather you might choose more roundabout routes through the Region and discover scenic and historical wonders which we have not had space to mention. The countryside is uniformly picturesque and endlessly varied. There is exhilarating moorland in the Ettrick Forest (from which the trees vanished long ago), south and west of Selkirk; also between Gordon Arms, where Scott took a last farewell of James Hogg the "Ettrick Shepherd," and Traquair and Borthwick (B709, B7007); also on the bleak unfenced roads (beware of sheep!)

which rise to the sources of the Lammermuir burns north of Duns (B6355) and Longformacus ("Longfor-make-us") (unclassified).

# PRACTICAL INFORMATION FOR BORDERS

**HOW TO GET THERE. By train.** Services from London's King's Cross and from the major cities in northeast England pass through Borders en route to Edinburgh. From London to Berwick-on-Tweed by high-speed Inter-City train takes 4¼ hours, on to Edinburgh another 45 minutes (or 1½ hours by stopping train). There is no other railroad in Borders Region.

**By bus.** From larger centers within Scotland, particularly Edinburgh, *Eastern Scottish* run many day and half-day bus tours through the Border country. On the various routes between Edinburgh and Newcastle-upon-Tyne, buses pass through Berwick, Coldstream, Kelso and Jedburgh. There are also frequent services between Edinburgh and the towns of the middle and upper Tweed: Melrose, Galashiels, Selkirk and Peebles.

**HOTELS AND RESTAURANTS.** Borders Region is a great tourist area but it is not well equipped with accommodations and eateries—gourmets make for Edinburgh. Towns are small and country hotels traditionally cater for fishermen who tend to require meals at odd hours. It is bed-and-breakfast country, and few places are accustomed to long-stay visitors. A selection of the better establishments is given below.

**BLYTHE BRIDGE. Restaurant.** *The Old Mill* (M), tel. Drochil Castle 220. Festooned in horse brasses and similar rustic bric-a-brac. Good fresh food. Busy at weekends.

**COCKBURNSPATH. Restaurant.** *Cockburnspath Inn* (I), tel. 217. Good stop on A1 highway for a bar lunch. Excellent fresh fish.

**COLDSTREAM. Restaurant.** *Collingwood Arms* (M), tel. 2424. Over Coldstream Bridge, technically a few miles into England. First-class menu and service.

**DRYBURGH ABBEY** *see* Newtown St. Boswells.

**EDDLESTON. Restaurant.** *Horseshoe Inn* (M), tel. 225. Genuine coaching house on Peebles–Edinburgh road; smart but not flashy. Sophisticated cuisine.

**KELSO.** *Woodside* (M), tel. 2152. 11 rooms, all with bath. Superior, well-conducted hotel.

**MELROSE.** *Waverley Castle* (M), tel. 2244. 104 rooms, 34 with bath. Heart of Walter Scott country.

**NEWTOWN ST. BOSWELLS.** *Dryburgh Abbey* (E), tel. 22261. 29 rooms, 16 with bath. Bogus baronial, but very civilized. Fine gardens next to abbey in bend of Tweed. Excellent restaurant, very handy for lunch.

**PEEBLES.** *Peebles Hydro* (E), tel. 20602. 144 rooms, 127 with bath. Two miles from town near Tweed bank. Heated pool, sauna, sports facilities. Popular conference center.

**ST. MARY'S LOCH.** *Tibbie Shiels Inn* (I), tel. Cappercleuch 231. 4 rooms, no private baths. Historic fishing/drovers' inn set between two lochs. Tibbie was old-time proprietress, a martinet who stood no nonsense from Scott, Hogg, Wordsworth and other literary folk. A young couple are now in charge, and they have made it a cheerful little oasis on the moorland. Magnificent fishing.

**TWEEDSMUIR.** *Crook Inn* (M), tel. 272. 8 rooms, 4 with bath. Renovated 17th-century "howff." Outlook bleak but spacious, cozy inside.

**WALKERBURN.** *Tweed Valley* (M), tel. 220. 14 rooms, none with bath. Pleasant atmosphere, few frills, fishing and shooting during season.

**HOW TO GET ABOUT. By bus.** Country people depend on buses and services are therefore quite comprehensive, especially on Saturdays and market days; reduced services operate on Sundays. Most isolated villages have their bus connections with some main-route town at least once or twice a week. The Tweedside roads described in the first half of the chapter are also busy bus routes and you could travel downriver from Peebles to Coldstream in a day, stopping off at one or two places on the way.

The *Harrier* bus service, operating summer Tuesdays and Thursdays only, covers a scenic route that includes Peebles, Gordon Arms, St. Mary's Loch, Yarrow, Abbotsford, Melrose, Galashiels and Kelso—and back—all in five hours; there are connections at various points with *Border Courier* buses to more-out-of-the-way places.

**By car.** This is excellent motoring country, though strangers should beware the surprising ups-and-downs and sharp bends, even on the major roads. Self-drive automobiles are available from Chalmers McQueen Ltd, Albert Place, Galashiels (tel. 2729); George Murray, Netherdale Industrial Estate, Galashiels (tel. 55172); and Smith's Motor Services, Elcho Street, Peebles (tel. 20217). The last-named company also provides chauffeured automobiles for renting by the day or longer.

**TOURIST INFORMATION.** There are Tourist Board information centers for visitors entering Scotland by road at Jedburgh (A68) and Southwaite (Cumbria, M6). Local information centers are at Peebles, Melrose, and Newtown St. Boswells.

**FISHING.** The chief fishing rivers are the Tweed, Teviot, Ettrick and Whiteadder, but every hill-stream has brown trout and sometimes salmon too. On the Tweed the salmon season runs February through November. The heaviest hauls come with the fall run (September and October) when salmon of 20–25 pounds are caught.

Most beats are strictly preserved or very expensive but on the Tweed at Peebles and certain stretches of the Teviot the visiting angler can buy a permit quite cheaply. Trout fishings are mostly in the hands of local angling associations who welcome casual visitors. Many hotels offer trout fishing. Fishing-tackle shops provide information and issue the permits. The trout season is effectively April to September. Dry fly on June, July or August evenings achieves the best results.

For the stillwater fisherman many lochs and reservoirs are stocked and managed by district angling societies. The best are St. Mary's Loch (A708), Coldingham (A1107) and Lindean (B6360). Sea-angling is offered at Eyemouth, weekends only. For a boat and boatman, contact Eyemouth Sea Angling Club. Whitefish angling off the rocks is free everywhere all the year round.

**GOLF.** There are 17 golf courses in the Region, most of them in attractive surroundings. Galashiels, Hawick, Kelso, Minto, Peebles and West Linton all have 18-hole courses. Golf is not a costly game in Scotland and at smaller courses you pay about $2 a day, perhaps a little more on Sat. and Sun. (Where the steward is not full time, put your money in the trust box.)

Drinks and meals, or at least sandwiches, are available at clubhouses. Peebles municipal course is the only one with caddy cars for hire. At Peebles you pay $6 for the day or $4 a round; $9 and $5 at weekends.

**HISTORIC HOUSES AND GARDENS.** The following are but a few of Border properties open through the summer. Many more open periodically, details being advertised in the local press and in shop windows. Entrance, where charged, is usually less than $2.

**Abbotsford,** on the Tweed near Melrose (B6360). Mementos of Sir Walter Scott and many historic relics. Open mid.-Mar.–Oct., weekdays 10–5, Sun. 2–5.

**Bowhill,** near Selkirk (A708). Grandiose mansion dating from 1812 and the home of Dukes of Buccleuch. Extravagant furnishings and fine pictures. Woodland play area for children. Pony-trekking. Open May, June, Sept., Wed., Thurs., Sat., Sun. only; July, Aug., daily except Fri.; all 12.30–6 (Sun. 2–6).

**Dawyck,** on the Tweed near Peebles (B712). Choice collection of trees and shrubs, gathered over 300 years. Herons and deer. Open daily Apr.–Sept., 10–5.

**Floors Castle,** near Kelso (A6089). Great 18th-century mansion with Victorian embellishments. Valuable paintings. Garden center. Open May–Sept., daily except Fri., Sat., 1.30–4.45.

**The Hirsel,** near Coldstream (A697). Ancestral home of Earls of Home. Colorful gardens and birds. Estate interpretation center. House not open but you may walk in the gardens any time. Box for charitable donations.

**Lothian Estates,** Ancrum (A68). Visitor center, woodland interpretation center, walks. Open Easter–mid-Oct., daily except Mon. and Sat., 2–5.30.

**Manderston,** near Duns (A6105). Much-lived-in Edwardian mansion. Rooms, kitchens, stables, dairy etc. open to parties by appointment. No entrance charge. Open mid-May–mid-Sept., Sun. and Thurs. only, 2–5.30.

**Mellerstain House,** near Gordon (A6089). One of the finest creations of Robert Adam. Outstanding furnishings and pictures of his era (late 18th century). Beautiful gardens. Open May–Sept., daily except Sat., 1.30–5.30.

**Neidpath Castle,** on the Tweed near Peebles (A72). Splendid situation, 14th-century tower. Open Easter–mid-Oct., weekdays 10–1, 2–6, Sun. 1–6.

**Priorwood,** Melrose, next to abbey. Flower garden, picnic area, pretty views. Open mid-May–Oct., weekdays 10–6, Sun. 1.30–5.30; Apr.–mid-May, Nov.–late Dec., Mon.-Fri. only, 10–1, 2–5.30. N.T.S.

**Traquair House,** near the Tweed at Innerleithen (B709). Claims to be the oldest house continuously inhabited in Scotland. Furnishings reflect 10 centuries of domestic life. Brewhouse and craft workshops. Open Easter–early Oct., daily 1.30–5.30—in July and Aug., 10.30–5.30.

 **MUSEUMS.** There are museums all over Borders Region, often attached to public libraries in towns and villages, where admission is free. We include the following because they illustrate particular aspects of regional life.

**Castle Jail,** Jedburgh (A68). Local lockup, but a model of prison reform when opened in the 1820s. Open Apr.–Sept., Mon.–Sat., 10–12, 1–5., Sun. 1–5.

**Coldstream Museum,** Coldstream (A697). Local crafts and curios, history of Coldstream Guards. Open May–Sept., daily except Thurs., 2–5.

**Commendator's House,** Melrose (A6091). Monastic relics from the abbey. Open Apr.–Sept., Mon.–Sat., 9.30–7, Sun. 2–7; winter months, Mon.–Sat. 9.30–4, Sun. 2–4.

**Jim Clark Memorial Room,** Duns (A6105). Jimmy Clark was the quiet-spoken local sheepfarmer who went on to become motor-racing champion of the world and one of the all-time greats, before his tragic death at Hockenheim in Germany, in 1968. The room contains trophies and cups from his many victories (including the *Indianapolis 500*); also personal items. Open Apr.–Sept., Mon.–Sat. 10–6, Sun. 2–6.

**Scottish Wool Textiles Museum,** Walkerburn (A72). History of Borders woolen industries, old machinery, spinning and weaving demonstrations. Open Mar.–Oct., 10–5 daily.

**Selkirk Museum,** Selkirk (A7). Life of a community dedicated to shoemaking in ancient times. Open May–Sept., Mon.–Fri. 2–4.45.

**Wilton Lodge,** Hawick (A7). Social, industrial and archeological history of town. Handsome building in parkland on Teviot bank. Open Apr.–Oct., Mon.–Sat. 10–5, Sun. 2–6; winter months, weekdays only 10–4.

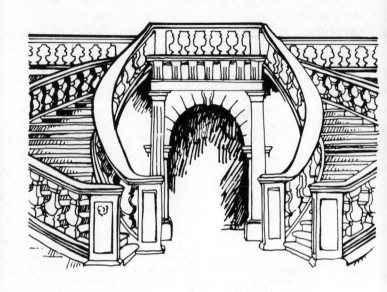

# SCOTLAND'S DEEP SOUTHWEST

## *Dumfries and Galloway*

This Region was for many years neglected by tourism. It lies away from the major England–Scotland routes and travelers to Glasgow and Edinburgh have usually been more concerned with getting to their destinations than with turning aside to explore it. One historic line of communication does pass through it: the road from Carlisle to Stranraer and Cairn Ryan, two harbors which offer the shortest sea crossings, 40 and 35 miles respectively, between the United Kingdom and Ireland.

Of the rich pre-history of this Region very little of substance remains. Scotland's first settlers, about 4000 B.C., had villages on Luce Bay and beside the banks of the River Annan; flint implements, now in museums, have been recovered. There are small chambered cairns of the Neolithic period (2000 B.C.) at Cairnholy near Gatehouse of Fleet and at Windy Edge near Langholm. The sites of "crannogs," lake villages on stilts, have been identified on the lochs of Milton near Crocketford, Carlingwark near Castle Douglas and the Castle at Lochmaben. They have rotted away but you can still see the low, brushwood-covered isles on which they were built.

In the second century A.D., the important Roman camp of Blatum Bulgium stood at Burnswark in Annandale. The name means "Flour Bags" and presumably it was a grain stockpile. But afterwards a thoughtless Duke of Buccleuch took the stones away to build walls; and Birrens, as the place is now called, has only a mound and a hollow to show for its Roman past.

The large decorated Celtic cross (7th century) of Ruthwell near Annan was also destroyed. The shaft, pieced together again, now stands inside the parish church.

The Region's outstanding ancient building was a small church built about 410 at Whithorn, south of Wigtown, by Ninian, Scotland's senior saint (c.360–432). It replaced his temporary wooden building on the Isle of Whithorn, three miles away, which the chroniclers called "Candida Casa" or White House. The Whithorn church is thought to have been sited where a ruined 12th-century priory now stands. The priory, at any rate, has been one of the holy places of Roman Catholic pilgrimage since medieval days.

Castles and abbeys abound, especially around river estuaries on the Solway Firth. The former lack the grandeur and the latter the ethereal grace of military and ecclesiastical architecture elsewhere in Scotland. Caerlaverock, Threave, Cardoness and Castle Kennedy are symbols of Scots–English struggles and wars between kings and unruly barons. The principal abbeys, Lincluden, Dundrennan, Luce and Sweetheart have also known moments of turbulent history. No building, however, attracts more attention than the blacksmith's shop at Gretna Green on the Cumbrian border with its tales of marriages between eloping English couples.

There are no large towns. Dumfries ("Dum-freess") has fewer than 30,000 inhabitants and Stranraer, the next largest, only 10,000. The Dumfries district is split by the valleys of three rivers, the Nith, Annan and Esk. Their courses reach back into the Borders and Strathclyde hills and their sources are lost in the lonely lochs of Tweedsmuir and Lowther.

West of Dumfries the land is called Galloway. In these parts mild temperatures, copious rainfall, well-drained hills and shelter from northerly winds favor arable and dairy farms. The black rough-haired Galloway pony is not so common now and on the pastures the belted Galloway cattle—black with white belly-bands—are giving way to heavier imported stock like the Charollais. But cattle-raising, agriculture and forestry are still the traditional industries. There are shiny silo towers but very few factory chimneys.

The central districts cover the old county of Kirkcudbright ("Kircoobry"), commonly called the Stewartry because from early times it was governed by a Steward directly answerable to the King. For more than 200 years the Steward was a Maxwell, a name you will often come across. The Maxwelton Braes of *Annie Laurie* rise above the Cairn valley north of Dumfries.

The Glen Trool National Forest Park occupies a large area in the middle of Galloway. Here the scenery is of Highland character. Large lochs appear in unexpected places and many of them have been harnessed for hydroelectric schemes.

Coastal areas are pleasantly pastoral. The coastline is deeply indented with sandy or muddy river mouths on the southern shore and low cliffs on the western. Around the hammer-head isthmus called the Rhinns (hill ranges) of Galloway you will find sub-tropical gardens. One of Scotland's most exhilarating coast drives is the 18 miles from Gatehouse of Fleet to Newton Stewart.

Old-time occupations—farming and smuggling—were portrayed in the novels of S.R. Crocket (1860-1914), who was born at Balmaghie near Castle Douglas. His sentimentality is mawkish to modern readers but *The Raiders* and *The Lilac Sunbonnet* were extremely popular in their day. Scott's *Redgauntlet* and *Guy Mannering* are both set in the Region and his character "Old Mortality" (Robert Paterson, 1715–1801) is buried at Caerlaverock. R.L. Stevenson's *The Master of Ballantrae* (actually a picture of Borgue near Kirkcudbright rather than Ballantrae) illustrates the deep-dyed conservatism of Galloway folk. Stevenson himself was stoned in the village streets in 1878 for some slight eccentricity of dress.

Thomas Carlyle was born at Ecclefechan, J.M. Barrie went to school at Dumfries Academy and Robert Burns lived, died and was buried in the same town. James Clerk Maxwell the 19th-century physicist was brought up near Corsock and Thomas Telford the 19th-century engineer was born near Langholm. Inhabitants of Eskdale have made much in recent years of the fact that Neil Armstrong, the first man on the moon, claims a local ancestry.

In this chapter we shall take the trans-Regional roads from Gretna to the Mull of Galloway, then retrace our steps and examine the dales north of Dumfries.

### Marriage à la Mode

Traveling along the A74 from Carlisle, over the border in England, to Glasgow, the first village in Scotland you reach is Gretna, a junction of routes among the marshes at the head of the Solway Firth. For 200 years it was the goal of eloping couples from England who could take advantage of Scots law and marry by simply making a declaration before a witness—such as the village blacksmith. After 1939 such marriages were made illegal, but young English and foreign couples continued to flock to Gretna Green because in Scotland you could marry without parental consent at 16 while in England and most Continental countries the age was 21. Today at the Old Blacksmith's, one of two smithies at Gretna Green, mock ceremonies are performed daily as entertainment for bus parties.

### Dumfries

From Gretna via the small town of Annan, where the River Annan checks its headlong rush from the uplands and winds soberly to the sea, it is 24 miles to Dumfries (A75). Like Annan it is an estuary town, seven miles from the sea, spread over the bends of the canal-like River Nith; a busy agricultural center with traffic congestion on market days.

Dumfries became a royal burgh 700 years ago. The foundation of its Greyfriars monastery off Buccleuch Street near the river bank dates back almost as far. It was there in 1306 that Robert the Bruce, pressing for recognition as Scotland's rightful king, stabbed his rival John Comyn. As Bruce fled with his supporters, one Roger Kirkpatrick turned back and drove his dagger again into the dying man "to mak siccar" (make sure). The Dumfries Kirkpatricks have ever since borne a bloody hand with a dagger for their coat-of-arms with the motto: "I mak siccar."

In the 1870s, the playwright J.M. Barrie spent his childhood in Victoria Terrace, Dumfries, and attended Dumfries Academy. The garden of Moat Brae House is supposed to have been the playground which inspired his boyish dreams of Peter Pan. In his memoirs Barrie wrote of running to the street corner to doff his cap to the literary giant of the age, Thomas Carlyle. "I dare say I paid this homage 50 times, but never was there any response."

Dumfries's real lion is Robert Burns. His last and most lyrical songs and poems were written while he lived in and near the town. Burns gave up his third unsuccessful farming venture at Ellisland, six miles upstream on the Nith, in 1791. *Tam o' Shanter, Of A' the Airts, Jo Anderson my Jo* and *Auld Lang Syne* belong to that period. He and his wife Jean Armour took a house in the Wee Vennel, afterwards moving to what is now called Burns Street. For the first time in his life Burns had a steady salaried job. He was a customs officer at the port of Dumfries. Here he wrote, among scores of songs, *Ae Fond Kiss, Duncan Gray, The Lea Rig* and—possibly the most perfect of 18th-century love-poems— *O, wert Thou in the Cauld Blast.*

To the doctor who attended him on his deathbed in 1796 he described himself as "a poor pigeon not worth the plucking." He was only 37. The cause of death has been variously diagnosed as rheumatic fever, endocarditis and a diseased nervous system. "Who dae ye think'll be oor poet now?" said a man in the Dumfries streets as the cortège passed by. The funeral was gorgeous but when a grand meeting was called to raise a monument only three citizens turned up. It took 30 years to reach the target of £3,000 ($15,000 in those days) for the mausoleum, most of the money coming from England.

Dumfries has many Burns relics in its civic museum, which is a converted 18th-century windmill. The house in the Wee Vennel (now Bank Street) is not visitable. The house in Burns Street, formerly Mill Vennel, where Burns died is the poet's official museum. You may visit the Globe tavern, his regular "howff" in the last years, and the mausoleum in St. Michael's churchyard where he is buried. His farm at Ellisland has been transformed into a showcase of agricultural methods of Burns's time and is open to the public.

## Between Nith and Solway

South of Dumfries, where the Nith widens to the mudflats of the Solway Firth, a number of castles resistant to the "crumbling touch of Time" dot the shoreline. Caerlaverock, noble in decay, islanded in a lake-like moat, in the 13th century was the Maxwells' proudest stronghold. King Edward I of England took it with battering-rams and catapults in 1300. The Covenanters accomplished its ruin in the wars of 1639–40. "Old Mortality," who crops up everywhere in the moss-grown corners of Scotland, is buried in Caerlaverock churchyard.

On the opposite bank of the Nith (A710), under the dome of the solitary mountain Criffell (1,868 feet), stand MacCullock's Castle, Wreath Castle and Auchenskeoch Castle. The proximity of England, only ten miles across the Firth, accounts for the prodigality of fortresses round these vulnerable Scottish promontories.

On the A710, before you reach these ruins, you come to a foundation worth more than a passing glance. New Abbey, otherwise Sweetheart Abbey, points a gaunt red sandstone tower and colonnades of broken arches to the sky. It was founded in 1273 by Devorgilla, a descendant of the ancient lords of Galloway who married John Balliol (founder of Balliol College, Oxford) and gave birth to the more historic John Balliol, puppet king of Scotland before Bruce. The lady also built Dumfries's first bridge, precursor of the 15th-century "Old Bridge" which pedestrians use to this day, and the Greyfriars monastery. It seems that Devorgilla herself was not particularly devout, but her husband had insulted a bishop and after his death these penances devolved upon her. She carried her husband's embalmed heart in a casket wherever she went. She was buried with it in 1289 in her own New Abbey: hence the place's popular name of Dulce Cor or Sweetheart.

Kirkbean, also situated where Criffell's skirts brush the sea, was once a seaport. (All round the Galloway coast you may trace the beach mark, about 25 feet above sea level, up to which the sea used to rise.) Here was born Dr. Craik, personal physician to George Washington. Arbigland, right next door, was the birthplace of John Paul ("I have not yet begun to fight") Jones, the gardener's boy who became an American citizen and is sometimes called the founder of the U.S. Navy. One wonders if the two men ever met.

For several weeks in 1778 in the *U.S.S. Ranger,* the first ship to wear the Stars and Stripes, Jones bombarded ports and harried shipping in the Solway Firth and Irish Sea in pursuance of orders to "distress the enemies of the United States." The propaganda effect was considerable: not for 100 years had any foreign vessel dared attack a British coast.

Jones, who died in Paris in 1792, is commemorated with a plaque on his birthplace, a font in Kirkbean church presented by the U.S. Navy in 1945; and a museum at Kirkcudbright's 16th-century Tolbooth, the gaol where he was once imprisoned.

## Castle Douglas to Newton Stewart

Castle Douglas takes its name from a 14th-century castle called Threave, a stronghold of the Black Douglas on an island in the River Dee. So powerful was this medieval warrior-lord that King James II had to bring an army to Threave in 1455 to teach him a lesson; an occasion on which the "bombard" (cannon) was first used in Scotland. You can see one of the cannon-balls, 17 inches in diameter, in the Dumfries Burgh museum. Modern Threave, three miles south of the ruined castle, is a showplace of rhododendrons and rock plants. This is where the National Trust for Scotland trains its gardeners. The watery neighborhood is a great place for greylag geese.

Threave's river, the Dee, flows down from Loch Ken and the Water of Ken, an elaborate system of hydroelectric reservoirs and barrages; down from New Galloway, population 300, the smallest royal burgh for miles around; and down from Carsphairn among Galloway's highest and wildest hills. This was the country of the Macadams, of whom John Loudon Macadam (1756–1836), inventor of carriageable roads, was the most distinguished son. Tradition says the family were MacGregors, a name proscribed by law after the Jacobite risings, and that John's grandfather called himself Macadam because none could deny that all men were "sons of Adam." It is a coincidence that the other pioneer of road engineering, Thomas Telford, was born in the same region at about the same date (1757). Telford was a shepherd lad from Eskdale.

The Dee meets the sea at Kirkcudbright (A711), chief town of the Stewartry and best-looking of Galloway burghs—at least when the tides is in. As in all Solway estuaries there is a lot of mud about at low water. Kirkcudbright is an 18th-century town of unpretentious houses, some of them color-washed and roofed with the blue slates of the district. The Tolbooth is a good example of 16th–17th-century public building with a plain facade and an outside stairway. The slender Mercat Cross in front of it dates from 1610. Witches were tried there. The last witch to be burned was one Elspeth McEwen in 1698, but as recently as 1805 a Jean Maxwell was convicted of witchcraft at Kirkcudbright and sentenced to a year's hard labor.

Kirkcudbright's L-shaped main street is full of craft and antique shops. The castle, called Maclellan's Castle, is the shell of a once-elaborate castellated mansion dating from the early 17th century.

Below the town, on the shores of the estuary, you will see herons. For centuries there has been a heronry on St. Mary's Isle in the bay. There are priory ruins too on this small island; and some years ago the Canadian government decided to set up a monument at the site of a demolished house. It was the home of Lord Selkirk, who helped establish the Red River colony, afterwards Winnipeg, in 1817.

A few miles east (A711) stands ruined Dundrennan Abbey, founded 1142, where Mary Queen of Scots spent her last night in Scotland. At Port Mary, a mile away, you can see the stone from which she stepped into the boat which took her to England and delivered her to the mercy of her cousin Queen Elizabeth I: the spot where she left Scotland never to return.

For Kirkcudbright bridge, the A755/A75 leads west to Gatehouse of Fleet, Creetown and Newton Stewart, three insignificant townships situated among quiet waters. Cardoness Castle (15th century) south of Gatehouse, overlooking Fleet Bay, has associations with the "Young Lochinvar" of the well-known poem; as has Rusco Castle, a few miles northwest. Only fragments survive of these formerly important towers of the Gordons of Lochinvar.

## St. Ninian's Chapel

Newton Stewart, largest of the three townships, is an obvious touring center for Galloway's far west. South of the town, the A746 winds above the shores of Wigtown Bay on a promontory called The Machars —sometimes rendered "Machers," an instance of the confusing Scots habit of finding alternative spellings for place-names wherever possible. Wigtown is another royal burgh in name, a sleepy village by nature. Both in the churchyard and on the mudflats of the shore are memorials to the Wigtown Martyrs, two women tied to stakes and left to drown in the incoming tide during the anti-Covenant witch-hunts of 1685. Much of Galloway's history is linked with Border feuds; but even more with the ferocity of the Killing Times. Wigtown, like several other places in the Region, is dominated by a hill-top Covenanters' Monument, a reminder of the old persecutions.

The A746 was a pilgrim's way and a royal route. It ends at Isle of Whithorn (which is not in fact quite an island), a place which early Scottish kings and barons sought to visit at least once in their lives, as Moslems seek to visit Mecca. The pilgrimage was often prescribed as a penance, but these pleasant shores impose no penance today. The goal was St. Ninian's chapel, the 4th-century cell of Scotland's premier saint. Some pilgrims made for Whithorn village and others for the sandspit "isle." Both places claimed to be the site of the original "Candida Casa" of the saint. As you approach Whithorn's 12th-century priory, observe the royal arms of pre-1707 Scotland (that is, Scotland before the Union with England) carved and painted above the arch of the Pend (covered way).

## Newton Stewart to Stranraer

The abbeys of Galloway, like the castles, have all been scarred and beaten down, but are nowadays oases of tranquillity once more, carefully maintained and surrounded by lawns. Luce Abbey near Glenluce beside the Water of Luce and close to the A75 belongs to the 12th century; Carscreuch Castle, three miles northeast on an unclassified road, to the 17th. From Glenluce you cross a neck of water-meadows and pools which just saves the Rhinns of Galloway from being an island; and then you are at Stranraer.

Ferry ports, designed to speed the traveler away in one direction or another, are rarely worth visiting on their own account. Stranraer is an exception. Having been in existence long before steamer piers and customs sheds were thought of, it has a life of its own. "Bluidy" Claverhouse, scourge of the Covenanters in the Killing Times, made his headquarters at the 16th-century castle in the middle of the town. Another "castle," on the waterfront, bears the curious name of North West. It was built by Rear-admiral Sir John Ross (1777–1856), explorer of the Canadian Arctic and born four miles away at Inch. The "castle" is now a hotel.

The ferry port for Ireland used to be Portpatrick, now a neat little holiday village on the western side of the Rhinns, 12 miles nearer the

Irish ports. But the harbor proved too exposed and when regular ferry schedules were introduced the port of Stranraer, well sheltered at the head of its sea-loch, was chosen. More recently a rival ferry company has developed Cairn Ryan, halfway down the loch, as an alternative ferry station.

You will find Irish and British currency circulating in the Stranraer and Cairn Ryan districts: check your money before you leave, because the Irish coins and notes will not be accepted elsewhere in Scotland; note also that the Irish pound (punt) is worth about 20% less than its British equivilent.

### The Rhinns

Stranraer is the doorway to the T-shaped peninsula of the Rhinns of Galloway, which appear to have been stuck on to the mainland as an afterthought. The Rhinns are a bright patchwork of cultivated land with quiet open roads and calm little villages. Sandhead (A716), where a battle once took place between Scots and Picts, nestles at one end of the eight-mile-long sands of Luce. Among Kirkmadrine's chapel ruins, two miles from Sandhead, early Christian inscribed stones are preserved, hinting at a possible saintly settlement as old as St. Ninian's.

Climate and soil have produced subtropical vegetation like that of the western isles and the southwest of Ireland. A Galloway landowner, Lord Stair, demonstrated the agricultural potential of the area in 1770 when he planted the Lochinch gardens at Castle Kennedy near Stranraer (A75). They have since been matched by brilliant displays at Ardwell House south of Sandhead (A716) and Logan House near Port Logan (B7065). There is an avenue of palm trees at Logan House which looks as though it might have come from the French Riviera. At Port Logan itself, in the small tidal basin, there is a fishpond to which cod and other saltwater fish have been attracted for 200 years to feed out of visitors' hands.

Run on another four miles from Port Logan to see the sculpted stones in the churchyard of Kirkmaiden, the most southerly parish in Scotland (not to be confused with Kirkmadrine above). The greatest continuous distance in Scotland, 280 miles in a straight line, is the proverbial "Maiden Kirk to John o' Groats"—the extreme southwest to the extreme northeast.

### Heart of the Stewartry

The road for Glasgow (A77) goes north from Stranraer along a coastline which offers fine views in clear weather of Northern Ireland and the hills and isles of the Firth of Clyde. This road links up with Girvan, Ayr and the Clyde coastal towns, described in our Strathclyde chapter.

To return to Dumfries from Stranraer you must take the A75 again at least as far as Newton Stewart. This once-peaceful route is sometimes heavily trafficked with commercial vehicles for the Irish ferries. But from Newton Stewart you may strike northeast along the A712 for New Galloway, passing through part of the Glen Trool National Forest

Park. Glen Trool itself lies north again, beyond the ridges of Galloway's highest hills; accessible on unclassified roads from the A714.

Scenically, the A712 is one of the Region's best roads, reminiscent in parts of the Highlands; although the large-scale afforestations on the hills and the hydroelectric dams on the lochs give the landscape more of a man-made look. These areas are well furnished with picnic places and marked nature trails, but they are among the least-frequented districts in southern Scotland. All the way to Dumfries the nearest thing you will see to a town will be a tightly-knit little cluster of cottages here and there.

East of New Galloway on the A712 an unfenced road (B794) goes south, bounding down a valley with a little stream called the Urr Water. Follow this stream through its wooded length and you will pass close to the Mote, or Moat, of Urr, an important Saxon fortification. Continue through Dalbeattie, another old-fashioned little burgh, and you will reach the coast again on a typical Solway inlet (reeds, weeds and mud) near Palnackie. The 15th-century tower of Orchardton, one mile south, is circular: a unique feature for Galloway. Across the water you look towards Kippford and see the yachts and the cocktail terrace of the hotel: a sophisticated oasis in a land of rustic seclusion.

A remarkable openair display of stone sculptures can be seen on the hillside above Shawhead (off the A75 soon after it joins the A712 to take you the final 10 miles to Dumfries). The sculptures were placed there by the local landowner, Sir William Keswick, in the 1950s and include a head by Rodin and two large groups of figures by Henry Moore.

## Drumlanrig

From Dumfries there are several roads to Glasgow and Edinburgh. They follow the dales, climbing out to surmount the masses of overlapping hill ranges which separate the English border from the Forth–Clyde valley.

The A76 goes via Thornhill, a place to which, to borrow the words which the Scottish judge Lord Cockburn used of another town of the Region nearly 200 years ago, "decent characters with moderate purses might retire for quiet comfort." Chief among the stately homes with which the village is ringed is Drumlanrig Castle, a square-built, turreted, shocking-pink 17th-century palace, elegantly planted on well-manicured parkland beside the River Nith.

Happy the owner, you might imagine, who could choose such an idyllic spot and maintain such a handsome pile. But gruesome tales are told of Drumlanrig. Its builder, the first Duke of Queensberry, lived there for one night and fled. In the 18th century an idiot heir of the Queensberrys escaped from his tower prison, seized a kitchen-maid and boiled her alive in the supper cauldron. In the park are the ruins of a much older castle called Tibber's, badly knocked about by Bruce in 1311.

The inventor of the bicycle in 1842 came from Keir, two miles west of Thornhill. He was Kirkpatrick MacMillan (1813-1878), locally known as "Daft Pate." On his prototype velocipede he raced the mail-coach to Glasgow; but unluckily knocked a child down while traveling at the dangerous speed of nine miles an hour.


## Grey Mare's Tail

From Thornhill the A702 goes by the Dalveen pass, an awesome defile to Elvanfoot in Strathclyde Region; and so to Edinburgh or Glasgow. The A701 is an equally fine road with dramatic changes of scenery. Moffat, 20 miles from Dumfries, sits in a bowl of the hills where several torrents splash down to form the Annan River. Roughly halfway between Carlisle and Edinburgh, this comfortable-looking small town, with its exceptionally pretty public park, makes a good touring center for the southern uplands of Scotland. Its original *raison d'être* is expressed by the statue of a ram in the square at the end of its broad main street.

At Moffat House in 1759 the literary impostor James "Ossian" MacPherson produced the Gaelic epic poems which brought him into conflict with Dr. Johnson. The road-builder John Loudon Macadam is buried in Moffat kirkyard. Robert Burns and James Boswell both came to Moffat to seek relief from their digestive troubles.

The place has a spa air, and was indeed at one period regarded as Scotland's answer to Bath, Cheltenham and other English watering-places. Other Scottish springs have been claimed as the "St. Ronan's Well" of Scott's novel of that name—but it is most likely that he had Moffat in mind. From chalybeate waters discovered in the 1780s miraculous cures of scurvy and scrofula were reported. Baths, hotels and a *kurhaus* sprang up, but suddenly Moffat's fame subsided. Possibly invalids found the remedy worse than their diseases: the taste of the waters was officially likened to "rotten eggs beaten up in the scourings of a foul gun."

Or maybe the gold rush trampled fashionable hypochondria out of existence. In 1863 a nugget containing seven grains of pure gold was exhibited in the window of Moffat's Black Bull hotel; it had been found in the Moffat Water. Prospectors, professional and amateur, descended on the town. Miners with their picks and sieves trekked down from Fife to pan the hill-burns. Quantities of yellow-grained rock were brought in. But geological analysis destroyed all dreams: the pure gold was pure iron pyrites, fool's gold. (20 miles away at Wanlockhead and Leadhills gold has been found, though in uneconomical amounts.)

There are some obscure but charming glens in Moffat's neighborhood. Raehills, seven miles south on the Dumfries road, is worth looking at. Among notable topographical curiosities are the Devil's Beeftub, two miles north on the Edinburgh road, a fearsome hollow once used by cattle-rustlers as a hiding-place for stolen herds; and the Grey Mare's Tail, a streaming 200-foot cascade on the wild road to Selkirk (A708). The latter has been taken over by the National Trust for Scotland and in summer there is an information office at the roadside. The path to the cascade is short but treacherous in wet weather. After heavy rain, however, a close-up view of the waterfall repays the ordeal.

## Ecclefechan

The plain two-storied house where Carlyle was born stands on the main A74 (Glasgow-Carlisle road) in Ecclefechan village, nine miles north of Gretna Green. No historic site in Scotland could be more accessible, but it has the distinction of being the least-visited of all the National Trust for Scotland's properties.

Thomas Carlyle (1795-1881) is thought of, if at all, as the sage of Chelsea in London, and indeed his years of distinction were spent at 5 Cheyne Row in Chelsea. But before his *History of the French Revolution* and *Frederick the Great* established him as one of the most influential of the 19th-century philosopher-historians, he lived penuriously at Craigenputtock in the Cairn valley (B729) north of Dumfries; and before that he taught at Annan Academy (A75). In 1837 a young American admirer, Ralph Waldo Emerson, came to see him at Craigenputtock. "I found the house amid desolate heathery hills," Emerson recalled, "where the lonely scholar nourished his mighty heart . . . tall and gaunt with a cliff-like brow, holding his extraordinary powers of conversation in easy command. . . . "

## Langholm

Cross the empty moorland routes of the B725 and the A709 from Ecclefechan or take the main A7 Edinburgh road from Carlisle and you arrive at Langholm, a little metropolis of the dales, strung out along the Esk River. Langholm is called the "Muckle (big) Toon"—surely for its length, certainly not for its size. But this tiny Eskdale community supports woollen mills and tweed shops; a golf course, two bowling greens and a cricket ground, all delightfully situated by the rippling mountain river; and a great Scottish rugby football team. There are four hotels, much patronized by trout fishermen.

The Langholm Monument, commemorating locally-born General John Malcolm, crowns the 1,200-foot Whita Hill above the village and is a focal point of the Langholm Common Riding, held annually on the last Friday in July: one of those picturesque Borders cavalcades which patrol the parish boundaries.

In Borders history, Langholm was the stamping-ground of Johnny Armstrong, a 16th-century desperado whose dubious activities are celebrated in popular ballads. From the Armstrongs, a name distributed throughout Eskdale, sprang the family of Neil Armstrong, the first man on the moon. When he came to be sworn a freeman of the burgh in 1972 the local mill wove a special Moon tartan for him.

Scotland's major modern poet, Hugh MacDiarmid, was born in Langholm in 1892, the son of the local postman. As was the case with Burns at Dumfries, this poet is too recently dead to be thought much of in his native town.

The main road for Edinburgh (A7), an appetizer for the romantic scenery you will feast on in the Highlands, climbs through an ever-narrowing gorge and crosses the watershed at a historic travelers' rest, the Mosspaul Inn, at around 1,600 feet. By following the Esk from

Langholm on the B709 you come, after seven miles, to Westerkirk, birthplace of Thomas Telford the "Colossus of Roads." Farther on is Eskdalemuir with its observatory. So by lonely dales full of color you eventually reach Lothian Region. This is a slow, unfamiliar but outstandingly beautiful approach to Scotland's capital city.

Liddesdale (B6357) is another south–north thread tying England to Scotland. Ruined forts and peel towers dot the harsh landscape of the "Debatable Lands." One of them (B6399) is Hermitage Castle, a 13th-century Douglas stronghold with a long and cruel history. It still looks menacing. Newcomers to Scotland who make Hermitage their first stop will get a vivid taste of something they will get used to as they travel on: the influence of history on the landscape. In few countries of Europe has a stormy past left more indelible marks on the present.

# PRACTICAL INFORMATION FOR DUMFRIES AND GALLOWAY

**HOW TO GET THERE. By train.** Two main inter-city railroads pass through the eastern part of the Region: Carlisle to Glasgow via Annan, Dumfries and Kirkconnel; and Carlisle to Glasgow via Lockerbie. These are the routes by which you enter the Region from London (Euston), Birmingham or Manchester. From London to Dumfries takes 5½ hours. Another railroad links Stranraer with Glasgow; on this line there are no intermediate stations in the Region.

**By boat.** *British Rail Sealink,* 24 Donegal Place, Belfast, Northern Ireland (tel. 27525), operate ferry services for passengers and vehicles between Larne and Stranraer, voyage time 2¼ hours; *Townsend Thoresen,* The Harbor, Cairn Ryan (tel. 276) between Cairn Ryan and Larne, voyage time 2 hours. There are up to 10 crossings a day in the tourist season.

**By air.** Nearest airports are actually outside the Region: Prestwick (55 miles from Stranraer) and Glasgow (82 miles).

**By car.** Main routes from Carlisle (Cumbria) pass through the Region on their way to Glasgow and Edinburgh. The main east–west road is the A75, Carlisle–Dumfries–Gatehouse of Fleet–Stranraer. From Newton Stewart and Stranraer in the far west there are main roads (A714 and A77) to the Clyde coast and Glasgow. Dumfries is 33 miles from Carlisle, 73 from Edinburgh, 74 from Glasgow, and 69 from Stranraer.

**HOTELS AND RESTAURANTS.** The Region is relatively inexpensive for accommodations and food. Standards are adequate but luxurious hotels are few. However, guest-houses have improved in recent years. Of the many restaurants in the hotels and inns on the touring routes, those we have listed below have all received good reports.

**AUCHENCAIRN** (off A711). **Restaurant.** *Balcary Bay* (M), tel. 217. On seashore south of Dalbeattie. Local beef, seafood, Scottish specialties.

**DALRY** (A713). **Restaurant.** *Lochinvar* (M), tel. 210. In small country hotel among winding lanes of Glenkens.

**DUMFRIES** (A75). *Cairndale* (E), English Street (tel. 4111). 44 rooms, 29 with bath. In town center. Pleasant atmosphere, excellent meals.

**GATEHOUSE OF FLEET** (A75). *Murray Arms* (M), tel. 207. 22 rooms, 16 with bath. Typical main-street coaching inn, expensively restored. Here, it is said, Robert Burns wrote *Scots Wha He'e.* Old-fashioned rooms but first-class service and imaginative cuisine.

**LANGHOLM** (A7). *Holmwood House* (I), tel. 80211. 7 rooms, 2 with bath. Exceptionally good cooking and baking; local produce, fish and steaks.

**MOCHRUM** (off A714). **Restaurant.** *Greenmantle* (M), tel. Port William 357. Also a peaceful bed-and-breakfast stop.

**MOFFAT** (A701). *Beechwood Country House* (M), tel. 20210. 8 rooms, 6 with bath. All-round excellence in attractive surroundings. *Craigieburn* (I), Selkirk Road (tel. 20229). 6 rooms, 2 with bath. Small, family hotel; attentive staff.

**NEWTON STEWART** (A75). *Galloway Arms* (M), tel. 2282. 21 rooms, 14 with bath. Another venerable staging-post on the route to Ireland. Fishing clientele and, as usual with fishing hotels, generous country cuisine.

**PORTPATRICK** (A75). *Knockinaam Lodge* (E), tel. 471. 12 rooms, 8 with bath. Victorian country house set in 30 acres with lawns sloping to beach. Young resident owners have genuine interest in food and wines.

**ROCKCLIFFE** (off A710). *Baron's Craig* (E), tel. 225. 27 rooms, 20 with bath. On coast south of Dalbeattie near lively yachting center. A large 19th-century house of character in spacious grounds.

**STRANRAER** (A77). *North West Castle* (M), tel. 4413. 83 rooms, all with bath. Historic house with Arctic exploration connections, hence the name. High standard of comfort and amenities. Curling holidays offered.

**WHITHORN, ISLE OF** (A750). **Restaurant.** *Queen's Arms* (M), tel. 269. An old inn on remote but popular harbor. Fish, lobster, Galloway beef, regional cheeses.

**HOW TO GET ABOUT. By car.** Communications through the Region are swift: long, fast stretches of roadway, few towns. You can hire a self-drive automobile from *SMT Self-Drive,* York Place, Dumfries (tel. 5291), *Galloway Motor Co.,* Creebridge, Newton Stewart (tel. 3101) or *Godfrey David Europcar,* Belvilla Road, Stranraer (tel. 5254).

**By bus.** The bus network is comprehensive and in summer there are many excursions on offer, both daily and for longer periods, from the Bus Station, Whitesands, Dumfries.

**TOURIST INFORMATION.** The local centers, open 10–6 Apr.–Sept., are: Castle Douglas, Dalbeattie, Dumfries, Gatehouse of Fleet, Gretna, Kirkcudbright, Langholm and Moffat. They operate booking services for local accommodations.

The Information Center, Dashwood Square, Newton Stewart, is open daily: 9.30–6 Apr.–Jun. and Sept.; 9.30–8 Jul.–Aug.; and 10–4 Oct. The National Information Center at Port Rodie, Stranraer, is open daily 10–6.30 Jun.–Sept.; weekdays 10–5 and Sun. 10–4, May and Oct.; and weekdays 10–5 Nov.–Apr. The offices sometimes close for an hour at lunchtime. The National Trust for Scotland operates an information service at Threave Gardens, open daily 9.30–7 Apr.–Oct. At Carsphairn on the A713 there is a tourist information noticeboard.

For visitors heading toward the Region on the M6 in England there is a National Information Center at Southwaite (Cumbria), 8 miles south of Carlisle.

**FISHING.** The rivers of the Region, especially the Annan, Cairn, Cree, Esk, Nith and Urr, are very good for salmon, sea trout and brown trout. Hotels at Beattock (A74), Canonbie (A7), Gatehouse of Fleet, Moffat, New Galloway and Newton Stewart have their neighboring beats and offer fishing to non-residents for $4 or so per day, $15 or so if hire of boat is involved. The small lochs and reservoirs of Galloway's highlands are stocked with brown trout. The Newton Stewart Angling Association, Arthur Street, Newton Stewart, controls many of them and issues daily and weekly permits. Farther west, a good contact is the Stranraer & District Angling Association, 90 George Street, Stranraer. Permits for fishing the Water of Ken and large Clatteringshaws Loch may be obtained from the Ken Bridge Hotel, New Galloway (A712). The average rate for permits is $2–5 per day.

North and south of New Galloway the natural and artificial loch and river systems attract pike, perch and roach anglers. For coarse fishing permits, about $1 per day; contact hotels, grocery store or post office at New Galloway.

The Solway Firth is good for cod, bass and flatfish. Kippford (off A710), Kirkcudbright (A711), Port William (A747), Portpatrick (A77) and parts of Loch Ryan near Stranraer (A77) are becoming sea angling centers of a casual and informal nature: go down to the harbor and ask the first weatherbeaten sea-dog you meet! Tackle, bait and boats are always available Jun.–Sept. at Isle of Whithorn where there are good rock marks and sheltered waters. Boatwork generally is for experts: the coast is notorious for reefs, strong tidal streams and shifting sands.

**GOLF.** The Golf Coast (see Strathclyde chapter) ends north of this Region, but Stranraer and the Rhinns of Galloway have their courses, as do most towns along the south shore from Wigtown (A714) to Annan (A75). Dumfries has two courses with the usual amenities, around $5 per day, book in advance if possible. Moffat (A701) and Thornhill (A76) have attractive 18-hole courses. Elsewhere in the northern districts golf courses are nine-hole or nonexistent.

**HISTORIC HOUSES AND GARDENS.** Long ago, when the Maxwells and Douglases ruled the land from Annan Water to "bonnie Doon," a lengthy chapter might have been written on the once-formidable stately homes of Dumfries and Galloway. But the medieval castles are now empty shells, and, sad to say, the Region is no longer rich in living, visitable properties.

**Drumlanrig Castle,** Thornhill (A76, 4 miles north). Imposing house and grounds. Notable collection of paintings, furniture, plate. One silver chandelier weighs 120 pounds. Open May and Jun., Mon., Thurs., Sat. 12.30–5, Sun. 11–6; Jul. and Aug., daily except Fri., 11–5.

**Ellisland Farm,** Holywood, Dumfries (A76, 7 miles north). The farm Burns rented 1788–91. House and granary sympathetically restored. Poetic associations in grounds. Open at all reasonable times.

**Lochinch Castle,** Stranraer (A75, 4 miles east). 19th-century (1867) house next door to ivy-clad ruin of Castle Kennedy. Famous for gardens and shrubbery. Woodland and lakeside paths. Open Apr.–Sept., daily except Sat., 10–5.

If great houses are few, the gardens of the flowery southwest—and public parks—are rich and colorful. **Threave** near Castle Douglas is where the National Trust for Scotland trains its gardeners. The house, a pseudo-baronial extravaganza, is a school where soil science and plant genetics are taught; it has a two-way student exchange link with Longwood Gardens in Pennsylvania. There are rose gardens, rock gardens and heather and woodland gardens laid out in 65 acres. A Visitor Center has interpretative displays. Gardens open daily 9 to sunset, Visitor Center daily 9.30–7, Apr.–Oct.

Other gardens frequently open are the **Dickson Garden,** Moffat (A701), next door to Moffat Weavers' shop, a walled smalltown garden; **Arbigland,** Kirkbean (A710), where John Paul Jones worked as a boy; **Ardwell House,** Stranraer (off A716), and **Lochinch,** Stranraer (A75), two splendid azalea and rhododendron gardens best seen in late May and early June; **Galloway House,** Garlieston (B7004 south of Wigtown), with fine trees and shrubs round a severely classical mid-18th-century house; and **Kirkdale,** Creetown (A75), with a magnificent setting on Wigtown Bay.

The great subtropical garden of the Region is at **Logan House** near Port Logan (B7065), but it is open only occasionally, usually around the end of May.

**MUSEUMS.** Several towns and rural centers in Galloway and Dumfries Region have interesting local museums and art exhibitions. The following selection should be of general interest.

**Burns' House,** Burns Street, Dumfries (A756). The house where Robert Burns died in 1796. Period furnishings and relics of the poet. Open Apr.–Sept., weekdays 10–1 and 2–7, Sun. 2–7; Oct.–Mar., weekdays 10–12 and 2–5.

**Carlyle's Birthplace,** Ecclefechan (A74). A neat cottage appropriately furnished. Manuscripts and relics of the historian. Open Apr.–Oct., weekdays 10–6. N.T.S.

**Deer Museum,** Clatteringshaws (A712 west of New Galloway). A Forestry Commission display covering red deer, wild goats and other regional fauna. Open Apr.–Sept., daily 10–5.

**Famous Old Blacksmith's Shop,** Gretna Green (A74). Marriage registers, documents relating to elopements, a collection of horse-drawn carriages. Open Apr.–Oct., daily, 9 in morn. to 10 at night.

**Gem and Rock Museum,** Chain Road, Creetown (A75). Large collection of minerals, precious stones, walking sticks and drinking mugs. Open daily 9.30–5.30.

**Maxwelton House Museum,** Moniaive (B729). Pageant of domestic life from 14th century. Birthplace of Annie Laurie. Open May–Sept., Wed., Thurs., and last Sun. of month, 2–5.

**Stewartry Museum,** St. Mary Street, Kirkcudbright (A711). Historical material including John Paul Jones relics. Open Apr.–Oct., weekdays, 10–1 and 2–5.

CHARLES
RENNIE
MACKINTOSH

DOORS:
WILLOW TREE
TEA ROOMS

# HEARTLAND OF INDUSTRY

## *Glasgow*

"Surely they're not going to slide that great ship into that trout stream?" a guest at the launching of the 80,000 ton *Queen Elizabeth* was heard to say. The workaday part of the Clyde, before it enters the Firth (which we describe in the Strathclyde chapter), is remarkable for its extreme narrowness. The double line of navigational bouys marks a channel only a few hundred yards wide and the bouys look gigantic. This part of the Cylde was once a sandy salmon river, shallow enough to wade across. Glasgow put it to work by making a canal out of it, to bring the tobacco and sugar clippers into the heart of the city and begin an era of prosperity. Hence the saying: "Glasgow made the Clyde and the Clyde made Glasgow."

In Glasgow, the river presents a dismal foreshore to its Firth, with no hint of the stunning scenery on which it is to open. Here are Clydebank, Renfrew, Linthouse and Govan, all shipyards on both sides of the river, and the cranes at full stretch could almost entangle their jibs with those opposite. This is where you used to hear the "symphony of the Clyde" or, as shipyard workers would put it, "a helluva bashing din." The environment was deafened day and night by the clashing of ships' platings, the hammering of pile-drivers and the chattering of the riveters. For five and a half years in World War II the five miles below

Glasgow called Clydeside built and repaired 13 ships every day. But things are quieter now.

Where the docks, basins and slipways congregate round the black and sluggish river, two centuries of war and commerce, adventure and exploration have begun. James Watt of Greenock solved the problems of steam propulsion in 1765. Henry Bell in 1812 offered Scotland the world's first steamship service in his three-horsepower *Comet*, every lawful day (that was, not Sundays) from Glasgow to Greenock. There is an obelisk to Henry Bell near Bowling (A82) and the timbers from his *Comet* paddle-wheeler, eventually wrecked in the Firth of Lorne, are laid in the floor of the Queen's Hotel at Helensburgh (A814). The ship's flywheel stands in Helensburgh's Hermitage Park.

Glasgow's dockland was a cradle of disaffection in periods of economic depression. In the early 1930s the legend of "Red Clydeside" was born and the district returned Communist members to the Westminster parliament. Radical dreams have now come true, for the famous old shipyards are in public ownership. Historic yards which built battleships and liners for the maritime nations of the world have diversified, not always successfully, into special jobs for gas and oil seabed exploration. The best-known firm of all, John Brown of Clydebank which built the Cunarders, is now the Texas-owned Marathon yard, making oil drilling rigs and production platforms.

## No Mean City

Glasgow, with nearly a million inhabitants, is the biggest city in Scotland and the third biggest (after London and Birmingham) in Britain. Writers of earlier periods, even up to the late 18th century, rarely failed to admire her neat, well-paved streets and well-built houses and the way the salmon leapt up the rapids of the crystal-clear Clyde on their passage through the city. Later the picture changed. The river was dredged and deepened. Industry crowded its banks. A large influx of peasants from Ireland and the Highlands did not settle down too happily. Scandals arose in public affairs, slum districts spread out from the lower waterfronts, dirt and soot (made worse by the steady drizzling rain which Glasgow knows so well) painted layers of ugliness on an urban scene which had become a chaotic mass of unplanned streets and factories.

Until fairly recently Glasgow has been a byword for civic corruption, petty gangsterdom and abysmal squalor. If you have read the novel *No Mean City* by Alexander MacArthur (who ended up taking poison and throwing himself in the Clyde) or seen the ballet *Miracle in the Gorbals,* you will already have a picture of Glasgow which you might have recognized as you walked her streets any time in the first half of this century.

Things are different now. There are black spots. There are some areas of inner and outer urban deprivation, some skylines of factory chimneys and concrete cooling towers and shabby high-rise apartment blocks; some waste ground and blank walls frescoed with aerosol. But you can walk through the infamous Gorbals and wonder when you are coming to the Gorbals and your lasting impression of that quarter may

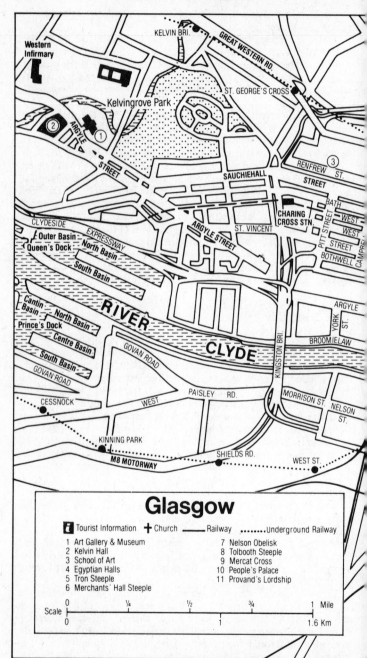

Western
Infirmary

KELVIN BRI.

GREAT WESTERN RD.

ST. GEORGE'S CROSS

Kelvingrove Park

②
ARGYLE
①
STREET

RENFREW ST.
③

SAUCHIEHALL
STREET

BATH
CHARING
CROSS STN.
WEST
PITT
STREET
WEST
STREET
BOTHWELL
CAMPBELL

CLYDESIDE
EXPRESSWAY
Outer Basin
Queen's Dock
North Basin
South Basin

ARGYLE STREET
ST. VINCENT

Cantin
Basin
North Basin
Prince's Dock
Centre Basin
South Basin
GOVAN ROAD

RIVER

ARGYLE

YORK ST.
BROOMIELAW

CLYDE

KINGSTON BRI.

GOVAN ROAD

PAISLEY RD.

MORRISON ST.
NELSON ST.

CESSNOCK

WEST

KINNING PARK

M8 MOTORWAY

SHIELDS RD.

WEST ST.

# Glasgow

**i** Tourist Information   ✝ Church   —— Railway   ······· Underground Railway

1 Art Gallery & Museum
2 Kelvin Hall
3 School of Art
4 Egyptian Halls
5 Tron Steeple
6 Merchants' Hall Steeple

7 Nelson Obelisk
8 Tolbooth Steeple
9 Mercat Cross
10 People's Palace
11 Provand's Lordship

Scale
0    ¼    ½    ¾    1 Mile
0        1        1.6 Km

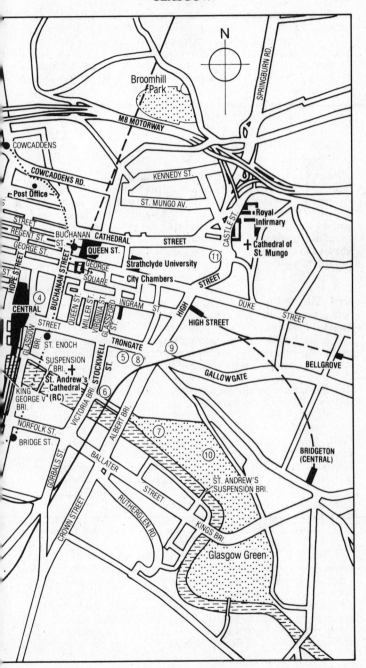

be of the graceful suspension bridge over the Clyde, the fine Victorian facades of Carlton Place and the gardens which slope to the river.

Glasgow has 260 parks and areas of public gardens, more per head of population than any other European city. She extends over 16 hills (at least, there are 16 Hill Streets in different areas) and she throws 15 bridges over the Clyde, not counting those above Rutherglen, outside the main downtown area.

## River of Glasgow

Since we came in on the river, let us continue upstream through the heart of the city. No boat can take us, unless we are among those dozens of rowing-club members who ruffle the surface night and morning. No paddle-steamer will carry us "doon the watter" from the Broomielaw landing-stage as once it did: new bridges prevent ships coming into town. But promenades and walkways are pushing among derelict warehouses and one day it will be possible to walk the Clyde on either bank from Renfrew Castle to Rutherglen and beyond.

Near Old Kilpatrick (A814), 11 miles from the city center, the Erskine road bridge (toll) replaces a fond old landmark, the Erskine ferry. The next road crossing, going upstream, is the Clyde tunnel; actually it's two tunnels, one for northbound and one for southbound traffic.

Renfrew and Govan, just above the tunnel, are the first of the shipyard complexes. For all their cheap and dingy housing they are ancient settlements. Renfrew is the cradle of the royal house of Stuart: Walter the Steward acquired his first Scottish lands there in the 13th century. The Inchinnan church, one mile west of the town center, stands on 800-year-old foundations and in the churchyard there are Celtic stones, tombs of the crusading Templars and several "mortsafes"—iron cages built over graves to deter body-snatchers. Govan's kirkyard too has Celtic crosses and monuments. Here the numerous bridges of central Glasgow begin. You can see Glasgow University—founded 1451, not here but in the High Street farther east—on the more respectable north side, above large buildings which include the city art gallery and museum, and Kelvin Hall, the largest covered arena in Britain. Round them flows the Kelvin River through the park called Kelvingrove, down to the Clyde. In 1967 salmon reappeared in the Kelvin, giving hopes that antipollution measures were succeeding; but the environmentalists still have a lot of work on their hands.

If the river is not too clean, at least it flows fast, swerving among gentle hills. You may walk its banks for four miles without more than a distant glimpse of buildings, passing through Glasgow's botanic gardens. The large palm-house, Kibble Palace, once did duty as an assembly hall where Disraeli and Gladstone, 19th-century Prime Ministers, delivered their election addresses to the Scottish nation.

Near the Kelvin's confluence with the Clyde is a system of crescents and terraces which would not look out of place in the New Town of Edinburgh.

## Charles Rennie Mackintosh

If we leave the Clyde and climb through those terraces we shall soon be within sight of Renfrew Street, which runs parallel with a famous Glasgow thoroughfare, now partly pedestrianized, called Sauchiehall Street.

Cultural tourists and architectural students in Glasgow give Renfrew Street a high priority. There stands the prestigious Glasgow School of Art, the creation of Glasgow-born Charles Rennie Mackintosh. The building incorporates the Mackintosh Library. Like the Adam brothers 150 years before him, Mackintosh also designed the furniture and interior decor for his buildings, to make them one harmonious whole.

When he died in 1928 his name was scarcely known, least of all in Scotland. Now he is confirmed as a distinguished innovator in art and architecture. Deceptively plain kitchen cabinets by Mackintosh, which used to be broken up for firewood, now fetch high prices; and the discovery of a lost piece excites the international art markets. There is a Charles Rennie Mackintosh Centre at Queen's Cross, Glasgow and you may see examples of his work in the city art galleries and museums and at the University. Tearooms in the city, now converted to other uses, were also his work—notably Miss Cranston's Willow Tearooms, today part of a department store in East Sauchiehall Street.

## The Hielandman's Umbrella

Back to the Clyde. At the Broomielaw quay we pass under three bridges close together. The middle one, which carries a multitude of railroad tracks, also crosses the main shipping thoroughfare of Argyle Street to enter Glasgow Central station and is known to Glaswegians as the "Hielandman's Umbrella"—a draughty shelter for poverty-striken immigrants of long ago in the heart of Britain's wettest city.

Here there are promenades on either side of the Clyde, currently being extended. Near Victoria Bridge, in Stockwell Street, you will see a plaque on the birthplace of James McGill, founder of the Canadian university which bears his name. But an even more distinguished Glaswegian James was James Watt the engineer. And it was in Glasgow Green above Albert Bridge (with the exception of London's royal parks, Glasgow Green is the oldest public park in Britain) that James Watt walked one Sunday morning completing the calculations that were to bring about the advent of steam as motive power. It has been pointed out that in the strict Presbyterian climate of the day he risked a fine and a public rebuke for idling on the Lord's Day.

## "Dear Old Glasgow Toon"

We may continue along a riverside path to Rutherglen Bridge and on through Motherwell and Wishaw, the steel and coal towns. But it is not tourist country. Though we shall meet the Clyde again in more salubrious surroundings, for the present our route takes us uptown from Glasgow Green into the crisscross pattern of streets which constitutes the commercial, shopping and historic nucleus of "dear old Glasgow toon."

The Glasgow comedian Will Fyffe had a song in which those words occurred. And Glasgow is indeed dear to her inhabitants. Like some other ugly cities, the redeeming features of Glasgow are the warmth, cheerfulness and wry humor of the citizens and their love for their town, with all its faults. Once you have penetrated the accent, Glaswegians are the wittiest and most outgoing of all Scots. They do not sneer at culture either. Glasgow has one of the best civic collections of European paintings in Britain.

The Burrell art treasures, the nation's finest private collection, were bequeathed to Glasgow in 1945 but the city's atmosphere was not clean enough to receive them for open display. In 1983 a specially-built gallery in Pollok Park, three miles south of the city center, was completed. To celebrate the event, the trustees of the bequest bought a large and famous pot, the Warwick Vase. As we go to press, the Burrell gallery is due to open in October 1983 (opening hours as for other civic galleries and museums).

Continuing the city's surprisingly rich cultural vein, Glasgow is also the headquarters of the Scottish Opera and Scottish Ballet Companies and the Scottish National Orchestra.

## Historic Glasgow

For an ancient foundation, Glasgow is short on historical sights. In her palmy days the tobacco lords and sugar tycoons, rich on the Virginia and West Indies trade, destroyed whole streets to create mansions worthy of their status. We can only speculate what Candleriggs, Clayslaps, Cowcaddens and Goosedubs looked like in their heyday. St. Andrew's church, patronized by the rich merchants, stands forlorn on Glasgow Green. It is the oldest surviving classical church in Scotland, built 1739–1756. A short way north, beyond the Tolbooth steeple (1626) and modern Mercat Cross at the intersection called Glasgow Cross, you come to the High Street and the Old College, original site of Glasgow University, today reduced to a couple of plaques outside a railroad freight yard. But if you visit the present University in Kelvingrove, have a look at the porter's lodge which is built with stones from the original foundation.

In Castle Street, a continuation of the High Street, stands the house called Provand's Lordship. Built in 1471, it is probably Glasgow's oldest dwelling and it is believed that Kings James II and IV and Mary Queen of Scots lodged there at various times. It was a church house attached to Glasgow Cathedral and inhabited by a prebendary of Provand, the old name for the parish of Barlanark. Northwards again, near the disused Monkland Canal (off B806) stands Provan Hall (also 15th century), twin buildings on a courtyard, once the country retreat of the same prebendary. Both houses are open to the public.

Opposite Provand's Lordship you see the Cathedral, the only large Scottish church apart from St. Magnus Cathedral in Orkney to have survived the Reformation intact. It is dedicated to Glasgow's patron saint, Mungo (sometimes also known as St. Kentigern) and is said to stand on the site where that wandering monk built his humble chapel on the banks of the Molendinar Burn: the beginnings of Glasgow. The chapel has gone, the Molendinar is piped underground, the plain Gothic 12th- to 14th-century Cathedral itself has lost its main bell-tower and undergone changes for the worse . . . but the crypt, consecrated in 1197, adorned now with murals of the legends of St. Mungo, is worth a visit.

Castle Street and the High Street may well be the oldest thoroughfares in Scotland. A document refers to the existence in 540 of this route between Clyde and St. Mungo's chapel, a pathway known as the "King's Highway."

Glasgow's civic arms originate in a typical St. Mungo legend. The King of Strathclyde gave his wife a ring which she was rash enough to present to an admirer. The King obtained it by a ruse and threw it in the Clyde, then asked his wife what she had done with it. In her distress the Queen went to her confessor, St. Mungo, and asked his advice. He instructed her to fish in the river and—surprise!—the first salmon she landed had the ring in its jaws. If you study the Glasgow coat-of-arms you will see that the supporters are three salmon, one with a ring in its mouth.

## Let Glasgow Flourish!

Architectural vandalism has disturbed the plan, but you can still detect signs of a once-elegant city. Trongate, with its steeple dating from 1637 (a steeple without a church) and Argyle Street gradually converge on Sauchiehall Street as they march westward. Major shopping streets with Scotland's biggest department stores connect them. Glasgow, you are reminded, gave birth to Thomas Lipton, the grocer turned America's Cup yachting millionaire; and John Anderson the universal provider, the "inventor of elevenpence three-farthings," the canny marketing dodge whereby a price is made to sound less by quoting the nearest possible figure down the scale—as it might be 99 cents instead of a dollar.

The city's official center is George Square, between Argyle Street and Queen Street station. It is a large quadrangle banked with flowers and shrubs and lined with the florid variegated marble of the City Chambers (Town Hall). More interesting is the network of streets which call back the yesterdays of mercantile wealth: Virginia Street, Miller Street, Glassford Street, all off George Square. The French-style palaces with their steep mansard roofs and cupolas were once tobacco warehouses. Inside them are shops and offices, while here and there you may trace the elaborately-carved mahogany galleries where the auctions took place. Two large prestigious libraries, Stirling's and the Mitchell, enshrine the names of two 18th-century tobacco barons who built them as their private residences.

Westward again you negotiate rows of blackened tenements which on closer inspection turn out to be dignified Victorian terraces. Their tiled halls and spacious apartments amaze visitors. Still moving west, you arrive at Kelvinside and the western parkland, the quarter we started at.

#### "A Sweet Green Place"

"All Glasgow needs," said an architectural pundit, "is a bath and a little loving care." She is getting her bath; even the Clyde is getting a bath and one day we shall see riverside drives comparable to those along the Seine in Paris and the Danube in Budapest; glass-canopied river boats are already promised. One day Glasgow may be again the "sweet green place" which the word is supposed to mean.

The city aspires to be a tourist center, having now acquired what she has long lacked, some first-class city-center hotels. She is ringed with splendid scenery and has always been a wonderful starting point for day trips: Loch Lomond half an hour; Clyde coast 40 minutes; Trossachs 50 minutes.

If you still feel that Glasgow is not for you, remember that the best urban expressway in Britain soars across the city and you may traverse the whole conurbation east to west without meeting a stop light.

# PRACTICAL INFORMATION FOR GLASGOW

 **GETTING INTO TOWN FROM THE AIRPORTS.** A frequent express coach service links Glasgow airport with all major bus and rail termini in the city. From the airport to Buchanan Street bus station takes 25 minutes and costs 60p. There are also bus and rail services several times a day between Prestwick international airport and central Glasgow. (For timetables contact the Anderston Cross bus station or Buchanan Street Travel Center.) The bus fare for the 33-mile journey (70 minutes) is £2.20. Taxis are available from both airports. Expect to pay around £4 from Glasgow airport and £21 from Prestwick.

 **HOTELS.** The city is now better equipped with hotels of all categories than it has ever been—but that is not saying much. Glasgow was historically a very poor oasis for the traveler. Nonetheless there are now some big city-center hotels of both expensive and moderate character and some good and reasonable small hotels and guest-houses in the suburbs, with easy transportation into town. A feature of Glasgow's hotels is the excellent breakfasts, normally included in the price of the room. All the larger hotels have restaurants which are open to non-residents.

*Deluxe*

**Albany,** Bothwell Street (tel. 248 2656). 251 rooms, all with bath. Glasgow's latest hotel, centrally situated. Its two restaurants are highly praised.

**Holiday Inn,** Argyle Street (tel. 226 5430). 311 rooms, 305 with bath. Another city-center innovation of the most up-to-date kind. Has French restaurant, coffee shop and terrace buffet.

# GLASGOW 151

## *Expensive*

**Beacons,** 7 Park Terrace (tel. 332 9438). 26 rooms, 25 with bath. Quiet and dignified hotel overlooking rustic Kelvingrove Park yet close to main downtown area.

**Bellahouston,** 517 Paisley Road West (tel. 427 3146). 72 rooms with bath. Close to big park, palace of art, all-weather sports center. Impressive range of amenities considering it is at lower end of price scale.

**Central,** Gordon Street (tel. 221 9680). 211 rooms, 170 with bath. Typical Victorian railroad hotel with thick carpets, mob-capped chambermaids and ample rooms from another era. Its *Malmaison* restaurant has venerable ultra-respectable dinner-date reputation.

**Ingram,** 201 Ingram Street (tel. 248 4401). 90 rooms with bath. In a city-center street restricted for space. Business people crowd its public rooms. A friendly, well-run place.

**North British,** George Square (tel. 332 6711). 130 rooms, 90 with bath. Another old-fashioned railroad hotel, but with updated decor. Continuous meals and drinks service, 7 A.M.–11 P.M.

**Pond,** Great Western Road (tel. 334 8161). 137 rooms, all with bath. The pond it overlooks is no Loch Lomond but it is well sited for heading that way, on main exit from city.

**White House,** 12 Clevedon Crescent (tel. 339 9375). 35 apartments, all with bath. Stately terraced houses converted into luxury hotel suites. Maid service. No evening meals.

## *Moderate*

**Buckingham,** 31 Buckingham Terrace (tel. 334 4847). 31 rooms, 13 with bath. Meal service does not quite match standards of room comfort and amenities.

**Burnside,** East Kilbride Road (tel. 634 1276). 16 rooms, 13 with bath. Some distance from center, but highly rated for all-round quality.

**Cavendish,** 1 Devonshire Gardens (tel. 339 2001). 13 rooms, 1 with bath. Near western exit from city. Quiet situation, helpful staff.

**Glasgow Centre,** 377 Argyle Street (tel. 248 2355). 122 rooms, 120 with bath. New construction on main shopping thoroughfare. Traditional Scottish and vegetarian options in restaurant.

**Kenilworth,** 5 Queen Street (tel. 221 5151). 38 rooms, 4 with bath. Not very spacious but good for meals and has long had its faithful clientele.

**Royal,** 106 Sauchiehall Street (tel. 332 3416). 45 rooms, 15 with bath. Much of this city-center street is all-pedestrian. The hotel has been commended for its rooms, services and especially food.

**Royal Stuart,** 318 Clyde Street (tel. 248 4261). 112 rooms, 70 with bath. Exceptionally efficient service—and needs to be, since this hotel is the venue for many receptions and large functions.

**Tinto Firs,** 470 Kilmarnock Road (tel. 637 2353). 30 rooms, 24 with bath. More country-house than city style, on park-like south side but handy for center. Good reports of food and room furnishings.

## *Inexpensive*

**Apsley,** 903 Sauchiehall Street (tel. 339 4999). 17 rooms, 5 with bath. Comfort and cuisine well above its price level.

**Crookston,** 90 Crookston Road (tel. 882 6142). 23 rooms, 10 with bath. Quiet atmosphere. Food writers have praised generous cuisine.

**Devonshire,** 5 Devonshire Gardens (tel. 334 1308). 20 rooms, 3 with bath. Pleasant situation just out of earshot of city bustle. Evening meal 6 P.M. sharp.

**Hazelcourt,** 232 Renfrew Street (tel. 332 7737). 9 rooms. Better-than-average rooms, friendly staff, but best to eat out.

**Marie Stuart,** 46 Queen Mary Avenue (tel. 423 6363). 23 rooms, 1 with bath. Excellent service, popular bar.

**Queen's Park,** 10 Balvicar Drive (tel. 423 1123). 37 rooms. Good all-round standard, flexible meal hours.

**Smith's,** 963 Sauchiehall Street (tel. 339 6363). 28 rooms. Not highly rated for food but otherwise comfortable and conveniently situated. No evening meals.

### Guest Houses

**Belle Vue Guest House,** 163 Hamilton Road (tel. 778 1077). 11 rooms, 1 with bath. Rather out of the way but reasonable value for modest price.

**Chez Nous Guest House,** 33 Hillhead Street (tel. 334 2977). 14 rooms. Attentive staff, imaginative menu, meals until 9.30 P.M. (many guest houses serve only high tea in evenings).

### Student Halls of Residence

Accommodations at around £5 to £10 per night bed and breakfast (£33 to £87 per week full board) per person are offered at the city's educational establishments during vacation periods, usually a month at Easter and three months in summer. Single and double rooms are available, also a full meal service. Rooms are bright and modern, but bathroom facilities must be shared. Applications are made to the Warden of each establishment.

**Baird Hall,** University of Strathclyde, 460 Sauchiehall Street (tel. 332 6415). 190 rooms. In city center. Open all year round.

**College Hostel,** Jordanhill College, 76 Southbrae Drive (tel. 959 7057). 50 rooms. Jul.–Aug. only.

**Dalrymple Hall,** Glasgow University, 22 Belhaven Terrace West (tel. 339 5271). 134 rooms. Easter and summer.

**Queen Margaret Hall,** Glasgow University, 55 Bellshaugh Road (tel. 334 2192). 340 rooms, nearly all single. Meals highly rated. Easter only.

**Queen's College,** 183 Dorchester Avenue (tel. 339 8481). 89 rooms. Inexpensive. Open Jul.–Sep.

Glasgow University has other accommodations in west and central locations, including the self-catering **Maclay Hall.** For information contact the Accommodation Office, 4 University Gardens, Glasgow G12 8QJ (tel. 339 8855).

### Youth Hostels

Up to £4.25 per night. Contact Scottish Y.H.A., 10 Woodlands Road, Glasgow G3 (tel. 332 3004).

 **HOW TO GET ABOUT. By bus.** Glasgow and suburbs are served by a comprehensive network of city buses, fares averaging 10p–15p per mile. Short journeys to outer suburbs begin at Anderston Cross (tel. 248 7432) and Buchanan Street (tel. 332 7133) bus stations. The former serves west and south, the latter north and east. Buses for Glasgow airport leave from both stations. Day and half-day tours in and around Glasgow are operated by W. Alexander & Sons, Buchanan Street bus station (tel. 332 0025) and Haldane's of Cathcart, Devlin Road (tel. 637 2234) at fares of £1.50 upwards.

**By subway.** Glasgow's Underground (subway), built when Victoria was Queen, was completely modernized and reopened in 1979. It consists of a circle embracing the city center and going under the Clyde. Two of its 15 stations give

Craigievar Castle (Grampian) — one of the fairytale castles belonging
to the National Trust for Scotland.

The Forth Rail Bridge, with its slender modern sister, the Road Bridge, behind.

Edinburgh — The Castle Rock with National Gallery of Scotland in the foreground.

The Brig o' Doon (Alloway) — a celebrated spot in the heart of Burns' country.

Melrose Abbey — One of several great ruined abbeys in the Border country.

The Standing Stones of Callanish (Lewis) — neolithic monuments in the Outer Hebrides, which run Stonehenge a close second.

access to British Rail stations: Queen Street on the east and Partick on the west. Fares average 20p between stations.

There are surface rail connections between central Glasgow and the suburbs with very frequent commuter services. Queen Street station serves five routes to west, north and east; Central station nine routes to west and south. A bus service links the two stations.

**By taxi.** Glasgow's taxis are like London's and Edinburgh's; black and old-fashioned-looking with yellow TAXI signs on their high roofs. When the TAXI light is on the vehicle is available for hire. Taxis cruise the city and there are ranks at all rail and bus stations and in the principal squares. Fares for one adult passenger are 50p for the first mile and 35p thereafter, with a 10p per mile surcharge between midnight and 6 A.M. Additional passengers pay 5p each, however short or long the journey.

**By car.** Unlike Edinburgh, Glasgow is well organized for the motorist. The trans-city expressway has removed much through traffic and parking is easy in most central districts except around George Square, where it is controlled and parking meters are extensively used. There are multi-story parks open 24 hours a day at Anderston Cross, Cambridge Street, George Street, Mitchell Street, Port Dundas Road and Waterloo Street; and many surface short-term car-parks.

**By boat.** New Clyde bridges have effectively sealed off central Glasgow's river from all but light private craft. In summer there are down-river cruises from Stobcross Quay.

 **TOURIST INFORMATION.** Head Post Office, George Square (tel. 248 2882). Canadian Consulate, 195 West George Street (tel. 248 3026). (The American Consulate is in Edinburgh.) Customs & Excise, 21 India Street (tel. 221 3828). Greater Glasgow Passenger Transport Executive, 103 St. Vincent Street (tel. 248 3371). (For city bus and Underground enquiries.) British Airways, 85 Buchanan Street (tel. 332 9666). British Rail passenger enquiries 221 3223, sleeper reservations 221 2305.

The principal Information Bureau is in George Square, tel. 221 7371. Guide books, maps, calendars of events and timetables are supplied. You may book accommodations here for Glasgow or other parts of Scotland. Open Jun.–Sept. weekdays 9–9, Sun. 2–9, Oct.–May weekdays only, 9–5.

Remember that if you are calling a Glasgow number from anywhere outside the Glasgow area you must prefix it with the Glasgow code 041.

 **MUSEUMS. City Art Gallery and Museum,** Kelvingrove. Magnificent fine arts collection, notable displays of silver, jewelry, ceramics, arms and armor. Open weekdays 10–5, Sun. 2–5.

**Haggs Castle,** 100 St. Andrew's Drive. Museum of social history, emphasis on children at work and play through the centuries. Activities for young visitors. Open weekdays 10–5, Sun. 2–5.

**Hunterian Museum.** Glasgow University, Gilmorehill. Glasgow's oldest museum (1807). Zoology collection bequeathed by famous royal physician William Hunter. Incorporates new *Hunterian Art Gallery* with rare works of James McNeill Whistler and Charles Rennie Mackintosh. Open weekdays 10–5, Sat. 9.30–1.

**Museum of Transport,** 25 Albert Drive. Trains, buses, bicycles, streetcars, horse-drawn vehicles and model ships. Old subway station. History of Scottish automobile industry. Open weekdays 10–5, Sun. 2–5.

**People's Palace,** Glasgow Green. A 100-year-old city museum illustrating textiles and shipbuilding, feminist movement, landmarks of Glasgow's political and cultural history. Open weekdays 10–5, Sun. 2–5.

**Pollok House,** 2060 Pollokshaws Road. An Adam mansion in parkland, housing important fine arts. Open weekdays 10–5, Sun. 2–5.

**Third Eye Centre,** 350 Sauchiehall Street. Continuous exhibitions and music recitals, concerts etc. Open Tues.–Sat. 10–5.30, Sun. 2–5.30.

**ENTERTAINMENT AND NIGHT LIFE. Theaters.** Glasgow is home to the Scottish Opera, the Scottish Ballet and the Scottish National Orchestra. There are winter and spring performances in the *City Hall* and the *Theatre Royal* (which a leading music critic has described as "the most enchanting opera theater in the United Kingdom"). The huge *Kelvin Hall* stages promenade concerts in June, noted for their informality and the enthusiasm of a young audience. More than a million people pass through the Kelvin Hall's massive doors every year to attend a variety of events.

There are five other theaters: the King's for light entertainment and musicals; the *Apollo,* mostly rock and jazz celebrity concerts; the *Pavilion,* traditional variety shows; the *Mitchell* at the Mitchell Library, straight plays; and, most prestigious of all, the *Glasgow Citizen's Theatre* in the Gorbals, which has built a reputation for serious and experimental drama.

**Movies, Dancing, Discos.** The city has a good choice of cinemas. The big ones are the *ABC Centre* and *Scala Centre* in Sauchiehall Street. Three large cinemas in Renfield Street are the *Odeon Centre, Regent* and *Classic.* At 97 Eglinton Street is the *Coliseum.* The *Glasgow Film Theatre,* noted for important Continental and avant-garde movies, is on Rose Street, just off Sauchiehall Street.

Discos abound in clubs and pubs. You will see them advertised principally along Argyle Street, Sauchiehall Street and connecting streets. The free monthly events guide called *Glasgow Leisure,* which you may pick up in hotel lobbies and at stationers and bookstalls, gives details of disco dates month by month.

The principal dance halls are *Tiffany's* in Sauchiehall Street and the *Plaza* at Eglinton Toll.

**SHOPPING.** Glasgow is the best city in Scotland for inexpensive shopping. You will find some of Britain's largest and most up-to-date department stores in the pedestrian areas of Sauchiehall Street and Buchanan Street and along the Argyll (note spelling!) Arcade. Among larger stores which have preserved their Scottish character is Arnott's in the Sauchiehall Street Centre. Smaller old-established businesses and modern boutiques are also plentiful in this area and along Argyle Street and the narrower streets running north.

For jewelry, craft items and souvenirs, go to the Argyll Arcade, or to the Robin Hood gift house at 11 St. Vincent Place of (for more precious items) to Reid & Todd at 202 Sauchiehall Street.

At 57 West Regent Street you will find Glasgow's "Victorian Village" of 25 antique shops and a tea room, all under one roof. A picturesque survival of another Glasgow—but only a pale shadow of its former self—is the age-old Saturday flea market of the "Barrows" in the Gallowgate east of Glasgow Cross.

**DINING OUT.** There are a few old-established restaurants in Glasgow and a great number of fairly new ones which have yet to prove themselves. The prestige rendezvous are in, or annexed to, the large city-center hotels. But there are others, and recent years have brought a few good Indian, Pakistani and Chinese restaurants; also a mixed bag of Italian ones. Most restaurants are licensed to sell liquor up to 11 P.M., but evening meal service tends to cease at a much earlier hour.

### Deluxe

**Ambassador,** 19 Blythswood Square (tel. 221 3530). International cuisine. Pre-theater meals. Dancing every evening except Mon.

**Four Seasons,** Albany Hotel, Bothwell Street (tel. 248 2656). Continental and Scottish cuisine. Impressive layout and discreet atmosphere. Dancing.

### Expensive

**La Bonne Auberge,** 7a Park Terrace (tel. 332 9438). Quiet surroundings and discriminating French menu.

**Fountain,** Charing Cross (tel. 332 6396). Used by Glaswegians for special occasions. Cheaper *Pub Bistro* downstairs.

**Il Pescatore,** 148 Weedlands Road (tel. 332 3045). Italian seafood.

**Malmaison,** Central Hotel, Gordon Street (tel. 221 9680). International cuisine à la carte in refined surroundings, ideal for tête-à-tête.

**Rogano,** 11 Exchange Place (tel. 248 6687). An old favorite of Glasgow's diners-out. Specializes in French dishes and elaborate seafood.

### Moderate

**American Burger and Wine Cave,** Broadway Hotel, 80 Glassford Street (tel. 552 5761). Open all day and half the night. Emphasis on Burgundy and beef, from fillet steaks to hamburgers.

**Berkeley,** 229 North Street (tel. 221 1555). Large licensed restaurant open till midnight with cabaret. Bar lunches. Open Sun.

**Buttery,** 652 Argyle Street (tel. 221 8188). Good plain cooking in a civilized atmosphere. Vegetarians catered for.

**Ceilidh Place,** Lorne Hotel, 923 Sauchiehall Street (tel. 334 4891). Open till 10 P.M. daily with average cuisine but interesting musical entertainment, mainly Scottish.

**La Costiera,** 51 West Regent Street (tel. 331 1980). Continental and predominantly Italian. Good place for a civilized meal late Sun. evening. Open till midnight.

**Danish Food Centre,** 56 St. Vincent Street (tel. 221 0518). Open sandwiches and cold buffet the specialties. Open till 11 P.M., not Sun. À la carte *Copenhagen Room,* verging on expensive. This Scandinavian invasion has been welcomed by staid Glaswegians.

**La Fourchette,** Central Hotel, Gordon Street (tel. 221 9680). Superior quick-lunch buffet offering Scottish culinary specialties.

**Lanterna,** 35 Hope Street (tel. 221 9160). Italian trattoria, very good home-made pasta and country dishes. Wines not remarkable.

**Marigold,** 96 Renfield Street (tel. 332 5261). Chinese food. Popular with young Glaswegians. Dancing some evenings. Open late, including Sun.

**Moussaka House,** 36 Kelvingrove Street (tel. 332 2510). Greek and other Continental food with suitable music and decor. Open till midnight, also Sun. evenings.

**Rock Garden,** 73 Queen Street (tel. 221 2200). Good à la carte. Alternatively, American-style buffet midday and early evening. Open late, including Sun.

**Sloan's,** Argyll Arcade (tel. 221 8917). Sturdy British cuisine among unique decor of etched glass and Victorian mahogany panelling. Proletarian delicacies of yesteryear figure on the menu: pig's trotters, sheep's head, mutton pies.

*Inexpensive*

**Ad Lib,** 111 Hope Street (tel. 248 7102). American-style hamburger joint; open to 2 A.M., Sun. 1 A.M.

**Arnott's,** Sauchiehall Street Centre (tel. 332 6833). Example of the department-store restaurants where most Glasgow shoppers and business people go for an alcoholic lunch or a pot of tea with buttered scones. Arnott's is not licensed to sell liquor but has lunch tables fastidiously laid, waitress service, nice cutlery and china. Evening openings till 7, Thur. only.

**Fraser's,** 21 Buchanan Street (tel. 221 3880). Another city-center department store which makes a feature of Scottish dishes.

**Mario's,** 168 Ingram Street (tel. 552 2636). Adequate for a swift or leisurely lunch or tea. Unlicensed, but you are welcome to bring a bottle of wine.

**Lahore Tandoori,** 253 Argyle Street (tel. 221 5325). Punjabi and European cuisine; open late, closed Sun.

**Lucky Star,** 84 Sauchiehall Street (tel. 332 6265). Big and unpretentious with good Chinese food from extensive menu; open late, closed Sun.

 **PUBS.** There are 1,300 in Glasgow, 260 in the central square mile, so the best advice is to look in and see if you like what you see. Visitors cannot honestly be recommended to the traditional Glasgow pub. Many appear to be run by ex-prizefighters and superannuated soccer players for the exclusive benefit of burly shipyard workers and aged problem drinkers and have not altered much since a 19th-century French visitor described them as "a living illustration of some unwritten page of Dante's *Inferno.*" Though some formerly notorious dives have gone stridently upmarket with gaudy tartan-and-plastic decor, Glasgow pubs lack the individualistic character of those of Edinburgh; and a request for anything but whisky or "half and half" (whisky and strong ale) is likely to brand you a suspicious stranger. The best places to drink in, particularly for women, are the well-stocked, well-run bars and lounges attached to the larger hotels. In central Glasgow we recommend:

**Ambassador,** Blythswood Square. Sophisticated cocktail bar.

**Charlie Parker's,** 21 Royal Exchange Square. American bar and diner, open to midnight or later, Sun. included.

**Curlers,** 256 Byres Road. Scots nights, music and song, inexpensive restaurant upstairs.

**De Quincey's,** 17 Renfield Street. Open Sun. evening, has cold buffet lunch weekdays.

**Devil's Elbow,** North British Hotel, George Square. Probably the most popular bar in central Glasgow. Good selection of malt whiskies.

**Le Provencal,** Royal Exchange Square. Bistro-type bar, good selection of beers and wines.

**Tavern in the Town,** 152 Bath Street. Attached to a privately-owned hotel. Real ale, genuine atmosphere.

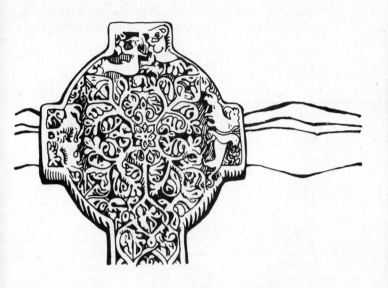

# A COAT OF MANY COLORS

## *Strathclyde*

Those grand solitudes you see when you fly in to Glasgow airport or Prestwick, that jigsaw puzzle of firths and straits and interlocking islands: that is Strathclyde. There must be some mistake, you feel. Is not Strathclyde the most densely-populated Region in Scotland? Yes, it contains more inhabitants than all the other regions of Scotland put together. But it also contains large areas of no population at all.

Strathclyde wears a coat of many colors. Every aspect of Scottish life, character and scenery is to be found in a 400-mile-journey through the Region (the same distance as from Edinburgh to London), from the northern tip of the island of Coll in the western isles to the Pentland Hills not far south of Edinburgh and on by the source of the Clyde to the coast again a short way north of Stranraer, Scotland's most southerly harbor.

Historically, Strathclyde embraces two of the four ancient kingdoms into which Scotland was once divided: a territory called Strathclyde, maintained by the original Britons in cooperation with their kinfolk of Cumbria (England) and Wales, a land they had to defend against Picts from the Highlands and Scots from Ireland; and Dalriada, afterwards Argyll, the kingdom established by those same colonizing Scots. It is only 13 miles across the sea from the Mull of Kintyre in Strathclyde to Torr Head in Antrim, Northern Ireland. The place-names of

Strathclyde commemorate many Irish saints—eight of them on the island of Bute alone—and they have left their stones and ruined chapels in many rural places.

Glasgow, once proclaimed the second city of the British Empire, has shrunk a little but she still sprawls over the middle belt of the Region. Her river, the Clyde, comes in from Tweedsmuir 60 miles away and flows out down a channel which has been Scotland's industrial gateway to the world for 200 years. A maze of sinuous channels breaks its northern shores: the sea-lochs which take you deep into Highland glens and mountains. The southern shores are smooth, prolific with greenery and dotted with white houses and small towns: commuter country, the yachting-and-golfing enclave.

This country gets a lot of sunshine, a lot of rain and little frost. At certain seasons an almost embarrassing wealth of primroses, wild cherry blossom, bluebells and anemones are reflected in loch water of astonishing clarity. In March and April the turreted country houses are immersed in drifts of daffodils, while palmettoes and eucalyptus trees grow in sheltered places. If the Scots of this western lochland could live on scenery they would be rich indeed. Instead, Strathclyde is one of the most deprived regions in the European Economic Community.

This is the country of Scott's *The Abbot* (which describes Cathcart Castle and the battleground of Langside, afterwards swallowed up by Glasgow); of the humorous tales of the coasting skipper "Para Handy," told by Neil Munro; of the novels *Kidnapped* and *Catriona* by Robert Louis Stevenson; of James Boswell the biographer and David Livingstone the explorer; of James Watt and Henry Bell and William Symington and many other pioneers of the industrial revolution; and above all of Robert Burns the national poet.

Strathclyde's offshore islands, like those of Highland and Islands Region, are barriers against the Atlantic. They include the geological freak of Staffa and the holy isle of Iona, burial place of Celtic kings. They also include away-from-it-all corners which rock stars, politicians, actresses and north-country industrialists have made their own. Fingers of mainland can easily be mistaken for islands, so tenuous is their grasp. Down the Kintyre peninsula, which is attached by a strip of land narrow enough for fishermen to drag their boats across it, you may drive 75 miles and dabble your toes in salt water at every pause before you come to the open sea.

In Strathclyde the smell of the sea is always in your nostrils. You can spend a whole day disentangling yourself from the skeins of lochs and isthmuses, looking for the sea. And when you reach it (on the Firth of Lorne, for instance, when you come to the tiny stone link with Seil island, known correctly as the "Bridge over the Atlantic") it is still hard to see past the crowding islands on the western horizon.

We cover Glasgow and Clydeside in the previous chapter. Here we cover the rest of Strathclyde Region, firstly the districts north of Glasgow, secondly the southwestern area and thirdly the islands.

### South from Glencoe

South from Glencoe, the A82 is a fast winding road over the Black Mount to Tyndrum, thence by winding valleys to Crianlarich and down the full length of Loch Lomond (see Central Region chapter); and so to Glasgow. Many Glaswegians make the 150-mile round trip on winter weekends to sample the rudimentary—but improving—winter-sports facilities in the Glencoe area.

Near Kingshouse Hotel at the top of Glencoe a minor road (unclassified) meanders away through savage Glen Etive to the head of Loch Etive where, it you had a boat, you could sail 20 miles through the loneliest country to the sea at Connell Ferry near Oban (A85). In the other direction, from Taynuilt (A85), you can do this trip in summer on a regular small-boat service—as Wordsworth and his sister Dorothy did early in the 19th century. They loved it.

### Oban

We meet the A85 by continuing down the A828 from Ballachulish instead of turning left for Glencoe. It crosses Loch Etive at Connell by a bridge built for trains; the railroad is now closed.

Oban, most lively of West Highland mainland resorts, faces a bewildering tangle of isles in the Firth of Lorne. It is a great yachting port—for the experienced!—as well as a ferry port for the islands and a collection point for cargoes of shellfish. With its russet-stone, white-painted houses it has a venerable air, but most buildings were the result of an influx of early-20th-century vacationeers. The only ancient monuments are slightly suspect ones: the Dog Stone east of the bay, where the hero Finn MacCool (in Scotland called Fingal) tethered his mastiff Bran; and Diarmid's Pillar at the head of Loch Nell, two and a half miles from town, where Diarmid the founder of the Clan Campbell is said to be buried (date unknown, but long before Colin Campbell from whom the present chief takes his name was slain hereabouts in 1294).

The Roman Coliseum lookalike on the hill above the town is no antiquity. It was the unfinished masterwork of a 19th-century Oban banker named MacCaig and is known as "MacCaig's Folly." He went bankrupt trying to immortalize himself with that grandiose temple and simultaneously provide work for distressed fishermen. The portholed shell on the hill symbolizes more than one set of wrecked hopes.

### Campbell Country

All this is Campbell country. The Campbell's war-cry is "Cruachan!", the name of a mountain above the A85 near Loch Awe. The great seat of the Campbell chiefs, currently the Dukes of Argyll, is at Inveraray near the head of Loch Fyne at the end of the A819, a roundabout route from Oban. Inveraray Castle is a smart place with a self-satisfied air, dominating a well-disciplined town. Here Dr. Johnson was entertained in 1773 and here, as Boswell tells, the celebrated lexicographer first tasted Scotch whisky. At the castle you can inspect

items which successive Dukes of Argyll have salvaged from the Tobermory galleon, a vessel from the Spanish Armada which sank (legend
says it was blown up by a daring Scot) in the Sound of Mull near
Tobermory. The turmoil of the years round Inveraray is introduced
into Scott's *The Legend of Montrose,* Robert Louis Stevenson's *Catriona* and Neil Munro's *John Splendid.*

Going round the head of Loch Fyne from Inveraray, you have a
choice of several routes, all leading towards Glasgow or the shores of
the Firth of Clyde. The lochs are deeper, the mountains steeper and the
landscape more compressed than in the relatively wide open spaces of
Highland Region, There is more traffic at weekends and there are more
walkers and cyclists in summer. Far from the sea you may hear the
bleat of a steamship's siren, for all the harbors along the lochs are
served with ferryboats and cruising vessels.

The short run to Glasgow from Inveraray (44 miles) goes over Rest
and be Thankful, notorious in days of automobile reliability trials, a
shoulder of Ben Arthur (2,891 feet), which from the configuration of
its peak is affectionately known as The Cobbler; and joins the Loch
Lomondside road (A82). Proceeding a little farther down the Loch
Fyne shore opposite Inveraray (A815), you can thread the chopped and
broken hills of the Argyll National Forest Park—locals call it the
"Duke of Argyll's Bowling Green"—and come out at Dunoon on the
Firth of Clyde at another delta of intricately-winding lochs. In this
district you are for ever taking sharp turns as the shimmering tentacles
of the sea cut into your path. Every lochside village has its steamer pier
and every pier its scheduled service of passenger boats to another quiet
little place round the corner. At some, nothing ever seems to happen
apart from the coming and going of the ferries.

## Mull of Kintyre

We retrace our steps, as you often must if you are to give this
labyrinthine land of Argyll its due, and go south again from Inveraray
to the peninsula of Kintyre (A83), which is 70 miles long. First stop
is Crarae Lodge, the horticulturist's challenge to the myriad wild flowers which Nature has assembled on the shores of Loch Fyne. Crarae's
exotic blooms and shrubs, notably azaleas, at their best in June, help
explain why rich English landowners for two centuries have sought
Scottish gardeners. The setting, under hills on the loch shore, comple-
ments the floral display.

Kintyre's chief town is Campbeltown but long before you arrive
there the intrusive sea-lochs have almost cut through the peninsula.
The nine-mile neck of land at Lochgilphead (A83) was severed by
Thomas Telford between 1793 and 1817 when he built the Crinan
Canal. Nowadays it is used by yachts and the Loch Fyne fishing fleet.
Tarbert (still A83) straddles a narrow saddle of land. Like other Scottish Tarberts it was a place where fishermen could manhandle boats
from one coast to another and save themselves long voyages—an
etymological connection, perhaps, with the Latin *traho,* "I drag."

Campbeltown, at the end of a narrow corniche road (B842) which
runs for 30 miles only a few yards above the sea's edge, is an anchorage

for fishing vessels. Superior whiskies are distilled here. A richly decorated Celtic cross overlooks the harbor: not of great antiquity but a reminder that Kiaran, a saint who antedated Columba himself, made this inlet his home. The hamlet of New Orleans four miles away (unclassified road) appears to have no connection with its transatlantic namesake.

From Campbeltown, the B843 and a disused railroad cross to Machrihanish on the west side of the peninsula. This was a historic railroad, the only narrow-gauge system in Scotland, only six miles long but grandiloquently known as the "Railway of the Atlantic." It was detached from the nearest mainline station by 100 miles and up to 1932, when the last train ran, the small resort and golfing center of Machrihanish could boast itself the westernmost railroad station in Britain.

The B842 from Campbeltown terminates at Southend. You may take a fairly rough track to the Mull (promontory) of Kintyre. The cliffs here are imposing and honeycombed with stalactite caves. The coast of Antrim in Northern Ireland and Rathlin Island where Bruce shared a cave with the spider seem only a jump away.

If you return north by the west-coast road (A83) up Kintyre you will find at Tayinloan a small ferryboat which serves Gigha ("Gear") three miles away; an isle whose owner at Achamore House created famous subtropical gardens.

## Bute and Arran

On the sea-route from Kintyre to Glasgow lie two easily accessible islands folded in the arms of the Argyll mainland. Arran, bold and shapely with several summits of 2,500 feet and glens with steep torrents rushing seawards on all sides, is the sort of place where city-dwellers aspire to own holiday cottages—and many do. Lamlash, Brodick and Lochranza are vacation resorts too and Brodick Castle is one of the commanding stately homes of the west.

Bute also has its aristocratic establishments: Mount Stuart, ancestral home of the Marquesses of Bute; and Kames Castle, which competes with Dunvegan (Skye, Highland and Islands) and Traquair (Borders) for the title of oldest continuously-inhabited house in Scotland. Bute is undulating and pastoral, a stopover for migratory geese and other wildfowl and a vacation isle with a long history. The early Stuart kings, 600 years ago, relaxed at Rothesay Castle. One of them made his eldest son Duke of Rothesay, a title still borne by the Prince of Wales, the monarch's eldest son. These old Firth of Clyde castles give the heir to the throne no fewer than three out of his five titles. He is Duke of Rothesay. He is Earl of Carrick, from Robert the Bruce's Carrick Castle whose ruins you can see on the west side of Loch Goil near Lochgoilhead. And he is Baron Renfrew, from the castle in the ancient burgh of Renfrew, close to Glasgow, which was the feudal citadel of Walter the Steward, progenitor of the Stuart dynasty.

If you hear the expression "doon the watter" from the lips of Glasgow people it refers to the beloved excursion to Rothesay in the old Clyde steamers from the city's Broomielaw landing-stage. One of them, the *Waverley,* the oldest paddle-steamer afloat, still operates in the Firth of Clyde.

Rothesay town presents a facade of hotels and boardinghouses to its bay. Up steep wynds you see the castle ruins and cameos of an introverted past. If you walk across the island you will pass silent lochs, hedgerows loaded with autumn fruits; and, two miles from Rothesay, the cottage called Woodend in which Edmund Kean the English tragedian, satiated with London's acclaim, found in 1826 his "loophole of retreat."

Bute's scenic wonder is the Kyles, a narrow strait between the mainland and the island's northern corner. On a boat-trip through the Kyles of Bute you can almost reach out and touch the rocks on either side as your skipper twists and turns among them. Two lifelike pinnacles, the "Maids of Bute," have been painted up to look like real female figures. One charming little port of call is Tighnabruaich, the archetypal lochside village, on the mainland shore. Until recently it was virtually inaccessible by land, but now there is a road (A886) from Strachur on Loch Fyne.

If you have an automobile on Bute, the Kyles ferryboat will deliver you in five minutes to the districts of the Argyll Forest Park.

## Firth of Clyde

Shipping entering the Firth of Clyde has Arran and Bute on one side and the coastal towns of Ardrossan, Largs, Fairlie and Wemyss Bay ("Weems") on the other—all of them delightful little ferryports for the islands in the Firth. At Largs in 1263 King Alexander III of Scotland repelled the last Norse invasion. From that harbor and also from Brodick on Arran you may cross to the two Cumbrae isles and their town Millport. The larger has a marine biology station and a kirkyard with the tomb of the 19th-century minister James Adam who used to pray for "the Great and Little Cumbraes and adjacent islands of Britain and Ireland."

The gentle air of this stretch of the Firth, for many years an innocent playground, is now mocked by the expanding NATO base and deepwater harbor works at Fairlie; by the nuclear power station of Hunterston near Largs; and by the Polaris nuclear-submarine base in Holy Loch above Dunoon on the opposite shore. It is said that the loch took its name from a consignment of earth from the Holy Land, destined for the foundations of Glasgow cathedral but sunk off Dunoon in the wreck of the ship which carried it.

Sailing higher up the Firth, shipping for Glasgow turns east at the Cloch lighthouse. The Cloch is the first, or last, of a dead-straight line of lightships and lighthouses down the British and Irish coasts which lead from the Bay of Biscay to the narrows of the Clyde. The Cloch stands beside the A78, which runs from Gourock to Wemyss Bay, and is visitable.

Here the Firth is two miles wide. On the north bank stands Dunoon with all the trappings of a seaside resort—pier, promenade, gardens, theater, cinemas, bowling greens, golf courses—but little of noise or stridency except on days of the Cowal Highland Gathering (annually, end of August) when upwards of 150 pipe bands compete for trophies. The town is an excellent touring center with many opportunities for bus and boat excursions, the most popular Clyde resort after Rothesay.

On Castle Hill, see the monument to "Highland Mary," whom Robert Burns loved and lost ("Highland" because she worked on the south side of the Firth, south of the Highland line; but came from Dunoon, which is north of that once-important divide).

Dunoon Castle, now a heap of ruins, was once the principal Campbell residence. In 1646 that clan which has so much blood on its hands treacherously murdered a glenful of Lamonts against whom they had some grudge. The then Earl of Argyll, the Campbell chief, hanged 36 Lamont clansmen from one tree in Dunoon and shot or stabbed the rest.

## Helensburgh

Sailing up the Firth or motoring along the south shore (A8) towards Glasgow we see Loch Long tapering away beyond Dunoon; maybe an oil-tanker inward or outward bound, to or from the terminal at Finnart, to which oil is piped across Scotland from the North Sea. The model residential town of Helensburgh lays a gridiron pattern on the hill-slope. It is something of a cultural shock, to embark in a gloomy cavern of a Glasgow station and ride with the commuters, arriving within the half hour at this sparkling burgh which resembles a segment of Georgian Edinburgh transported to the western mountains. This is one of Glasgow's superior satellite towns. James Logie Baird, the television pioneer, was born here; Henry Bell of *Comet* fame was provost (mayor).

Helensburgh was also the birthplace of the stage and screen stars Jack Buchanan and Deborah Kerr, and is the site of Charles Rennie Mackintosh's most impressive work, the Hill House in Upper Colquhoun Street. "Here is your house," wrote Mackintosh when he handed it over to the Glasgow publisher Walter Blackie. "It is not an Italian villa, an English mansion, a Swiss chalet or a Scots castle. It is a dwelling house." The Hill House came into the care of the National Trust for Scotland in 1982.

Directly opposite Helensburgh is the very different and grimly industrial town of Greenock; and between them the Firth widens to provide the great anchorage called (from a long shoal in the fairway) the "Tail o' the Bank." Veterans of World War II might perhaps recall that this was the place where thousands of overseas servicemen and women had their first sight of wartime Britain.

The next landmark on the northern shore after Helensburgh is the Rock of Dumbarton with its memories of William Wallace and Mary Queen of Scots. Then comes Old Kilpatrick where the Antonine Wall ended and the Forth–Clyde canal came to the sea. And here we approach the gates of the Clyde river and the confines of Glasgow, which we deal with in our Glasgow chapter.

## Glasgow to Hamilton

We have to travel some 25 miles up the Clyde to see anything resembling those crystal founts and bosky arbors the old writers saw. By Rutherglen, Cambuslang and Bothwell the Clyde pours through a seemingly endless corridor of housing estates, steelworks and coalmining villages. Roadworks and repairs have erased all traces of the battle of Bothwell Brig (between Royalists and Covenanters in 1679). Next door to Bothwell (A74, Glasgow–Carlisle) is the cotton and coalmining village of Blantyre (A776). It was here, in 1813, that David Livingstone was born, and here that he went to school and started work at ten, in a cotton-mill. Self-sacrificing parents and sisters scraped to send him to Glasgow University. In 1840, as doctor and missionary, he went to Africa and in the course of the next 17 years crossed that continent twice, making important geographical discoveries. On a third trek he disappeared, to be found in 1871 by the Anglo-American journalist H.M. Stanley. He declined to come home, died two years later and is buried in Westminster Abbey.

Five miles from Blantyre is the new town of East Kilbride (A749). It is one of three new towns in Strathclyde Region, the others being Irvine on the Clyde coast (A71) and Cumbernauld (M80, Glasgow–Stirling). They were established in the 1950s to take pressure off the decaying hearts of Glasgow and Clydeside. Some say they prosper only at the expense of older communities, but Cumbernauld alone has attracted 55 English and 29 foreign businesses, something the tired old industrial centers round Glasgow could not have done. Having now grown to their fixed limits, the new towns have achieved a social balance and one-quarter of their houses are privately owned—a high proportion by Scottish standards.

Hamilton (A74) is the next place upstream on the Clyde. The Mausoleum, burial-place of the Dukes of Hamilton, faces the river, looking like a large classical beehive. The caretaker does not fail to astonish you with the acoustics: his voice echoes like the sound of military bands and massed choirs. An inn and assembly hall which one of the Dukes of Hamilton put up for his guests is now a museum where you can inspect relics of Harry Lauder the singer and comedian (in his youth a Hamilton miner); Hamilton lace, once prized, no longer made; and memorabilia of the Cameronians (Scottish Rifles) regiment.

The great Hamilton Palace, built on the profits of coal and undermined by coal workings, had to be pulled down earlier this century. One of its smaller rooms contained the whole of the Beckford Library, 15,000 rare volumes collected by the eccentric early 19th century Romantic, builder of impossible follies and author of *Vathek*. Being hard up, the Duke auctioned it in 1882 and was disgusted with the mere £ 400,000 ($2 million at that time) it fetched.

## Hamilton to Lanark

Upstream again, Cambusnethan Priory (A72) is a hotel where today medieval banquets are served. It was owned by Sir James Craig the industrialist, who covered this landscape with steel strip- and rolling-mills. Here the Clyde begins to look like the sylvan stream the old-timers praised. Soft-fruit gardens and apple orchards and red sandstone bridges decorate the banks. Near Crossford on the Nethan Water the ruin of Craignethan Castle recalls Scott's novel *Old Mortality*, in which he fictionalized it as Tillietudlem Castle. After her escape from Loch Leven (Tayside), Mary Queen of Scots took refuge there.

The most interesting town on the upper Clyde is Lanark (A73), built across one of a series of romantic gorges. Here are Cartland Crags (also A73) at the north end of the town; and the Falls of Clyde—Cora Linn and Bonniton Linn—a short distance south; natural beauties commemorated in verse by Wordsworth, Coleridge and others and painted by Turner. Lanark is a proud weaving and fruit-growing town with the oldest race course in Scotland. The town also celebrates some tradition-al pagan ceremonies, of which Lanimer Day early in June is the most elaborate, and lays claim to memories of the medieval bully-boy "Sir" William Wallace. He came from Elderslie near Paisley, but at St. Kentigern's church in Lanark he married a Lanark girl and a building in Castlegate has the inscription: "Here stood the house of William Wallace who in Lanark in 1297 first drew sword to free his native land." He stabbed an English soldier who smiled at his foppish dress.

### New Deal for Weavers

"New towns" are not all that new. In 1797 a mill-owner named David Dale built one. It consisted of a textile mill and barracks for workers, one mile south of Lanark. He called it New Lanark. He envisaged a company estate on which employees would live as one happy family. His son-in-law and successor, Robert Owen, sometimes known as the father of the cooperative movement, took paternalism a few steps farther by introducing free health and education schemes. His ultra-progressive notions, such as reducing the working day to 12 hours and declining to employ children under 10, got him into trouble with fellow mill-owners. Nonetheless, New Lanark flourished until 1824, by which time Owen was involved with wider philanthropies. He after-wards started the first free-thinking commune in America.

The mills stand in picturesque isolation in a green wooded gorge of the Clyde. They were empty for years but have now been partly re-opened as craft workshops; and an energetic campaign has begun to revive New Lanark. A bus service connects the place with Lanark itself.

### Clydesmuir

The Clyde's early course is among the open dales and the amiable hills of Tinto and Lowther. You see the broad shallows of the infant river when you come north to Glasgow by road (A74) or rail from Carlisle. The river rises close to the well of the Tweed. It is a squelching walk to the source, itself a little bubbling pot. A Glasgow journalist put a cork in the hole and stopped the flow, visualizing a Clydeside covered in mudbanks with all the ships lying on their sides; but when he returned to Glasgow he found everything going on as usual.

## Alps of Strathclyde

West of the stripling Clyde lies another Strathclyde landmass: the districts historically known as Cunninghame, Carrick and Kyle. This is an area of rolling moorland and rippling streams, scarred here and there with coal-mining villages and peat bogs.

Road passes through gaps in the hills are often dramatic, none more so than the B797 and/or B7040 from the A74 Glasgow–Carlisle road. It takes you across the Lowther hills from Abington or Elvanfoot to Sanquhar ("Sankar") in Dumfries and Galloway. In about six miles it climbs, with many ups and downs, to nearly 1,600 feet. Incredibly, a railroad went this way in the 1930s and the blue-and-white railcar with its weekend loads of walkers and climbers gave the landscape the appearance of a scene in the Swiss Alps. The summit station, Wanlockhead (just inside Dumfries and Galloway Region), was the highest in the British Isles. The village, at 1,380 feet, is still Scotland's highest, and its neighbor Leadhills the second highest at 1,355—both are Lowland places, paradoxically, and not Highland.

These twin villages, with the regional boundary between them, make a miniature mountain kingdom, remote from other realms. Gold and lead were once mined and you may visit the old workings. At Leadhills (population a few hundred) Allan Ramsay the elder, poet and dramatist, was born in 1686 and William Symington, pioneer of steam navigation, in 1763. If that were not enough fame for one village, Leadhills has the highest golf course in Britain and the grave of Scotland's longest-lived person: John Taylor, died aged 137.

Green Lowther, a hill above Wanlockhead (2,403 feet), has a future as a winter-sports center.

Sanquhar puts us on the A76, a fast road back to Strathclyde Region and the coastal resorts of the Firth of Clyde. We pass Kirkconnell and then New Cumnock and the Afton Water, which recalls Robert Burns's *Sweet Afton;* then Auchinleck ("Affleck"), family home of Boswell, visited by Dr. Johnson; then Mauchline, renowned for lace. Now we are in the Burns country, conveniently laid out for tourists around the seaside resort of Ayr (A70) and the international airport of Prestwick, the most important in Scotland.

## Burns Country

English children know that Burns is a good minor poet. Scottish children know that he is Shakespeare, Dante, Rabelais, Mozart and Karl Marx rolled into one. As time goes by it seems that the Scots have it more nearly right. As poet and humanist, Robert Burns increases in stature. When you plunge into the Burns country, as plunge you must, do not forget that he is held in extreme reverence by Scots of all degrees. They may argue about Sir Walter Scott and Bonnie Prince Charlie; there is no disputing the merits of Burns.

A good starting point for the Burns itinerary is the Burns Monument and Land o' Burns Centre at his birthplace Alloway, a suburb of Ayr (off B7024). The Centre, run by the Scottish Tourist Board, has a theater with Burns documentaries, an agricultural museum, gardens sloping to the river—"Boonie Doon"—and a shopping area with approved souvenirs at controlled prices. Pick up the Burns Heritage Trail leaflet, which describes an elliptical route on the Ayr-Dumfries axis, a route of about 150 miles which takes in the towns, villages, farms and literary landmarks of the poet's life. You will meet pilgrims on this route from Burns societies worldwide, from Tokyo to Moscow to Vancouver.

Ayr (A77, five miles from Prestwick, Glasgow–Stranraer railroad) has a Burns statue, the Tam o' Shanter Inn of his best-known narrative poem, the Auld Kirk where he was baptized, the Auld Brig "where twa wheelbarrows tremble when they meet" and, four miles away on the A713, the farm at Mount Oliphant where he was brought up. At Alloway you may visit the Land o' Burns Centre and the poet's birthplace.

Kirkoswald, on the A77 near Maybole, has the graves of Souter Johnnie and Tam o' Shanter, two of Burns's best-loved characters, and in the garden of Souter Johnnie's museum-cottage you will see effigies of them, and of various other worthies immortalized by Burns. Tarbolton (B744) has the Bachelors' Club of which Burns was first president; it is now a museum maintained by the National Trust for Scotland. Mauchline (A76) has Burns's first married home, graves of his children and friends in the kirkyard, Poosie Nansie's tavern (his favorite "howff," still open) and the National Burns Memorial.

Two of the farms he failed to make a living at, Mossgiel and Lochlea, are near Mauchline. At Irvine (A78) on the coast road north of Ayr is the house he lodged at and the Burns Club museum. For the southern parts of the Burns Heritage Trail see the chapter on Dumfries and Galloway Region.

One word of warning: call him Robert, Robin, Robbie, Rob or Rab—but never Bobbie.

## The Golf Coast

Between Ayr and West Kilbride along the coast road there are 20 golf courses, one for every mile. South of Ayr as far as Girvan (A719, A77) they are hardly less numerous. This curving shoreline of the Firth of Clyde, flat with dunes and interspersed with bold headlands, is commonly called the Golf Coast. At Turnberry the railroad company built one of Scotland's finest hotels specifically for golfers. Turnberry, (A719) and to the south of Ayr, and Royal Troon, (B746) on a slender peninsula to the north, are among golf's major international championship venues.

It might be called the Castle Coast. On Turnberry's cliff-top in a now ruined castle, Robert the Bruce is believed to have been born. At Dunure a few miles north (A719) some medieval land-grabbers named Kennedy encouraged the local abbot to make over his castle by, says the chronicler, "rosting him in sope." Roasting in soup and similar ploys secured to the Kennedys a large slice of southwestern Strathclyde which they fortified with a string of coastal castles. In many places only ruined towers survive, but one place has blossomed. This is Culzean ("Cullane") off the A719 four miles north of Turnberry.

## Culzean Castle

The Kennedys prospered and were ennobled: their present-day representative is the Marquess of Ailsa. The 11th Earl was born and raised in America and had quite a good address: 1, Broadway, New York City. The troubles of 1776 drove him back to the land of his fathers, where he found himself heir to the seagirt fortress of Culzean which the celebrated architect Robert Adam was transforming into a civilized family house. Adam worked on Culzean, inside and out, even on follies in the gardens and neo-classical farm steadings, until 1792 when he died.

Culzean Castle today, despite being difficult to get at without an automobile, is the most-visited of all National Trust for Scotland properties. Its unique oval staircase leads to an oval dome and then to . . . well, not exactly an Oval Office but an oval presidential suite nonetheless. It's a penthouse apartment presented to President (then General) Dwight D. Eisenhower in 1947 as a mark of Scotland's gratitude to a great war leader. The President stayed once or twice at Culzean and his relations still do occasionally. Between visits it is used by the N.T.S. for official hospitality. Approach is by way of rooms evoking the atmosphere of World War II: momentoes of Glenn Miller, Winston Churchill, Vera Lynn and other personalities of the epoch all help create a suitably 1940s mood.

Culzean's "home farm," more pleasing architecturally than the Castle itself, is built round an octagonal courtyard where barns, stabling and swine pens have been upgraded into historical tableaux, educational displays and a restaurant. There is a country park with deer. The garden shrubberies reflect the essential mildness of this coast, though some visitors, meeting the full force of a westerly gale, might be inclined to think otherwise. Culzean's perpendicular sea-cliff offers views across the Firth of Clyde to Arran and the Irish coast. Not a stone's-throw away, it seems, the pinnacle of Ailsa Craig rears from mid-channel. It is halfway along the sea route from Greenock to Belfast and was known of old as "Paddy's Milestone." From Girvan (A77), excursion motorboats go to Ailsa Craig in summer, a round trip of 25 miles.

## Roads to Glasgow

From Ayr northwards the roads are drawn into Glasgow like spokes to a hub. The pleasantest is the longest, all round the Clyde coast (A78). After Greenock it is dull, but you have the compensation of Argyll's shifting panorama across the water. If you are in a hurry the M8 will take you from Greenock across Glasgow to Edinburgh or (M74, A74) to Carlisle.

An exceptionally pretty village called Eaglesham straggles along the B764 under bleak Fenwick Moor, an alternative to the main A77 Ayr–Kilmarnock–Glasgow road. Eaglesham has Covenanting memories in its kirkyard but the cottages make up a perfect late 18th-century planned village of the type devised by landowners desperate to tempt workers back to the land. Eaglesham also has the bizarre distinction of being the site where in 1941, Rudolf Hess, the German vice-fuehrer, landed in his bid to secure a peace agreement with Britain.

## Paisley

Another route from the Golf Coast (A737) comes into Glasgow by Paisley, a place not often dwelled on in guidebooks although it is the largest town in Scotland (100,000 inhabitants) after the four major cities. The first U.S. troops to reach Britain in World War II were stationed here in 1942. They could hardly have picked a less promising-looking part of Scotland.

But Paisley is worth pausing at if you are passing this way. It is the world's oldest and largest cotton-thread production center and a weaving town of great antiquity which gave fashion the famous Paisley pattern shawls and scarves—fine silk woven with Oriental peacock designs. Paisley Abbey, founded 1163, is the most imposing piece of architecture for miles around. An effigy in a side-chapel is thought to mark the tomb of Marjory Bruce, mother of the Stuart dynasty.

## Isles of Strathclyde

There are scores of islands in Strathclyde Region, a continuation of the groups we dealt with in the Highland and Islands chapter. Many are fragments of rock and bars of sand and others have only a seasonal population of fishermen or cattle. For practical purposes there are six Inner Hebridean isles in the Strathclyde Region worth visiting: Mull, Coll and Tiree west of Oban; and Colonsay, Jura and Islay west of Kintyre; plus two islets, Staffa and Iona.

These isles are microcosms of Scotland. Each has its jagged cliffs or tongues of rock, its smiling sands and fertile pastures, its grim and ghostly fortress and its tale of clan outrage or mythical beast. None is more microcosmic than Mull, a large island by Inner Hebridean standards and much penetrated by the Atlantic billows.

## Mull

Mull has something of an English air; it reminds people of Cornwall. Some English people make their homes there and others anchor their yachts in Tobermory harbor, which is situated at a junction of sea-lochs along the narrow strait between the island and the mainland.

Note the place-names: Mishnish, Quinish, Mornish, Treshnish . . . it could be a foreign island. (Note also Calgary, a seaside hamlet whose exiles founded a Canadian city far from the sea.) Tobermory means "Well of Mary." Its waterfront is a curious mixture of suave yachting folk and weatherbeaten fishermen. Crates of liquor for some floating gin-palace are piled beside an array of creels, scrubbed and tarred, ready for harvesting the lobster, crab, scallops, squid and scampi for which Mull's waters are known.

You may see divers preparing to hunt for bigger game round the hull of the *San Juan de Sicilia,* a treasure-ship of the Spanish Armada which anchored in Tobermory Bay in 1588 and suddenly exploded. Ever since that date she has attracted explorations, but the doubloons have not appeared. Meantime she sinks deeper into the mud.

On Mull you can fish, golf, pony-trek and even stalk deer. In summer there are boats to take you from Fionnphort (A849) to two islets of ecclesiastical, regal, geological and musical renown: Iona (one mile) and Staffa (seven miles).

## Staffa and Iona

Staffa consists entirely of basalt pillars stacked on a rock shelf; the very name means "isle of staves." Strangely this geological freak was unknown to the world until, in 1772, the English naturalist Sir Joseph Banks found it the hard way—he ran aground on it—while on a voyage to Iceland. The grotto on Staffa, known to locals as the "musical cave," and to the rest of the world as Fingal's Cave, was visited by several 19th-century romantics. John Keats wrote: "For solemnity and grandeur it far surpasses the finest cathedral." Mendelssohn said: "What a wonder is Fingal's Cave! this vast cathedral of the seas with its dark lapping waters within and the brightness of the gleaming waves outside!" They were two who were lucky enough to land—the ocean swell and slippery rocks can sometimes make landings impossible. Here Mendelssohn was inspired to write his *Hebrides* concert piece, which ended up as the overture *Fingal's Cave.* But it was not for this reason that it was called the "musical cave," rather for the strange Aeolian-harp effect of the wind through the basalt pillars.

Of Iona, Dr. Johnson said it all when he wrote the passage beginning: "We were now treading that illustrious Island which was once the luminary of the Caledonian regions . . . ." St. Columba chose Iona for his monastery in 563 and from it his monks carried Christianity throughout northern England and Scotland. Many Dark Age kings, 48 of them Scottish, are buried on this sacred islet; and many carved slabs commemorate clan chiefs. The present cathedral dates chiefly from the 15th and 16th centuries but fine decorated crosses from earlier periods stand round it. Of some interest to American visitors is the plot set aside for 19 victims of the *Guy Mannering,* shipwrecked in 1865. They were American sailors and the then American consul in Glasgow, the novelist Bret Harte, persuaded the Duke of Argyll to give them burial and a monument in the island graveyard.

## Coll and Tiree

Both Coll and Tiree are low-lying and exposed, an inadequate barrier for Mull against the Atlantic. Coll has pastureland and silver sands. Tiree, so flat that it was known to the Gaels as "the kingdom less tall than the waves," claims to be the sunniest spot in the west. The inhabitants of both islands are crofters (smallholders) but the boat from Oban brings mainland families for their vacations and if you talk to them you will hear that they would not dream of taking a holiday elsewhere.

## Jura and Islay

Jura lies south again and runs roughly parallel with the coast of Kintyre, only about four miles away. Its twin conical peaks, the Paps of Jura, are a landmark for sailors approaching the west coast and under them are two or three hamlets with hotel accommodations; even a road (A846) and a few vehicles. Islay, pronounced "Eye-la" and almost attached to Jura, is congested by comparison, with several small ports, a rudimentary road system and an airfield. Islay is flat and green, much frequented by Glasgow people, some of whom have been known to go over merely to play golf. Among the coastal villages are 12 hotels. Even so, you will always find peace and solitude if you want it.

## Colonsay

While not the largest or most important of Strathclyde islands, Colonsay represents the culmination of island charms. It has cliffs and moors, small stone walls, l chans full of waterlilies, woods embosomed in rhododendrons and sand-dunes infested with rabbits. Wild goats are seen in the north (A870 beyond Colonsay House) and on Oronsay, an islet which hangs from Colonsay's southern tip on a sand-spit.

Colonsay, west of Jura and south of Mull, is a resting-place for migrant seafowl. In early summer you find rare varieties of sea samphire, hellebore and orchis among the wild flowers. Offshore reefs are often occupied by gray seals, looking enviously shorewards. A scattering of ancient monuments, from a ruined chapel near Balnahard to the remains of a 15th-century priory on Oronsay, suggest a Celtic priestly occupation. There is a hotel on Colonsay and some self-catering accommodations in island cottages and at Colonsay House. You may take a car to the island but not a caravan. You may ride a bicycle but not pitch a tent!

# PRACTICAL INFORMATION FOR STRATHCLYDE

**HOW TO GET THERE. By air.** There are daily flights from Glasgow airport to and from Campbeltown, Islay and Tiree; and helicopter links with Rothesay, Lochgilphead and Oban.

**By train.** Stations which you can reach on the Carlisle–Glasgow section of the London–Glasgow main line are Kirkconnell, Kilmarnock, Lanark and Motherwell. For stations in other parts of Strathclyde you should go to Glasgow and take another train. Glasgow's Central station serves the country south of the Clyde and her Queen Street station serves all the districts north of the Clyde. There are several trains daily (reduced service on Sundays) to Dumbarton, Helensburgh and intermediate stations to Oban; to Gourock and Wemyss Bay on the Clyde coast; and to Irvine, Ardrossan, Largs, Troon, Prestwick, Ayr, Maybole and Girvan in the southwest. Train schedules coincide with boat connections to the western isles.

**By bus.** Long-distance coaches day and night connect London (Victoria and King's Cross), Coventry (Corley Service Station) and Birmingham (St. Chadsway) in England with Abington, Motherwell, Cumbernauld, Airdrie and Hamilton in Strathclyde. Excellent and inexpensive buses run very frequent services between Glasgow's Anderston Cross and Buchanan Street bus stations and most towns of the Region.

**HOTELS AND RESTAURANTS.** Accommodations in Strathclyde are numerous and of many types. Our small selection below provides merely a general outline of the choice available. It is a different matter as far as restaurants are concerned. Strathcylde is not one of the great gastronomic regions of the world, though some country restaurants and coastal hotels display an adventurous touch with local produce. But most are notable for providing proletarian cuisine at a reasonable price. The motherly familiarity of waitresses appeals to some and irritates others.

High tea flourishes between 5.30 and 7 in the evening, and at seaside stops you will find "cairry oot" (to go) teashops or stalls offering snacks and drinks. Cafes and pubs where you can stop for lunch line the touring routes, except in the loneliest parts of Argyll.

**ABBOTSINCH** (M8). *Excelsior* (E), tel. Glasgow 887 1212. 305 rooms, all with bath. One of the best British airport hotels and right next to the check-in desk. Discreet bars, average restaurant.

**AYR** (A77). **Restaurants.** *Bumbles* (M), tel. 60993. For fresh fish and steaks. *Bobby Jones* (I). Mucb-praised for food and value.

**CAMPBELTOWN** (A83). *Argyll Arms* (I). Fine and very inexpensive pub food.

**CRINAN** (B841). *Crinan* (E), tel. 235. 22 rooms, all with bath. Newly rebuilt where canal meets the sea. Large, well-furnished rooms. Rooftop restaurant with views over Firth of Lorne.

**EASDALE** (B844, south of Oban). *Dunmor House* (M), tel. Balvicar 203. 11 rooms, 5 with bath. Converted hill farm on islet joined to the mainland by the tiny "Bridge over the Atlantic."

**GALSTON** (A71, near Kilmarnock). *Cobwebb Tea-Shoppe* (I). Reasonable prices for fine homemade teas.

**KILMORY** (Isle of Arran, A841). **Restaurant.** *The Lagg* (M), tel. Sliddery 255. A 16th-century smugglers' inn; sophisticated cuisine—good trout and scampi.

**LANGBANK** (B789 off M8). *Gleddoch House* (E), tel. 711. 18 rooms, all with bath. House of dignity and exclusive character on south Clyde shore, 13 miles from Glasgow. Fine views across Clyde; large lawns and gardens. Country club adjacent.

**LOCHAWESIDE** (B845). *Taychreggan* (E), tel. Kilchrenan 211. 22 rooms, 11 with bath. Old drovers' inn on lochside, enlarged and carefully modernized. Comfortable but not luxurious.

**PRESTWICK** (A77). *Carlton Motor Hotel* (M), Ayr Road (tel. 76811). 37 rooms, all with bath. Superior modern stopover but you might get bored on a long stay.

**TIGHNABRUAICH** (A886). *Royal* (M), tel. 239. 10 rooms. Focus of rural life on a remote Argyll peninsula. Looks across narrow strait to island of Bute (ferry). A new road is bringing in more strangers.

**TOBERMORY** (Isle of Mull, A848). *Western Isles Hotel* (M), tel. 2012. Offers seafood, festive evenings, gastronomic nights, ceilidh (Gaelic songs and story telling) suppers. Sensitive guests wear earplugs on weekends.

**TURNBERRY** (A77). *Turnberry Hotel* (L), tel. 202. Scenic outlook from famous golfing hotel. Expensive international menu. New management yet to be put to the test.

**HOW TO GET ABOUT. By boat.** No passenger boats sail from Glasgow. The major sea-ferry route is Ardrossan to Douglas (Isle of Man), by the Isle of Man Steam Packet Co., Imperial Buildings, Douglas (tel. 3824). Western Ferries, 16 Woodside Crescent, Glasgow (tel. 332 9766) operate a trans-Clyde ferry between Gourock (A8) and Hunter's Quay (A815).

The principal ferry operator is Caledonian MacBrayne, The Pier, Gourock (tel. 33755), with car and passenger services on weekdays as follows. *From Oban:* to Lochboisdale (South Uist), Castlebay (Barra), Craignure (Mull), Coll, Tiree, Colonsay and Lismore. *From Tayinloan* (Kintyre, A83): to Gigha. *From Kennacraig* (Kintyre, A83): to Port Ellen and Port Askaig (both Islay) and Feolin (Jura). *From Wemyss Bay* (A78): to Rothesay (Bute). *From Largs* (A78): to Millport (Great Cumbrae). *From Ardrossan* (A78): to Brodick (Arran). *From Claonaig* (Kintyre, B842): to Lochranza (Arran), May–Sept. only. *From Colintraive* (B8000): to Rhubodach (Bute). *From Fionnphort* (Mull, A840): to Iona, no automobiles. *From Lochaline* (B849): to Fishnish (Mull, B8035). *From Gourock* (A8): to Dunoon (A815) and Kilcreggan (B833).

There are numerous small-boat excursions in summer between mainland vacation resorts and offlying islands.

**By bus.** The main bus station in the Region is on Buchanan Street, Glasgow, with services to all parts of Scotland and many day excursions and longer tours.

**By train.** Both Central and Queen Street mainline stations have Blue Trains to Helensburgh and Balloch (Loch Lomond), as well as to outlying towns including Lanark, Cumbernauld, Kilmalcolm and Milngavie.

**By car.** The M8 is a great boon to motorists going to, from or across Glasgow, but driving in the city and its satellite towns can be slow and depressing; and signposting is not clear. In the countryside the roads are good, with some fine fast stretches to south and west and some twisting and at weekends heavily-trafficked sections to the north. Fish trucks from Oban and other ports are a hazard; car-and-caravan drivers an irritation in summer.

There are many car-rental firms in Glasgow and all the well-known operators are represented at the airports of Glasgow and Prestwick. In other towns you may rent an automobile from: James Laidlaw, South Biggar Road, Airdrie (tel. 64702); Budget Rent-a-Car, 196 Prestwick Road, Ayr (tel. 264087); Kenning

Car Hire, Station Hotel, Ayr (tel. 81529); International Car Rental, Thawbank Road, East Kilbride (tel. 33111); Budget Rent-a-Car, 1 Ker Street, Greenock (tel. 21313); Swan National, Bothwell Road, Hamilton (tel. 286644); Isle of Coll Hotel, Coll (tel. 334); Appleyard's, Western Road, Kilmarnock (tel. 35911); Godfrey Davis, 477 Windmillhill Street, Motherwell (tel. 66534); Godfrey Davis, Marchfield Avenue, Paisley (tel. 8359); and James Dodds & Son, 70 Portland Street, Troon (tel. 312312). Dodds of Troon deliver and collect at Prestwick airport.

**TOURIST INFORMATION.** You will find tourist information offices at Abington, Ayr, Balloch, Biggar, Bowmore, Brodick, Campbeltown, Culzean, Cumnock, Dalmellington, Dunoon, Girvan, Glasgow, Gourock, Greenock, Helensburgh, Inveraray, Largs, Lochgilphead, Luss, New Cumnock, Oban, Prestwick, Rothesay, Tarbert (Loch Fyne), Tobermory and Troon. In larger towns such as Glasgow (George Square, tel. 221 7371) they are open all year round, usually 9–6; and in summer months on weekday evenings also and Sun. afternoons. Smaller places keep shorter variable hours. In the islands, except on Bute, you will not find offices open on Sun. At all tourist information centers you may obtain accommodations locally or "book-a-bed-ahead."

**FISHING.** In northern and western districts most hotels offer free fishing to guests for salmon, sea trout, rainbow and brown trout. Loch Awe southwest of Dalmally (A819 and B840), the River Awe and lochans of the area are particularly good: permits around $20 per day from Inverawe Fisheries, Taynuilt (A85), or the Chief Forester, Dalavich, Taynuilt. The Clyde above Glasgow is noted for brown trout and grayling—tackle dealers in Edinburgh, Glasgow and Clyde towns will provide permits for about $1 per day or $8 the season. The Loch Lomond Angling Improvement Association, 224 Ingram Street, Glasgow, issues permits for salmon and brown trout fishing in various parts of Loch Lomond, as do the hotels at Luss and Ardlui (both A82 lochside road). There is good trout fishing in the lochs and burns of Mull: contact Tobermory Angling Association, c/o Brown's Shop, Tobermory, or the Western Isles Hotel, Tobermory. On Bute the Glenburn Hotel, Rothesay, can arrange fishing for island and adjoining mainland lochs at about $8 per day.

Coarse fishing for pike, perch and grayling is popular in the Glasgow and Greenock areas and farther south in rivers, canals, lochs and reservoirs. Spring and fall are best. Contact tackle shops or hotels in the areas or apply to British Waterways Board, Applecross Street, Glasgow. Permits cost about $2 for the season.

There is good sea-angling (facilities provided) from Port Charlotte (Islay), Salen and Tobermory (Mull), and the Coll Hotel (Coll). Local hotels supply boats and tackle. Fishing from pier-end or from boats locally available is a major pastime on the Clyde coast at Girvan, Ayr, Prestwick, Troon and Ardrossan (all on or near A78/A77); also in villages of Bute and Arran. The long, deep Loch Fyne, with depths of 600 feet even at the head of the loch, is fine sea-angling ground and you can hire boats on the quays of Tarbert (A8015) and Inveraray (A83). Elsewhere on Loch Fyne it is hard to launch a boat on account of the rugged coastline.

**GOLF.** Notable among Glasgow's 20-odd golf courses are Haggs Castle, Cathcart Castle, Cawdor (Bishop-briggs) and Pollok (men only). Visitors require introductions through member or home club secretary. Fees around $8 per day. Every town and many villages of southern Strathclyde have golf courses, the greatest concentration being around Glasgow and on both sides of the Clyde coast. There are few courses in northern Strathclyde. Among the islands there are two on Bute, six on Arran, two on Mull, one on Tiree and one on Islay.

The small town of Troon (B746) has five courses. Among Scotland's famous championship courses are Royal Troon, Turnberry and Old Prestwick. You must have an introduction to them and will pay up to $25 per day. At most other clubs and all municipal courses you can play without formality for a maximum of $6 per day.

**HISTORIC HOUSES AND GARDENS.** Of the many historic houses and castles found in Strathclyde Region, the following are particularly noteworthy and well worth visiting.

**Brodick Castle,** Brodick, Isle of Arran (A841). Long, severe, island citadel of ducal families, formerly Hamilton and now Montrose. Sporting prints. Silver and porcelain from William Beckford's amazing collection. Open May–Sept., daily, 1–5; mid–end-Apr., Mon., Wed. and Sat., 1–5. N.T.S.

**Cameron House,** near Balloch, on banks of Loch Lomond (A82). A showpiece on the loch shore. Historical material includes old whisky bottles and relics of 18th-century novelist Tobias Smollett, owner's ancestor. Open Apr.–Oct., daily, 11–6.

**Culzean Castle,** Maybole (A719). Large, castellated mansion on 150-foot headland. Medieval tower, Robert Adam additions. Farm complex also styled by Adam. Woodland, lake, picnic areas. Open Apr.–Sept., daily, 10–6 (10–4 Oct.). N.T.S.

**Dean Castle,** Dean Road, Kilmarnock (A77). Castle dates from 14th–15th centuries, with period furnishings, medieval musical instruments. Open May–Sept., Mon.–Fri. 2–5, Sat. and Sun. 10–5.

**Duart Castle,** near Craignure, Isle of Mull (B8035). This grim seat of the MacLean chiefs has commanded the entrance to the Firth of Lorne for 600 years. Furnishings reflect the clan's changing fortunes. One room devoted to history of Boy Scout movement—Lord MacLean was Chief Scout of the Commonwealth in the 1960s. Open May–Sept., daily, 10.30–6.

**The Hill House,** Upper Colquhoun Street, Helensburgh (A874). Splendid art deco suburban chateau, Charles Rennie Mackintosh's greatest work. Open Apr.–Oct., Mon. 12.30–5, Tue. 12.30–7, Wed. 9.30–5, Sat. and Sun. 2–6.

**Inveraray Castle,** Inveraray (A83). Four-square, conical-towered home of Duke of Argyll, chief of Campbell clan. Tapestries, armor, 18th-century furniture. Open Jul.–Aug., weekdays 10–6, Sun. 2–6; Apr.–Jun. and Sept., weekdays except Fri., 10–1 and 2–6, Sun. 2–6.

Mild, moist air and sunlight reflected off deeply winding lochs contribute to the wonderful displays of azaleas, rhododendrons, fuchsias, camellias and other blooms in Strathclyde not seen much in Britain outside botanical gardens. Of the properties listed above, Brodick Castle has Himalayan, Chinese and Burmese plants, vast shrubberies, and 250-year-old formal gardens; and Culzean

Castle has formal and walled gardens, as well as springtime arrays of snowdrops and daffodils in the woods.

Many gardens are open to the public on only one or two days a year—usually a Saturday or Sunday. For details, see advertisements in local newspapers or posters in shop windows etc. The following, which you will find open most days in summer, are of special note: **Achamore House,** Gigha (ferry from Tayinloan, A83); **Achnacloich,** Connel, near Oban (A85); **Ardanaiseig,** Kilchrenan, Loch Awe (B845); **Ardchattan,** North Connel (off A828); **Crarea,** Loch Fyne (A83); **Stonefield Castle,** Tarbert (A83); **Torosay Castle,** Craignure, Mull (B8035); and **Treshnish,** Calgary, Mull (B8073).

 **MUSEUMS. Burns Club and Town Museum,** Eglinton Street, Irvine (A78). History of burgh with graphics, audiovision and dioramas. Items include letters from U.S. presidents Teddy Roosevelt and Eisenhower, past members of the club. Open Sat. 2.30–5 or by request.

**Burns' Cottage and Museum,** Alloway, Ayr (B7024). Birthplace of poet, with large collection of books, letters, manuscript poems. Open May–Oct., daily, 9–7; Nov.–Apr., weekdays only, 9–7.

**David Livingstone Center,** Blantyre (A776). Birthplace and elaborate national memorial with relics of explorer's diaries and instruments. Open weekdays 10–6, Sun. 2–6.

**Gladstone Court,** Biggar (A702). A museum-street with shops, bank, school etc. illustrating country life of last century. Open Apr.–Oct., weekdays 10–5, Sun. 2–5.

**Glencoe and North Lorne Folk Museum,** Glencoe Village, Glencoe (A82). History of district including Jacobite relics and slate industry, housed in restored thatched cottage. Open Jun.–Oct., weekdays, 10–5.30.

**Museum and Art Gallery,** High Street, Paisley (A737). Paisley shawls, Scottish artists and craftspeople. Open weekdays 10–5.

**Museum of Scottish Lead Mining,** Goldscaur Row, Wanlockhead (B797). Museum on site with 1½-mile walkway through 18th-century mine and among 19th-century leadmining technology. Open Apr.–Oct., daily, 11–4.

**New Lanark Counting House,** Lanark (A73). Interpretative display on innovations of David Dale and Robert Owen between 1797 and 1824. Open on request; village open all times.

MR SERLE AS ROB ROY MACGREGOR

# BATTLEFIELDS AND BONNIE BANKS

## Central

Stand on a high point of Central Region—there are several, but Stirling Castle rock is as good as any—and you will survey the whole Region, provided there is not too much industrial smoke about. You will see Scotland coast-to-coast. This is where Scotland draws in her waist from the Clyde in the west to the Forth in the east. All the Lowland highways converge here and fan out again to the Highlands.

The Forth–Clyde belt, only 28 miles wide, was a cradle of Scottish industry, a forcing-house of that mechanical genius to which engineering science worldwide was indebted. On the Forth–Clyde canal in 1790 Patrick Miller demonstrated the first paddle-steamboat. In the same place 28 years later Sir John Robinson's *Vulcan,* the first iron ship, took the water. Iron foundries on the Carron River had by that time built the heavy guns for Nelson's warships: hence the term carronade. In 1850 James "Paraffin" Young, extracting oil from locally-mined shale, showed how it could be burned in lamps. That led to the decline of mineral oil as a patent medicine in America—and to the founding of the Rockefeller fortunes.

Central Region is still to the fore in oil technology. It has the petroleum refinery of Grangemouth, with a pipeline to the west coast for American tankers; and a petrochemical industry that ranks the top six in Europe.

But the Region is not all industry. As in Lothian and Strathclyde, wild scenery begins on the doorsteps of manufacturing towns and a sense of past intrudes on the present. Stirling's braes (hilly streets) ascend to a 900-year-old citadel which—like that of Edinburgh, but smaller and neater—holds a military garrison and dominates a landscape. From the ramparts you can see seven battlefields, including Stirling Bridge and Bannockburn, scenes of victories by William Wallace and his successor Robert the Bruce; and Sheriffmuir and Falkirk, which belong to the history of the Jacobite rebellions.

Under Stirling's fortifications the River Forth, not yet a firth, meanders about the meadows, taking 16 miles to do a journey of three as the crow flies. You may look westward to its source in a tangle of hills: Ben Lomond (3,192 feet), Ben Vrackie, Ben Ledi ("Lady"), Ben Venue and Ben More (3,843 feet). You cannot quite see Loch Lomond's bonny banks on the western edge of the Region but you can pick out the Trossachs (the word means "bristly country") and the hill pass called the Duke's Drive, winding down towards Loch Katrine.

Almost at your feet as you stroll round Stirling's battlements are Cambuskenneth Abbey where the Scottish Parliament once sat and the Gothic pencil of the Wallace Monument against the backcloth of the Ochil Hills. Eastward, the River Forth, widening to the sea, carries your eye towards a distant view (25 miles) of the Forth bridges.

The Highland Line, the geological boundary which in olden times was a sociological one too, slices through the Region. You will observe its effect when you travel. One moment you are gliding across flat meadowland, the next you are facing heather-covered moors or plunging into glens where the silver birches hang precariously above and a powerful little torrent leaps down beneath.

The Romans' Antonine Wall crops out in several places on its march across Scotland's wasp waist. The Celts are represented in the curious Stone of Mannan at the village of Clackmannan: the sea god Mannan also gave his name to the Isle of Man. There are medieval strongholds at Dollar, Fintry and Doune, an ancient cathedral at Dunblane, a modern university at Bridge of Allan, elaborate gardens at Keir and Gargunnock, Highland Games at various centers in summer and plenty of lochs for fishing, boating and boat excursions.

Memories of Wallace and the Bruce abound, but Central Region's folk hero is Rob Roy MacGregor, the Highland freebooter whose real-life exploits were concerned with cattle-rustling on the approaches to the trysts (markets) of Falkirk and Stirling. The novels *Rob Roy* and *The Legend of Montrose*, both by Sir Walter Scott, are set in the Region and Scott's *Lady of the Lake*, a long narrative poem, is almost a step-by-step guide to the Trossachs. Numerous regional place-names are immortalized in songs by Robert Burns and others: *Allan Water, The Battle of Sheriffmuir, Bruce's Address Before Bannockburn* ("Scots Wha Ha'e"), *Bonnie Strathyre* and, of course, *Loch Lomond* ("Ye'll tak' the high road and I'll tak' the low road").

High road or low, there is a microcosm of Scottish scenery and history in this Region which clasps the Lowlands to the Highlands.

## Stirling

As a motorail terminal with overnight trains from the south and west of England, Stirling is the first Scottish town many visitors see. It is the tourist capital of the Region, a little Edinburgh with "crag-and-tail" foundations and a royal half-mile. Stirling's strategic position, commanding the lowest bridge on the Forth, was appreciated by the Stuart kings and they spent a lot of time at its castle—a fact which, together with the relics of freedom fighters in the neighborhood, has led some Scottish Nationalists to declare that should Scotland achieve independence again Stirling must be her capital city.

Earlier in this chapter we were on the ramparts, admiring the view. Let us now look inside at apartments which hold memories of the unlucky Stuart monarchs. The Parliament Hall, recent recipient of major architectural surgery and restored now to something like its 14th-century glory (in the intervening centuries it had been an army barracks), belongs to the time of James III. The royal palace, still inside the castle walls, was built by James V and the chapel beside it by James VI. Several kings and queens were born or crowned in these buildings. Mary Queen of Scots lived there in her infancy before she was sent to France. An embrasure on the battlements with the inscription "MR 1561" is still called Queen Mary's Lookout.

Going downhill from the esplanade you pass the Landmark Visitor Centre, a garden, tearoom, bookshop and craftshop and an exhibition hall with a multiscreen theater showing historical films. On the right is Mar's Work, the ivy-covered ruin of a mansion which the Earl of Mar, premier earl of Scotland, put up in 1570. The building of slightly later date on the left, the Argyll Ludging ("ludging" was "lodging," a nobleman's town house), was for many years a military hospital and is now a youth hostel. Darnley's House at the foot of the street has an inscription: "Nursery of James VI and his son Prince Henry."

Before you descend to modern Stirling's shopping streets you pass the old Town House (City Hall), the Mercat Cross, where proclamations were made, and the parish church of the Holy Rude (rood, cross), a fine Gothic building dated 1414. Here King James VI was crowned at the age of one year; the presiding clergyman was John Knox.

Close by in Back Walk stands the gaunt 17th-century Cowane's Hospital, built as a refuge for the old. You can walk from here along the south side of the castle hill to the Smith Institute, the local museum and art gallery. As you start, note the square patch of ground beside the Dumbarton road (A811) called the King's Knot. It was once a garden of intricately intersecting paths and borders laid out by King James IV.

## Across the Forth

One mile beyond the convolutions of the Forth, a river which seems reluctant to leave Stirling, you come to the Wallace Monument on a crag above a loop in the river. (Take Wallace Street and cross by Stirling Bridge, A9.) The tower has a good view from its 220-foot balcony and a sword alleged to be Wallace's is kept in a small museum.

Inside another loop of the river (take Shore Road next to the railroad station) are the tower and ruins of Cambuskenneth Abbey, founded by the "sair sanct" King David I in 1147. It was briefly Scotland's House of Parliament 500 years ago. A tombstone marks the graves of James III (murdered after the battle of Sauchieburn, 1488) and of his queen, Margaret of Denmark.

## Bannockburn

The chief attraction within walking distance of Stirling and the most hallowed ground in Scotland for patriots is the field of Bannockburn, two miles south on the A872 road. But take a bus or taxi if you can: it is not a pretty walk. The scene of feints and withdrawals, charges and routs, heroism and sacrifice on a June day in 1314 is now threatened with a pincer movement of housing estates, half-made streets and gas stations. If Edward II of England had had a sense of the fitness of things he would have attacked over the Ochil Hills or across the windings of the Forth—poetic spots in keeping with the drama of the situation.

Here, however, he came with an army big enough to have brushed the Scots aside. He has been accused of joining battle too hastily, but time was pressing. English forces under siege in Stirling Castle had agreed to surrender if not relieved within two days. At first the English army seemed to gain the day. The fight went this way and that. The light cavalry of Randolph, Earl of Moray (his name is recalled in Randolphfield, the police headquarters on the outskirts of Stirling), nipped King Edward's outflanking movement. The turning-point was the appearance over the hill (still called Gillies' Hill) of some Scottish domestics and camp-followers whom the English mistook for reinforcements. Robert the Bruce from his vantage-point at the Bore Stone saw the enemy falter, give ground and run. This was Scotland's most decisive victory in all the medieval wars and it led to her independence eight years later.

The Bannockburn Monument on the hill consists of a curved wall, a flagged pavement, a flagstaff and a big black equestrian statue of Robert the Bruce, the work of Pilkington Jackson. Fragments of the Bore Stone, a boulder with a socket in it where Bruce set his standard, are preserved at the Visitor Centre on the site—but most of it has been chipped away by the souvenir-hunters of the last six centuries. The new Visitor Centre, inaugurated in April 1982 near the A872 at the entrance to the Monument, has transformed Bannockburn from a rather bleak 10-minute pull-up for tourists into an experience worth an hour or so of anyone's time. The continuous movie presentation describes the battle, with appropriate sound effects; the maps, diagrams and stunning wall-painting have earned British Tourist Authority awards. Every year on June 24, the anniversary of the battle, the site is a rallying-point for the Scottish National Party, who regard Bannockburn as a symbol of the Scots' determination to be Scottish.

Yet the battle is now believed to have taken place elsewhere, though no one says exactly where. But it was probably farther north, to the east of Stirling, where the little stream called Bannock Burn wriggles into the Forth.

The strategic center of the year 1314 has become a strategic center of motorways. Bannockburn is the point at which the M80 from Glasgow meets the M9 from Edinburgh and continues (as the M9) to Dunblane. Though set in a most unpicturesque landscape it is a tourist metropolis with, apart from the Visitor Centre, the large King Robert hotel, a restaurant, a major National Trust for Scotland information center and shop, and a major Scottish Tourist Board information center.

The somber majesty of Bannockburn, its panoply and glitter, are a loud shout for Scotland. One cannot help contrasting it with that other great battleground just across the English border, Flodden, where the victory went to the other side and where the commemoration is a simple stone: "To the Brave of *Both* Nations." But then, Flodden does not receive 50,000 visitors every year.

## Ironworks and Roman Camps

Five Scottish Regions surround Central Region. Journeying along them in turn, the first route is along the M9 motorway, or the accompanying A9, into Lothian Region (Edinburgh 37 miles). The horizons are lined with hills and with the shining lattice-work and flaming towers of Grangemouth oil port, but the immediate surroundings are heavily industrialized as you negotiate the coalmining and iron-founding sprawl of Stenhousemuir, Larbert and Camelon. Scotland's Arthurian students link the last-named place with Camelot, a theory which the density of factories makes impossible to disprove from evidence on the ground. It is no easier to reconstruct the past in Falkirk, though the place has a history. It was the chief Scottish market for sheep and cattle, which were driven down from the Highland fastnesses before the railways took over the transportation of livestock. Bonnie Prince Charlie slept the night at a shop in the main street before the battle of Falkirk (1746); and not long afterwards the Duke of Cumberland, commander of the Government forces, also stayed there in the "Great Ludging"—a room above a bootmaker's shop. The Jacobites were retreating towards their doom on Culloden Moor and Prince Charlie claimed the victory in this rearguard action; but Major James Wolfe (afterwards of Quebec), a down-to-earth officer of the opposing side, wrote: "'Twas not a battle for neither side would fight."

Three miles north of Falkirk the famous Carron Ironworks were established in 1760. To serve their needs brickworks and coal mines began to proliferate. The Carron Company in its prosperous days made every conceivable cast-iron object, from guns and bridge girders to fireplaces and kitchen pots.

Two miles east of Falkirk the Antonine Wall crosses the A9. It comes from the Forth shore near Bo'ness (Lothian), enters the grounds of Callendar House and then runs more or less parallel with the Forth–Clyde canal to Old Kirkpatrick below Glasgow. Most of the interesting finds in the Wall were made between 1769 and 1790, when the waterway was being excavated and people came from miles around to see the miracle of ships sailing through dry land. Now both canal and Wall are done for, killed by the march of science. You can pick up a leaflet at the Falkirk museum which shows where Roman remains are still visible. The most conspicuous of its 20 forts is Rough Castle, a mound of earth near Bonnybridge, six miles west of Falkirk on the A803. It is cared for by the National Trust for Scotland.

### "Look Aboot Ye"

Crossing the Forth at Stirling and turning east on the A91 towards Fife Region you enter the district of Clackmannan. Before regionalization, it was the smallest county in the British Isles. It was once thickly forested. Robert the Bruce lost a glove there while hunting and sent his lieutenant back to find it. "Go to a path near Clackmannan village," he instructed him, "and look aboot ye." The road is called Lookabootye Brae to this day and tourism has adopted the slogan, advising "Look aboot ye" as you travel the small burghs, old and new, rustic and industrial, threaded along the hillfoot road under the ridge of the frowning Ochils.

Menstrie, Alva and Tillicoultry are nothing much to look at from the main road, but among these villages the back streets are worth investigating. Menstrie has a 17th-century fortress, the birthplace and property of Sir William Alexander who founded the Canadian colony of Nova Scotia. Behind Alva and Tillicoultry two charming little glens climb up waterfalls into clefts in the hills. A glen with a mile-long footpath beside it goes up from Dollar to Castle Campbell, a former residence of the Clan Campbell chiefs. Perched on a crag above the meeting of two streams, the castle is like a woodcut in a Gothic novel. The streams are called Care and Sorrow, the fortress was originally Castle Gloom and Dollar itself was once spelled Dolour; yet the scene, though romantic, is not at all melancholy. Legend says the names were bestowed by a noblewoman kept captive there, but the likelier explanation would be some punning reference or corruption of forgotten Gaelic names.

Dollar has a peaceful early 19th-century air and some handsome buildings of that period, notably Dollar Academy, founded 1818 and built by Playfair. Now it is a fairly prestigious school for girls and boys. From here you pass on to the Yetts of Muckhart ("yetts" are gates; we are back to another old drove road) and the Rumbling Bridge beneath which the Devon River tumbles noisily in an echoing gorge. To stay in Central Region you now turn southwest on the A977 for Clackmannan village, Alloa and the riverside road (A907) to Stirling.

### The "Gret Schippe"

At Alloa (accentuate the "Al"), largest town of the district, they brew beer and make the glass bottles to put it in. Sluggish and muddy, the River Forth executes a horseshoe bend which, before it silted up, formed Scotland's naval base and dockyard. Here after her launching in 1511 by King James IV lay the *Great Michael,* flagship of the Royal

Scottish Navy. Shipwrights from France, gunners from Holland, iron-workers from Spain and tinsmiths from Cornwall helped native crafts-men to build her. Her 10-foot-thick sides were reported to have "wasted (consumed) all the woods in Fife," her copper sheathing came from Denmark and her anchors were brought from Cadiz. The caravels of Columbus, which were crossing the Atlantic when she was laid down, were toys beside her. She had 300 guns and, judging by the model in the Royal Scottish Museum in Edinburgh, almost as many flags and banners. Her main masthead ensign, the St. Andrew's Cross, required 24 yards of fine cloth.

Having emptied his treasury to build her, the King appeared not to know what to do with her. For two years she lay in the Pool of Alloa and at other berths up and down the river. The "gret shippe" was the talk of Scotland and the wonder of all who traveled to Scotland to see her. When she finally sailed for war it was the year of Flodden, a bad time for Scottish arms, and James had entrusted her command to a playboy courtier, the Earl of Arran, who had never been to sea. Alarm-ing reports of her maiden voyage prompted him to change his mind. He despatched Scotland's greatest sea-captain, Sir Andrew Wood of Largo, to take over—but the *Great Michael* could not be found. Like many another weapon designed to conquer the world, she cost the earth, achieved nothing and returned not a cent on the investment.

No one knows what happened to her. The best guess was that a rotting hulk discovered years later at the port of Brest in France was the remains of the *Great Michael.*

### Dunblane

Our third route from Stirling is also a short one. The north road (A9) soon passes into Tayside Region. Along with the M9 motorway it leads to Bridge of Allan and Dunblane, four and eight miles respectively from Stirling.

They are two suburban-looking towns, mainly populated by com-muters and retired people, pleasantly spread out on the banks of Allan Water, which Burns celebrated in song. Near Bridge of Allan in a fine waterside situation stands Stirling University, one of the newest and most progressive in Scotland. Its MacRobert Centre, open to non-students, offers jazz concerts, debates, avant-garde theater and films.

Dunblane is noted for its hydropathic establishment, a spa center built in the 19th century. There are quite a number of these centers in various Scottish towns, all dating from the days when the vogue for Scottish air and mountain water led some doctors to consider them a wonder cure for every complaint. Like most of the "hydros," Dun-blane's is now a hotel.

In the middle of the town stand the partly-restored ruins of a large cathedral. King David, the "sair sanct", built the existing structure on the site of St. Blane's little eighth-century cell. Dunblane cathedral is contemporary with the Border abbeys but more mixed in its architec-ture, part Early English and part Norman. The 19th-century art critic John Ruskin said of it: "I know nothing so perfect in its simplicity and so beautiful, as far as it reaches, in all the Gothic with which I am

acquainted." Restoration over the past century has been sensitive on
the whole. Dunblane ceased to be a cathedral, as did most others in
Scotland, at the time of the Reformation in the mid-16th century.

The moorland east of Dunblane, sloping up to the ridge of the Ochil
Hills, is the site of the battle of Sheriffmuir (1715) at which Government troops scattered the Earl of Mar's Jocobites and destroyed the
hopes of the Old Pretender, Bonnie Prince Charlie's father. The site is
marked with the so-called Gathering Stone (for gathering the clans)
near the unclassified Wallace Stones road, two miles from Dunblane.
A turning to the right would bring you down steeply among forested
slopes and small reservoirs into Bridge of Allan again.

## Rob Roy's Native Heath

The most heavily-trafficked road out of Stirling in the summer
months is the A84 to Callander and Lochearnhead. It is a section of
the main highway between Edinburgh and the western Highlands, and
near Fort William it joins up with the old Road to the Isles.

The first town is Doune, feudal seat of that "Bonnie Earl o' Moray"
who was treacherously slain near Aberdour in 1570. The incident
inspired one of Scotland's best-loved ballads:
"O lang will his lady
Look o'er the Castle Doune
Ere she sees the Earl o' Moray
Come sounding through the toon. . . . "
For every person who nowadays visits Doune to climb the massive
walls and descend to the reeking dungeons of the stronghold for a
glimpse of the harsh life of long ago, there must be a score whose
destination is the Doune Motor Museum, a collection of automobiles
ancient and modern, the lifelong labor of love of the late J.C. Sword.

After Doune you follow the Teith River to Callander, a well-built
townlet with a broad main street thronged in the season with visitors.
It is the base for the Trossachs, which we shall come to presently, and
it disputes with Pitlochry the claim to have more hotels per head of
population than any town in Britain. Just before you enter Callander
a signposted path takes you to the Roman Camp, a circle of earthworks
on the river bank. Another signpost on your right points up a steep brae
to the Falls of Bracklinn, one mile away. The cascade, falling down a
staircase of sandstone boulders, exposes the geology of the Highland
Line, the rock fault across Scotland which separates Lowlands from
Highlands. Callander, like Pitlochry, justifiably describes itself as a
Gateway to the Highlands.

Northward through Strathyre with the newly-afforested Braes of
Balquhidder sweeping up to the west, the road struggles to disentangle
itself from rock and torrent and overhanging rowan, oak and birch.
Two serpentine lochs spill down the glen, and it is fascinating after rain
to watch the stream racing beneath you in a succession of rapids and
waterfalls.

"My name is MacGregor," says Rob Roy in Scott's novel, "and my
foot is on my native heath". These rough ravines and the heather-
covered wilderness from which they radiate are his native heath. Rob

and his wife and two sons are said to lie under some stone slabs in Balquhidder ("Bal-hwidder") churchyard, the turning on the left after you pass through Strathyre; but the quaint carvings of weapons and animals suggest that the stones are a good deal older than those characters whose exploits belong to the early 18th century. Tales of Rob Roy MacGregor, a man of great physical strength and courageous energy, tend to romanticize him. In fact he was a medieval throwback, a cattle thief, an embezzler of lairds' rents and the operator of a vicious protection racket among poor farmers.

Across the watershed you arrive at Lochearnhead, a water-sports center on Loch Earn. Local hotels offer sailing lessons, canoeing, fishing, water skiing and suchlike. Your road, now the A85, continues north for another five miles to the Lix Toll (a reminder that the 59th—LIX—Roman legion was stationed there) and then, finding the going rather heavy, swings west to run along the softer, more open valley of Glen Dochart. It arrives at Crianlarich, another pocket of tourist hotels.

This is an important T-junction for tourists. The A82 from Glasgow comes in, having traveled the full 23-mile length of Loch Lomond, one of Strathclyde Region's famous routes. It, and the road from Lochearnhead, now continue northwest for Glencoe and Fort William in the Highlands.

On this historic route trodden by Romans and Picts, cattle drovers and cattle thieves, you must have an automobile or be a hardy walker. The railroad from Stirling to Crianlarich which used to accompany the highway has been closed down; although its continuation from Crianlarich to north and west was mercifully reprieved. The serenely remote vale from Crianlarich to Tyndrum has the strange distinction of being the only valley in Britain with two mainline railroads through it: Glasgow–Crianlarich–Oban and Glasgow–Crianlarich–Fort William.

Along the high road you note an agreeable aspect of Scottish travel. Every few miles, viewpoints and scenic spots are provided with parking places, picnic areas, tables and benches, perhaps a short nature trail, perhaps even a treehouse for the children; and nothing to pay. When a man or woman in uniform bears down on you, don't hurry away—it's only the district ranger, come to talk about the wildlife or to offer a loan of his binoculars or a plastic bag for your garbage.

For energetic tourists with time on their hands there are rewarding walks round the quiet riverine lochs of Lubnaig and Voil. To the summits of neighboring mountains it is usually quite a long walk, but nowhere is it difficult. Three miles north of Callander on the A84, an iron bridge crosses the river and, beyond the disused railroad, a fairly obvious route intermittently marked with a footpath leads in about 1½ miles to the top of Ben Ledi (2,873 feet), a magnificent viewpoint from which in clear weather you can see Arthur's Seat in Edinburgh and Goat Fell on the island of Arran, two places 100 miles apart. From Lochearnhead an unclassified road goes along the south shore of Loch Earn to Ardvorlich House, which is the starting point for Ben Vorlich (3,224 feet) with equally dramatic views of the approaches to the Highlands.

## The Trossachs

The popular road to the Trossachs from anywhere in the east of Scotland is via Callander on the A84, the road we have just traveled. One mile north of that town the A821, rather bumpy and narrow for its summer traffic, goes off to the left and almost at once you are coasting Loch Vennachar, the first of the Trossachs lakes. From here on the most comprehensive guide is Sir Walter Scott's poem *The Lady of the Lake:* it mentions every little bridge and farmhouse. Various engineering schemes of the Glasgow Water Department have rendered some of the topography out of date.

Loch Vennachar gives way to the beautiful little Loch Achray, shrouded in woodland; and Loch Achray leads on to the principal lake, Loch Katrine (pronounced "Kattrin"), where the road ends. Wandering byways in this area will take you to the smaller and more isolated Trossachs lochs: Arklet, Chon and Ard.

It is hard to describe the Trossachs or to account for their peculiar charm. They combine the wildness of the Highlands with the prolific vegetation of an old Lowland forest. Their open ground is a dense mat of bracken and heather, their woodland is of silver birch, dwarf oak and hazel which fasten their roots into every crevice of the rocks and stop short on the very brink of the lochs. The most colorful season is the fall, particularly October when the visitors have departed and the hares, deer and game birds have taken over. But the district is rich in color from early spring onwards with the variegated greens of the leaves and the grays and blues of the crags gradually yielding to the browns and purples of bracken and heather, soft and bright as an old tartan.

In rainy weather the Trossachs are a sponge and the water which filters through the rocks comes out so pure and clear that the lochs are like sheets of crystal glass. When Glasgow folk, who draw their water from this area, want distilled water for their automobile batteries they simply get it from the kitchen tap.

Throughout the summer the steamboat *Sir Walter Scott* plies between the Steamer Pier, one mile from the Trossachs hotel on the A821, and the hamlet of Stronachlachar, seven miles away near the head of Loch Katrine. You can also reach Stronachlachar by the minor B829 from Aberfoyle. Another tiny road continues beyond Stronachlachar and beside Loch Arklet for five miles to Inversnaid on Loch Lomond, where the landing-stage is a port of call for summer steamboats from Balmaha and Balloch (Strathclyde Region).

The district is well furnished with hill and forest paths. Parts of the loch shores are denied to the public, being the private territory of Glasgow's waterworks, but you will find dozens of little crags and clearings from which the ever-changing panorama of loch, heath and woodland opens out.

Place-names and topographical features commemorate Rob Roy, whose stamping ground this was. His supposed cave is close to Inversnaid on Loch Lomond. The old Highland word for a roughneck marauder like Rob Roy was "cateran," and that is said to be how Loch

Katrine got its name. When you take a walk and find the going tough, think how it was in this brigand country when Rob was an outlaw— when, as Scott says, "there was no mode of issuing from the Trossachs except by a sort of ladder composed of the branches of roots and trees."

An area of 45,000 acres covering most of the Trossachs, the two high hills of Ben Lomond and Ben Venue and a stretch of Loch Lomond's eastern shore has been designated the Queen Elizabeth Forest Park.

## Aberfoyle

When motoring for pleasure you can hardly go wrong on the scenic drives in the Trossachs. The lanes are narrow, with passing places; sometimes they end abruptly and you have to turn back. But to delay or retrace your steps is no hardship in this fresh, picturesque and varied landscape.

In the Pass of Achray, between Lochs Achray and Katrine, the A821 turns south for Aberfoyle. Old inhabitants can remember when this seven-mile road was the "Duke's Drive" and no automobiles were allowed on it. Bus-loads of vacationeers from Glasgow had to walk or travel in horse-drawn wagonettes. But now the Duke's Drive is a fine skyline route, snaking up to 800 feet and down again with panoramas of all the Trossachs lakes. Three miles from Aberfoyle, near the David Marshall wildlife park (hillpaths and picnic lodge) you may detour round the Achray Forest Drive (toll road, pay as you enter with two 50p pieces) and relax on a loch shore among the birds and beasts of the forest.

Aberfoyle village is popular with pony-trekkers. If you are only passing through, the focal point of interest is the local inn, with its supposed relics of the brawl in *Rob Roy,* when Bailie Nicol Jarvie of Glasgow set the Hielandman's kilt on fire with a red-hot poker.

Here you are on the road for Stirling (A873). It runs level along a broad valley, rather humdrum after the Trossachs scenery. It skirts the Lake of Menteith, often described as the only "lake" in Scotland (there are others in fact) and a venue for an occasional Grand Match between curlers, Highlands against Lowlands, whenever winter frosts permit the ice to bear. At a priory on one of the two islands in the lake the five-year-old Mary Queen of Scots was taken for safe keeping after the battle of Pinkie (Lothian) in 1547—a foretaste of the island prisons of her later captivity.

The serene parkland around Blair Drummond, where you rejoin the A84, contains lions, giraffes, dolphins and other exotic fauna. It is Scotland's first safari park. (Drive through, keep the windows closed and do not stop; should the monkeys tear off your windshield wipers, the gatekeeper has a sackful of spares for you to choose from.)

It is now eight miles to Stirling, our starting-point. The round trip, Stirling–Callander–Trossachs–Aberfoyle–Stirling, is only 52 miles, so if you devote the day to it there is plenty of time for exploring byways.

## Loch Lomond: the Eastern Shore

Our last Central Region route travels due west (A811) towards Strathclyde Region. A group of smooth rounded hills separates it from the Forth–Clyde valley where the Roman Wall, the canal and now the invisible oil pipeline from Grangemouth to Loch Long and the M80 to Glasgow run. The mini-massif has different names on its different sides: Fintry Hills, Campsie Fells, Kilsyth Hills. One minor road (B818) crosses them east to west and another (B822) north to south. They are relatively quiet alternatives to the arterial roads of the Region and not without charm. Northern slopes look towards the Highlands, southern slopes over the central-belt industrial conurbations.

Drymen ("Drimmen"), 23 miles from Stirling, is a pleasant-looking village built round an open square. The fast-flowing Endrick River runs close by, coming out of the Fintry Hills and heading for Loch Lomond. This is Buchanan country, as the name of the hotel tells us. Buchanan Castle stands aloof in its neighboring park. George Buchanan (1506-1582), scholar, poet and tutor to Mary Queen of Scots, was born at Killearn, two miles from Drymen.

At Drymen you are only three miles from Balmaha Pier on the east bank of Loch Lomond (B837); and Balmaha is the place at which all the loch steamboats call and from which a delightful trail, narrow and much-trafficked in summer, goes along the loch shore to Rowardennan (eight miles).

The boundary between Central and Strathclyde Regions is an imaginary line down the middle of Loch Lomond. It divides a pattern of islands opposite Balmaha. They look like clumps of forest lifted from the Trossachs and dumped in the lake, and the steamboat threads its way through them. Most have Gaelic names, but note two little rocks which do not: St. Rosalind's and St. Winifred's. There is a sentimental tale attached to them. In the 1880s the great map-maker John Bartholomew took his girl friend, suitably chaperoned, for a sail. They picnicked on one of those tufts of greenery. Maybe they managed to maroon the chaperone on another—at all events, two islets were involved in the happy memories that came back to John Bartholomew years later when he drew up the new map of Loch Lomond. Discovering that the islets had no names, he named one for his girl friend and the other for the chaperone.

Note also Bucinch and Ceardoch. They are washed by the passing boats but their dense foliage and lack of a boat landing make a visit difficult. They belong to the National Trust for Scotland. Legend says Robert the Bruce planted Bucinch's yew trees to provide weapons for his bowmen. Legend and history have stuck their labels on all the isles of this little Lomond archipelago: this one has a ruined château, that one a ruined nunnery, this one was the scene of a massacre, that is the old burial ground of the MacGregor chiefs . . . to visit them you would have to hire a boat and that is best done from Luss on the opposite shore.

Here at Balmaha and all the way up the track to Rowardennan they are part of the embroidery of the loch, anchored for eternity in the shimmering water, calm and mystical like green stones in a Zen garden.

To reach Rowardennan with an automobile is no problem, but beyond that point you have to walk; and it is another 16 miles on a forest path, under the bluff rocks of Craig Rostan (the Craig Royston of Scott's *Rob Roy*), before Loch Lomond—barely a mile wide at Rowardennan—eventually tapers to a stream at Ardlui. But climb Ben Lomond if you can (3,192 feet, not a difficult walk from Rowardennan) and from its summit you will see the whole of Loch Lomond, the biggest lake in Great Britain, retreating north and south beneath your gaze. At weekends there is a good deal of boating, skin-diving, fishing and rock-climbing going on; but somehow these activities never disturb the essential tranquillity of the loch.

From Stirling to Balmaha by the direct A811 route and back by the more roundabout routes over the Campsie fells would be a total journey of 70 miles. The boat trip from Balmaha Pier to Inversnaid and back takes nearly three hours.

# PRACTICAL INFORMATION FOR CENTRAL

**HOW TO GET THERE. By train.** Mainline railroads connect Stirling with Edinburgh (intermediate stations at Larbert, Falkirk and Polmont); with Glasgow (intermediate station at Croy); with Carlisle; and with Perth (intermediate station at Dunblane). From London (Euston) via Glasgow or from London (King's Cross) via Edinburgh the train takes about 7 hours. There is a direct overnight motorail service—it takes passengers *and* cars—between Stirling and London (Euston); Stirling and Newton Abbot (West of England); and Stirling and Inverness (Highland).

In the northwest of the Region there are rail connections from Tyndrum and Crianlarich to Glasgow in the south, Oban (Strathclyde) in the west and Fort William (Highland) in the north.

**By car.** Stirling is 37 miles from Edinburgh, 27 from Glasgow, and 35 from Perth. The M9 and M80 motorways from Edinburgh and Glasgow respectively pass one mile west of the town and continue to Dunblane; they are gradually being extended to Perth and Dundee.

**By air.** Airports for Central Region are Glasgow (M80, M8), 31 miles from Stirling; and Edinburgh (M9), 30 miles from Stirling.

**HOTELS AND RESTAURANTS.** Central Region's main touring bases are Stirling and Callander. There, and at small towns and villages throughout the Region, you will find a spread of tourist accommodations out of all proportion to the size of the communities. (The industrial towns are the exceptions.) Standards of inexpensive and medium-price establishments have improved in recent years and are still improving. The grand hotels, though few, were brought into existence by the rich "carriage trade" of the 19th century, when travel in Scotland was the fashion, and their services have not slipped. But you will also find that numerous country hotels match them for comfort and hospitality.

Like hotels, the restaurants of the touring districts are many and competitive, and continually improving. Regional country delicacies like loch trout, river salmon, mutton and venison are found regularly on modest menus, something extremely rare 20 years ago. The urban areas south and southwest of Stirling, in contract, lack refinement in matters of eating and drinking. There you will find simple low-built pubs, often crowded and noisy, but serving substantial food at lunchtime (often eaten balanced on your knee, or at a shared table). Three heavy courses at one of these pubs will cost you all of $2 or $3.

**ABERFOYLE** (A81). *Bailie Nicol Jarvie* (M), tel. 202. 33 rooms, 25 with bath. The wild men of Rob Roy's "clachan" (tavern) would not recognize their old drinking den on the fringe of the Trossachs, now enlarged and attractively modernized.
**Restaurant.** *Old Coachhouse* (M), tel. 535. Fishing net hangs on wall, but menu is cosmopolitan.

**BLAIR DRUMMOND** (A84). **Restaurant.** *Broughton's Country Cottage* (M), tel. Doune 897. Quite small (prior booking advisable). Prices are low for this category.

**CALLANDER** (A84). *Glenorchy* (M), Leny Road (tel. 30329). 15 rooms, 3 with bath. Large, cozy guest-house with superior amenities.
**Restaurant.** *Pip's Coffee House* (I), Ancaster Square (tel. 30407). Good lunch stop. Wide choice of dishes, despite name.

**DRYMEN** (A81). *Buchanan Arms* (E), tel. 60588. 23 rooms, 21 with bath. Imposing building, high standard of cuisine.

**DUNBLANE** (A9). *Hydro* (E), tel. 822551. 126 rooms, all with bath. Ample caravanserai of well-heeled hypochondriacs of long ago, today replaced by delegates of high-powered conferences. Beautiful situation. Elaborate venison, salmon and seafood dishes.

**LOCHEARNHEAD** (A85). *Craigroyston House* (M), tel. 229. 12 rooms, 4 with bath. Warm, friendly, family-run; with cordon bleu and traditional Scottish cooking. Steak and fish bar open 12 hours a day. Own foreshore on Loch Earn, boats, water sports.

**POLMONT** (A9). *Inchyra Grange* (E), tel. 711911. 30 rooms, all with bath. Solid stone country house, secluded but handy for motorway. Quiet luxury. Large wine cellar.

**ROWARDENNAN** (on unclassified road from Balmaha). *Rowardennan* (I), tel. Balmaha 273. 9 rooms, 1 with bath. A homely, whitewashed inn at the ferry slip, halfway along Loch Lomond. Surprisingly sophisticated cuisine, attracts many visitors at weekends for drinks and lunches. Other times this is a place to unwind amid unforgettable scenery.

**STIRLING** (A9). *Golden Lion* (E), King Street (tel. 5351). 75 rooms, 43 with bath. Venerable staging post with much coming and going, but efficiently run. First-class cuisine.

**Restaurant.** *Heritage* (M), 16 Allan Park (tel. 3660). Elegant, French-owned 18th-century establishment; fanlights and candles. Not surprisingly, there's a Gallic flavor to its cuisine.

**THORNHILL** (A873). **Restaurant.** *Lion and Unicorn* (M), tel. 204. A place of real character. Try the fillet steak on a cast-iron platter.

**TROSSACHS** (A821). *Loch Achray* (I), tel. 229. 52 rooms, 3 with bath. Another unpretentious but perfectly adequate stopover for meals or beds in a magnificent situation beside the Duke's Drive.

**HOW TO GET ABOUT. By car.** The road network in the Central Region is excellent. Though it may sometimes be hard for the stranger to extricate himself from the industrial towns south of Stirling, traffic pressure on the narrow streets of the old burghs has been much relieved by the construction of the motorways. In July and August the roads west and northwest of Stirling are busy by Scottish standards, especially at weekends. On a fine Sunday afternoon you will find the minor roads in the Trossachs and Loch Lomond areas quite congested: they were built for cattle, not vehicles.

You can rent an automobile in Stirling or Falkirk—see local telephone directory for names of firms.

**By bus.** There are service buses on all the routes described earlier in the chapter. Dark blue in color, they are operated by *William Alexander & Sons,* Bus Station, Stirling (tel. 3763—prefix with 0786 if calling from outside Stirling). This company also runs excursions and tours of the Region, as does *Scottish Omnibuses,* St. Andrew Square, Edinburgh (tel. 556 8231—031 prefix if out of town).

**By boat.** A scheduled boat service operates on Loch Lomond between Inversnaid, Balmaha and Balloch (Strathclyde).

**TOURIST INFORMATION.** Central Region's principal information centers are at Stirling (Dumbarton Road, tel. 5019) and Callander (Leny Road, tel. 30342). There you can "book-a-bed-ahead."

Stirling is open Apr.–Sept. with a restricted service Oct.–Mar. Callander is open Apr.–Sept. only, as are the district centers at Aberfoyle, Clackmannan, Dunblane, Killin, Kincardine Bridge and Tyndrum. Opening hours are usually weekdays, 10–6. In Jul. and Aug. some centers open Sun. 10–6 or 11–6.

The Scottish Tourist Board operates an information center at Bannockburn (tel. 814026), open daily 10–9, Apr.–Sept. The Forestry Commission maintains a Forestry Information Service at Strathyre (A84), where there are also forest cabins to rent. Open Easter–mid-Oct.

**FISHING.** There is salmon fishing in the upper Forth, Teith and Devon rivers and in Loch Lomond (from Inversnaid hotel). Day or season permits may be obtained from or through local fishing-tackle shops. Sunday fishing is prohibited in most parts of the Region.

Sea trout and brown trout are fished in the Allan Water (permits from Stirling and Bridge of Allan tackle shops). The Lake of Menteith is stocked with brown and rainbow trout: fly fishing only, from boats at Lake of Menteith hotel, and rather expensive at around $18 per day. The Carron Valley reservoir in the Fintry Hills has brown trout; fly fishing from boat around $12 per day (permit from Director of Finance, Central Regional Council, Viewforth, Stirling). Two good inexpensive lochs for brown trout are Loch Achray in the Trossachs ($2 per day, permits from Loch Achray hotel, some pike, bream and perch also); and Banton Loch ($1 per day, permit from Kilsyth Fish Protection Association, 24 Kingston Flats, Kilsyth, or Colzium Service Station, Stirling Road, Kilsyth).

Hotels that offer fishing to residents in own grounds or nearby include Forest Hills, at Aberfoyle; Winnock, at Drymen; Inversnaid, at Inversnaid; Lake, at Port of Menteith; Loch Achray, at Trossachs; Glazertbank, at Lennoxtown; and Rosebank House, at Strathyre.

**GOLF.** As elsewhere in Scotland, every town and many a village has its nine- or 18-hole course. You can normally turn up and play a round without formality on payment of a fee of $6–9 a day. Caddy cars, snack meals and drinks are usually available. The three smart clubs are at Dollar, Drymen (Buchanan Castle) and Dullatur. These clubs require an introduction from a member or a golf club secretary and do not welcome casual clothes in their lounge bars, or visitors at weekends.

**HISTORIC HOUSES AND GARDENS.** The northern parts of Central Region were too close to the predatory Highlanders to encourage much building of elegant houses or the laying out of woods and estates; while southern parts were completely overlaid by industry in the 19th century. Nonetheless, there are some attractive houses and gardens in the valleys of Forth and Teith, west of Stirling, but most are privately-owned and open on specified days only, in spring and summer. Consult local newspapers or information centers for details.

**Doune Castle,** Doune (A84). Ruins of a 14th-century stronghold, massive in decay. A descendant of the earls of Moray, who owned it, now has the *Doune Motor Museum* close by. Open Apr.–Oct., daily, 10–5.

**Gargunnock House,** 6 miles from Stirling (A811). Entrance to the house itself is by written appointment only. The gardens are especially worth visiting and are normally open Apr.–Oct., Wed. only, 1–5.

**Menstrie Castle,** Castle Road, Menstrie (A91). 16th-century fortress almost completely modernized. Part is privately-occupied, but you can visit the Nova Scotia commemoration rooms with relics of Sir William Alexander (1567–1640) and the history of the colonial baronetcies. Open May–Sept., Wed., Sat. and Sun., 2.30–5. N.T.S.

**MUSEUMS. Falkirk Museum,** Orchard Street, Falkirk (A9). Social, industrial and archeological history of the district, including material on Antonine Wall. Open weekdays 10–12.30 and 1.30–5.

**Grangemouth Museum,** Bo'ness Road, Grangemouth (A904). History of Forth–Clyde and Falkirk-Edinburgh canals. Open weekdays during library hours, currently 10–7.

**MacRobert Arts Center,** 3 miles along road to Bridge of Allan, University of Stirling (A9). Enterprising exhibitions of many kinds in a lively cultural center. Open Jan.–May and Sept.–Dec., weekdays 11–5, Sun. 2–5.

**Scottish Railway Preservation Society Depot,** Wallace Street, Falkirk (A9). Fine collection of historic locomotives, coaches, wagons. Open Sat. and Sun., 11–5.

**Smith Art Gallery and Museum,** Albert Place, Stirling (A9). History of district; various temporary exhibitions. Undergoing extensive renovation. Open 2–5.

Andrew Carnegie

# KINGDOM OF THE PICTS

## *Fife*

"Fareweel Scotland, I'm awa' to Fife," cried the fishwife of Newhaven, setting sail for the opposite shore of the Firth of Forth. It was all of six miles away but she expressed what many Lothian people used to feel: that Fife was a foreign place. Since her time, communications between Fife and the rest of Scotland have been made easier. There are the one and a half-mile-long Forth rail and road bridges to join her to the south, and the longer but less spectacular Tay rail and road bridges to the north. Travelers in a hurry to get across one or other of these bridges are out of Fife before they realize they are in it.

It is called the Kingdom of Fife. It is the only remaining kingdom of the seven into which Scotland fell when the Romans went home in the 4th century A.D. and the Picts moved in. That distinction was remembered when local government in Scotland was reorganized in 1973. Of all the county councils which put up arguments against merging with their neighbors to form Regions—and most of them did—only Fife won the day. Plans to divide her between Central and Tayside Regions were abandoned. She kept her kingdom intact and the eight Regions became nine. This tells us something about Fife folk: they are stubborn, even among Scots, and will go to greater lengths than most to preserve their independence.

Until recently, the main touring routes avoided Fife. The great northern highway from Edinburgh to Perth and Inverness (M90) now runs along its western borders. Its northern and southern limits are the Firths of Tay and Forth respectively; its eastern border is the open sea. Not surprisingly, fishing and seafaring have played a role in its history. At an earlier period a large population lived and worked in the small ports and harbors which form a continuous chain round its coasts. James V called Fife "a beggar's mantle fringed with gold."

That was before the exploitation of another kind of gold, black gold, began in the western parts of the Region. Coal from the West Fife coalfields provided the energy which got Scotland moving in the Industrial Revolution in the late 18th century. As in West Lothian across the Forth, this industry was now declined and you will see more disused pits than working ones. Fife's industrial hopes these days are pinned to 20th-century black gold—oil, petrochemicals and liquid gases from the North Sea. A large liquid-gas development is proposed for Moss Morran near Aberdour (A92) to produce propane and butane for export to North America from the nearby Braefoot tanker terminal. Westward along the same shoreline, off the A895 road near Culross, the biggest power station in Great Britain (2,400 megawatts) pours its hot effluent into the Forth.

## Around and About

The industrial corner of Fife, a depressed and depressing district, occupies only a small part of the Region. The rest is pleasant agricultural country, not sensational but never monotonous. And the whole Region is still ringed with those fishing villages which, weathered down by the centuries, have become antiques of domestic architecture.

At Castle Law near Abernethy (A913) you will find a pre-Roman hill fort. Pictish names are common and you may be shown the occasional Pictish stone built into the wall of a church or cottage. There is one at the gates of Upper Largo church (A915). In Dunfermline and St. Andrews, Fife has the two senior religious settlements in Scotland; and at Lindores and Balmerino near the Tay shore (A913) the ruins of two large Norman abbeys.

There are no commercial airports in the Region. Fife people use either Edinburgh or Dundee. The main railroad from Edinburgh to the north, coming in by the Forth bridge, passes through the middle of the Region, where it divides in two, one track curving away to Perth for the old Highland line and the other going forward to the Tay bridge, Dundee and Aberdeen. There is also a branch line from the Forth bridge to Dunfermline and the mining towns of Cowdenbeath and Cardenden.

South to north through the Region, from Forth bridge to Tay bridge, is 40 miles, that is, about the same distance as the route west to east, from the M90 motorway to the promontory of Fife Ness.

The M90 cuts off a corner of the Region but the best road south to north through Fife is the A92, which takes in an old-fashioned little burgh called Cupar ("Cooper"), the "capital of the kingdom." The main west–east routes leave the M90 at different points for the coastal towns of the Forth (A911, A921); St. Andrews (A91); and the coastal villages of the Tay (A913).

## West Fife

Coming off the Forth bridges by road or rail you plunge into a short stretch of uninspiring, rather tired-looking industry. On your left is the naval base of Rosyth, the Royal Navy's most junior home port, founded 1912. It ought to have been on the opposite shore, more convenient for Edinburgh and the south, but the Marquess of Linlithgow at Hopetoun House would not have it; and in those days the noble landowner's word was law. Rosyth has often been threatened with closure but it is now a refitting yard for nuclear submarines and its future seems assured.

On your right you glimpse the reverse side of the naval coin: the shipbreakers' yards at Inverkeithing, where famous old battleships were brought to end their days. The first of them were the surrendered units of Germany's High Seas fleet in 1919.

Dunfermline, five miles beyond the bridge going north, lifts her head proudly above the dismal coalmining scene round about. Her abbey, built on the site of a Celtic church, was a favorite shrine of Queen Margaret. She was married there to King Malcolm Canmore, who made some solid Romanesque improvements to the building to remind her of the ecclesiastical jewels of her own country, England. They must have seemed a strange innovation for Scotland.

Malcolm and Margaret had a small palace at Dunfermline (you can see its remains inside the abbey walls) and both of them were buried there in 1093, the Queen having died of grief at hearing of her husband's death. Scottish monarchs, who had up to that date always gone to Iona for burial, were thereafter interred at Dunfermline. There are 15 royal graves in the abbey, including that of Robert the Bruce. But the place suffered in the English wars and at the hands of John Knox's reformers and what we see today is chiefly an early 19th-century renovation. Purists consider the stone lettering "Robert the Bruce" round the parapet of the tower to be in rather poor taste.

Dunfermline's modern "patron saint," the man most responsible for its air of comfortable self-satisfaction, is Andrew Carnegie. His birthplace (1835) was a small house, now a museum, in Moodie Street. His parents rented the attic. As a steel baron in the States, Carnegie wielded power that the old Scottish kings would have envied, but he never forgot Dunfermline. He created the Carnegie Trust (1903) which enabled his native town to enjoy social and educational amenities and he bought and gave to the town the beautiful private park through whose heavy locked gates he had hardly dared look as a child. Pittencrieff Glen is still open to the public and is probably the most lavishly-endowed public park in Britain.

Seven miles west of Dunfermline, just off the A985, the 17th-century burgh of Culross ("Coo-russ") nestles beside the Forth. Its cottages, wynds, miniature abbey, town house and palace are like scenes from an old engraving: hard to believe that Culross 350 years ago was a bustling seaport and a pioneer of the coal trade. The National Trust

for Scotland saved Culross from decay, restoring its houses and preserving its bumpy cobbled lanes with their characteristic plainstanes,
the strips of level paving reserved for local gentry. Culross is a three-
dimensional document in which you may read the social history of a
vanished era.

## Old Hills and New Towns

Rejoining the M90 in the direction of Perth you pass by Loch Leven
and come to the next main road into Fife, the A911. Vincenzo Lunardi,
the first aerial traveler in Britain, floating toward Fife in his balloon in
1785, wrote: "I saw huge hills which I took to be the Highlands." They
were not. They were the Lomonds (nothing to do with Loch Lomond)
which curve up from the Howe of Fife, the agricultural heart of the
Region, to heights of about 1,700 feet. They have lately taken on
another aeronautical connection: they are a venue for the Scottish
gliding and hang-gliding clubs.

As the Lomonds sink behind you in the west you approach some
towns of fairly innocuous industry, a small complex of which Glenrothes is the center. Glenrothes is a startling intruder in this archetypal
Lowland scene: a new town, developed since 1950 and originally designed to meet the housing needs of new colliery workers. But coalmining has declined and Glenrothes instead has attracted the trailblazers
of Scotland's most important new industry, electronics. Most of its
35,000 inhabitants are employed in factories which manufacture com-
puters, office machinery and rocket and satellite systems. Having seven
universities within a 90-minute drive of its center, it has also become
an exchange-and-mart of scientific research. Glenrothes boasts the Fife
airport, for light aircraft only.

The neighboring communities at Leslie and Markinch depended on
papermaking at mills powered by the streams which flow from the
Lomond Hills. For two centuries the big name hereabouts has been
Tullis Russell, makers of quality paper and cardboard.

Following the A911 and its continuation A915 and A917 we come
to the Firth of Forth, with views of Edinburgh 15 miles across the
water, and enter the East Neuk ("nook") of Fife.

## The East Neuk

This is James V's "golden fringe." Although it is a Scottish equivalent of the Italian riviera, a series of waterfront villages darkened by
the shrubbery of masts and rigging, little seaside places which can never
be grand because they have no room to expand, the East Neuk is not
all that "golden" in terms of sand or sunshine. You may think the
outlook of black rocks and seaweed rather dreary. But the villages have
character, with their brownstone or color-washed fronts, their rusty
pantiled roofs, fishy weathervanes, outside stone stairways to upper
floors, no two windows or chimney pots alike and crude carvings of
anchors and lobsters on their lintels—all crowded on steep narrow
wynds and hugging pint-sized harbors which, in the golden era, supported village fleets of 100 ships apiece.

At one period the East Neuk boats traded with Holland and Denmark and its fishermen followed the herring down the east coast of England as far as Lowestoft in Suffolk. The village girls went down to meet them, on foot, to mend the nets and cure the catch.

The first place you come to is Largo, popular with the bucket-and-spade brigade. Here a juvenile delinquent named Alexander Selkirk grew up, terrorized the neighborhood and departed to sail the seas. In 1704, having quarrelled with his captain, Selkirk was put ashore on the isle of Juan Fernandez off the coast of Chile. Four years later a British privateer picked him up; his rescuers found him dressed in goatskins and surrounded by tame goats. Piratical adventures on the way home earned him a fortune and he returned to Largo so richly dressed that his mother did not know him. It is said that he could not settle down in the house, so built himself a hut in the garden—where the writer Daniel Defoe found him. He listened to his story, and out of it made the tale of *Robinson Crusoe*.

After Largo comes Elie, where there is good golf, and then the archaic villages of St. Monance (or St. Monans—the village roadsigns spell it both ways), Pittenweem, Anstruther and Crail, each on its diminutive inlet. The boatyard of Miller of St. Monance has been building Fifies, traditional high-stemmed, broad-beamed, three-man fishing boats, for more than two centuries. Nowadays they do yachts and cabin cruisers as well. Pittenweem (it means "place of the cave") has part of the Dark Age hermitage of St. Fillan built into its harbor wall. Anstruther (locally called "Anster") is the site of a Fisheries Museum. Crail, oldest and most aristocratic of East Neuk burghs, was the place the fish merchants retired to and built cottages, palatial by local standards. The Devil came to the Isle of May, six miles offshore, and threw a boulder at them. Half of it lies in the market-place and you can see his thumbprint on it.

Local history says that Crail once had the biggest fishmarket in Europe. Certainly the disproportionate size of the tolbooths (town halls) and market crosses in all these little harbors is significant; and so are the large houses and their doocots (dovecots, where pigeons were kept for winter meat) of the country round about. According to an old saying, the Fife landowner's possessions amounted to "pickle (small) land, muckle (large) debt, a doocot and a lawsuit"—Fifers were great litigants. From somewhere around here in the 19th century came "Muck Andrew," a figure all too well known at the court of session in Edinburgh, for he was there year in year out until the law finally beggared him; and all for a trivial squabble with a neighbor over the ownership of a farmyard manure-heap.

## "Little City, Worn and Gray"

From Crail to St. Andrews is only 10 miles but we shall return to the M90 turn-off and approach that cathedral city by the A91, along the crop-growing Howe of Fife ("howe" is hollow). The road passes through Auchtermuchty (something of a joke in pronunciation for the English, but locals call it "Auchmewty") and through Fife's capital city, the royal burgh of Cupar. Royal burghs abound in Fife, though

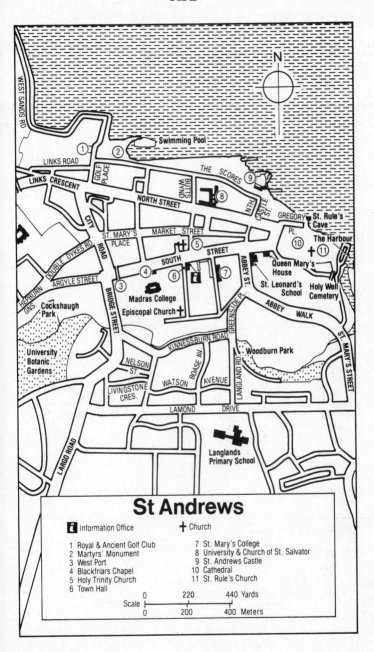

# St Andrews

**i** Information Office          **✝** Church

1  Royal & Ancient Golf Club      7  St. Mary's College
2  Martyrs' Monument              8  University & Church of St. Salvator
3  West Port                      9  St. Andrews Castle
4  Blackfriars Chapel            10  Cathedral
5  Holy Trinity Church           11  St. Rule's Church
6  Town Hall

Scale
0        220        440 Yards
0        200        400 Meters

they rarely look regal. The hard-up Stuart kings bestowed charters with suspicious generosity; it was a cheap way of supplementing the royal income.

Cupar is a venerable market center with something of a neo-classical air. More than 900 years ago it was the seat of those thanes (earls) of Fife who are mentioned in Shakespeare's *Macbeth*. A conspicuous landmark one mile south is the 16th-century castellated mansion of Scotstarvit. From the top of its five-storied tower you can see most of the Kingdom of Fife, including "St. Andrews by the northern sea . . . a little city, worn and gray."

That poem by Andrew Lang (1844-1912) expresses the affection that almost everyone who lives or studies there seems to feel. Possibly the most-visited town in Scotland after Edinburgh, though rather out of the way, St. Andrews is spread out above a wide bay, open to the northeast breezes. Its oldest monuments are the Celtic church ruins above the harbor; St. Rule's tower (1126); the castle (about 1200), the cathedral (dedicated 1318) and the West Port, the only original town gate in Scotland which is still in use.

St. Andrews came into prominence as the first bishopric of Scotland in the reign of Mary Queen of Scots. By that time the legend of St. Rule, or St. Regulus, had taken root. Briefly, Regulus was a 7th-century Greek monk divinely inspired to steal some of St. Andrew's bones from Patras cathedral where the apostle had been martyred; and to take them on a journey. Led by dreams, Regulus ended up on the Fife coast and managed to convert the Pictish king to Christianity. There is some debate where, if anywhere, St. Andrew's bones lie: most of the skeleton is in Amalfi cathedral in Italy.

St. Andrews in plan is pure Middle Ages, three main streets converging on a cathedral. Like most of the town's ancient monuments the cathedral is impressive in its desolation—but this is no dusty museum-city. The streets are busy, the gray houses sparkle in the sun and the scene is brightened during the academic year by bicycling students in scarlet gowns.

The ghost of a "white lady" periodically moans from the cathedral ruins in the direction of the castle, which was also a bishop's palace in bygone days and now covers a grassy headland with its remaining stones. Here, during the Reformation, there were savage struggles between Catholic bishops and Protestant extremists. The Cardinal-bishop Beaton was murdered and his murderers occupied the palace, where they were joined by John Knox. In August 1547 some French galleys appeared in St. Andrews Bay and their gunfire broke down the walls. Knox and his companions were transported to France and Knox himself spent 18 months as a galley slave.

In those fights the delicate stonework of St. Andrews University was damaged. The oldest of the Scottish universities, founded 1411, it now consists of two fine old colleges in the middle of the town and some attractive modern buildings on the outskirts. A third old college (1512) has become the fashionable girls' school of St. Leonard's.

And so to golf. The Royal & Ancient Golf Club of St. Andrews is the ruling house of golf worldwide and the spiritual home of all who play or follow the game. Its clubhouse on the dunes—a building of some dignity, more like a town hall than a clubhouse—is a treasury of golfing relics but you may enter only by invitation. Anyone, on the other hand, can play on the four courses at St. Andrews, even the famous Old Course itself.

In the churchyard near St. Rule's tower and also on a wall tablet in Holy Trinity church you will see memorials to Tommy Morris. Tommy's father, old Tom, was the greatest golfer in the world—until his son reached the age of 17, won his first professional title and went round the Old Course in 47. That was when fairways were not mown and greens were cut with a hand-scythe. Next year, 1868, Tommy won the Open Championship and held the title for five years. Then he died, aged 24, unchallenged supremo of golf, whose like the game will never see again.

St. Andrews prospers on golf, golf schools and equipment. The manufacture of golf balls has been a local industry for more than 100 years. But it is also a popular seaside resort; and at the Lammas Fair, held in early August, half the population of East Fife seems to be in town.

## The "Lang Toun"

Now we return to the Forth bridge to take the main route (A92, A914) through Fife, which accompanies the principal rail line to the Tay bridges. The first town is Inverkeithing, oldest royal burgh in Scotland, but its period charm smothered by factory development. After the commuter suburb of Dalgety Bay you pass through Aberdour, where a steep little street leads down to a beach and harbor which even Fife people think small; but those few square yards of sand are immortalized in two famous old ballads: *Sir Patrick Spens* and *The Bonnie Earl of Moray.*

Aberdour, a family vacation resort on a small scale, at one period supported an artists' colony. Now there is a sailing school for beginners. The boat service to Inchcolm, isle of Columba, two miles offshore is suspended but you will find boatmen willing to take you out. The island is little more than a rock, quite bare apart from its ruined 12th-century church. Inside its walls the earliest known Scottish fresco, a 13th-century scene of priests in procession, was discovered.

Burntisland ("Burnt Island") comes next; a shipyard and a restored tower house which Mary Queen of Scots used as a staging-post on her journeys into Fife. Here her impetuous French admirer Chastelard propositioned her and was promptly beheaded for it. The incident taught Mary how vulnerable a beautiful 19-year-old could be, even if she were a queen, and prompted her to embark on the rash marriages which split the nation.

At the next coastal village, Kinghorn, a tablet beside the railroad commemorates Alexander III's fatal fall over the cliff. A short steep lane leads down to the firm crystalline beach on which he landed.

Kirkcaldy ("Kirkawdy"), 15 miles from the Forth bridge, is the "Lang Toun" (Long Town). Its main street measures four miles and somewhere along it, according to an old tradition, St. Serf wrestled with the Devil. "The Deil's dead, the Deil's dead / And buried in

Kirkcaldy" goes the children's song and some say it must have been the stench which killed him. What with rotting flax for the linen industry and the Spanish cork and Greenland whale oil used in the manufacture of linoleum, Kirkcaldy used to have an aroma which strangers found hard to take. To inhabitants who knew the old days, the fumes from the large Coal Board installations at Seafield, one mile from the town, are mild and pleasant.

Kirkcaldy and Dunfermline, each with 50,000 inhabitants, are the largest towns in Fife Region. Kirkcaldy used to be the principal port, but her shipping connections with numerous North Sea ports are virtually reduced to a dilapidated sign above the harbor office announcing long-discontinued passages to London. Some of the little angular streets and alleyways have curious names. What, one wonders, was the origin of Prime Gilt Box Street? The houses of Sailor's Walk have been restored by the National Trust for Scotland with the usual pleasing result.

Where the High Street swings round into the Esplanade you will find the birthplace of Adam Smith, pioneer economist and author of *The Wealth of Nations*. At the old Burgh School there is a plaque recording that both he and Robert Adam the architect were pupils there in the 1730s; and that Thomas Carlyle the historian and essayist taught at the school nearly 100 years later.

If you leave Kirkcaldy by the Dunfermline road (B925) you will pass by two handsome public parks on left and right: Beveridge, gifted by the local linoleum tycoon; and Raith, the old feudal demesne. Raith House was formerly one of the many defensive strongholds of this coast, property of that Shakespearian MacDuff who was urged to "Lay on!"

## The Right Royal Burgh

Heading now for the Tay bridges we come to a crossroads and old coaching station, the New Inn. (Fife is a land of historic intersections marked with stagecoach houses.) At this point you should detour two miles to Falkland, another royal burgh of twisting streets and crooked stone houses.

Falkland is more royal than most royal burghs, for here stands the great courtyard palace of the Stuarts, one of the earliest examples in Britain of the French Renaissance style. Of the original not much remains. It belonged to the 12th century but was badly damaged by the English in 1377. The really imposing survivals, the gatehouse and flanking towers and the pit dungeon, were chiefly the work of James IV and James V, who were especially fond of Falkland. The most attractive feature is the south range of walls and chambers, rich with Renaissance buttresses and stone medallions and built for James V in 1539 by French masons. It has been described as the outstanding symbol of the "Auld Alliance" between Scotland and France.

Why build a palace here in the dangerous backwoods of the medieval Howe of Fife? It was primarily a hunting lodge, a center for such royal pleasures as hawking, archery, deer-slaying and pig-sticking in the Falkland Forest. It still has its "real" tennis court, like that at Hampton

Court on the Thames near London; but no mementoes of the lions and performing seals which James V kept in a private zoo. In Falkland's beautiful walled garden, overlooked by turret windows, you may easily imagine yourself back at the solemn hour when James V on his death-bed pronounced the doom of the house of Stuart: "It cam' wi' a lass and it'll gang wi' a lass."

And all of this, palace and fortifications and garden, agreeable to the old Scottish fashion, is embedded in the heart of the burgh. Whatever else you miss in Fife, do not miss Falkland.

## Northeast Fife

From the New Inn to the Tay bridge is 21 miles of undulating, cultivated country. The road and rail bridges, each two miles long, are low-built and workmanlike, lacking the photogenic appeal of their Forth counterparts; and lacking also the flimsy latticework of that notorious first Tay bridge, miracle of 19th-century technology, which collapsed in a storm in 1879 while a train was crossing it. Shortly before that, General Ulysses S. Grant was among the celebrities who had come to view it: a wall-tablet at Tayport, the old ferry station two miles east, recalls his visit. That bridge's replacement, built 1883-88, still carries the railroad to Dundee. The modern road bridge (1966) crosses the Firth a short distance downstream and delivers motorists into the heart of Dundee.

Newport and Tayport are firthside towns, residential suburbs of the Dundee conurbation of which they have close-up views. Near the bridge is a T-junction of interesting roads: first, the one we have trav-eled from Kirkcaldy; second, a 10-mile route to St. Andrews (A919) past the wild flats of Tentsmuir with its bird sanctuary, the Royal Air Force's strike command headquarters at Leuchars and the five-arched medieval bridge and ultra-modern paper mill at Guardbridge; third, a delightful winding route westward along the Firth, which here resem-bles a small inland sea, to the M90 and Perth.

On that unclassified but perfectly smooth and safe byroad you may inspect fragments of the 13th-century monastery at Balmerino ("Bal-merry-no"), the 14th-century Rothes fortress at Ballinbreich, and the ruins of the once-lordly red-sandstone abbey of Lindores, overthrown in 1559 by John Knox and his crusaders in an excess of reforming zeal. You encounter hardly any traffic. Fife, which began with a sprawl of industry, ends here in a landscape of rustic charm and tranquillity. Newburgh, a royal burgh sunk in the decrepitude of old age, despite its name, is where you join the A913 road for the motorway and Perth and Dundee to the north, Edinburgh to the south.

## PRACTICAL INFORMATION FOR FIFE

**HOW TO GET THERE. By train.** Fife Region is well served by British Rail (see beginning of chapter). There are passenger stations on the main London–Edinburgh–Dundee line at Aberdour, Burntisland, Kinghorn, Kirkcaldy, Markinch and Cupar; and at Dunfermline, Rosyth Halt and Leuchars. It takes 5¾ hours by fast train from London (King's Cross) to Kirkcaldy.

**By bus.** W. Alexander & Sons, The Esplanade, Kirkcaldy, have bus services from London (Victoria) and Coventry (Corley Service Station) daily to Dunfermline and Glenrothes; and return. The same company operates buses between Glasgow (Buchanan Street) and Dunfermline, Leven and St. Andrews. Eastern Scottish, St. Andrew Square bus station, Edinburgh, operate services between Edinburgh and Dunfermline, Kirkcaldy and St. Andrews. All the Fife towns have their own services to neighboring towns. The journey from London to Dunfermline takes 11 hours and costs about £11. The journey from Edinburgh to St. Andrews takes 90 minutes and costs £2.25.

**By car.** Fife is accessible from the south by the Forth road bridge and from the north by the Tay road bridge. The Edinburgh–Perth motorway (M90) crosses the western side of the Region and from numerous points on it there are good main roads to Kirkcaldy, the "East Neuk," Dunfermline, Culross, Cupar, St. Andrews and Newburgh.

**HOTELS AND RESTAURANTS.** If you are staying in Fife the obvious base is St. Andrews, where you will find ample accomodations of all kinds, except possibly when the Open Championship or some other important golfing event is taking place. Other towns do not offer a wide range, but you will find hotels and guest-houses at Dunfermline and Kirkcaldy; and all the royal burghs have hotels or inns in the town or the neighborhood. Along the coastal strip and in the Howe of Fife between Strathmiglo and Cupar there are some superior country-house hotels and restaurants.

In Kirkcaldy, Dunfermline and West Fife towns in general, you will find Italian and Chinese restaurants, and cafes of all kinds. Bar lunches are becoming the rule in hotels large and small throughout the Region, while in seaside places the "carry oot" (to go) meal is an old tradition.

**ANSTRUTHER** (A921). **Restaurant** *Craw's Nest* (I), tel. 310691. Old property sensitively modernized. King Charles II dined here and praised the fresh farm produce.

**DUNFERMLINE** (A823). *Keavil House* (M), Crossford (tel. 36258). 12 rooms, all with bath. Old-fashioned, intimate, country-style hotel, triumphing over drab surroundings. *King Malcolm* (M), Wester Pitcorthie (tel. 22611). 48 rooms, all with bath. Spacious hotel, popular with conference organizers, business executives.

**ELIE** (A917). *Golf* (M), tel. 330209. 21 rooms, 7 with bath. Exposed situation but warm and pleasant with excellent cuisine; fish dishes a specialty.

**FALKLAND** (A912). **Restaurant.** *Covenanter* (I), tel. 224. In town center. With good wine list. Also some rooms.

**KIRKCALDY** (A92). *Station* (M), Bennochy Street (tel. 62461). 34 rooms, 9 with bath. Provincial version of the big Edinburgh railroad hotels; something of an air of somber dignity.

**LARGO** (A915). **Restaurant.** *Crusoe* (M), tel. Lundin Links 320759. Renowned for elaborate seafood confections. Lobsters landed daily.

**LUNDIN LINKS** (A921) *Lundin Links* (I), tel. 320207. 16 rooms, 8 with bath. Large Victorian villa near beach and golf course; friendly relaxed atmosphere. Praise-worthy steaks and seafood.

**NEWPORT-ON-TAY** (A914). *Sandford Hill* (M), at Wormit (tel. 541802). 16 rooms, 15 with bath. Typical of several Fife country hotels that have been expensively modernized. Small rooms, labyrinthine passages, courtyard; even a wishing well. High-class cuisine attracts a discriminating clientele.

**ST. ANDREWS** (A91). *Old Course* (E), tel. 74371. 71 rooms, all with bath. Biggest and newest hotel in St. Andrews with balcony views over Old Course. Sliced drive from 17th tee has been known to land in soup. *Argyle Guest House* (I), North Street (tel. 73387). 18 rooms. Good amenities, reasonable rates. Bar.
**Restaurant.** *Grange* (I), tel. 72670. Old farmhouse-type building; excellent bar lunches individually prepared. Candlelit dinners; good selection of malt whiskies.

**HOW TO GET ABOUT. By car.** The Region is so small and has such good roads that if you are motoring you might well choose to make your base in Edinburgh, Perth or Dundee and cover Fife in the course of a few daily excursions. Conversely, you could take accomodations at St. Andrews or some other royal burgh of the Region, and explore the previous three cities along with Fife itself.

**By train.** The main Edinburgh–Dundee railroad has stations in Fife at Kirkcaldy, Markinch (for Glenrothes), Ladybank, Springfield, Cupar and Leuchars; with a loop from Markinch (southbound traffic only) to Cardenden and Dunfermline. Trains from Edinburgh to Perth and the Highlands also follow this route as far as Ladybank.

**By bus.** Dunfermline and Kirkcaldy are the chief centers of local buses and day or half-day touring coaches in Fife. In summer, there are also excursion buses from St. Andrews.

**TOURIST INFORMATION.** These are located in the following places: The Fisheries Museum, Anstruther (tel. 310628); Bridge Car Park, Dunfermline (tel. 20999) (Apr.–Sept.); Falkland Palace, Falkland (tel. 397); Kingdom Center, Glenrothes (tel. 754954); Esplanade, Kirkcaldy (tel. 67775) (Apr.–Sept.); South Street, Leven (tel. 26533); South Street, St. Andrews (tel. 72021); Forth road bridge (on M90, north side of bridge) (tel. Inverkeithing 417759).

From any of these centers you can get a free *Accomodation Register* and the *Fife Holiday News* booklet.

**FISHING.** River and loch fishing is controlled by local angling associations from whom permits may be obtained. Consult Eden Angling Association, Braehead, Cupar, for salmon and trout fishing on Eden River and Ceres Burn; and the Fishing Lodge, Lochore Country Park, Lochgelly, for trout fishing in the Ore Loch. At Tayport, St. Andrews, Pittenweem, Anstruther and Methil you may fish from hired boats or harbor walls. Mostly cod, flatfish and haddock. Fishing-tackle shops and strategically sited hotels provide information locally.

 **GOLF.** Every golfer's ambition is to play at St. Andrews and once you are in Fife the ambition is easily realized. Old, New, Eden and Jubilee, the four St. Andrews courses, are open to visitors, the charges varying between $4 and $12 a round. For details of availability—there is sometimes a waiting list—contact the Secretary, Links Management Committee, Golf Place, St. Andrews (tel. 75757). There are about 40 other courses in the burghs of Fife, from Tulliallan in the far west to Tayport on the Tay estuary. They have restaurant and/or bar facilities, and all offer golf to the visitor by the round or the day.

 **HISTORIC HOUSES AND GARDENS.** Houses grand and not-so-grand, public and private, are to be found all over the Region. Prime visiting is in spring and summer, when the flower gardens are looking their best (usually open Saturday and Sunday). Opening details can be found in local shop windows and the Scottish national and local press.

**Falkland Palace,** Falkland (A912). Seat of kings and childhood home of Mary Queen of Scots. Rare plants in gardens. Open Apr.–Oct., weekdays 10–6, Sun. 2–6. N.T.S.

**Hill of Tarvit,** Cupar (A916). Ancient mansion house remodeled in 1908 for a millionaire. Fine tapestries, paintings, furniture. Superb views. Open May–Sept., daily except Fri., 2–6. Gardens and park open all year, 10 to sunset. N.T.S.

**Kellie Castle,** Pittenweem, 3 miles from town (A921). Tower house of the Siwards who came to Scotland in Macbeth's time. Carefully enlarged in 16th century and since 1875 restored by the well-known Lorimer family of Scottish architects. Good plasterwork, colorful garden. Open Apr.–Sept., daily except Fri., 2–6. Gardens Apr.–Sept., 10 to dusk. N.T.S.

**Pittencrieff Park,** Dunfermline (A823). Formal gardens, nature walks, aviary and animal center, maze, and romantic glen set in 76 acres on edge of town. Open all year during daylight hours.

 **MUSEUMS. Carnegie Birthplace Memorial,** Moodie Street, Dunfermline (A823). Personal relics of the Scottish-American industrialist. Open May–Aug., weekdays except Sat., 11–1 and 2–6; Sept.–Apr., weekdays except Sat., 11–1 and 2–5; Sun. 2–5 all year.

**Fife Folk Museum,** Ceres (B939). Domestic and agricultural life of long ago. Open Apr.–Oct., daily except Tues., 2–5.

**John McDouall Stuart Museum,** Rectory Lane, Dysart (A92 near Kirkcaldy). Relics and audiovisual presentation at birthplace of Australian explorer (1815–66). Open Jun.–Aug., daily, 2–5.

**Laurie Auchterlonie Golf Museum,** Pilmuir Links, St. Andrews (A91). History of the game. Open May–Nov., weekdays 10–1 and 2.30–6.

**Light Vessel and Scottish Fisheries Museum,** on harbor front, Anstruther (A917). Illustrates aspects of Scotland's fishing industry: actual boats stripped down, an aquarium, logbooks of the Greenland whaling skippers, and other historical items. Open all year, weekdays 10–12.30 and 2–6, Sun. 2–5; closed mornings and Tues., Nov.–Mar.

**Lochty Railway,** Lochty Farm, Pittenweem (B940). Steam railroad, standard gauge, a reconstruction of old Fife industrial lines. Operates mid-Jun.–Aug., 2–5.30, Sun. only.

**North Carr Lightship,** East Pier, Anstruther (A917). Anchored in North Sea 1938–75, now a floating museum. Open daily April–Oct. 10–5, June–Aug. 10–7.

**St. Andrews Cathedral,** St. Andrews. Ruins of the largest church in Scotland. Displays of Celtic and medieval monuments, pottery, glass. Open May–Sept., weekdays 9.30–7, Sun. 2–7; Oct.–Apr., weekdays 9.30–4, Sun. 2–4.

**The Town House,** Culross (off A985). One of several 17th-century dwelling houses in this "museum burgh" with painted ceilings and audiovisual historical program. Open Apr.–mid-Oct., weekdays 9.30–12.30 and 2–5.30, Sun. 2–5.30. N.T.S.

# LANDSCAPE IN ROSE AND GRAY

## Tayside

On a world scale of rivers, the Tay is a trickle; 119 miles long from source to mouth. But it is Scotland's longest river and it pours a greater volume of water into the sea than any river in Britain.

The land drained by the Tay and all its lochs, streams and tributaries is Tayside Region. Its western border is Rannoch station, a desolate outpost of the West Highland railroad, 17 miles from the nearest village. Its boundary with Highland Region runs north through virtually inaccessible tracts of the Forest of Atholl, crossing the Great North Road (A9) by the Boar of Badenoch and Atholl Sow mountains and the 1,506-foot Drumochter pass, the highest point reached by trains on British railroads.

Across the headwaters of four torrents in four long secluded glens—Esk, Prosen, Clova and Isla—the boundary descends to the terracotta-colored cliffs of Angus, turns south to the seaport of Dundee, carves a hunk of territory out of Kinross-shire south of Perth and makes its way westward again, enclosing the sinuous lochs and wooded valleys of the south-central Highlands.

The Highland Line cuts across Tayside Region, with some lonely mountain country on one side of it and some fertile stock-breeding and market-gardening districts on the other.

Tayside Region has two cities, large by Scottish standards: Dundee and Perth. It has the oldest Scottish capital at Scone ("Scoon"), where Dark-Age kings were crowned on what was popularly thought to be Jacob's pillow—the Stone of Destiny, which now lies under the coronation throne in Westminster Abbey, London. Legend says that Scotland received her national flower, the thistle, from this Region. In 990, before the battle of Luncarty near Perth, a barefooted Dane trod on one and gave early warning of a surprise attack. Legend also affirms that the gnarled yew tree in Fortingall churchyard is the oldest tree in the world; that Pontius Pilate, offspring of a Roman centurion and a local girl, was born under it; that the sculpted stones of Meigle lined the grave of Guinevere, King Arthur's faithless queen; that the bones of St. Columba who brought Christianity to Scotland lie under Dunkeld cathedral. . . .

It is hardly surprising that Tayside is a region of legend. It has the antiquities and folk memories to sustain them. It seems to have been one of the first Scottish areas to be settled by Mesolithic man, around 6000 B.C. In several places now known only to the golden eagle and the mountain hare are to be found the prehistoric stone circles, hill forts and flint implements of a sizeable population.

The Romans established a presence in Strathearn and Strathmore— the vale of the River Earn, and the Great Vale which leads from Perth towards Aberdeen. Pictish remains are too numerous to list; you will come across them everywhere. Of especial note are the souterrains (sunken shelters) of Ardestie and Carlungie near the A92 road two miles north of Monifeith.

An early Pictish king set up his capital near Forteviot, southwest of Perth (B9112) and soon afterwards Scone became the political, and Dunkeld the spiritual, centers of Pictland. The word Pict means "painted" (the Picts tattooed themselves). And studying the rich decoration and complicated draughtsmanship of Tayside's Pictish stones, you realize what great pictorial artists they were.

Christianity came with the Irish monks; and the first churches, Abernethy, Dunkeld and Brechin, were built on their cells. The Tayside-Irish connection is venerable. The round towers of Abernethy and Brechin, unique in mainland Scotland, are an old Irish ecclesiastical feature. In more recent times, Dundee's shipyards attracted hosts of immigrant Irishmen.

Outside Dundee and Perth, the towns of the Region are either small holiday resorts or small agricultural centers. As you tour them you will see one huge medieval abbey (Arbroath); a dozen castles, including the showpieces of Blair and Glamis; a pink sandstone coastline ribboned with firm sands; a winter playground in Glenshee; numerous Munros— mountains of more than 3,000 feet, named for the Scottish geographer who classified every 3,000-foot-plus summit in Scotland; and the birthplaces or graves of a few celebrities, from Sir J. M. Barrie the playwright to William MacGonagall, the "world's worst poet."

Sir Walter Scott used the Region's scenery and folktales in his novels *Waverley, The Antiquary, The Abbot* and *The Fair Maid of Perth.* The moorland west of Dunkeld is featured in R. L. Stevenson's novel *Kidnapped.*

The Region is both cooler and drier than most parts of Scotland. It enjoys plenty of sunshine, winter and summer, but the coast is notorious for cold winds.

## Kinross to Perth

Traveling north from the Forth bridges you enter Tayside Region at Kinross, once an important stopover for stagecoach passengers, as its two hotels with their stabling and haylofts indicate. Kinross's back gardens are washed by Loch Leven, renowned among anglers for its strain of pink-bellied trout. In summer you can take a boat trip round the castled island, 20 minutes each way, from which Mary Queen of Scots made a daring escape in 1568, having exerted her powerful charms on her gaoler's impressionable son.

If you are on the M90 motorway, avoiding the small towns of this district, you will ride high over Glenfarg. But if you are not in a hurry it is worth your while to tackle the tortuous descent through the wooded gorge to the flat meadows of the River Earn. At its foot you could turn right for Abernethy (A913) and its round tower.

The Earn is a central river of Tayside, as is the Tay, and they meet near Abernethy. Upstream, Strathearn is rich in prehistoric and Roman remains. Forteviot (B935) was once a metropolis of Fortrenn, the Pictish kingdom. Two miles away, across the A9, are the mounds of a Roman station and a stretch of Roman road. Much history is still buried under the road as you approach Perth, for centuries the lowest crossing-place on the Tay.

At first glance this ancient foundation appears to consist of railroad yards, distilleries and dyeworks. But Perth is a civilized place. It is the "Fair City"; and a seaport, though only just. Below its trio of bridges, the Tay becomes a navigable waterway, above them it is a shallow, canal-like stream. The flood levels of two centuries are marked on the arches and it is for good reasons that the open parklands north and south of a compact city center are called the "Inches"—islands. Two Perth bridges were built and washed away before the present mainroad bridge, built in 1771, at last provided a safe exit from downtown Perth's rectilinear streets.

## Battle of the Clans

The Inches, with their massive beech and chestnut trees, now enclose golf courses and cricket grounds. Games of a more murderous kind were played in 1396, when Robert III decided to settle once and for all the quarrels between the Clans Chattan and Kay. He staged a mass trial by combat, a pitched battle between 30 champions from each side. In the specially-built wooden enclosure ringed with an invited audience of noblemen and women on the North Inch it must have been something like a Roman circus. The fight went on all day until the last Kay escaped the 11 surviving and desperately-wounded Chattans by diving into the Tay. The Clan Chattan had arrived that morning one short but a Perth man, Hal o' the Wynd, volunteered to make up the number. It was said that he had no idea who was fighting whom, that he committed mayhem on both sides and that he came out without a scratch. Scott tells the story in *The Fair Maid of Perth*.

Nothing now survives of the Blackfriars monastery from which King Robert watched the battle of the clans. It was one of four great Perth monasteries of the middle ages. Visiting kings took to lodging at Blackfriars amid "sweet arbours and soft flower-beds" after the royal castle on Tay bank collapsed in the spate (flood) of 1210. Forty years after the clan fight, James I was assassinated there by a party of courtiers led by his uncle the Earl of Atholl. This was the occasion of the well-known tale of Catherine Douglas—"Kate Bargate"—the brave lady-in-waiting who used her own arm as a padlock for the door in an effort to give His Majesty time to escape.

## Pearls, Policies, and Port Wine

Perth is recommended as a shopping center. No other Scottish city preserves more individually-owned stores, many of which have been in the same family for generations. They sell typical products: meats, cakes, shortbread, tartan and woollen goods, pebble and silver jewelry. One notable city-center jeweler, Cairncross, displays the Abernethy pearl, the largest of the lustrous seed-pearls found in the freshwater mussels which are still picked out of the Tay. These days the hauls are not so exciting, since too much polluted water is mixed with the mud where the mussels grow, but a few old gypsy families still make a living hunting for pearls.

Some of Perth's little shops seem to belong to the countryside; and in the countryside round about you find the urban factories and offices which have made Perth an international capital of investment and insurance (a fifth of Britain's automobile policies are processed in Perth); of dyeing and dry-cleaning; of port wine and whisky.

The big name in port is Sandeman's, a firm whose founder established the first connections between Britain and Oporto (Portugal) in 1765. Two famous brands, Bell's and Dewar's, represent the whisky trade. Their Perth origins go back nearly two centuries and the polite rivalry between the first Bell and the first Dewar, two devout churchmen, is anecdotal in Perth. Example: on their way together to a meeting of church elders they stopped off for a drink. Bell: "What will ye have, Dewar?"—Dewar: "I'll have a Bell's. It wouldna do tae go tae the meeting smelling o' strong drink."

All these successful businessmen were benefactors to their town. The schools, libraries and public parks of Perth, like those of Dunfermline, give the city an air of distinction and prosperity.

## The Fair Maid

A walk of one and a half miles takes in the best of Perth. Start at the Fair Maid's house in Curfew Row, just opposite Perth bridge on the edge of the North Inch. The young lady so renowned for her gentle beauty was Catharine Glover; her father a glover by trade. By way of George Street you come to St. John's, most historic of Perth's churches. Eight of the oldest bells in Britain are in its carillon, having been spared when other treasures were thrown down by Protestant extremists after John Knox's sermon there on 11th May 1559, when he challenged the Catholic regent, mother of Mary Queen of Scots.

Off the High Street, near St. John's, the old vennels (French *venelle* meaning a funnel or narrow passageway) are worth exploring. A diagram of them is on the wall of Fountain Close at the end of South Street. Two famous inns of different character are in this quarter of Perth: the Salutation, looking much as it did when Bonnie Prince Charlie sought lodgings; and the more stately Royal George hotel, renowned for its breakfasts in a land of substantial breakfasts.

Around the northern end of George Street lies the classical Perth of terraced streets and crescents. You might inspect Barossa Place and Atholl Crescent and then look at Rose Terrace where John Ruskin the 19th-century art pundit lived when young and met the girl he disastrously married. Another handsome terrace is Marshall Place, which faces the South Inch, with a stone-crowned church (like St. Giles's in Edinburgh) at one end and a well-proportioned rotunda at the other. This latter building, called the Round House, was for years Perth's Fire Brigade headquarters and is now the city's tourist information center: ideally suited to the panoramic displays and audiovisual presentations which you can see when you call there.

## Jute, Jam, and Journalism

Cross the Tay by Perth's Victoria bridge and turn sharp right and you are on the A85 to Dundee (22 miles). The sights of the route are at either end of this fast road: first a pretty stretch of the Tay under wooded crags on which the hill of Kinnoul juts out (take the signposted road off Gowrie Street for the summit and fine views of the Firth of Tay and of the labyrinthine motorway interchange on the opposite shore); and at the other end a dramatic prospect of the open firth and the two Tay bridges (see the chapter on Fife Region).

In between the A85 traverses the Carse (alluvial valley) of Gowrie, a district which made Dundee a great place for raspberry jam. The fruit gardens nowadays extend north to Blairgowrie and Coupar Angus and in the season, June and July, motorists are invited to stop and pick their own strawberries and raspberries, paying a nominal price for them.

Now the road enters Dundee, which is more than many guidebooks do, for Scotland's fourth city has somehow acquired a reputation of being unworthy of tourists' attention. It is at first sight a rather shabby industrial complex; though the redeveloped city center, with throughways leading straight to the Tay bridge tollgates, has brightened it up. Much Scottish history is written into the grim stonework of old Dundee. The place has been a royal burgh since 1190. William Wallace the patriot attended Dundee Grammar School and about 1465 the historian Hector Boece ("Boethius") was born there. It has associations with the Covenanters, the Cromwellians and both Pretenders. A plaque on

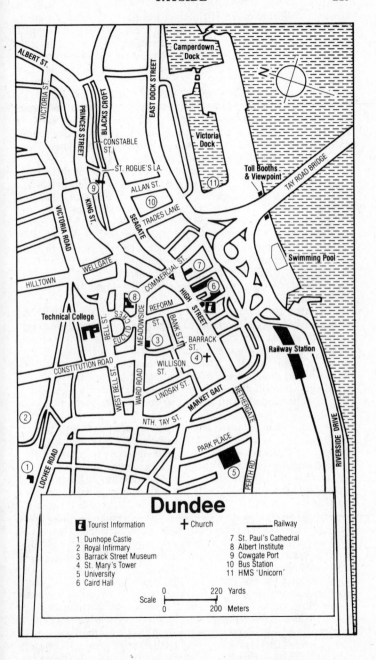

# Dundee

| i Tourist Information | + Church | —— Railway |
|---|---|---|

1 Dunhope Castle
2 Royal Infirmary
3 Barrack Street Museum
4 St. Mary's Tower
5 University
6 Caird Hall

7 St. Paul's Cathedral
8 Albert Institute
9 Cowgate Port
10 Bus Station
11 HMS 'Unicorn'

Scale

0       220 Yards
0       200 Meters

St. Paul's cathedral in the High Street records that on the site where Dundee Castle used to stand, Wallace "struck the first blow for Scottish independence" in 1288; that the Old Pretender lived there in 1715 until his defeat at Sheriffmuir exiled him from Scotland for ever; and that Adam Duncan, famous admiral and victor of Camperdown in 1797, lived next door.

Admiral Duncan's son bought Camperdown Park (off Kingsway, the city ring route) and built a great mansion, Camperdown House. Nearly a century later another rich Dundonian, the industrialist Sir James Caird, bought Caird Park close by, where the gaunt, four-gabled, six-storied tower of 16th-century Mains of Fintry Castle stands. These two beautiful areas of greenery are now public parks.

The city has had its economic ups and downs. Through an early connection with Calcutta, citizens made fortunes in the jute and indigo trade. Dundee shipyards specialized in tough vessels for whaling and Polar exploration. The soft fruit poured in, and it also became a center for the manufacture of jam and marmalade. Valentine's of Dundee were pioneers of the picture-postcard industry, and from the 1870s onwards—when the education laws made schooling compulsory and literacy almost universal—Dundee's publishers issued torrents of cheap weekly papers, a large number of which are still going strong. The business of Dundee was encapsulated in the slogan "Jute, jam and journalism."

Sir James Caird gave the city its great civic center, Caird Hall. Not all the tycoons were so benevolent. Socially, Dundee was divided into the greedy and the needy and so many robber barons of commerce and industry elbowed their way to political honors that it came to be known as the "City of Dreadful Knights." Ostentatious wealth went with harsh working conditions and bad housing. It is significant that even in the very different social climate of today, Dundee is a bastion of radical politics, usually with one or two Communists on the city council.

The jute and jam industries employed many women. In former times the female population greatly outnumbered the male and by some mysterious natural law standards of feminine beauty rose. Dundee has the most beautiful girls in Scotland, as Nottingham, for similar reasons connected with the lace and tobacco industries, has in England.

Dundee University, with its almost rustic campus, is set in the city's heart, at the west end of Nethergate. Also in Nethergate is the 15th-century Old Steeple, massive yet stylish, once an umbrella for no fewer than four churches. The East Port off the Cowgate is the only remaining covered port (gate) of the old city walls. Here, the reforming preacher George Wishart delivered a sermon in 1544 to the plague-stricken inhabitants.

As you leave the east end of the city, rejoining the A972 ring road, a perfect Scottish-baronial fortress-house rises above the roofs of bungalows. Grim and workaday, with the vertical proportions of some Aberdeenshire castles but none of their frivolities, Claypotts was built for defense, not for show. It originally belonged to the Grahams of Claverhouse ("Clavvers") and that cruel Jacobite general ironically known as "Bonnie Dundee." It subsequently belonged to the Douglases, a loyal but consistently unlucky clan, and then to the Earls of Home, the well-known Borders family. Today, it is in the hands of Scotland's Department of the Environment.

The view from Dundee is tremendous. Like Athens, the city drops from a hill and spreads out along a broad waterfront. The summit, Law Hill (571 feet), offers a wonderful panorama of Tayside and Fife Regions, including the inland sea of the Firth of Tay and the strips of coastline bending north and south as the estuary opens to the North Sea.

## The Sandstone Coast

If it were the Mediterranean they would call it the Vermilion Coast or the Costa Rosa or something of that sort. It is the pink sandstone littoral which curves away northward by the cold sea. The A92, from Dundee to Aberdeen, hugs it closely.

Beyond the championship golf course of Carnoustie (A930), lying among the dunes, is Arbroath, 17 miles from Dundee. Here the characteristic scenery of Scotland's northeastern shores begins: blunt cliffs, ragged watch-towers and castles. Arbroath recalls that poetic line "a rose-red city half as old as time," for the sandstone arches, pillars and cloisters of an abbey founded by William the Lion in 1178 still dominate several acres, with a tangle of narrow streets and cottages clustered round them for protection.

In 1320 Abbot Linton of Arbroath drew up on behalf of Robert the Bruce a letter to Pope John XXII in Rome, affirming Scotland's rights to independence: the Declaration of Arbroath. As far as we know the letter was not acknowledged or acted on, but every Scottish schoolchild learns the more stirring passages of it by heart. It is declaimed at the Arbroath Pageant, an annual and much-publicized tourist spectacle on the Abbey lawns (early September).

In that inimitable setting, the floodlit ruins and locally-made costumes are a memorable sight. Unfortunately the acting is amateurish and the script more hysterical than historical: another example of the "Wha's like us?" syndrome and strident xenophobia which make some Scots the despair of their more enlightened countrymen. The Abbey, incidentally, is dedicated to an Englishman, St. Thomas à Becket.

Arbroath has a flourishing fishmarket. In side streets which lead to it you may enter the little kiln-sheds where haddock are turned into "smokies," the local delicacy. Try a smoky with your high tea at 6 P.M., a meal of cakes and scones and one hot dish for which it might have been invented.

## "Down Sank the Bell"

In the Abbey's great sea-facing rose window, the "Round O of Arbroath," monks of the middle ages kept a bonfire burning to light the fishermen home. They also placed a bell on the Inchcape Rock, 12 miles offshore, which thereafter became the Bell Rock. It lay athwart the tracks of vessels making in or out of the Firths of Tay and Forth and was the subject of a legend (and a popular recitation-piece by

Robert Southey: "Down sank the Bell with a gurgling sound . . . ")
about a pirate who cut the Bell and later drove his ship on the rock for
want of the warning signal.

More than 70 ships were wrecked on this coast in the great storms
of December 1799. When the Commissioners of Northern Lighthouses
were appointed, their first priority was a light-tower on the Bell Rock;
a job they entrusted to their new engineer, Robert Stevenson, grandfather of R. L. Stevenson. He began work in 1807 and completed the
115-foot tower in 1811. For the first year or two he and his workmen
had to travel back and forth daily. They subsequently lived on a floating
pontoon anchored to the Rock, able to work only at the lowest state
of the tide, half an hour or so a day. Faced with tasks of unprecedented
difficulty, Stevenson invented solutions to his problems as he went
along: underwater cement, lifting appliances, a method of dovetailing
masonry for an immovable foundation. The Bell Rock tower was a
prototype for semi-submerged buildings the world over and its beam,
flashing red and white, was the first two-color light in the mariner's
almanac.

Stevenson's tower is still there, just as he built it. Only the lantern
has been modernized and made more powerful. In summer, weather
permitting, Arbroath boatmen run trips round the Bell Rock. The
lighthouse itself is not visitable except by special permission from the
Northern Lighthouse Board, 84 George Street, Edinburgh. (There are
about 30 manned lighthouses round Scotland's coasts which you may
visit. Afternoon, up to sunset, is the preferred time. It is best to phone
the head keeper in advance: see under Lighthouses in the telephone
directories.)

## Montrose

Between the headlands of the Angus coastline are crescents of sand
firm and expansive enough for an attack on the world's land-speed
record. Tourist propaganda describes Lunan Bay and Montrose Bay as
bracing—meaning that they are cursed with icy winds. But on a calm
summer day there are no more desirable bathing beaches. At other
times, wise holidaymakers wrap up well and engage in energetic activities.

Behind a four-mile sweep of sand, between two river mouths, South
Esk and North Esk, stands Montrose, four-square on its promontory.
The A92 enters by a structure of startling ugliness, a sort of art-deco
suspension bridge made of concrete. The South Esk is tidal and behind
the town it widens to several square miles of mudflats, covered at high
water. This Montrose Basin is a bone of contention between conserva-
tionists who want to protect the wildlife and local sportsmen who have
hereditary privileges of shooting it.

Montrose is a plain, handsome, unpretentious town: as long ago as
1684 local regulations prohibited the use of any building material
except sandstone. In the Town House in 1773 the gentry entertained
Dr. Johnson and his biographer James Boswell as they passed through
on their Highland jaunt. Robert Burns was in Montrose in 1787 and
Queen Victoria in 1848. Scotland's best—some say only—modern poet,

Hugh MacDiarmid, worked as a cub reporter on a Montrose newspaper in the 1920s.

From town center to beach is a long trek, with only the splendid golden cupola of Montrose Academy, the neo-classical high school, to vary the monotony of the walk; but this place has long been a favorite vacation spot with city dwellers, especially families from Glasgow—and from much farther afield, you might imagine, when you hear American accents floating up from the doors of Montrose's little pubs. But these are servicemen from the U.S. Army Air Force's security base at Edzell, 15 miles up country. Dozens of local girls have married Americans, which has resulted in some comings and goings between the States and this little windblown town they call "East Nowhere."

Montrose's fishing community, or what is left of it, inhabits Ferryden across the estuary, a double line of white-painted, low-built cottages. The serious maritime action takes place in Montrose harbor, which you approach by way of Baltic Street. The name hints at a far-flung trade of long ago, when Montrose's imports read like a bill of lading of argosies: flax from St. Petersburg, tar from Stockholm, tea and cloves from Antwerp and Amsterdam. Now she exports paper, barley and potatoes and does business with the oil rigs, 50 miles beyond the North Sea horizon.

Her most celebrated son, James Graham, Marquess of Montrose, was born in 1612 at Maryton on the south side of the Basin. He joined the Covenanters in 1638, fighting against his king, Charles I, in defense of Scottish Presbyterianism. Disillusioned with the Covenanters' bigotry, he then led a royalist army and virtually pacified Scotland for Charles I. But his victories came to nothing; in England the King was defeated and eventually executed at the hands of Cromwell's republicans.

After Charles II's restoration, the "Great Marquess" as he was called fought again for the Stuarts against the rebels. But private intrigues took precedence over national politics. Montrose fell into the clutches of a personal enemy, the Duke of Argyll, and in 1650 he went to the scaffold in Edinburgh: a military genius who never lost a battle and an idealist who never won a debate.

## The Great Vale

At the North Esk bridge one and a half miles north of Montrose, the A92 swings into Grampian Region. However, our route turns inland on the A935 for Strathmore, the Great Vale of Angus, which runs southwest to Perth, 43 miles away. We have finished now with the real towns of Tayside: all the burghs to come, though important enough in their way, are little more than villages.

The first is Brechin, technically a city because it is an episcopal see and whose cathedral, founded about 1150, lies on the site of a 10th-century monastery. Of the monastery nothing survives and the cathedral's original structure is camouflaged by later "improvements." Adjoining it is the 87-foot round tower, tallest and most complete of the three in Scotland. (We have already mentioned Abernethy's; the third is on Egilshay island in Orkney.)

Pictish and Danish crosses and stones in the cathedral chancel proclaim Brechin's stormy ecclesiastical history, but on the whole it is a place of small industries and few buildings of note, a place the centuries have bypassed and left behind.

Forfar (A94), the county seat of Angus before regionalization, is a livelier town. It even has a culinary specialty: the Forfar bridie, a spiced minced-beef pasty. The town grew up round a castle of William the Lion (12th century), long demolished. At that period Forfar was an island in a swamp from which, now that it is drained, several Pictish stones have been recovered. Good examples are at Dunnichen off the A958 and Aberlemno on the B9134. Close to Dunnichen was Nechtans Mere (mere meaning lake) where the Picts gained a crushing victory over King Egfrith of Northumbria in 685. A tower-base and archway, dating from about 700 at Restenneth one mile east of Forfar on the B9113, are the oldest pieces of church masonry in Scotland.

## Glamis

Continuing through Strathmore (A94), while the blue ridge of the roof of Angus falls away to the west, you enter the cattle-breeding country around Glamis. On those neat farms and well-kept policies, among the belts of trees and freshly-painted white five-barred gates the famous polled (hornless) Aberdeen-Angus bulls are bred. Stockbreeders come from all over the world to bid for them at the Perth livestock sales. The strain originated north of Aberdeen but was developed in Angus: hence the name. The stock descends from the black cattle which used to roam the Highlands, famous for their efficiency in converting sparse pasture into good Scotch beef. (It was an old jibe that Scotland had the best meat and the worst butchers in the world.)

Glamis (pronounced "Glahms") is a village green, a line of grace-and-favor cottages and the tall gates of Glamis Castle, the residence which, after Balmoral, most visitors to Scotland want to see. They have heard of its dark secret, its inaccessible chamber and the warning passed to Lord Strathmore's heir when he comes of age. A warning so dire that the heir never smiles again. From the look of the place, its gloomy turrets have heard the tale too; but your guide will smile and change the subject. The fact is that he knows no more about it than you do.

Glamis Castle connects Britain's royalty throught ten centuries, from Macbeth ("thane of Glamis") to the present Queen's sister, Princess Margaret, who was born there in 1930, the first royal princess born in Scotland for 300 years.

All this region conveys an agreeable impression of rural stability, simple lives and a disinclination to move with the times—a contrast with the humming traffic on the highways to Scotland's boomtown, Aberdeen. In the Glamis street called Kirkwynd, the Angus folk collection is kept, something out of the ordinary in folk museums. It portrays old country values, old notions of thrift and sobriety; not so different from the life around you in the calm little world of Strathmore.

Five miles northwest (A928) of Glamis is Kirriemuir, the weaving town wich Sir J. M. Barrie immortalized as "Thrums." Peter Pan's creator was born and buried there. Seven miles south (A94) is Meigle, rich in Pictish stones. The museum is an old village school. Meigle is also the burial-place of a British Prime Minister (1905-08), Sir Henry Campbell-Bannerman.

Blairgowrie, 15 miles west of Meigle (A926) is the starting point for the wild ascent of Glenshee, the steep twisting section called the Devil's Elbow (no problem now, but a stern test on reliability trials in pioneer automobile days) and the lonely road past the ski slopes to Braemar (A92). It can be a busy road on winter weekends: Glenshee has the nearest natural winter-sports grounds to Edinburgh, Perth, Dundee and Aberdeen. Blairgowrie boasts a couple of good hotels and restaurants and excellent fishing in the contortions and cascades of the Ericht River above and below the town. If you have time to spare and the season is right you can get a holiday course in Pictish and Roman remains, and go blackberry, raspberry and strawberry picking in the lanes and market gardens.

Four miles south of Blairgowrie on the Perth road (A93), slow down to admire the remarkable beech hedge of Meikleour. It is 110 feet high and still growing, half a mile long and needing an army of gardeners to clip it every three years. It is said to have been planted in 1745, the year of Bonnie Prince Charlie. Continuing down the A93 you enter Perth near the old palace of Scone, one of the important house-and-garden sites of Tayside Region.

## Glens of Angus

If possible, when you are in the northern parts of Strathmore, try to see at least one of the glens which penetrate the roof of Angus to the west. Long, silent and gently-winding, they were frequented until recently only by deer-stalkers and grouse-shooters. Now they are appreciated by touring motorists, but not in large numbers. One or two of the former shooting lodges—sizable little mansions, some of them—have become successful hotels.

Try Glen Esk, north from Brechin on an unclassified road; or Glen Clova (B955), Glen Prosen (unclassified) and Glen Isla ("Eye-la") on B951, all from Kirriemuir. After 12 miles or so they climb out of the Vale and approach the ridge of the high Grampians, growing rough and chilly. By the source of the Isla you may go (but only on foot) over the old robbers' road of the Monega Pass; at 3,300 feet, it is the highest right of way in the British Isles.

## Dunkeld

The Great North Road (A9) leaves Perth by Atholl Street and the barracks of Perth's own regiment, the Black Watch, and after 14 miles comes to Birnam in the densely-wooded valley of the Tay. The Dunsinane ("Dun-synan") of Shakespeare's *Macbeth* is near Coupar Angus, 15 miles from here; a long march with a tree in your arms. But this riverside woodland, just opposite the larger town of Dunkeld, is the authentic Birnam Wood and on the Tay bank, behind the Waterbury Guest House, are two hoary trees, an oak and a sycamore, to prove it.

The main road bypasses Dunkeld. It crosses the turbulent Bran River west of the town and from the parking area at the roadside you may walk half a mile through larches and cedars (the first in Scotland, introduced by an arboricultural Duke of Atholl, affectionately known as Planter John, 200 years ago) to a small stone-built folly called The Hermitage. Tales of old-time travelers mention this place: it was a mandatory sight, a tiny summary of what Scotland had in store for them. Underneath the balcony the Bran foams and fusses among black rocks where you will often see fishermen precariously balanced, fighting the huge eels they have hooked while angling for salmon.

Spare half an hour, however, for Dunkeld, a charming town wedged among high hills. Its "little houses"—a row of 18th-century cottages along the cathedral approach—are one of the National Trust for Scotland's most successful renovations. In the ruined cathedral (12th–13th century), romantically situated in beautifully kept grounds on the river bank, lies Count Roehenstart of Bavaria, killed in a coach accident on Dunkeld bridge in 1854. He is described as the last descendant of Bonnie Prince Charlie.

A curious little museum in the square where the little houses begin is devoted to the history of the Scottish Horse, a yeomanry (rural volunteer) regiment raised by the Duke of Atholl's son. It started off on horses and ended up on bicycles.

Throughout the summer at the Loch o' the Lowes, one mile from Dunkeld on the A923, you may view ospreys and assorted waterfowl from a cleverly-constructed hide 200 yards from the car park. This is one of two excellent public osprey-viewing sites in Scotland (the other is near Boat of Garten, Highland Region).

## Pitlochry

Hotels and guest-houses in the main streets of little towns on Scotland's Great North Road no longer tremble to the midnight passing of fish trucks and oil tankers from the north: that highway, Edinburgh–Inverness–John o' Groats, which used to negotiate every insignificant village of the route, has, since 1976, been straightened out and carried clear of all bottlenecks.

It sweeps round Pitlochry, passing close to the Festival theatre, sometimes called the Theatre in the Hills, on a forest slope worthy of an Ibsen drama; but this summer theater goes in more for unadventurous family-type plays.

Pitlochry's main street, a tartan bazaar in a graystone corridor, has become almost a pedestrians-only precinct. The small town is generally taken to be the midpoint of Scotland, though the geographical center is a few miles northwest, around Dalnacardoch. Pitlochry is equidistant from the three major winter-sports areas of Britain (about 40 miles from each): Glenshee, Aviemore and Glencoe.

Now the Highland fastnesses begin to crowd in. From here on, going north, you climb steadily. The town is well-built, with some comfortable stone villas of late-Victorian date. Among the many hotels which sprang up at that period is the inevitable Hydro, with a healing spring nearby. Forest paths to the deer-stalking country have now become nature trails. The salmon which used to make their way up the Tummel River into Loch Faskally above the town now go by way of a glass box, so you can see them.

## Atholl

From Pitlochry to the northern boundary of Tayside Region lie hundreds of square miles of antediluvian forest and bare moorland. You are in Atholl country, the feudal domains of the Murrays of Atholl, offspring of royal Pictish lines and ancestors of the pre-Stuart monarchs. Medieval spellings have bequeathed a few inconsistencies. The Duke is "Atholl", but the whisky they distill at Pitlochry is "Athol." And the famous oatmeal-honey-and-whisky pudding, once the Hielandman's iron ration and now a delicacy of Taste of Scotland cookery, is "Athole" brose.

At Blair Atholl, seven miles north of Pitlochry, stands the clan seat, Blair Castle, in an estate of 300,000 acres. It is a building of suitable size and magnificence; and was the last British castle to be laid under siege (by its owner Lord George Murray when he returned from the Jacobite campaigns in 1746 and found strangers in possession). In and around Blair you may see something of the extravagant garb and stiff pageantry of an ancient body of troops: drums piled, pipes wailing, flags heaped and banners furled, possibly some antique piece of ordnance being touched off by the Master Gunner. These are the Atholl Highlanders, first formed under the "fire-and-sword" commissions which kings gave to self-governing lairds and now the last private army in the Queen's dominions. They pose no threat to the security of the state. They are recruited from among the Duke's own friends and tenants. Retired generals and high court judges consider it an honor to serve as common soldiers. Their functions are to be His Grace's bodyguard, to wear pre-Culloden fancy dress and to preserve the old ceremonies.

It is another 15 miles to the watershed and the regional boundary (with Highland) at the Drumochter Pass. Here the winter snows linger late into the spring. A tough fence, built to protect the highway and the railroad from the weather, adds to the wildness of the scene. Those who regard Britain as over-populated might take a walk in these tree-less wastes of Atholl. They may easily walk where no human foot has trodden before them.

## Lochs Earn and Tay

We now return to Perth and complete our roundup of the Region with a few excursions into the western districts. First we go south towards Stirling on the A9, turning at Auchterarder to the A824 and A823. For a rather dull mainroad village, Auchterarder has a lot of antique shops. The reason is that Gleneagles hotel, with its clientele of well-heeled foreign visitors, is just up the road. This most prestigious caravanserai in the British Isles comprises 700 acres of parkland, 209 luxurious rooms, acres of gardens, a shopping complex, four 18-hole golf courses—and its own railroad station.

At Crieff, another clean, graystone, health-resort town on a hillside, we turn west (A85) to follow the River Earn to its loch, passing through Comrie, which is noted for slight earth tremors, being on an unstable plate of the Highland Line, and St. Fillan's. The healing saint Fillan had his cell here around the year 500 and his well, on the far side of the golf course, was at one period almost a Scottish Lourdes, to which invalids from all over the country were brought. The local archeological attraction is Dundurn, a hill close to the well. As a Pictish fort, Dundurn controlled the western approaches to the capital at Forteviot and the chronicles record a great battle there between Picts and Scots in 683.

Loch Earn, a typically long, thin loch embedded in steep hills, is becoming a notable water-sports venue. From here it is a short step to Killin (A827) where a rattling torrent bubbles over rapids in the main street. Then you coast the more elongated, more richly-wooded Loch Tay. Roads border each side of the loch for its whole 16 miles and then you are at Kenmore, which some have called Scotland's prettiest village. It is undoubtedly one of the most antiseptic; a tribute to the wealth and influence of the Marquess of Breadalbane who built it for the estate-workers at Taymouth Castle a half-mile away. The Breadalbanes (accent on the "al") were originally of the Campbell family, the Dukes of Argyll, the most rapacious landowners in Scotland and the most ruthless in holding their land down. "From the greed of the Campbells, good Lord deliver us" went the prayer of the inhabitants of the south-central Highlands. In 1842 the Marquess was still living in feudal splendor. He entertained young Queen Victoria at Taymouth that year with fireworks, gold plate and a procession of decorated barges on the loch.

An unclassified road out of Kenmore doubles back to the west and dives into the hills for a tranquil journey past Fortingall's yew tree of incalculable age and along Glen Lyon, on and on, a single track with occasional passing places, chopped and intersected by streams which race down from 3,000-foot heights. Glen Lyon, the longest accessible glen in Scotland, goes on for 27 miles until you come to a hydroelectric barrage and have to turn back on the route by which you came.

Six miles east of Kenmore on the A827 is Aberfeldy, yet another smart little town in an idyllic setting.

### "Bless General Wade!"

The most-photographed feature of Aberfeldy is the Wade bridge over the River Tay, a neat pillared structure built in 1733 by General George Wade, and built to last.

Wade was the soldier whom the British Government commissioned to make roads and bridges through the Highland passes where no roads but the paths of cattle had existed before. "If you'd seen these roads before they were made / You would lift up your hands and bless General Wade" says the couplet. While building his roads Wade lived at Weem, close to Aberfeldy, and after his death in 1748 he was buried in Westminster Abbey, London. His Scottish monument is the Wade Stone on a hillside near Dalnacardoch (A9).

The first map of the military roads of Scotland, published in 1755, computed their total length at 1,103 miles. Of the innumerable fine bridges that Wade built, Aberfeldy's is the most elaborate. Many others cross deep ravines, where you ought to stand in the torrent bed underneath to appreciate the magnitude of Wade's tasks. A few stand dilapidated at the roadside, having been rendered obsolete by the new lines of highway.

A Wade road will take you back from Aberfeldy to Dunkeld and Perth via Ballinluig, where a cottage claims the distinction of having provided breakfast for Bonnie Prince Charlie in 1746. That road follows the Tay all the way, but a more interesting route is the A826 to Amulree, joining the A822 to Crieff: two cattle passes, one bosomed in rich foliage and the other winding among stony hills. In the latter, the Sma' Glen, you can usually count on seeing a herd or two of genuine Highland bullocks; small, golden, shaggy, photogenic beasts and extremely docile despite their ferocious branching horns.

## Roads to the Isles

"By Loch Tummel and Loch Rannoch and Lochaber I will go" says the old song, *The Road to the Isles*. The isles are the Hebrides and the first part of the road is in Tayside Region, starting close to the pass of Killiecrankie, becoming the A9 three miles north of Pitlochry.

At Killiecrankie in 1689 a Jacobite army under Bonnie Dundee, supporting their exiled monarch James II and VII, attempted an ambush of Government troops. They succeeded, but their leader was killed and they failed to press home the advantage. A soldier named Donald MacBean, chased by the Jacobites, saved himself by leaping an 18-foot-wide chasm over the River Garry at the narrowest point of the pass. The "Soldier's Leap" is a short walk from the car-park at Killiecrankie.

Half-a-mile south, the Road to the Isles goes off west by Loch Tummel and the Queen's View: the spot at which Queen Victoria on her journeys north used to stop her carriage to admire the variegated forests mirrored in the loch. The road (B8019, B846) winds along the loch shore to Kinloch Rannoch, then follows a longer loch, Rannoch, for another 16 miles to Rannoch station, a wayside halt on the West Highland railroad (Glasgow–Fort William). Beyond that you must go on foot. In dry weather a walk of about four hours would take you across Rannoch Moor to Kinlochleven among the western sea-lochs.

From Rannoch station a minor road returns to Kinloch Rannoch on the other side of the loch, with close-up views of Schiehallion's pyramidical peak (3,547 feet), most graceful of Scottish mountains.

These cross-country routes are among the most scenic in the central Highlands: undulating forests of birch and pine, riverine lochs, crumbling packhorse bridges, green turf and fast-flowing streams, broad prospects through gaps in the harsh hills. On tinier trails which trickle away from your road you may voyage into the territories of an undisturbed wildlife—deer, hares, pheasant, grouse, eagles—without seeing either humans or their habitations. This is a land where the Roads to the Isles are like roads to the world's end.

# PRACTICAL INFORMATION FOR TAYSIDE

**HOW TO GET THERE. By train.** Perth is a motorail terminal (from London's Euston station) and an important rail junction with mainline trains from Edinburgh (1½ hours), Inverness (3 hours), Aberdeen (2 hours), Dundee (½ hour), and Kirkcaldy (1 hour). The journey from Euston or King's Cross in London to Perth takes 7½ hours.

There are several trains per day to Perth from Arbroath and Montrose on the east-coast line, and from Dunkeld, Pitlochry and Blair Atholl on the picturesque Highland line. Rannoch station gives Tayside a toehold on the West Highland line, with access to Fort William in the north and the Clyde coast in the south.

**By coach.** W. Alexander & Sons, Riggs Road (tel. 26122), and Stagecoach, Friarton Road (tel. 33481), both in Perth, run daily express coach services between Perth and London's Victoria, a 12-hour journey.

**By air.** There is an airfield for light private aircraft at Scone, and a small commercial airport at Dundee for Air Ecosse flights from Aberdeen, Wick, Orkney and Shetland. But for practical purposes the airports to and from Tayside are Edinburgh and Aberdeen.

**HOTELS AND RESTAURANTS.** The number of hotels, inns and guest-houses in Tayside's many country routes is ample proof of the Region's popularity as a touring area. Pitlochry alone—a mere village—has 30 hotels, more even than Perth! Coastal places like Dundee and Arbroath have been slower to catch up with demand.

Eating and drinking present no problems. Dundee, Perth, and the main routes all have restaurants and teahouses of a fairly stereotyped character, while country pubs offer bar lunches and snacks at reasonable prices—but sometimes in rather dingy surroundings.

**ABERUTHVEN** (On A9, 10 miles southwest of Perth). **Restaurant.** *Smiddy Haugh* (I), tel. Auchterarder 2013. Low cost, superior value.

**AUCHTERARDER.** *Gleneagles* (E), tel. 2231; 209 rooms with bath. One of the most famous hotels in the land, stands among endless golf courses and gardens with wonderful view, heated pool, tennis, squash, sauna. It remains to be seen what the new ownership will mean to the standards of this old favorite. Closed in winter.

**AUCHTERHOUSE** (A927, midway between Dundee and Meigle). *Old Mansion House* (L), tel. 366. 7 rooms, 6 with bath. Small, luxury mansion with an expensive V.I.P. suite. Nice lawns and shrubbery. Tennis, squash courts, heated outdoor pool.

**BLAIRGOWRIE** (A923). *Altamount House* (M), tel. 3512. 7 rooms, 2 with bath. Well-proportioned house secluded in large garden. Noted for imaginative cuisine.

**CRIEFF** (A85). *Murraypark* (M), Connaught Terrace (tel. 3731). 15 rooms, 10 with bath. High standard of comfort and service.

**DUNDEE** (A85). *Angus* (M), tel. 26874; 57 rooms, 43 with bath, modern, comfortable, and well-run. *Ivercarse* (M), tel. 69231; 27 rooms, all with bath. Excellent restaurant. In grounds overlooking the River Tay, fishing.
   **Restaurant.** *Raffles* (I), Perth Road (tel. 26344). Deservedly popular pull-up on main road.

**FORTINGALL** (on unclassified road off A827 near Kenmore). *Fortingall* (M), tel. Kenmore 367. 21 rooms, 2 with bath. Old Highland inn in reconstructed village of character. Fishing, golf on doorstep. Wild scenery.

**GLEN CLOVA** (B955, 15 miles into the wilds from Kirriemuir). *Rottal Lodge* (E), tel. Clova 224. 12 rooms, 9 with bath. Stone-built former shooting lodge with elegant cuisine and good cellar. An attractive but lonely spot.

**GLENFARG** (A90). **Restaurant.** *Bein Inn* (I), tel. 216. Low-built historic "clachan" (tavern) isolated in wooded glen. Quiet weekdays, noisy on Saturday and Sunday.

**KINCLAVEN** (A93 near Meikleour). *Ballathie House* (E), tel. Meikleour 268. 39 rooms, all with bath. Fantastic pseudo-French-baronial chateau, but nothing bogus about comforts and amenities. Own kitchen-garden produce. Trout fishing.

**KINROSS** (A9). *Green* (E), tel. 63467. 43 rooms, all with bath. Venerable stage-coaching inn on Great North Road. Tradition of unostentatious excellence. Indoor curling. Fishing on Loch Leven.

**KIRKMICHAEL** (A924). *The Log Cabin* (M), tel. Strathardle 288. 13 rooms, 8 with bath. A ranch among the pines. Cordon bleu cooking makes it a popular stopover, halfway between Pitlochry and Blairgowrie. Tourist information center on premises.

**LUNAN BAY** (A92). **Restaurant.** *Lunan Bay* (M), tel. Inverkeillour 265. Prominent on headland overlooking wide expanse of beach. Seafood.

**PERTH** (A9). *Salutation* (M), South Street (tel. 22166). 62 rooms, 55 with bath. Well-worn and slightly creaky, but still earns praise of hotel inspectors and food writers.
   **Restaurant.** *Hunting Tower* (M), Crieff Road (A85), tel. Almondbank 241. Superior country restaurant in historic center close to city.

**PITLOCHRY.** *Green Park* (M), tel. 2537. 37 rooms, 17 with bath. Overlooking Loch Faskally, good touring base. *Hydro* (M), tel. 2666. 71 rooms, 33 with bath. In own grounds above town and a bit old fashioned. Tennis. Full board only during season.

**HOW TO GET ABOUT. By car.** Main roads through Tayside are the A9 (Edinburgh–Perth–Inverness), A93 (Perth–Blairgowrie–Braemar), A94 (Perth–Forfar–Aberdeen), A85 (Perth–Dundee) and A92 (Dundee–Aberdeen). They are fast and not heavily trafficked. The principal touring center, Perth, is 40 miles from Edinburgh, 115 from Inverness, and 81 from Aberdeen.

Minor roads throughout the Region are uniformly good. In the Angus glens and the western valleys toward Rannoch Moor it is possible to travel 20 miles without seeing a gas station; elsewhere the byways lead from village to village. Facilities for both people and automobiles are adequate.

Godfrey Davis Europcar have an office in Perth (tel. 36888), in Dundee (tel. 21281), and at Gleneagles Hotel (tel. Perth 31322). Budget Rent-a-Car are at Dundee (tel. 644664). Ritchie's Self-Drive operate out of Arbroath (tel. 72850), Brechin (tel. 2343), Carnoustie (tel. Arbroath 72850), and Montrose (tel. Brechin 2343).

**By bus.** There are bus services on all the major routes in Tayside, and mail or mini buses on most of the minor ones. The principal company is W. Alexander of Perth (see How to Get There for address).

**TOURIST INFORMATION.** If you enter Perth from the south by road, the Round House is one of the first buildings you see after crossing the South Inch. This is the Region's most impressive information center, serving Perth and district. You can "book-a-bed-ahead" and view audiovisual travelogues while you wait. Open Mon.–Fri. 9–7, Sat. 9–6, Sun. 12–6, Jun.–Sept.; normal office hours Oct.–May.

Other information centers are at Aberfeldy, Arbroath, Blairgowrie, Carnoustie, Crieff, Dundee, Dunkeld, Glenshee, Kinross, Montrose and Pitlochry. They are also the accomodations bureaux for their districts and most of them will "book-a-bed-ahead." Opening hours are normally 10–6 daily except Sun. from May to Sept., with shorter A.M. and P.M. openings in winter months.

Most village post offices and some pubs and newsagents' shops supply leaflets and other tourist information.

**FISHING.** The Tay, its tributaries and their lochs provide rich salmon, brown and rainbow trout and sea-trout fishing. On certain Tay beats at Killin and Dunkeld you may fish for about $1 per day; permits available locally. Fishing on lochs Tay, Earn, Tummel and Faskally, with boatman or self-drive motor boat, may cost up to $30 per day; permits from lochside hotels.

If you like the look of a particular stream or loch, enquire at the nearest village post office, fishing-tackle shop or hotel. Among the hotels that offer excellent fishing to residents and nonresidents are Bridge of Cally, Blairgowrie; the Log Cabin, Kirkmichael; Fortingall, Fortingall; Ben Lawers, Aberfeldy; Dunkeld House, Dunkeld; Grandtully, Strathtay; and Ballathie House, near Meikleour. Permits for the Tay within Perth city boundaries are issued by the Director of Finance, 1 High Street, Perth.

Crab boats at Arbroath will take you out for a day's sea-angling—cod, mackerel, haddock, flounder. There are good marks round the Bell Rock, 12 miles offshore. Sea fishing is available from central Dundee to the suburbs of Broughty Ferry and Easthaven: tackle, bait and local wisdom from Gow's, 12 Union Street; Shortcast, 8 Whitehall Crescent; and McGill's, 18 Victoria Road.

**GOLF.** There are about 50 golf courses in the Region; three good ones in Dundee and three more in Perth. Perth's King James VI club on Moncreiffe Island in the Tay (not really an island) has associations with that golfing monarch of 400 years ago. Carnoustie (A930), 11 miles east of Dundee, is Tayside's answer to St. Andrews, and you will pay around $9 for a round on the Medal (championship) course. The four 18-hole golf courses at Gleneagles are more costly still: apply to Golf Secretary in advance (tel. Auchterarder 3543).

The superb and scenic small-town courses—Arbroath, Brechin, Forfar, Montrose, Aberfeldy, Comrie, Crieff, Dunkeld, Kenmore, Pitlochry and others—come much cheaper for the casual visitor. It is best to make arrangements beforehand if possible with the local secretary or professional.

**HISTORIC HOUSES AND GARDENS. Blair Castle,** Blair Atholl (A9). One of Scotland's great houses, with baronial-style enlargements on a tower dating from 1269. Apartments furnished in period manner. Important Jacobite relics. Open weekdays 10–6, Sun. 2–6, May–mid-Oct.

**Glamis Castle,** Glamis (A94). Much-visited 14th-century tower house with chateau-style additions. Old tapestries and needlework. Scene of Duncan's murder in *Macbeth,* repository of romantic legends. Open May–Sept., daily except Sat., 1–5.

**Kinnaird Castle,** Brechin (A94) (castle is 3 miles south on A933). 15th-century fortified house. Good paintings, furniture, domestic records. Open May–Sept. by arrangement (tel. Bridge of Dun 209).

**Scone Palace,** Scone (A93) (2 miles from Perth). Gothic house of early 19th century on ancient monastic structure. Large garden with Douglas fir raised from seed that David Douglas himself sent from U.S. in 1834. "Monks' Playground," "Friars' Den." Moot hill where Celtic kings were crowned. Indoors, bed hangings embroidered by Mary Queen of Scots. Rare porcelains and ivories. Open mid-Apr.–mid-Oct., weekdays 10–6, Sun. 2–6.

Private gardens open under Scotland's Gardens Scheme are **Bolfracks,** Aberfeldy (A827, 2 miles on Kenmore road), and **Cluny House,** also Aberfeldy (A827, 1 mile on Ballinluig road). Both open Apr.–Oct., daily 2–6.

Gardens that open occasionally in spring and summer include those at **Abercairny,** Crieff; **Airlie Castle,** Kirriemuir; **Battleby,** Redgorton near Perth (headquarters of the Countryside Commission for Scotland); **Branklyn,** Perth; **Cortachy Castle,** Kirriemuir; **Drumkilbo,** Meigle; **Meikleour,** near Blairgowrie; and **Stobhall,** Guildtown, Perth. Consult Scottish or local press for opening details (normally weekends, once or twice a year).

**MUSEUMS.** You will find that virtually every town in Tayside Region offers a choice of interesting museums, while in most villages of the Region there are displays of local antiquities and curiosities. Among the more notable of the museums is the following selection.

**Angus Folk Museum,** Kirkwynd, Glamis (A94). The simple life of times gone by displayed in farmworkers' cottages. Open May–Sept., daily 12–5. N.T.S.

**Barrie's Birthplace,** Brechin Road, Kirriemuir (A926). The humble cottage of Peter Pan's creator, with his homemade theater and costumes. Open May–Sept., weekdays 10–12 and 2–6, Sun. 2–6. N.T.S.

**Black Watch Museum,** Balhousie Castle, Perth (A9). Story of the Black Watch regiment from 1739 to present day. Open Mon.–Fri. only, 10–12 and 2–4.30 (Nov.–Mar. to 3.30).

**Broughty Castle,** Broughty Ferry, Dundee (A930). History and ecology of the Tay, whaling industry, old armor, in 15th-century castle. Open weekdays except Fri. 10–1 and 2–5.30, Sun. (May–Sept. only) 2–5.

**Clan Museums.** These include *Clan Menzies,* at Weem, Aberfeldy, and *Clan Donnachaidh,* at Bruar Falls, Blair Atholl.

**Frigate "Unicorn,"** Victoria Dock, Dundee. Britain's oldest warship still afloat; served Royal Navy for 140 years. Shipboard life of Nelson's era. Open weekdays except Tues., 11–1 and 2–5, Sun. 2–5.

**Glenesk Trust Museum,** Tarfside, Glenesk (off A94). Old-time shepherd and farming life imaginatively reconstructed in a former shooting lodge, 10 miles into the hills beyond Edzell.

**Meigle Museum,** Meigle (A94). One of the best collections of Celtic sculptured stones in Europe. Open weekdays by arrangement (contact caretaker in village).

**Museum of Scottish Tartans,** Comrie (A85). All you need to know about clans and their costumes. Open weekdays 9.30–5, Sun. 2–4.

**Scottish Horse Museum,** Dunkeld (A9). Memorabilia of the checkered history of Tullibardine's Horse, a volunteer cavalry regiment. Open Easter, then May–mid-Oct., daily 10.30–12.30 and 2–5.

**Spalding Golf Museum,** Camperdown House, Dundee (A923). History and traditions of golf. Open daily except Fri., 10–1 and 2–5 (Sun. 2–5 only).

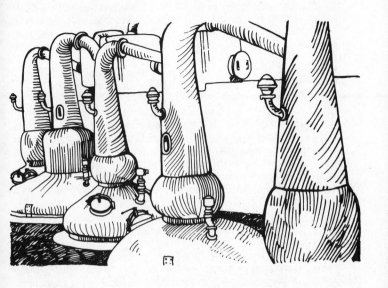

# SCOTLAND'S GRANITE
# SHOULDER

## *Grampian*

Scotland's most easterly Region has an east-facing seaboard of about 70 miles and a north-facing one of about 60. The former is a continuation of the sandstone coast of Tayside Region but in Grampian there are cliffs and headlands of granite, sometimes of a formidable grandeur. Frequently they stop short on the sea's edge. Sometimes they are lined with strips of hard pale sand. (The strip which runs north from Aberdeen is 25 miles long.) On the north-facing coast you find fishing villages which appear to have been hollowed out of the cliffs. And there is also a stretch of wooded shoreline rooted in deep sand which owes its existence to the vagaries of Gulf Stream offshoots.

The Region is almost entirely north of the Highland Line, although much of it has Lowland characteristics. There are fertile river valleys, many square miles of agriculture and forestry, and, like the Lowland districts of Tayside, these areas are dotted with large farms and small hamlets and are the breeding-grounds of prize pedigree cattle, chiefly the Aberdeen Shorthorns.

But Grampian is not without Highland scenery. It takes its name from the highest mountain range in the British Isles. It shares with

Highland Region a string of flat-topped 4,000-foot summits (heights exceeded only by Ben Nevis). It contains Ben Macdhui (4,296 feet) and the dark and forbidding Lochnagar (3,786 feet). The Cairnwell pass, south of Braemar (A93), crosses into Tayside Region at 2,199 feet, the highest main road in Britain.

Grampian Region's A939 road, Cockbridge to Tomintoul, is invariably the first British road to be snowbound in winter and the last to be snow-free in spring.

By contrast, the Moray coastline on the northern shore, visible from the Grampian heights, is a strip of sand-dunes and pinewoods of almost subtropical prodigality. The twin rivers Don and Dee flow out of Grampian gorges and make their way east to Aberdeen by scenic routes. Balmoral Castle, the Queen's summer residence, and Crathie church, which the royal family attends, stand beside the Deeside road; and Braemar, host village of the most renowned of Highland Gatherings, lies at the end of it. Not so many tourists know the country of the Don, or are aware of what they have missed. But, regarded purely as rivers, Scotland's most attractive pair are the Spey and the Findhorn, running north to the Moray coast.

The Dee and the Don are each 90 miles long—a good length for Scotland. Grampian is primarily a land of short rivers. They proceed in a series of linns—a topographical feature of the Region, a combination of deep pool, cascade and swirling channel. The atmosphere above these streams and the peat and melted snow which impregnate them are the secret of pure malt whisky production.

The chief city is Aberdeen which, if the recent rate of expansion is maintained, will in due course supersede Edinburgh as the second largest city in Scotland. Since 1969 Aberdeen has become Britain's metropolis of North Sea oil and natural gas, a base for offshore operations and oil-related construction industries and the pipeline terminus for the rich Forties field. Outside Aberdeen, no town of Grampian Region has more than about 13,000 people; though Peterhead is also riding the oil boom and steadily expanding.

Among the relics of primitive man are the Neolithic long cairns of Macduff (north coast, A98), Gourdon (near Inverbervie, A92) and Cults (near Aberdeen, A93). They date from around 3000 B.C. There are Bronze Age (1500 B.C.) stone circles at Old Keig (Alford, A944), Sunhoney (Echt, A974) and Tomnaverie (Tarland, A974). The hills above the Don have numerous Iron Age forts (A.D. 100-200) and the whole Region is strewn with Pictish stones of the period A.D. 600–1000, some of them intriguingly decorated. The best-known is the Maiden Stone at Chapel of Garioch, four miles north of Inverurie, off A96. The ruins of Deer Abbey (13th century) near Mintlaw on the A950 from Peterhead are close to the site of a vanished Celtic monastery where the precious *Book of Deer* (now in Cambridge University Library) was compiled and illuminated.

The Region is remarkable for the splendor of its many baronial castles. Among them you will see mottoes carved on stone shields and door-lintels which summarize a native philosophy of life. Inside the ancient Mitchell Tower, for example, in Aberdeen's Marischal College, is inscribed: "Thay haif said. Quhat say thay? Lat thame say." And above the staircase at Craigievar Castle: "Do not vaiken sleiping dogs."

The character of the people was formed by Grampian's geography: cut off by wild mountains on two sides and an inhospitable sea on the other two. Danes and Norsemen fought over it. Peterhead is only 300 miles from Stavanger in Norway. Grampian people have Scandinavian blood in their ancestry and they have tended historically to be slow, stolid, thrifty, industrious, self-sufficient and resentful of interference; paradoxically the least parochial people in Scotland.

Sir Walter Scott's *Old Mortality* and *The Legend of Montrose* are associated with this Region. The simply country life of the Mearns (the valley south of Stonehaven) is portrayed in Lewis Grassic Gibbon's trilogy *A Scots Quair*.

## Stonehaven

The roads from the south, the A92 and A94, converge on a steep winding gradient at Stonehaven, a clean, breezy little fishing town with some old-fashioned wynds and pends (passages) between main street and harbor. You see plenty of evidence of its popularity as a resort in its crowded caravan park and often-congested seafront swimming pool.

Stonehaven, like Montrose 23 miles south and Aberdeen 16 miles north, is built along a stretch of beach between two river mouths. The ruins of one of Scotland's biggest medieval castles are spread over a belligerent headland south of the town. Dunnottar Castle was the frontier post and toll-gate from which the Keith lords, hereditary Earls Marischal of Scotland, commanded the nation's eastern approaches. William Wallace captured it from the English in 1296, firing the interior and roasting alive the soldiers who had fled into the chapel for sanctuary. The armies of Balliol, Bruce, Montrose and Cromwell besieged it in their turn.

During the interregnum when Cromwell ruled in England, the Scottish regalia of crown, scepter and sword of state were deposited at Dunnottar for safe keeping. While under siege the defenders managed to smuggle out the regalia to the parish church of Kinneff (on the coast, six miles south), where they lay buried until the restoration of King Charles II. During the subsequent witch-hunt for the Covenanters the deepest dungeons of Dunnottar were a prison in which 167 men, women and children were starved and suffocated. They lie under the Covenanters' Stone in Dunnottar churchyard. This is where Sir Walter Scott first saw Old Mortality, the pious graybeard who went round Scotland tidying up the graves of the Covenant martyrs and who flits through the pages of Scott's novel of that name.

Northwest from Stonehaven, a wild road called the Slug (A957), more beautiful than its name, cuts across heather-covered Grampian foothills to Banchory—a short route to Deeside if you wanted to avoid Aberdeen. The Camp of Raedykes, a Roman station four miles along this road, interests archeologists. Some say that this must have been Mons Graupius where, in A.D. 84, the Romans under Agricola defeated the Picts. It is the Grampian massif's nearest approach to the sea, a fairly plausible site for the greatest battle in terms of numbers fought on British soil. What the Roman historian Tacitus called "Graupius", the Scottish historian Hector Boece misread as "Grampius"—thus the word "Grampian" came down to us.

## Granite City

Lewis Grassic Gibbon, kailyard fiction supremo and local boy, called Aberdeen "the one haunting and exasperatingly lovable city in Scotland." Glaswegians of course say much the same sort of thing about *their* native town.

In many respects Aberdeen is an archetypal British city and governments recognize this. When sociological experiments or nationwide surveys have to be carried out, Aberdeen is often the guinea-pig. Yet few British cities have undergone more violent changes in the past half-century and none have withstood the impact of change more successfully. Grim under low cloud or sparkling gray in the sunlight, Aberdeen still looks impregnable against the influx of the oilmen and their technology.

The gently undulating ground on which the city is built divides the estuaries of the Dee and the Don, two fine salmon rivers. (The city was called Aberdon long ago, and the citizens are still Aberdonians.)

She is the third city of Scotland, with cathedral and university (which is actually two universities combined) and clean, broad beaches on her doorstep. She is the Granite City, and has for centuries exported the durable, glittering stone of her suburban quarries which at the same time supply her own building needs. In her docks and harbor, which you reach simply by following the main street to its end, you find yourself in the middle of all kinds of maritime construction and repair, from dinghies to drilling rigs. The quays and markets support a deep-sea white-fish fleet (her herring fishery is temporarily in abeyance). She is the chief mainland terminal for car-ferries and passenger boats to the Shetland isles.

Most of central Aberdeen on either side of the mile-long straight thoroughfare called Union Street was built around 1800–1820: not as startling architecturally as Georgian Edingurgh, but handsome enough in its sparkling block granite. Union Street is carried downhill on low piers and where the main railroad goes under the viaduct there are flanking gardens like those of Edinburgh's Princes Street, but on a more modest scale. Note the solid range of buildings at the north end of the gardens. They comprise public library, church and theater: a landmark which Aberdonians know affectionately as "Education, Salvation and Damnation."

The city's modern appearance is deceptive. Ancient treasures are embedded in her canyon-like streets near the waterfront, from the point where the "Auld Brig" of Don steps back more than 600 years to the point where the "new" bridge of Dee has stood for a mere 450 years.

Stand at the Market Cross at the foot of Union Street—it's one of the finest civic crosses in Scotland, dated 1686, with carved medallions round it representing ten Stuart monarchs. Face Union Street with the Custom House, quays and fishmarket on your left hand. The prominent

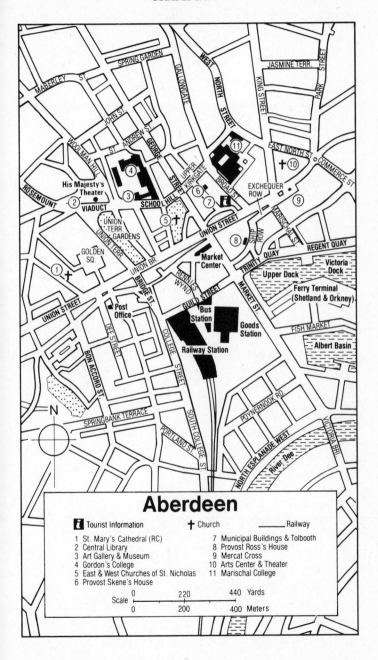

# Aberdeen

**i** Tourist Information     **†** Church      ———— Railway

1 St. Mary's Cathedral (RC)
2 Central Library
3 Art Gallery & Museum
4 Gordon's College
5 East & West Churches of St. Nicholas
6 Provost Skene's House
7 Municipal Buildings & Tolbooth
8 Provost Ross's House
9 Mercat Cross
10 Arts Center & Theater
11 Marischal College

Scale
0     220     440 Yards
0     200     400 Meters

building in front is the Athenaeum, built in the 1820s as a library and reading room, subsequently converted into a restaurant.

The old Shiprow, the main road into town in bygone days, goes off to the left. Here the house of Provost Ross, built in 1593, is worth looking at. The oldest house in Aberdeen is to your right, on the other side of Union Street, half-encircled by the city's administrative offices in St. Nicholas Street. This is Provost Skene's house, built in about 1540. Both Ross and Skene were hardheaded Aberdonians who made their fortune in the import-export business, chiefly with the Baltic countries. The Government commander-in-chief, the Duke of Cumberland, stayed at Provost Skene's house in 1746 during his pursuit of the retreating Jacobite army.

Aberdeen's outstanding building in gleaming white granite and in a flamboyant Gothic style, is Marischal (pronounced "Marshal") College, founded in 1593 as the city's second university. It was amalgamated with the first, King's College off King Street on the way to Bridge of Don (founded 1494), in 1826. Marischal College faces the north side of St. Nicholas House on the site of an ancient monastery. When the new building was opened in 1906 it was the second largest granite hall in the world, the first being Spain's Escorial.

In Union Terrace Gardens you will find a number of statues, including monuments to William Wallace and Robert Burns (portrayed addressing the Daisy of his well-known poem). The Art Gallery on the other side of the railroad tracks contains sculptures by Epstein and Henry Moore and some good Impressionist and Post-impressionist paintings.

Aberdonians have a reputation for ultra-Scottish parsimony. They share it with citizens of several European cities and it usually stems from envy at their success in developing meager resources. Perhaps in Aberdeen they were once more thrifty than most and more inclined to drive hard bargains in commerce. They capitalized on the slur: the penny-pinching Aberdonian became an industry, and Aberdeen the fountainhead of jokes and comic postcards on the subject.

In truth Aberdeen is renowned for its generosity in entertaining delegations, visiting firemen and so forth and in contributing to worthy causes. She is not the tidy, sober city she used to be. Oil has sprayed her with something of a Klondike aroma, there is much movement of strangers at all hours of the day and night and the quarter we have just described, round the Market Cross, is a riot of discos and nightclubs. Prices of foodstuffs and services approach capital-city level, and if you come looking for accomodations in the tourist season you may be disappointed or have to pay extortionate prices, if you insist on a city-center hotel. On the whole, however, Aberdeen is the best-organized of the four large Scottish cities and her resilient citizens, like their tough stone, have stood up well to the socioeconomic earthquake of North Sea oil.

### Scotland's Oil

As an energy source, oil is an infant barely 130 years old. We saw in the Central Region chapter how James "Paraffin" Young launched the world's first oil industry in Scotland after 1850. So rapidly did the demand increase with the invention of the automobile that by 1919 fuel economists were giving the industrial nations another 30 years before their oil ran out. Since then it has been discovered in previously undreamed-of quantities. The date of final exhaustion at current and projected rates of consumption keeps moving forward and now it stands somewhere in the second quarter of the 21st century.

North Sea oil was discovered in 1969 while engineers were prospecting for natural gas. Quantities have proved greater than forecast. Equally important, the oil is of very superior quality.

Scotland's oil lies in a straggling ribbon about 100 miles offshore, from a point southeast of Aberdeen to a point northeast of Shetland. There are about 70 exploration rigs continually working along this line and about 20 oil fields already in production.

The vision of a race of tartan sheikhs in Scotland has now evaporated somewhat, especially as the projected oil bonanza has not noticeably benefited the British taxpayer at large. But it has certainly benefited the economy in the east of Scotland and has created thousands of well-paid jobs.

## Buchan

From Aberdeen you can coast the rugged northeast shoulder of Scotland on the A92 road to Fraserburgh and the A98 to the Moray Firth. This corner of Grampian Region is called Buchan. All the way north there is a whiff of oil in the air; many coastal places have acquired small stakes in the construction and repair services which rigs, platforms and modules require. But the coastline itself is peaceful and rather featureless, while the hinterland is covered with oatfields and woods which gradually thin out as they rise to the blue foothills of the mountains in the west. There are some farms and cottages built in granite, which in this district has a rosy tinge.

At Newburgh, the mouth of a sandy estuary, the B9000 runs inland to one of Scotland's great formal gardens, Pitmedden, and on to the picturesque burgh town of Old Meldrum, set in almost southern-English countryside. There are examples hereabouts of the older style of Aberdeenshire castle in various states of disrepair: Udny, Barra, Toquhon and Mounie. If you cut across country to Banff by the A947 you will pass close to the castles of Gight, Towie-Barclay and (most impressive of all) Fyvie, which has been called the crowning glory of Scottish baronial architecture. To the east of Turriff (B9170) stand the castles of Delgatie and Craigston.

All these places were strongholds of the barons in the lawless period between the 14th and 16th centuries, and what now look like quaint decorative turrets and parapets can be seen on closer inspection to have had a part to play in the defense of the building against surprise attack.

The landscape is smiling and fruitful now but once it was poor barren land. The labor which excavated peat and rock and exposed potential agricultural soil has been compared to the slave labor which built the Egyptian pyramids; and the fortitude and stamina of the smalltime farmers of the 19th century are part of the folklore of the district. Some villages, New Pitsligo (A950) is a good example, were planned communities, built in the late 18th and early 19th centuries to tempt peasant workers to stay on the land. That hard life also attracted volunteers from among the Highland families who were evicted from Sutherland and Wester Ross (both Highland Region) during the Clearances which the great landowners carried out when they replaced labor-intensive cattle with free-ranging sheep.

## The Rockbound Coast

Peterhead and Fraserburgh are sturdy little ports with a life of their own, most of it concentrated on fishing. Yet in this remote corner of Scotland a university was set up in 1595 (at Fraserburgh). With the two in Aberdeen, this short stretch of Grampian coast had for a few years more universities than in the whole of England and Wales, though not for long. Fraserburgh University's principal quarrelled with his patron, King James VI, and in 1605 the charter was withdrawn. Not to be outdone, Peterhead set itself up as a health resort on the strength of the curative properties of local springs. Around 1780 the town was doing good business with invalids from the south, but the vogue did not last.

As its name implies, Fraserburgh was the seat of the Fraser clan and the coastal castles are relics of their history. Kinnaird Castle, built in 1569 on Fraserburgh's promontory, is now scattered in ruins round the lighthouse; and Inverallochy (two miles south on the B9107) is also a ruin. But there are still Frasers at Cairnbulg (same road), where that Anglo-Norman family have been since 1375.

Around Cairnbulg and St. Combs or on the golf course at Fraserburgh you may trace the line of Scotland's last light railway, closed in 1973—a railroad remarkable for having locomotives with cow-catchers on them.

A breezy, hilly, zigzag road (B9031) touches at several coastal villages on the way to Macduff and Banff. These are two of the area's idiosyncratic fishing harbors, where the plan of life is stark and simple, ruled by stern evangelical faiths. Most inhabitants are Plymouth Brethren of the Close or Exclusive order. The annual Temperance Walk (usually January) is the big event in the village calendar. Curious totems and taboos, once common all along the east coast of Scotland from Dunbar to Wick, remain among fishermen: they will not utter the words "pig," "salmon," "salt" or "minister" and some will postpone their voyage if they catch sight of the minister, or if a woman crosses their path, as they go down to their boats.

Strange beliefs and superstitions seem almost credible among the twisting byroads of cliff and cove and the huddles of cottages sheeted down against wind and spray. But not at Banff, a fishing village of amazing elegance, part Georgian like Edinburgh's New Town and part 16th-century small burgh like Culross. In the 18th century, Banff was a real spa town, a rival to Bath and Cheltenham. Among the Palladian buildings from that period are several fine churches, a Town House, an academy, a hotel and a clutch of mansions put up by fashionable devotees of the "Banff springs."

Old Banff is arranged on terraces above the gorge where the Deveron River enters the sea. Some of the cottages date from the early 17th century.

Banff grew organically through the centuries. Macduff, which faces it across the river-mouth, was custom-built late in the 18th century and has become the base of the local fishing fleet. Both places build small ships and both have a look of modest prosperity, as do nearly all the tiny ports along this coast. Nature was unfriendly but the works of man have many amiable features.

## Grampian Riviera

The A98 is a corniche road in places, winding west of Banff to what passes for a riviera in these parts. The wayward Gulf Stream begins to take effect and all the way to Inverness you will feel the mild air and see the foliage breaking out. Cullen's white crystalline sands and red sandstone rocks give the shoreline quite a Mediterranean look. These are singing sands. The breeze produces a wailing sound from them, and you can achieve the same result by striking them with a towel.

Still traveling west you enter the fertile "laigh" (low ground) of Moray which stretches between the lower courses of the great salmon rivers Findhorn and Spey. Follow these rivers into the hills if time permits and admire their glens and rapids and old castles hung on crags. The most beautiful reach of the Findhorn is between Sluie and Relugas on a footpath, accessible from the minor road out of Forres (off A96) which passes by Darnaway Castle and through the Darnaway Forest.

Forres is a small dignified town loaded with antiquities and surrounded by gardens and forest trails. The Findhorn, winding majestically to the sea, makes a curve round sand-dunes which 300 years ago began to shift inland, eventually overwhelming the cornfields of Moray. The Culbin sands are still on the move, but scientific afforestation has slowed them down. Once a week in summer the Forestry Commission arranges tours of the area (contact the Information Centre, Falconer Museum, Forres). On the opposite side of the estuary the Findhorn Community has taken root; this is a semi-religious colony which claims to achieve phenomenal market-gardening results through living in quiet harmony with Nature. Cabbages the size of hot-air balloons have attracted nationwide publicity, but it seems that nobody outside the Community has actually seen one.

## Elgin

The ideal touring center for the district is Elgin, a cosy little market town which, by virtue of having a 13th-century cathedral, styles itself "city." The cathedral's interior was accidentally burned out in 1270 and deliberately fired in 1390. In 1506 the steeple fell down and 60 years later the Earl of Moray sold all the lead off the roof to clear a debt. The place now stands in fairly impressive but melancholy decay.

The ruins are associated with General Anderson (died 1824) who bequeathed his fortune to the town. His mother, left homeless and penniless at his birth, crept into a cell among the cathedral's wreckage. It is said that a stone basin in the vestry was Anderson's cradle. He enlisted in the East India Company's army as a drummer boy, made a great deal of money and retired at the top of his profession. The ornate Anderson Institute, a Corinthian building of 1831-1832, established to give the young an education and make the old comfortable, stands opposite Panns Port, the cathedral's entrance gate.

South of Elgin on a roundabout route on the B9010 to Forres, is the hamlet of Dallas, prettily situated but otherwise quite insignificant. The Dallas which its emigrant families founded on the other side of the Atlantic was destined to be an entirely different sort of place. If you go to Dallas, Grampian Region, have a look at the parish cross in the kirkyard and then drive four miles north to Pluscarden Abbey, a foundation dating from 1230, and now undergoing substantial renovation by its community of Benedictine monks. It is open to visitors at all reasonable hours and its surroundings in the valley of the Lossie River, rich in both castles and distilleries, attract many visitors.

Elgin's north road (A941) brings you to the fishing harbor of Lossiemouth, lying on what its most famous son, Ramsay MacDonald, called "our Bay of Naples." MacDonald (1866-1937), first Socialist Prime Minister of Britain (1924 and 1929-31) was born in Gregory Place, Lossiemouth—a stone marks the cottage—and is buried in Spynie churchyard on the road to Elgin.

Lossiemouth had a naval air station during World War II, and this has since become an important Royal Air Force base. But the town and bay are also developing as a holiday resort. Five miles west, off the B9135, stands Gordonstoun, a 17th-century country house converted to a school in 1934 by the educationist Kurt Hahn. He attracted a royal pupil, Philip Mountbatten, later Duke of Edinburgh, and since then Prince Charles, and his brother Prince Andrew, have each received part of their education there.


## The Whisky Trail

South of Elgin and Banff, where the peaty streams jostle for elbow room on their race down from the Grampian heights to the sea, the glens embrace Scotland's greatest concentration of malt whisky distilleries.

Millions of people the world over know Scotch whisky as a serious adjunct to gracious living. The word is a corruption of *uisgebeatha,* the Gael's "water of life." Tradition says that Scottish doctors practicing in London first popularized the drink outside the Highlands by recommending it as medicine: they all had shares in the whisky firms. Subsequently, for almost 200 years, while fashions in liquor have come and gone, Scotch has maintained a steady and increasing popularity. Since 1960 it has been top of the world list for sales. The blending, bottling, transporting and selling keeps 20,000 Scots employed—rather more than does the fishing industry.

Yet the whisky most people drink is not, according to purists, the real stuff. Ordinary Scotch is blended from a variety of grain spirits in relatively large-scale operations. The real stuff, the connoisseurs say, is the unblended or single malt whisky produced in a small distillery or, better still, one of the very few illegal pot-stills said to exist in out-of-the-way places.

Memoirs of the Highland lairds nostalgically recall the "bothies" (mountain huts) of old with their well-built stone walls, watertight thatches and arrays of casks and tubs and iron pipes leading the cold spring water to the still-rooms. The permanence of the layout revealed that the one-man distillery stood in little danger of the law—maltster and excise officer were generally on the best of terms as the latter, appointed to some remote glen for life, soon learned discretion if he wanted to live peaceably with his neighbors.

The single malt distillery of today is a modest little building with pagoda-like chimneys. There are about 90 in Scotland, most of them scattered about the Grampian foothills, set on the banks of streams in the neighborhood of Elgin, Rothes, Keith, Dufftown, Tomintoul and Grantown-on-Spey. Their hygenic environment and sophisticated equipment are a world away from the "bothy" but the pale, sometimes colorless liquid which emerges is fundamentally the same as ever.

There are about 112 brands of malt whisky, but only some 20 are marketed commercially. They are usually matured for eight to 20 years and they cost about half as much again as blended Scotch. The best-known brands (Glenfiddich, Glen Grant, Glen Moray, Cardow, Glen-farclas and a few more) originate within a few miles of each other but they differ as subtly as do the great wines produced in adjacent vine-yards of Burgundy or Bordeaux. The most famous malt whisky is Glenlivet—"The Glenlivet," if it comes from Smith's distillery which, founded 1823, is the only one licensed so to describe the product, though several neighboring distilleries also take their water from the Livet stream. You will meet the Livet Water near Tomnavoulin on the minor road B9008, Dufftown to Tomintoul. It rises in the Ladder hills and finds its way into the Avon River and then the Spey.

The tourist Whisky Trail starts at the Glenfiddich distillery in Duff-town and proceeds south to Tomintoul, then north to the Glenfarclas distillery, then to Knockando on the Spey for the Tamdhu distillery; north again past Craigellachie to Keith for the 18th-century Strathisla distillery and back south to Dufftown—an attractive run of 65 miles in green and hilly country, even if whisky does not interest you. The Trail is signposted and all the distilleries named have a traditional welcome for visitors on weekdays (10–12 and 2–4).

Among distilleries not on the trail but also open to visitors are Glendronagh at Forgue (B9001 near Huntly); Glengarioch at Old Meldrum (A947 from Aberdeen); Glen Grant at Rothes (A941 from Elgin); and The Glenlivet (B9008 from Dufftown). Opening hours are normally 10–4 on certain weekdays only, mid-April to mid-October.

The drive down Strathavon from Tomintoul (B9136) and along the Spey to its narrow estuary (A95, B9103) is of high scenic quality. The sights of the route are Ballindalloch Castle at Bridge of Avon, built in 1546 but enlarged many times; and the iron bridge which Telford, a 19th-century pioneer of civil engineering in Britain, constructed across the Spey under the Rock of Craigellachie in an exceptionally romantic setting. The main A941 road used to cross it, but now you have to make a short detour.

## Disneyland Castles

The Grampian summits are the backcloth of the malt whisky country, and on a day of rain and sleet it sometimes seems a long way round them to the hamlets of the upper Don and Dee, the nearest habitable valleys. On the Lecht road, Tomintoul to Cockbridge (A939), you may find snow as early as October and as late as April; you will certainly see it on the hills as your road wriggles round their thrusting shoulders.

The Don valley is a soft, bright enclave which Scots love and strangers hardly know. The river is deep and swift and flows past farms and villages and great menacing fortresses like 13th-century Kildrummy (A97) and modern replicas like 19th-century Forbes (B992), where the road climbs out of a ravine called My Lord's Throat. Nearby is Alford ("Affad") on the A944 where the "Great Marquess" Montrose fought a battle in 1645 for the lost cause of Charles I; and a little farther south Lumphanan (A980) with a peel tower and the wood where Macbeth suffered defeat and was killed in 1057 at the hands of Malcolm Canmore. There are a Macbeth Stone, a Macbeth Cairn and a Macbeth Arms hotel here—but nothing of Macbeth himself, despite what self-appointed guides may say. That man of blood, along with other Celtic kings of Scotland, was buried on the isle of Iona (Strathclyde).

Here we approach Deeside and the land of fairytale castles. The most perfect of them, said to have been Walt Disney's model for the fairytale castles of his movies, is Craigievar, six miles south of Alford. It is one of those strange, pale-stone conglomerations of tall slender walls and turrets, winding stairs and crooked chambers that are the epitome of early 17th-century "Scottish baronial." They are found at their most graceful and esthetically satisfying in the valleys of Dee and Don. "Quite perfect, lightly poised on the ground . . . no infelicity of mass or exaggeration of detail . . . a serene assurance . . . a symphony in stone"—critics of various nations and centuries have enthused over Craigievar. Indoors the medieval and Renaissance elements are just as daring as the main fabric of the building. Until quite recently the castle was lived in by the Forbes-Sempill family. Older people can remember when rushes were freshly gathered in the meadows every morning and strewn on the floors. The place is now in the care of the National Trust for Scotland.

## George Bell, Master Builder

The most eye-catching of the Grampian castles were built between 1550 and 1630 by a family of master masons called Bell, the first of whom, George, lies at Midmar (B9119, ten miles west of Aberdeen) in the shadow of the magnificent tower house of Midmar Castle. He was probably working in it in 1575 when he died. Not all of those who inherited such fantastic residences appreciated their intricate design. The Grants in the 18th century complained of being saddled with "an old castle which had battlements and six different roofs of six different heights and directions, confusedly and inconveniently combined." That was Monymusk beside the Don (B994 from Kintore). The other Bell castles, apart from Craigievar and Midmar, were Crathes Castle near Banchory (A93); Castle Fraser (off A944, 15 miles from Aberdeen); and Glenbuchat (off A97, ten miles west of Alford).

All the Donside and Deeside castles are individually styled, all are picturesquely sited and all have their tales of ghosts and bloodshed, siege and torture, witches and warlocks. The booklet *Grampian the Castle Country*, available at tourist information centers in the Region, gives details of all visitable castles.

## Royal Deeside

We have left the Region's principal touring route until last. For the motorist—unhappily no longer for the rail traveler—the Deeside stretch divides into four: Aberdeen to Banchory (18 miles); Banchory to Ballater (25 miles); Ballater to Braemar (17 miles); and the minor road from Braemar to Linn of Dee, where the infant river comes bursting out of the Forest of Mar.

There are two Deeside roads and it makes sense to go up to Braemar on the A93 and return by the B976. The Dee itself has no great attraction, except for the angler, but the valley is richly clothed with woodland and lit with constantly changing colors.

Several beautiful houses cling to the lower banks. Note especially Drum Castle, a 13th-century hunting lodge with 17th-century additions (A93 near Peterculter); and Crathes, which has been in the hands of the same family, the Burnetts of Leys, since 1323 (A93 near Banchory).

All the valley towns are well-groomed and fresh-looking and the mica in their granite sparkles in the sun. They always look as though smartened up for a royal visit, as indeed they have often been in the past, for the Deeside roads have brought the crowned heads and potentates of Europe and farther afield to share a summer holiday with the reigning monarch at Balmoral. The Tsar and Tsarina of Russia once came this way and the cottages along Deeside were festooned in black and gold. In 1889 the Shah of Persia made a memorable visit to Queen Victoria and for him the color scheme was applegreen and pink. "What a beautiful climate," the Grand Vizier said enviously. "In our country it never rains like this."

Banchory is a modern village, though its golf course dates back to 1799 and the little monastery of St. Ternan stood in the 5th century where the churchyard is now. The Nature Conservancy Board studies the habits of grouse in a converted stables south of the river. The nearest thing Banchory has to an industry is the local lavender factory, to which tourists are admitted.

At Torphins, a little way off the A93, you can see the artificial canyon called Satan's Den which carried the Deeside railroad under some hilly obstacles. The line, closed in 1966, had many royal connections. Around Ballater station, the terminus where visitors for Balmoral disembarked and waited for their carriages to the castle, there survives some faded grandeur of the amenities provided for them.

Aboyne has a castle, some Bronze Age and Pictish remains, and there is also an annual Highland Gathering which usually takes place on the first Wednesday in September. The highlight is the opening procession, traditionally led by the "Cock o' the North" (the head of the ducal family of Gordon) and his attendant chiefs. All the route between here and Ballater is dotted with handsome country houses and mock-baronial châteaux. When Queen Victoria acquired Balmoral, a number of self-made men with social and political ambitions thought it wise to stake a claim in the neighborhood.

On a plaque on Ballater's river bridge the disastrous history of several previous bridges is outlined. The Dee in spate is an awesome sight and there is said to be the masonry of a dozen castles as fine as Crathes or Craigievar rolling in its bed. Ballater is becoming devoted to tourism: every house a guest-house.

This is Royal Deeside. Ten miles on you pass Crathie church and know that you are almost at Balmoral. Crathie is the royal family's parish church and when they are holidaying at Balmoral crowds of 10,000 people have been known to line the road on which they walk to and from Sunday worship. Few locals join the crowds. One of Balmoral's great attractions for the monarch has always been the villagers' respect for royal privacy. In Queen Victoria's time there used to be an undignified scramble to go to church with Her Majesty; nowadays seats are reserved for parishioners.

## Balmoral

Some credit Sir Walter Scott with having opened up Scotland for tourism through his poems and novels. Others say General Wade did it when he built the Highland roads. But it was probably Queen Victoria who gave tourism its real momentum when, in 1842, she first came to Scotland and when, in 1847—on doctor's orders: he thought the relatively dry climate of upper Deeside would suit her—she bought Balmoral.

At first sight she described it as "a pretty little castle in the old Scottish style." The pretty little castle was knocked down to make room for a much grander house in neo-baronial style. Year by year Victoria and her German husband Albert added to the estate, took over neighboring houses, secured the forest and moorland round about and developed the deerstalking and the grouse-shooting. Balmoral is now a large property: the grounds run for 12 miles along the Deeside road. Its privacy is protected by belts of pinewood and the only view of the castle from the A93 is a partial one, from a point near Inver, two miles west of the gates. But there is an excellent bird's-eye view of the castle in its wooded surroundings from an old military road, now the A939, which climbs out of Crathie, northbound for Cockbridge and the Don valley. This view embraces the summit of Lochnagar (3,786 feet) in whose "corries" (hollows) the snow lies all year round; and, behind the castle, the Forest of Ballochbuie, known as the "bonniest plaid in Scotland" from the alleged fact that its purchase price long ago was a length of tartan cloth.

As time went by the Queen and Prince Albert bought or leased for their relations and guests Birkhall House, Abergeldie Castle and Mar Lodge, all in the Braemar area. The royal connection brought prosperity to upper Deeside. It is now one of the most civilized districts of Scotland, in spite of the wildness of the scenery. In the early days, thanks to the Prince Consort's enthusiasm for the Highland tradition, a bad rash of tartanitis broke out. Stags' heads abounded, the bagpipes wailed incessantly and the garish Stuart tartan was used for every item of furnishing—carpets, curtains, chair-covers, wallpaper. Even the train which brought distinguished visitors and royal couriers to Ballater from Aberdeen had a tartan locomotive. The dress Stuart of its paintwork frightened the cattle and after a time the more somber Duff hunting tartan, black and green to blend with the environment, was adopted.

From the brief glimpse the visitor is today allowed of Balmoral's interior, it is clear that royal taste today is more restrained. The Queen and other members of the royal family, however, follow their predecessors' routine in spending a holiday of about six weeks on Deeside, usually mid-August to the end of September; and these days the Queen often arrives as her great-great-grandmother did when she first came to Balmoral: by royal yacht to Aberdeen and then along the Deeside roads.

## Springs of Dee

Nine miles west of Balmoral is Braemar, where the A93 takes a sharp turn south for the Devil's Elbow and Glenshee (Tayside Region). Here are the ruins of another royal seat, Kindrochit Castle, said to have been built by Malcolm Canmore in the 11th century.

The noisy torrent of the Clunie froths under an ancient bridge and Braemar village manages to look suitably dour although it consists largely of hotels, guest-houses and cafes. Convalescing at The Cottage in Castleton Terrace in 1881, Robert Louis Stevenson wrote most of *Treasure Island*.

The Highland Gathering arena is half a mile west of the village. This biggest of clan events, always attended by a member of the royal family and sometimes by other, more exotic guests as well, takes place on a Saturday early in September. On that day the village is closed to automobiles and the prices of food and accommodations are scandalously inflated.

Follow the Dee upstream into Mar Forest and within five miles you may see four boisterous "linns"—of Quoich, Corriemulzie, Garrawalt and Dee. Hereabouts the poet Byron, crippled but a compulsive swimmer nonetheless, narrowly escaped drowning.

The straight journey from Aberdeen to Linn of Dee and back would be 130 miles but if you are going to explore Deeside thoroughly the byroads would add a good deal of mileage to that.

# PRACTICAL INFORMATION FOR GRAMPIAN

**HOW TO GET THERE. By air.** The airport for Grampian Region is Dyce, 7 miles north of Aberdeen. It has flights from Glasgow and Edinburgh (British Airways), Wick (Air Ecosse), and Orkney and Shetland (British Airways); also connections from London (Gatwick and Heathrow), Newcastle, Leeds/Bradford, East Midlands, Birmingham, Humberside, Manchester, Isle of Man and Norwich, and also from Amsterdam, Bergen, Stavanger and Copenhagen.

**By train.** There is a main railroad to Aberdeen from Stonehaven and the south via Dundee and Perth. The journey from London (King's Cross) by Inter-City express takes 9 hours. There is also a King's Cross–Aberdeen motorail service carrying passengers and their vehicles. Frequent trains leave Inverness for Aberdeen with intermediate stations in Grampian Region at Inverurie, Insch, Huntly, Keith, Elgin and Forres. The journey takes nearly 3 hours.

**By bus.** The principal bus company in the Region is W. Alexander & Sons, Guild Street, Aberdeen (tel. 51381). This company operates a daily express service between London (Victoria) and Aberdeen, a 14-hour journey. Stagecoach, Friarton Road, Perth (tel. 33481) runs express coaches from and to Aberdeen/Stonehaven and London (King's Cross)/Birmingham (St. Chadsway). There are several direct bus services between Edinburgh/Glasgow and Aberdeen.

**By boat.** P. & O. Ferries, Jamieson's Quay, Aberdeen (tel. 572615) operate passenger and automobile shipping services to Lerwick in the Shetland Islands three times a week; journey time 10 hours.

**HOTELS AND RESTAURANTS.** The Region has some splendid country hotels with log fires and rich furnishings, where you can be sure of eating well if you have time for a leisurely meal. Restaurants of quality are otherwise rather sparse throughout the Region, though every town has its cafes and every village its pub, serving snacks and bar lunches.

In and around Aberdeen a number of places are springing up and some have interesting cuisine. The hotels listed below are all specialists in good food, Scottish and cosmopolitan.

**ABERDEEN** (A93). *Royal Darroch* (E), Cults (tel. 868811). 67 rooms, all with bath. In the suburbs on North Deeside road. Maintains impressive standards. *Westhill Inn* (M), Skene (tel. 740388). 53 rooms, all with bath. 8 miles from city center on A944. Luxury at a reasonable price.

**Restaurant.** *Mr. G's* (M), tel. 572112. Should be well worth trying. Let us know if it is maintaining its early promise.

**BALLATER** (A93). **Restaurant.** *Tullich Lodge* (I), tel. 55406. Local produce, superior cuisine.

**BALLINDALLOCH** (A95). *Delnashaugh* (I), tel. 210. 6 rooms, 4 with bath. Peaceful spot in distillery country. Warm and friendly, local produce.

**BRODIE** (A96). **Restaurant.** *Brodie Countryfare Restaurant* (M), tel. 339. A very good lunch stop near Forres on the main road. Quick and efficient service.

**BUCKIE** (A98). **Restaurant.** *Old Monastery* (M), Drybridge (tel. 32660). Excellent for fish. Atmospheric surroundings, wild coastal scenery.

**CRUDEN BAY** (A975). *St. Olaf* (M), tel. 3130. 5 rooms, 2 with bath. Above broad sweep of sand near the 18th-century village of Port Erroll. Delicious fresh fish on short but select menu.

**DYCE** (A947). *Skean-Dhu* (E), Farburn Terrace (tel. Aberdeen 723101). 222 rooms, all with bath. The larger of 2 airport hotels. Impersonal but less dehumanized than most.

**ELGIN** (A96). *Eight Acres* (E), Sheriffmill (tel. 3077). 40 rooms, all with bath. Admirably furnished with modern taste.

**ELLON** (A92). *Ladbroke Mercury Motor Inn* (E), tel. 20666. 40 rooms, all with bath. Company consider this the brightest jewel in their upmarket motel chain.

**FORRES** (A96). *Heather* (I), Tytler Street (tel. 72377). 6 rooms, 3 with bath. Not much to look at outside but comfortable and cheerful within. Might raise prices shortly.

**GLENLIVET** (B9008). *Blairfindy Lodge* (M), tel. 376. 12 rooms, 7 with bath. Shooting and fishing. Small rooms but first-class cuisine with venison and other country dishes. Not the large malt whisky collection you might expect from the address.

**HUNTLY** (A96). *Castle* (M), tel. 2696. 24 rooms, 9 with bath. Town center, some traffic noise. Cuisine designed for strong, hungry people in a cold climate.

**INSCH** (A979). **Restaurant.** *Rothney Coffee House* (I), Commercial Road (tel. 604). Light meals the specialty, but also offers lunch and dinner menu at reasonable prices.

**OLD MELDRUM** (A947). *Meldrum House* (E), tel. 2294. 9 rooms, all with bath. Best type of country-house hotel with much-praised cuisine, especially game pie and venison.

**PITCAPLE** (A96, north of Inverurie). *Pittodrie House* (E), tel. 202. 14 rooms, 7 with bath. Secluded 15th-century tower. Spacious rooms with tapestries and antiques. Cordon bleu chef.

**TOMINTOUL** (A939). **Restaurant.** *Glenmulliach* (I), Lecht Road (tel. 356). Home cooking. Lunch is good but tea and high tea with buttered scones and homemade shortbread are even better, and all at remarkably modest prices.

**HOW TO GET ABOUT. By car.** By road, Aberdeen is 120 miles from Edinburgh, 80 from Perth, and 105 from Inverness. Good centers for the coastal areas of the northeast are Fraserburgh, Macduff, Banff and Elgin; for the Grampian highlands and the whisky country, Keith, Huntly and Tomintoul; and for Deeside the small towns of Aboyne, Ballater and Braemar.

A dozen automobile hire firms operate from Aberdeen or Dyce (Aberdeen Airport) including Hertz, Avis, Godfrey Davis and Swan. You can also rent an automobile at Elgin (Budget Rent-a-Car, Macrae & Dick, Station Road, tel. 45281, or S.M.T. Self-drive, Elgin Motors, South College Street, tel. 7561) and at Stonehaven (Mitchell's Garage, Barclay Street, tel. 62077). Grampian roads are sometimes lonely and tortuous but always in reasonable condition. Even in the wildest places a faint dotted line on your map probably indicates a good usable road.

**By boat.** P. & O. Ferries of Aberdeen offer weekly cruises in summer round Scotland's northern coastline.

**TOURIST INFORMATION.** The Tourist Information Office for Aberdeen is at St. Nicholas House, Broad Street (tel. 23456). It is open Mon.–Sat. 9–5 in Jun. and Sept., Mon.–Sat. 9–8 Jul.–Aug., and Mon.–Fri. 9–5 Oct. –May. In summer there is also an information caravan on the Stonehaven road near the city limits, open 9.30–5.30 Jun. and Sep., 9.30–9 Jul.–Aug.

The Information Office at 17 High Street, Elgin, opens weekdays 9.30–5 Apr.–May, daily thereafter until Sept. and 9.30–7 Jul.–Aug.

Other local information offices are at Ballater, Banchory, Banff, Braemar, Crathes Castle, Cullen, Dufftown, Ellon, Forres, Fraserburgh, Huntly, Inverurie, Keith, Stonehaven and Tomintoul. Normal hours 10–5, sometimes later in midsummer. All centers except Crathes Castle offer local accomodations and "book-a-bed-ahead" facilities.

Leaflets and booklets on the Grampian castles, malt whisky distilleries and other special features are available.

**FISHING.** The Region is rich in rivers and in burns and streams. The Spey, Dee, Don, Findhorn, Ythan and Deveron provide excellent sport for salmon and trout fishermen. At Bridge of Feugh (A943 near Banchory) you can see salmon leaping up slippery rocks. Prime beats tend to be privately owned or rather expensive, up to $30 per rod per day, but most large hotels along the river can arrange permits. Try Mar Lodge and Invercauld Arms, Braemar, and Banchory Lodge, Banchory, for the River Dee; Castle Hotel, Huntly, and County Hotel, Banff, for the Deveron; Grant Arms at Monymusk and Kildrummy Castle near Alford for the Don; and Craigellachie Hotel, Craigellachie, and Palace Hotel, Grantown-on-Spey, for the Spey. The Clerk of Fishings, Duke Street, Huntly, issues permits for stretches of the Deveron and Isla rivers. Where local fishing-tackle shops sell permits they sometimes restrict them to visitors actually lodging in the district.

There is good sea-angling for cod, haddock, pollock and flatfish from rocks and harbor jetties at Lossiemouth, Buckie and Portsoy. Tackle, permits and information from The Angling Center, Moss Street, Elgin. You can fish from the long breakwaters of Peterhead and from boats at Fraserburgh and Stonehaven. Tackle, bait and list of local boatmen from sports shops or from the Information Caravan, The Square, Stonehaven.

The salmon/trout season runs February through September, with no Sunday fishing. Sea-angling is possible all year round, May to October being preferred. But among the old wrecks off Stonehaven there have been phenomenal catches of cod, 25–35 pounds in February and March.

**GOLF.** Grampian Region has 51 golf courses so you will never be far from one or perhaps two. They include numerous championship courses. All towns and many villages have their 18- or nine-hole municipal links. Among the notable private clubs are Royal Aberdeen and Deeside, Aberdeen; Duff House, Banff; and Royal Tarlair, Macduff. At municipal courses you will pay $1.50–3.50 per round. The more prestigious clubs charge up to $12 a day and expect you to book by letter, or bring a letter of recommendation from a member.

**HISTORIC HOUSES AND GARDENS.** The medieval and Renaissance castles of Grampian Region are famous and a feature of the landscape everywhere. If you wish to explore them comprehensively, the booklet *Grampian the Castle Country*, available at information centers in the Region, is a useful guide. Many houses are also renowned for their gardens, and below we list some that are open under Scotland's Gardens Scheme.

**Balmoral Castle,** Ballater (9 miles west on A93). Exhibition in ballroom. Royal life of 19th century including Lanseer paintings. Open May–Jul., weekdays only, 10–5.

**Braemar Castle,** Braemar (A93). Castellated mansion of 17th and 18th centuries. Among family treasures is 52-pound Cairngorm stone (semi-precious), the biggest ever found. Open May–Sept., daily, 10–6.

**Brodie Castle,** Forres (3 miles west on A96). Ancestral home of ancient Brodie family. French furniture, plasterwork. Open mid-Apr.–mid-Oct., weekdays 11–6, Sun. 2–6. N.T.S.

**Castle Fraser,** Inverurie (8 miles south on B993). A great 17th-century tower house. Oak furniture and portraits. Open May–Sept., weekdays 11–6, Sun. 2–6. N.T.S.

**Craigievar Castle,** Alford (7 miles south on A980). Outstanding 17th-century tower house with fine plasterwork and furnishings of three centuries. Open May–Sept., daily except Fri., 2–7. N.T.S.

**Leith Hall,** Huntly (at Kennethmont, 7 miles south on A97). Turreted house set around a quadrangle, dating partly from 1649. Relics and keepsakes, chiefly military, of Leith-Hay family. Open May–Sept., weekdays 11–6, Sun. 2–6. N.T.S.

Gardens regularly open May to September, usually daily from 9 to sunset, are **Innes House,** Fochabers (off A96), and **Kincorth,** Forres (off A96). Their special features are herbaceous borders, roses and shrubs. The Region's most remarkable garden is **Pitmedden** (10 miles from Aberdeen off A920), an elaborate layout of lawns, flowerbeds and parterres in the formal 17th-century manner, and with exhibitions on Scottish farming and gardening history. Pitmedden is open May to September, daily, 11–6. N.T.S.

Among gardens open periodically under Scotland's Gardens Scheme are **Arbuthnott House,** Laurencekirk (A94); **Beechgrove,** Beechgrove Terrace, Aberdeen (B.B.C. Scotland's television garden); **Douneside,** Tarland (B9119); **Dunecht House,** Dunecht (10 miles west of Aberdeen on A944); **Gordon Castle,** Fochabers (A96) ; **Gordonstoun School,** Duffus (B9012); **Kildrummy Castle,**

Alford (A944); and **Tillypronie,** Tarland (A97). Details about opening days can be found in local newspapers and on posters in shop windows.

 **MUSEUMS. Adamston Agricultural Museum,** Huntly (A96). Working farm with large collection of agricultural and domestic implements from the past, showing how the northeast was tamed. Open Wed., Sat., Sun., 9–7.

**Aden Country Park,** Mintlaw (A950 from Peterhead). Large stable and reconstructed estate worker's cottage with interpretative display. Open daily, 9 to sunset.

**Artspace Gallery,** 37 Belmont Street, Aberdeen. Monthly exhibitions, emphasis on northeastern arts and crafts. Open Wed., Fri., Sat. 10.30–5.30, Thurs. 10.30–8, Sun. 2–5.

**Gordon Highlanders' Regimental Museum,** Viewfield Road, Aberdeen. History of Grampian's famous regiment from its formation in 1794. Open Wed. and Sun., 2–5.

**Maritime Museum,** Provost Ross's House, Shiprow, Aberdeen. History of fishing industry, shipbuilding, docks, gas and oil. A modern museum (1982) in an ancient setting. Opening times under review, weekdays 10–7 at presstime.

**Maritime Museum,** Clunie Place, Buckie (A942). History of local fishing industry. Adjoins *Peter Anson Gallery,* where paintings and drawings by that well-known marine artist are displayed. Open Mon.–Fri. 10–8, Sat. 9.30–12.30.

# GRANDEUR AND TRANQUILITY

## *Highland and Islands*

Broadly speaking, this Region includes all the landmass of Scotland north and west of the Grampian mountains as well as about 600 islands, most of which are gathered in four groups: the Inner Hebrides and Outer Hebrides to the west, the Orkney and Shetland isles to the north. Physically the Region occupies about one third of Scotland, but its population is small. If you take out Inverness (pop. 30,000) it is hard to find a population center which, in other parts of Britain, would be more than a village. Dingwall, Wick, Kirkwall, Lerwick and Stornoway, the next biggest towns, have around 5,000 inhabitants apiece. Their situations as market centers or island capitals, however, give them an importance out of proportion to their size.

With summer tourists these places more than double their populations. If you have not visited the "real" Highland, you have not seen Scotland. In this Region is concentrated much of the romance of "Caledonia stern and wild," the glamor of the clans, the cattle, the red deer and the golden eagles, the Celtic mists and legends and a mixture of splendor and tranquility found hardly anywhere else in the world.

The best and easiest way to approach the Highlands is from the southeast. From coastal roads of Grampian, by Elgin and Forres; from Edinburgh, by the Great North Road through Perth and Pitlochry; from Glasgow or Stirling via Glencoe . . . modern roads follow the robust trails and high-arched bridges which General Wade and his successors built when in the 18th century they opened up a land in which cannibals and barbarians were believed to roam. In those days the Highlands were more densely populated. The people were disturbed out of their primeval ways in the 19th century when the great landowners discovered that sheep were more profitable than cattle. The Clearances—forcible evictions of peasants from their glens—started waves of emigrations, chiefly to Canada, America, Australia and New Zealand. The way the exiles succeeded in new environments was as remarkable as the way they transmitted to their descendants a love of a homeland which had offered them only misery and betrayal.

Touristically, the great surprise is the changing scenery and the stunning effects of light and shade, cloud, sunshine and rainbows. In a couple of hours you may pass from heather, bracken and springy turf to granite rock and bog, to serrated peak and snow-water lake, to the red Torridon sandstone of Wester Ross and the flowery banks of Loch Ewe and Loch Maree. Sea inlets are deep and fjord-like. The black shapes of the isles gather like basking whales on the skyline. Cliffs where quartzite gleams above crescents of hard sand lead round a northern shore which looks from the air as though it was trimmed by an axe. Westward, the next parish is America. Eastward, from Sutherland to Caithness, you enter a windswept moorland country of Norse place names and across the sea horizon you scan the half-Viking archipelagoes, which Scots call Orkney and Shetland (on some official documents, Zetland).

In the northwest of the Region some people speak Gaelic, a language akin to Erse, Welsh and Manx. There is no universally agreed grammar and the definitive dictionary dates from 1845. Simple love songs from the loom-workers in Hebridean crofts are Gaelic's contribution to the cultural heritage. Understood by some 80,000 people, the language is a living reality for far fewer. But language societies campaign energetically and you may arrive in a Highland town where the annual *Mod* is being held—a competition for singers, pipers and bards, all in Gaelic.

Although the Region is rich in ancestral memories and folk tales, its art and architecture, with one or two exceptions, are negligible. The castles, mostly ruins now, were massive but not handsome. The outstanding ecclesiastical building is St. Magnus cathedral in Kirkwall, Orkney. In Glenelg and on Shetland there are a few Pictish brochs, ancient stone towers. Orkney and the island of Lewis have notable chambered tombs and standing stones. Coming to more modern times, the wanderings of Bonnie Prince Charlie through the western Highlands have added legendary and historical interest to many roads, houses and caves. And almost every visitor has some vague hope of catching sight of the monster when visiting Loch Ness.

### Inverness

By way of Nairn, a clean, mild, upmarket vacation town, the A96 enters Inverness from the east. You can cross a modern road bridge (opened 1982) and proceed north without entering the town at all: this route takes you through the Black Isle, which is neither black nor an

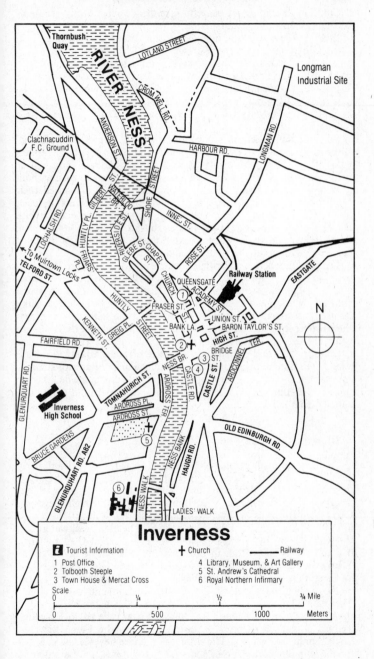

Thornbush Quay

RIVER NESS

LOTLAND STREET

CROMWELL RD.

Longman Industrial Site

ANDERSON ST.

Clachnacuddin F.C. Ground

HARBOUR RD.

LONGMAN RD.

GILBERT ST.

WATERLOO BRIDGE

SHORE STREET

INNES ST.

To Muirtown Locks

LOCHALSH RD.

HUNTLY PL.

FRIARS RD.

GLEBE ST.

RIVERSIDE ST.

CHAPEL ST.

CHURCH ST.

ROSE ST.

Railway Station

EASTGATE

TELFORD ST.

QUEENSGATE

ACADEMY ST.

(1)

FRASER ST.

UNION ST.

BARON TAYLOR'S ST.

KENNETH ST.

HUNTLY STREET

GREIG PL.

BANK LA.

(2)

HIGH ST.

N

FAIRFIELD RD.

NESS BR.

(3)

BRIDGE ST.

(4)

CASTLE ST.

GLENURQUART RD.

TOMNAHURICH ST.

ARDROSS TER.

CASTLE RD.

ARDCONNEL TER.

Inverness High School

ARDROSS PL.

ARDROSS ST.

OLD EDINBURGH RD.

BRUCE GARDENS

GLENURQUART RD. A82

(5)

NESS BANK

HAUGH RD.

NESS WALK

(6)

LADIES' WALK

## Inverness

**ℹ** Tourist Information    **✝** Church    ——— Railway

1 Post Office
2 Tolbooth Steeple
3 Town House & Mercat Cross

4 Library, Museum, & Art Gallery
5 St. Andrew's Cathedral
6 Royal Northern Infirmary

Scale

0     ¼     ½     ¾ Mile

0     500     1000     Meters

island, but an isthmus of peaceful farms and villages only gradually becoming known to visitors.

Inverness disappoints at first glance. It is an ordinary-looking place, though finely situated at the point where the River Ness and Caledonian Canal enter the narrows of the Inverness Firth; and its so-called castle, crowning a hill above the river bridges, is only a pseudo-Norman 19th-century edifice in red sandstone, housing local government offices. The most notable building is Queen Mary's House in Bridge Street, a lodging to which Mary Queen of Scots was reluctantly admitted for a few days in 1562.

But on a sunny day it is pleasant to wander round non-industrial Inverness, visiting old-established shops and admiring the paraphernalia of the clans, here displayed with an everyday air. You will be surprised at the accents of local people: a soft southern English without a trace of Scottish burr. The theory is that the Gaels learned their English from English soldiers, road engineers and post-Jacobite rebellion families who made fashionable little outposts of service life with the three garrisons the British Army established along the Great Glen: Fort George near Inverness, Fort Augustus in the middle of the Glen and Fort William at the southern end.

The cemetery here is also something of a tourist attraction. It spreads over the wooded slopes of Tomnahurich ("Hill of the Fairies") about a mile west of the town and overlooks a panorama of firth, river, canal and loch. It is not at all a melancholy spot and is well worth an evening stroll if you are staying in the town. At about the same distance from the town center, following the Ness upstream towards its loch, you come to the Ness Islands. They are neatly connected with each other by foot-bridges, and with either side of the river. Among them are bandstands and an open-air theater with regular programs of summer entertainment—nothing very sophisticated, but convincing demonstrations of the Highland capital's love and respect for the old piping and dancing traditions.

## Thomas Telford's Folly

On the west bank of the river, a street named after Telford, early 19th-century pioneer of civil engineering in Britain, leads to the Muirtown locks on the Caledonian Canal. Thomas Telford wore himself out designing and constructing this 60-mile waterway through the Great Glen, from Inverness to Fort William. He started it in 1803 and died in 1834; others completed the work by 1847. The twin breakwaters and the pair of locks by which the Canal enters the sea at Clachnaharry, one and a half miles from Inverness, alone took nine years to build.

Like the geological fault which formed the Great Glen, the Caledonian Canal runs in a fairly straight line, passing through the narrow lochs of Ness, Oich and Lochy and splitting Scotland into two portions. There are 29 locks to cope with variations in the water levels, and at the southern end, just above Fort William, a chain of eight locks (which Telford christened Neptune's Staircase) carries the Canal down to Loch Linnhe and the sea. The trip was therefore never a fast one; but for the shipping between east and west coasts it was an alternative to the dangerous passage round Scotland's northern shores, where the tides of the Pentland Firth run at 13 miles an hour.

The trouble was that in the 40-odd years between conception and completion ship sizes increased enormously; and steam replaced sail. By the time the Caledonian Canal was formally opened it was a picturesque white elephant, too narrow for anything bigger than inshore fishing boats. These, and holiday cruisers, are the traffic of the Canal today.

## The Great Glen

Loch and Canal excursions are available in summer from Inverness and Fort William. An excellent highway (A82) goes through the Glen, offering better views and a much faster trip. You hit the Loch Ness shore five miles from Inverness and in another ten you are at the Drumnadrochit inlet, the viewpoint for Nessie and site, at the Drumnadrochit Motor Inn, of the "official" monster exhibition.

Still hugging the shores of the loch, a further 13 miles brings you to Invermoriston where you can take the A887 and A87 into Glen Moriston, past the Five Sisters of Kintail (five peaks in a row) and along the banks of Loch Duich and Loch Alsh; a route which brings you to the ferry for Skye at Kyle of Lochalsh. This road is another "road to the isles"—perhaps the most scenic of all—and along it, near Dornie, you pass that sturdy little castle on the islet, with a causeway to the mainland, which features on the covers of so much tourist literature and in advertisements for Scottish products worldwide. It is called Eilean Donan. Empty and neglected for years, it is now a private house again. Bonnie Prince Charlie was never there, but the castle did have the distinction of being bombarded by frigates of the Royal Navy during an abortive Spanish-Jacobite landing in 1719.

As you pass through Glen Shiel (one of several glens of that name, easily confused) descending towards Loch Duich, observe the roadside boulder labelled "Clach Johnson." In 1773 the Grand Cham of English literature traveled this way with his biographer James Boswell, and they say that while resting beside this clach (boulder) Dr. Johnson determined to write his travel book *A Journey to the Western Isles.*

We have come some way from the Great Glen, so now we shall return to Invermoriston and continue down the A82 to the foot of Loch Ness: one of the largest freshwater lochs in Scotland, 24½ miles long and 750 feet deep in places; one of the loveliest too, with a width never greater than one and a half miles.

Fort Augustus is the small, rather withdrawn little town at the southern end of the loch. It was one of the forts built to accommodate the troops that pacified the Highlands after the first Jacobite rebellion of 1715. Much later (1876) it acquired a Benedictine monastery, which you may visit, though women are excluded from certain parts of it.

Here the Caledonian Canal and the A82 cut across a neck of valley, traverse the small Loch Oich where the Great Glen Water Park has been established, and run by Loch Lochy and Inverlochy to Fort William, a seaport 60 miles from the sea. The deep inlet, Loch Linnhe, is characteristic of the Region. Inland lochs have lengths disproportionate to their widths, but the sea-lochs seem to go on for ever. In the western Highlands, looking at the road ahead, it often seems impossible to find a way round all the water.

Fort William nestles on an elbow of lochs. It is a great tourist nexus in the season although it has only one real street. Ben Nevis, highest mountain in the British Isles (4,406 feet) looks over the town and if you do not want to make the climb (a surprisingly straightforward one) you should at least drive five miles up Glen Nevis (unclassified road) for a glimpse of the wild district of Lochaber. South of Fort William, the A82 turns at Ballachulish bridge for Glencoe and Strathclyde, while the A828 continues along the sea-loch shores, tortuous but smothered in flowers in spring, towards Oban and the hills of Lorne (Strathclyde).

The Great Glen roads and their offshoots are heavily-trafficked in summer and susceptible to flooding and landslips during torrential rains. For many visitors this Inverness–Fort William route is the base-line for explorations of Scotland's northwestern Highlands and islands.

## Glen of Weeping

South of Fort William the A82 crosses a modern bridge over the narrows of a loch at Ballachulish. (To go round the head of the loch would add 25 miles to your journey.) Here the main roads divide, the A828 going round the coast to Oban and the A82 climbing on the Rannoch Moor by way of Glencoe and heading for Loch Lomond and Glasgow.

There is always a chill in Glencoe (Glen of Weeping) even on the hottest day. The pass is hemmed in with 3,000-foot rocks and over the top, where the Kingshouse Inn (long ago the only tavern for miles around, therefore visited by every notable traveler) stands on an old disused road, the formidable rock bastion of Buchaille Etive Mor, the "Great Shepherd of Etive," frowns down from 3,345 feet.

Glencoe is the best-known of Highland passes as a result of the massacre of 1692. It involved fewer than 100 deaths, but has been remembered where many much larger and equally brutal clan massacres are forgotten. In a mix-up over an oath of loyalty, the chief of the Campbell clan saw an opportunity to pay off old scores against the MacDonalds. He led his men into Glencoe, was hospitably entertained and then fell on his hosts with fire and sword. Scarcely one of them survived. The enmity between the Campbells and the MacDonalds is hardly forgotten to this day.

The National Trust for Scotland now has care of 14,000 acres of rough moorland in Glencoe and neighboring Dalness. There is a NTS shop and visitor center at Clachaig on the old road halfway up the glen (open daily in summer 10–7 and in spring and autumn 10–5). The property includes a cave named for Ossian, a semi-mythical Gaelic bard, and a cascade called Ossian's Showerbath. The massacre took place near the foot of the pass, where a commemorative stone stands beside the Glencoe Hotel.

## Culloden

At the other end of the Great Glen, on the shores of the Inverness Firth, the pages of history flutter with other dark deeds of assassination and massacre. Cawdor Castle (B9090), scene of the murder in *Macbeth,* has been transformed into a well-organized house and park open to the public. You can eat in the castle restaurant or share a picnic with an amiable herd of Highland cattle; roam the gardens which hang above the River Nairn; and examine the domestic life of the laird from stable and kitchen to drawing-room and bedchamber. There are other fine castellated mansions in this district—Kilravock, pronounced "Kill-rawk," is a gem—and several of them will show you the room that Bonnie Prince Charlie occupied the night before Culloden. He must have had a restless time of it.

Culloden Moor is five miles east of Inverness. The B9006 crosses the battlefield. A short walk from the car-park are the Cumberland Stone, where the general staff of the Government forces took up its position; the cairn (a heap of boulders) and rough semicircle of Highlanders' graves marked with the names of the clans; and the Old Leanach farmhouse, a thatched cottage in the middle of the battlefield which somehow survived intact. The National Trust for Scotland has now prettified Old Leanach and made it even more intact.

Through January and February 1746 Bonnie Prince Charlie's Jacobite army continued its retreat from England, sporadically harried by the Duke of Cumberland's troops and steadily losing numbers as disenchanted Highlanders deserted and made for home. The Prince's idea was to recruit and re-form in the Highlands, to appeal to the French for reinforcements and launch another campaign. But first there had to be a confrontation with his pursuers, and it came in April on Culloden Moor.

When battle commenced the Jacobite command was gloomy, but the Prince was briefly his old optimistic self and full of dash. The skills and the numbers (9,000 against 5,000) were all on his opponents' side. It was over in 40 minutes. On the Moor lay 1,000 Jacobites, dead and dying, and the rest were scattered into hiding. Bundled away to safety the Prince stood dazed. "He neither spoke nor enquired after the absent."

## The Prince in the Heather

For six months after Culloden he wandered about the Highlands, a passive object, handed like a bale of contraband from one smuggler to another, numbed with constant applications of "mountain Malaga" (whisky)—the beginning of the chronic alcoholism which degraded and finally killed him. As you travel the northwest you will often cross his trail. From Culloden he found his way to Fort Augustus (A82), then to Loch Arkaig (off B8005), then to Arisaig (A830) where he escaped to the isles of Harris and South Uist. There he met Flora MacDonald, the young lady who took him, disguised as her maid, "over the sea to Skye" and back to the mainland.

The local lairds, Jacobites to a man, then cooperated in moving the Prince around the wastes of the central Highlands, first to Loch Affric (off A831) and to Loch Arkaig for a second visit (there was supposed to be a treasure-chest of louis d'or, French gold coins, waiting for him, but the lairds had shared it out among themselves) and at last to Loch nan Uamh on the Arisaig road (A830), close to the spot where he had landed 15 months earlier, to re-embark for France. "Never was there dawn so brilliant, never sunset so clouded," it was said of the Young Pretender's life. A biographer summed up his tragedy as: "In Rome a Protestant, in Britain a Papist"—in other words, fated always to be in the wrong place at the wrong time.

Despite a dragging sordid end which overshadowed The Adventure, the Prince remains a Scottish hero. He suits the pedestal on which song writers and sentimental novelists have placed him. His Scottish exploits were the stuff that myths are made of. *Will ye no' come back again* . . . *Speed, bonnie boat* . . . *Charlie is my darling* . . . the tunes and lyrics of Lady Nairne, jaunty or mournful, composed long after the events, are as good an epitaph as any adventurer could wish for.

Memories of the Prince cluster thickly on our West Highland routes, especially the 39 miles of the A830 from Fort William to Arisaig and Mallaig. The Fort William museum has a room dedicated to him; relics are shown at Culloden House (off B9006); Glenfinnan (A830) has the great monument to the clans who joined him there (a column aptly described by Queen Victoria as "rather ugly . . . like a sort of lighthouse surrounded by a wall"); seven beech trees at Kinlochmoidart (B850) commemorate the seven men of Moidart who befriended him; and there are numerous caves on coastline and loch shore which now bear his name.

Flora MacDonald has a statue in front of Inverness Castle; a memorial cairn at Milton, her birthplace on South Uist; and her last home and grave at Flodigarry and Kilmuir respectively (A855) near the northern tip of the island of Skye.

## The Highest Restaurant in Britain

The Great North Road (A9) and railroad come in from Tayside Region at the summit of the Drumochter pass. From that watershed they descend with the infant Spey in a valley which broadens quickly and acquires a green and golden fleece of pinewood and birch. We are as far from the sea as we can be in Scotland, yet there are tangs of ozone and the clean look of a maritime vacationland about us. Newtonmore and Kingussie depend almost wholly on tourism; on city people who want to unwind in the silence of the hills, to do a little fishing and play a little golf. From Newtonmore in the 1950s some riders set out to cross the mountains to Braemar; and the new activity called pony-trekking was born.

Kincraig (still A9) has the Highland Wildlife Park, open daily mid-March to October; and Carrbridge the ambitious Landmark Visitor Centre, a sculpture park, tree walks, nature trails, entertainments and a multivision theater with travelogues and narratives of Highland history.

Hereabouts you skirt the Cairngorm winter-sports complex, the biggest in Scotland. Access is from Aviemore (A9) and Coylumbridge or from Grantown-on-Spey and Nethybridge on two branches of the B970 road. A bus service links Aviemore with Coire Cas ("Corry Cass") at 2,000 feet, where there are parking lots, cafes and restaurants, two chairlifts and seven ski-tows. The principal chair-lift rises to 3,600 feet, only 500 feet from the summit of Cairngorm. At the halfway station there is a self-service restaurant. At the top stands the Ptarmigan restaurant, the highest in Britain, with a panorama of Strathspey and the blue hills beyond Inverness.

The Aviemore Centre has numerous modern hotels where lively evening entertainment is offered; ceilidhs (song-and-dance parties) and country dancing the specialties. There is a big ballroom, a theater, a cinema, a curling rink and facilities for children: the sort of things you will not see again in many miles of Highland travels. But not everyone comes here to ski, although all the villages up and down the A9 and A95 have their ski shops and ski schools. The district is busy with vacationeers old and young all year round.

## North of Inverness

At Inverness the A9 meets the sea and begins laboriously tracing the outlines of the firths of Beauly, Cromarty and Dornoch. From Inverness to Dornoch as the crow flies is 27 miles; by road it is three times as far. Most motorists, anxious to press on to John o' Groats, the most northerly point on the road, take short cuts: over the Kessock bridge and through the Black Isle to Dingwall (B9162); and over the Struie road (A836) to Bonar Bridge. They are pleasant roads and the view over Dornoch Firth from the Struie is one of the finest in Scotland. But this district, known as East Ross, should not be hurried through. If possible, go a little out of your way to see Cromarty (A832), once an important port on the narrows of its firth, now a sleepy period-piece; Fortrose and Rosemarkie (A832), also on the Black Isle, with their relics of 15th-century cathedral and 7th-century monastery, their Pictish stones and Fairy Glen and Eathie Burn, the stream in whose banks locally-born Hugh Miller "dug his reputation" as a renowned geologist; Contin church and Rogie falls near Dingwall; the lighthouse and ruined castle at Portmahomack (B9165); the spa town of Strathpeffer and its quaint Victorian railroad station (A834), locked in hills, dreaming almost undisturbed dreams of a fashionable 19th-century clientele; and Dornoch (B9167), population only 750 but cathedral city, county capital, golf mecca since 1619 and baronial stronghold.

North of Dornoch, near Golspie, the A9 passes through the woods of Dunrobin Castle ("o" as in "robe"), an ancient seat elaborated by its 19th-century lord, the Duke of Sutherland, into a flamboyant white-turreted enormity with more rooms than any hotel in Scotland. Trains so fascinated the Duke that he built his own railroad in the park and staffed and operated it with his own servants. If you travel by rail in these domains you will notice how the line follows the coast-road past Dunrobin, within sight of its windows, and a little farther north at Helmsdale takes a wide sweep across the heathery hinterland of Caithness, a detour which removes it from the view of the Langwell grouse moors and deer forests. Langwell was the stamping-ground of the Duke of Portland, who detested trains.

A branch road from the A9 accompanies that railroad, riding high over bare moorland to Kildonan (A897), where prospectors used to pan for gold, to a lonely hotel at Forsinard, and then to Melvich at the foot of Strath Halladale on the north coast of Sutherland. Staying with the A9, you run along a coast where cliffs are steep and harbors few. The best views are to be had from the Ord of Caithness, where you cross a 750-foot bluff within a mile of the sea before dipping perilously to the mouth of a glen at Berriedale. In the glen is Langwell House, a palace by ordinary standards, a mere hunting lodge for the ducal Portlands.

## Caithness

Dunbeath is another lost village, huddled in an angle of the cliffs where a torrent races down and with a castle ruin on the cliff edge. The castle was a fortress of the Sinclairs who controlled this country. The simpler life, everyday work and play of long ago, is displayed at the Laidhey Croft, a museum a few yards along the A9 from the village.

The largest of these little coastal refuges is Lybster, a center for archeological exploration. Within a few minutes of the village you may see the Camster cairns, dating from about 1000 B.C., the Standing Stones of Achavanich, the Hill o' Many Stanes and other relics of early Pictish and Norse occupation.

Wick, 121 miles from Inverness, lies on the coast athwart the Wick River. In the heyday of the Scottish herring it was a prominent port and it is still something of a metropolis for white fish and a market center for Caithness farmers.

Thurso, northernmost town on Britain's mainland, dates from Viking times. Its harbor too was once prosperous. From it was shipped the blue-gray Caithness stone which paved the streets and courtyards of many European towns. Like Wick, the place is developing as a modest family resort, its principal attractions the awesome cliff scenery and spacious firm sands. Considering the latitude (equivalent to that of Juneau, Alaska), the climate on this northern shore can be astonishingly mild. The port of Thurso, called Scrabster, is a terminal for Orkney.

Roads leading north from Wick and Thurso converge at John o' Groats, the Land's End of Scotland, though not precisely the most northerly point. The approach is shabby and dull. It is sad to see Caithness, not the most picturesque of Scottish counties at the best of times, petering out in a rash of shacks, small-holdings and caravan parks. But the beach and breakwater are usually remote from this unsightliness, while the cliff paths towards Duncansby Head on one side and Dunnet Head on the other offer dramatic seascapes. And at low tide you may find the lucky "groatie buckie," a type of cowrie shell found only here.

Summer boat-trips are offered from John o' Groats to Orkney through the swirling Pentland Firth. The tomb of Jan de Groot, the

Dutch settler who gave the place its name, is in Canisbay church, two miles west.

## Sutherland

Norse marauders gave the district its name: "Southland." But along with Caithness it forms the northern limits of Britain's mainland and it has the most savage and majestic of Scotland's sea-cliffs, cascades, caves and capes. From John o' Groats via Thurso, the A836 to Tongue and the A838 to Durness link the hamlets of the coastal strip. Ten miles from John o' Groats stands the Castle of Mey near a desolate foreshore. It is the property of the Queen Mother, to which she briefly retired after the death of her husband King George VI in 1952. A dangerous reef in the Pentland Firth, called the Merry Men of Mey, throws up spectacular fountains of spray in stormy weather.

Ten miles west of Thurso, at Dounreay ("Doonray"), you can stop for a conducted tour of one of Britain's earliest fast breeder nuclear reactors.

On the whole, however, these are sparsely-populated and neglected-looking regions. Fishermen, mountaineers and walkers have long visited them and the hotels and self-catering cottages are designed to meet their needs.

Sutherland's coastal backcloth is the mountain ranges of Reay Forest and Assynt, studded with glassy lochs and split with foaming torrents. Ben Loyal, south of Tongue, is called the "Queen of Scottish Mountains" for its grandeur rather than its height (2,504 feet). As you travel west, the peaks of Ben Hope (3,040 feet) and Foinaven (2,980 feet) are disclosed. Beyond them you may detour along the rough road from Durness to Cape Wrath; but the main A838 turns for Scotland's north-west frontier, meeting the Atlantic at Laxford Bridge.

Here, traveling south, you are at the first of a dozen long, deep and narrow sea-lochs which bristle with islets and are bordered by villages of low-built, white-washed stone cottages, the staging-posts for your journey back to such great places of the world as Ullapool and Kyle of Lochalsh. Some villages, marked in large letters on the map, turn out to be a road junction with a hotel and nothing else standing beside it. (There is always a hotel, often an amazingly comfortable one, too.)

"I would not exchange these lochs and isles with their passionate tides and skies loaded with mists for all the archipelagos of the eastern seas," wrote Jules Verne after his northwestern pilgrimage—sentiments echoed by some famous diarists who followed him. Splendor and tranquillity, an ever-changing sky, a kaleidoscope of brilliant colors revolving on the hills . . . there is something indefinable, too, which makes this district memorable for the visitor. Magical and eerie are words frequently used. Sunset over Badcall Bay (near Scourie, A894) has been known to inspire feelings too deep for words or tears in some fairly hard-bitten tourists. Now they know why a Highlander's nostalgia in exile lasts him all his life.

An occasional turning from the A9 on the east coast between Bonar Bridge and Wick takes the motorist across Sutherland to these western sea-lochs by way of mountain passes and serpentine lochs. Close to

Bonar Bridge at Carbisdale Castle (a modern building on the site of the last battle fought by the "Great Marquess" Montrose, 1650), the A837 crosses Scotland from east to west, passing through the wilderness of Assynt on its way to Lochinver. A branch of this road (A835) heads south for Ullapool on Loch Broom. Above the forest east of Inchnadamph the peak of Ben More Assynt (3,273 feet) is prominent; and the grim ruin of Ardvreck Castle sticks up from Loch Assynt as you descend towards the sea at Lochinver.

Another coast-to-coast highway, single-track for many miles, is the A838 from Bonar Bridge to Loch Laxford via Lairg. It is one of the most invigorating drives in Scotland, running along the rivers and riverine lochs which cut across a tough massif. The A894 down the west coast connects with the two roads described above, crossing a sinuous loch at Kylesku. Pause here for a sight of Eas Coulaulin, the highest waterfall in the British Isles, with a drop of 650 feet.

Lairg, which also has a fine cascade, the Falls of Shin, famous for its leaping salmon, is a grand junction of roads to far west and far north and is correctly called the gateway to Sutherland. From here the rough and hilly A836 and B873 make straight for the north coast at Tongue and Bettyhill respectively.

## Wester Ross

South of Sutherland and Caithness, the old country of Ross, formerly inhabited by the descendants of Celtic earls of that name, spreads across the full width of Scotland. Around the Cromarty and Dornoch firths on the A9 we traversed East Ross. The deeply-indented shores and multitudinous islets of the other side of Scotland, 80 miles away, are known as Wester Ross. The land is still rough and desolate and scenic, but the villages are more numerous than in the far north.

Ullapool was custom-built as a herring station in the 1780s. Then the herring vanished and for a time Ullapool was a ghost village. But its well-built stone cottages attracted inhabitants and now it deals in mackerel and seafood—and tourists.

From Ullapool the narrow fenceless roads wind round the shores or penetrate the glens of short sharp rivers, touching at places of extraordinary beauty but little importance. In spring and early summer a variegated botany springs to life. At a sheltered spot near Poolewe a sub-tropical garden has been created (A832). There is plenty of easy walking but the higher summits, such as the An Teallach ridge above Little Loch Broom and Slioch (3,217 feet) above Loch Maree, are best left to mountaineers.

Shieldaig and Applecross (B857 and an unclassified road) are well worth the diversion, though you must return by the same twisting roads. From Shieldaig you look back at the nine 3,000-foot summits of Torridon, a district of old rocks which has given its name to a whole geological classification. To Applecross your road goes over the historic Pass of the Cattle and on the descent you have before you the island of Skye, the seabird colonies on the stack rocks and the seals, perhaps even a shark, lazing by the shore.

Another memorable run is from Ullapool to Achiltibuie, either by unclassified road or by boat (the boat is the quicker). Sunset over the Summer Isles, a few miles offshore, is something that tourists drive long distances to see.

At the crofts of Lochcarron (A890) tartan is woven in the old manner. Prehistoric cairns and Pictish stones break the curve of hills in several places. The most remarkable antiquity in the northwest, however, is Dun Dornigaill, a beehive hut and enclosure 10 miles south of Eriboll in Sutherland (A838). Halt anywhere on the road and you will soon be made aware of a wealth of wildlife: red deer, eagles, even ospreys. (The osprey nest beside Loch Garten, off B970 near Aviemore, is under surveillance from thousands of tourists every summer; the birds seem quite unconcerned.)

In short, this northwestern land is an ecological paradise, 100% pollution-free; for many a harassed city-dweller the last great tranquilizer.

## Isle of Skye

Coming south down the west coast of Scotland you reach the first of the ferry ports to Skye at Kyle of Lochalsh, terminus of the A87 from Invermoriston in the Great Glen. On the five-minute boat trip to Kyleakin ("Ky-lakkin") your eye is caught by Moil Castle, a gap-toothed ruin. The owner was a Danish noblewoman of the Middle Ages called Saucy Mary, who stretched a chain to the mainland and demanded a toll from passing ships.

Skye is the largest of the Inner Hebrides group, 50 miles from tip to tip; celebrated for its Coolins, or Cuillins, a range of jagged black mountains which kill one or two rock-climbers every year. Roads are good. Castles, hotels and topographical features are soaked in the mystique of Bonnie Prince Charlie and Flora MacDonald but the person who did most to popularize the island by visiting it 30 years later and praising its landscapes and seascapes and natives' hospitality was Dr. Johnson. You may assimilate the violent history of the clans at the 800-year-old Dunvegan Castle (A850), ancestral seat of the MacLeods; at Duntulm (off A855), the ruin of a 15th-century citadel of the MacDonalds, Lords of the Isles; and at mock-Tudor Armadale Castle (A851) with its flower-beds and guided walks through a fertile strip of shoreline called the Garden of Skye.

You can make the crossing to Skye by the very frequent Kyle-Kyleakin ferry, but there are also ferries from Glenelg to Kylerhea (summer only) and from Mallaig to Armadale in the south of the island.

## The Cocktail Islands

South of Skye, across the Coolin Sound, lie the isles of Rhum, Eigg, Muck and Canna, a constellation known as the Small Isles. (The first three are sometimes facetiously called the Cocktail Islands.) Public access has long been restricted in the interests of conservation but nowadays Rhum attracts 4,000 visitors annually, some of whom stay a night or two at the ostentatious Kinloch Castle, which is part hotel, part hostel and part craft center. The wild life of Rhum includes goats and a peculiar breed of pony. Most of the isles are bare and rocky but low-lying Canna, now in the care of the National Trust for Scotland, has a farm, a bird sanctuary and a few Stone Age and Celtic remains. Canna House contains a library of traditional Gaelic songbooks and other literature. The National Trust for Scotland hopes one day to provide limited accommodations for ornithologists and folklorists.

Eigg is remarkable for its oddly-shaped sgurr (rock pinnacle) which rises to 1,289 feet. A 16th-century massacre by the MacLeods of Skye, who trapped and suffocated 395 of their hereditary foes the Mac-Donalds in a cave on Eigg, is described in Scott's long narrative poem *The Lord of the Isles.*

Visiting the Small Isles presents problems. It is best to adapt yourself to the schedules of mainland trains and inter-island mail-boats. You might, for example, leave Glasgow at 6 A.M., step aboard the Mallaig mail-boat at 11, having traveled the beautiful West Highland railroad; and spend the rest of the day island-hopping, calling at Skye and all the Small Isles and returning to the mainland about 7 P.M. But to stay more than a few minutes at each island might well involve staying several days, until the mail-boat calls again.

Mallaig, like Ullapool, is an important fishing harbor in a magnificent setting. Here you return to Bonnie Prince Charlie country. The A830 to Fort William passes, south of Arisaig, the cave where the Prince lived while awaiting the French ship sent to bring him off; and a tablet at the roadside in Borrodale, near the head of Loch nan Uamh ("Bay of Whales") marks the spot where he stepped on board and said farewell to Scotland. Halfway to Fort William you pass the Glenfinnan monument and Highland Gathering arena. In that bowl of the hills, where the view opens on Glen Shiel's misty length, the young Prince raised the standard of revolt in August 1745.

The land to the south, easier to penetrate than might appear from the tentative road markings on most maps, provides an abundance of heather-and-glen locations for the makers of Bonnie Prince Charlie movies. It is a fine blustery road to Salen and Ardnamurchan ("Cape of the Great Storms") by the A861 and B8007; and one to break the back of a snake as far as Lochaline in Morven (A884)—a route on which you pass through the disused lead mines of Strontian, where the rare mineral element (strontium) was first discovered. These western byways are as romantic and suggestive as the names of the districts they pass through: Moidart, Morven, Sunart, Ardgour. Their history is of the word-of-mouth kind, and it concerns murky clan feuds almost exclusively.

## Outer Hebrides

The oldest inhabitants call them the Long Island, this splintered line of many islands from the pugnacious Butt of Lewis in the north to the 600-foot Barra Head on Berneray in the south, whose lighthouse has the greatest arc of visibility in the world. They stretch about 130 miles from end to end, and lie about 50 miles from the Scottish mainland.

These are the Outer Hebrides. Lewis, the most northerly island, is the largest and also has the only town, Stornoway, on a big land-locked harbor. A few miles west (B8012) are the neolithic Standing Stones of Callanish—a central cairn surrounded by 13 monoliths and others which may have formed concentric circles dotted about—and the shapely broch of Carloway. These legacies of the aboriginal islanders are rated second only to Stonehenge in British antiquities.

Harris, which has the highest mountain in the islands (Clisham, 2,600 feet), was the home of the world-famous Harris tweed. A few weavers still practise their ancient craft, weaving and spinning by hand and coloring the material with natural dyes, but Harris tweed as an industry is now centered in Stornoway on Lewis, where mill shops have been established for individual sightseers and buyers.

From Leverburgh on Harris (a name which recalls the philanthropist Lord Leverhulme; his attempts to drag the islanders into the 19th century met with little success) a ferry-boat crosses to Newton in North Uist. From there you may travel through Benbecula and South Uist without stopping, thanks to connecting causeways.

North Uist is rich in monoliths and chambered cairns and other reminders of a prehistoric past. The temple of the Trinity (13th century) at Carinish, close to the southern causeway, is worth a visit.

Benbecula ("Mount of the Fords") is less bare and neglected-looking than the islands to the north; and in South Uist in summer there are wild gardens with riots of Alpine and rock plants. Ruined forts and chapels abound (this was a refuge of the old Catholic faith) and at Eochdar you will find the Black House museum, which gives a picture of Hebridean life as it was up to the 20th century. "Black" houses are cottages of undressed boulders, sometimes built half underground, sheeted down against the Atlantic gales with a dense straw thatch. The biggest religious monument in the isles, some say the biggest ever sculpted in Britain, stands on the Hill of Miracles at Rueval. It is the statue of Our Lady of the Isles and it was done by Hew Lorimer in 1957. South Uist's famous daughter, Flora MacDonald, was born at Milton; her cottage still stands. (All these hamlets are on or near the A865.)

Eriskay, known abroad for the haunting *Eriskay Love Lilt,* and its group of islets almost block the six-mile strait between South Uist and Barra.

Barra, an isle you can walk across in an hour, has formidable peaks, some sandy beaches and one huge old castle, the largest ancient monument in the western isles. This is Kishmul or Kismuil, on an islet in Castlebay, the principal harbor of Barra. The 45th MacNeil of Barra, its feudal laird, restored it earlier this century and local boats take visitors out to it on Saturday afternoons in summer. Barra is a friendly, flowery little island. Its airport is a stretch of sand, washed twice daily by the tide.

Within living memory it was hard to find a place to stay in the Outer Hebrides outside Stornoway. Now the hotels, guest-houses and self-catering developments proliferate and some natives complain that second-home buyers from other parts of Scotland are destroying a way of life. Communications by sea and air are excellent and you will have no difficulty with accommodations.

## Orkney

The northern archipelagos, two groups totaling 200 islands of which about 40 are inhabited, are linked historically with Scandinavia. "Shetland for scenery, Orkney for antiquities," the saying goes—and both for bird-watchers. The islands teem with sea-birds of many kinds, including migratory swarms of rare Arctic waterfowl.

Cartographical convenience usually dictates that Orkney and Shetland are tucked away in the corners of maps (as they are on ours), often on reduced scale. When you tour them you appreciate the spread of latitude that they cover: no hope of doing them justice in a couple of hours, or even in a couple of days.

Orkney's isles are mostly smooth and round-topped, enclosing bays and straits called flows. The off-lying stack rocks have land-based counterparts in important Stone Age and Old Norse monuments: Skara Brae, a 5,000-year-old complex of cottages; Maeshowe, of similar age, the finest chambered tomb in western Europe; the Ring of Brogar, 36 standing stones in a broken circle which once contained 60 of them . . . all these sites are close to, or on, the shallow loch of Stenness on Orkney mainland (A965 from Kirkwall). Local information leaflets will help you locate these antiquities and many more.

At Kirkwall harbor the lobster boats, coastal steamers and inter-island ferryboats come and go. Behind the waterfront the flagged streets and passageways resemble those of some prosperous little town of the Zuider Zee. The principal building, St. Magnus cathedral, is of modest and rather militant appearance, built in pink sandstone on foundations laid by the Norse Earl Rognvald in 1137. The St. Magnus Festival (arts, music, drama) takes place annually in June and its activities are centered on Kirkwall and the island's other "town," Stromness (A965), also on Orkney's mainland.

More recent history has left its mark. The twin Martello towers guarding Longhope, isle of Hoy (B9047) were built to stave off a possible French landing in the Napoleonic wars of two centuries ago. The Churchill Barriers across the eastern exits from Scapa Flow make it possible to drive 22 miles from Kirkwall across three islands. They are reminders of a nasty moment for the British Fleet in October 1939, when a German submarine braved ripping tides and hidden rocks to penetrate the great naval anchorage and sink a battleship.

## Shetland

Here the Norse heritage lives on as nowhere else, exploding in celebration in Lerwick on the last Tuesday in January at the winter fire festival of Up-Helly-Aa. But Lerwick is a cosmopolitan port all the year round. Flags of all nations fly at the mastheads of the fishing boats which come in to land their catches: Russian, Polish, Spanish, French, German. And if you travel Shetland's mainland as far as Sullom Voe ("voe" means inlet) on the A970 from Lerwick you will hear the accents of Texas and California at the great North Sea oil terminal.

Small ferries, taking automobiles, provide daily connections between Shetland's mainland, on which most inhabitants live, and some of the other 16 islands, from Yell (80 square miles) to Muckle Flugga (a quarter of a square mile). The nearer inhabited isles of Burra, Trondra and Muckle Roe are linked to the mainland of Shetland with bridges.

Stone towers or brochs keep watch from many headlands. That of Mousa, off the A970, 12 miles south of Lerwick, stands 43 feet high and you can climb the stairway in its walls. The most impressive archeological site is Jarlshof, close to Sumburgh airport in the extreme south: a village sunk to its roofs in the earth, inhabited by Bronze Age, Iron Age and Viking settlers.

The diminutive Shetland ponies are by no means extinct; but are kept more as pets in the south of England than as working animals on Shetland crofts.

## Fair Isle

Every year a handful of tourists visit the Fair Isle, midway between Orkney and Shetland; attracted perhaps by its reputation for the patterned knitwear which is still produced by a few of its 75 inhabitants, chiefly for mail-order customers. The distinctive patterns and the sheep with their exceptionally soft, shaded wool are not exclusive to the Fair Isle: Shetland does business in this kind of thing too. But Fair Isle patterns do retain a distinguishing mark—odd symbols of which the row of crosses and circles locally known as Oxo is most common.

If you want to visit the Fair Isle, a light aircraft connects with British Airways flights to Sumburgh (Shetland); or the island boat will take you there free, also from Sumburgh, a 24-mile trip. Accomodations are available at the Bird Observation Trust hostel (no single rooms).

## The Life Style

Looking round Highland graveyards, especially in Caithness, one gets intimations of near-immortality: some people live to a great age. Reflecting on that, and on the long summer days when, as the monkish chronicler wrote, you can see at midnight to pick the lice out of your shirt, one wonders how the population fills its time.

Those who work in the Highlands and islands are fully occupied wresting a living from barren land and inhospitable seas. Fishing is still vital to the economy of larger villages; and many girls, once unemployable, now find jobs in fish processing factories. Others work seasonally at hotels and guest-houses, which have multiplied rapidly since the 1960s.

Well-paid jobs, an influx of workers from far away and some disturbance in life-style and environment were brought in with the development of the major oil and gas terminals at Sullom Voe in Shetland and Flotta in Orkney and the oil-platform construction yard at Kishorn near Lochcarron (B857). Forestry is a growth industry too: you will notice as you travel the western Highlands how many neglected hill-slopes are being planted with Sitka spruce, Scots pine and Douglas fir.

Crofting, farming on a family scale, was once considered the solution to the problems of rural communities. It is nowadays practised only on a part-time basis. Very few Highlanders or islanders make a living from the land; but enough is produced to ensure that, wherever you stay, your breakfast egg will be fresh, while vegetables are delivered daily from a neighborhood plot.

Unemployment is higher than the national average. Drink is a problem. Old Roman Catholic traditions persist but life is influenced much more by the stern fundamentalism of the "Wee Frees"—the Free Kirk of Scotland which, among other restrictions, ensures that shops are shut on Sundays, that no frivolous activities take place on that day, that no ferries operate and that other transport services are cut to a minimum. The native Highlander and islander regards other Scots as foreigners, no better than the English or the Americans; but he is friendly and courteous as a rule. Satisfied with the simple life, augmenting the diet with some fishing and shooting, many who have resisted the temptation to emigrate to the south manage to pursue what appears to be an enviable *dolce far niente*. We tourists can envy them one thing at least. We soak up the beauties of this Region for a few days in June or September, perhaps—but we dream of them all year round.

# PRACTICAL INFORMATION FOR HIGHLAND AND ISLANDS

**HOW TO GET THERE. By air.** The principal airport in Highland and Islands Region is Dalcross, 8 miles east of Inverness. It has links within Scotland with Glasgow, Kirkwall and Stornoway; in England with London (Heathrow), Manchester, Newcastle and Tees-side; and abroad with Milan, New York, Paris, Reykjavik and Stavanger. London–Inverness by British Airways takes 70 minutes.

British Airways, Loganair, Air Ecosse and Burnthills Aviation (helicopters) will all fly you from Glasgow Airport to Fort William, Skye, Barra, Benbecula, Stornoway or Wick; or from Edinburgh Airport to Kirkwall, Sumburgh or Lerwick; or from Aberdeen Airport to Wick, Kirkwall or Sumburgh.

**HOTELS AND RESTAURANTS.** The Highland and Islands Region offer a wide range of hotels and guest-houses, as well as countless bed-and-breakfast places and caravans for short- or long-term hire. Alternatively, you can rent a self-catering cottage (contact local information center for details).

Most large country hotels have restaurants with international cuisine. Game, fish, seafood and venison are often presented in interesting forms. Town eateries tend to be unassuming (though Chinese and Indian cooking is becoming more prevalent, even in Stornoway), but—as at roadside pubs and cafes—you might be offered homemade soups, fresh salmon salads, fresh fried haddock and halibut, and scallops brought to the back door by a fisherman who collected them half an hour earlier. You may be agreeably surprised by the modest charges made for truly superb home cooking—even the bread and the breakfast marmalade may well have been made by your host or hostess. Much of the Region comprises countryside that has never known supermarkets, delicatessens or wine bars.

**AULTNAMAIN** (A836, on Struie Hill). **Restaurant.** *Aultnamain Inn* (M), tel. Edderton 238.

**AVIEMORE.** *Badenoch* (E), tel. 810261. 78 rooms, 60 with bath. Modern; in the Sports Center. *Coylumbridge* (E), tel. 810661. 133 rooms with bath; on A951. Tennis; close to Loch Marich for yachting and skiing on slopes above. French and English food. *Strathspey* (E), tel. 810681. 90 rooms, 89 with bath. *High Range* (M), tel. 810261. 25 rooms, 9 with bath. Central building with surrounding chalets, on outskirts of town, extensive mountain views, set in lovely wood. *Post House* (M), tel. 810771. 103 rooms with bath. Also in Sports Center, lively and modern with high-quality bedrooms; sauna.

**GAIRLOCH** (A832). *The Old Inn* (M), tel. 2006. 9 rooms, 7 with bath. Cheerful oasis in wilderness of the west.

**GOLSPIE** (A9). **Restaurant.** *Park House* (I), Main Street (tel. 3667).

**HALKIRK** (B874). *Ulbster Arms* (M), tel. 206. 30 rooms, 22 with bath. Modernized Victorian house on Thurso River. Saturday rendezvous for Caithness youth.

**INVERNESS** (A9). *Kingsmills* (E), Culcabock (tel. 37166). 58 rooms, 54 with bath. Country-house elegance in pleasant gardens. Squash courts. *Queensgate* (E), tel. 37211. 60 rooms, all with bath. Modern town-center hotel of highest class.

**LEWIS, ISLE OF.** *Caberfeidh* (E), Stornoway (tel. 2604). 37 rooms, all with bath. The most expensive hotel in Outer Hebrides.

**LOCHINVER** (A837). *Hillcrest Guest House* (I), tel. 391. 4 rooms. Friendly, willing service; home cooking.

**NAIRN** (A96). *Golf View* (E), tel. 52301. 55 rooms, all with bath. Famous seaside and sporting hotel, spacious location. Imaginative Highland cuisine. Gourmet nights and weekly Grand Buffet in paneled restaurant.

**NORTH UIST, ISLE OF.** *Langass Lodge* (M), tel. Locheport 285. 6 rooms. Seascapes, nature reserve, fishing. Good shellfish menu.

**ONICH** (A82, south of Fort William). *Onich* (I), tel. 214. 25 rooms. Family-run hotel on shore of Loch Linnhe; games room, putting green, fishing, boat trips. Venue for local dances and ceilidhs (Gaelic songs and stories).

**ORKNEY, MAINLAND OF.** *Ferry Inn* (I), Stromness (tel. 850280). 10 rooms, 6 with bath. Modernized fishing inn, strong nautical flavor. Late suppers served; home cooking with seafood specialties.

**ROSEMARKIE** (A832). *Marine* (M), tel. Fortrose 20253. 54 rooms, 13 with bath. Golfing and family hotel. Terraced lawns, handy for sailing and safe bathing.

**SHETLAND, NORTH MAINLAND OF.** *Busta House* (M), Brae (tel. 456). 13 rooms, 11 with bath. This historic building has its own harbor.

**SKYE, ISLE OF.** *Rosedale* (M), Portree (tel. 2511). 21 rooms, 7 with bath. *Roskhill Guest House* (I), Dunvegan (tel. 317). 5 rooms with 2 annexed holiday apartments. Homely hospitality, home baking.

**TONGUE** (A836). *Tongue* (M), tel. 206. 21 rooms, 9 with bath. Country house in splendid setting; rooms average but grills and baking good, and service beyond reproach.

**TORLUNDY** (A82, north of Fort William). *Inverlochy Castle* (L), tel. Fort William 2177. 13 rooms, all with bath. Regal welcome in a Highland castle where Queen Victoria once slept. Gastronomic cuisine, every reasonable whim satisfied. The costliest tariff north of Gleneagles Hotel.

 **HOW TO GET ABOUT. By car.** Vehicles towing caravans can be a nuisance on some Highland roads in summer, but in general motoring in this Region is a pleasure and principal routes are well-built and maintained. Inverness, Dingwall and Lairg are good centers from which to launch your assault on the wilds of Wester Ross and Sutherland; the nearest center for the island ferries is Fort William.

You can rent an automobile at Godfrey Davis, Aviemore (tel. 810696); MacLennan's, Balivanich, Benbecula (tel. 2191); Macrae & Dick, Station Road, Dingwall (tel. 63223); Gordon's, Birchen, Dornoch (tel. 503); Macrae & Dick, Gordon Square, Fort William (tel. 2345); Macrae & Dick, Railway Terrace, Inverness (tel. 39877); Swan National, Omnibus Station, Inverness (tel. 38084); Avis, Inverness Airport, Dalcross (tel. Ardesier 2787); Gordon Ritchie, Sunny Brae Road, Kirkwall (tel. 3220); Clan Garage, Kyle of Lochalsh (tel. 4328); Lewis Car Rentals, Bayhead Street, Stornoway (tel. 3760); Bolt's, Sumburgh Airport and Lerwick Ferry Terminal, Shetland (tel. Lerwick 2855); Dunnet's, Mansons Lane, Thurso (tel. 3101); and Macrae & Dick, Bridge Street, Wick (tel. 2195).

**By boat.** P & O Ferries, Jamieson's Quay, Aberdeen (tel. 572615) operate daily car-ferries between Aberdeen and Lerwick (Shetland); and between Scrabster (Caithness) and Stromness (Orkney). Caledonian MacBrayne, The Pier, Gourock, Strathclyde (tel. 33755) offer twice-weekly services from Mallaig to the Small Isles; four days a week from Mallaig to Armadale (Skye); a shuttle service on weekdays from Kyle of Lochalsh to Kyleakin (Skye); twice weekly from Sconser (Skye) to Raasay; three days a week from Oban (Strathclyde) to Barra and South Uist; daily from Uig (Skye) to North Uist and Harris; and daily from Ullapool to Stornoway; with appropriate return services. Caledonian MacBrayne also offer summer mini-cruises among the islands, with or without your own automobile.

Jacobite Cruises, Inglis Street, Inverness (tel. 33999) is one of several local companies offering trips on Loch Ness and the Caledonian Canal. Thomas & Bews, John o' Groats (tel. Barrock 619) have day tours of Orkney by boat (a 45-minute crossing) and coach, from John o' Groats.

**By train.** The islands have no railroads. The Region's mainland has three: the main line from Perth to Wick and Thurso, with intermediate stations at 22 places, including Inverness and Dingwall; the Kyle route, Inverness to Kyle of Lochalsh, with many stops at wayside halts (this is considered the most spectacular train ride in Britain); and the line from Fort William to Mallaig, a continuation of the dramatic West Highland route from Glasgow to Fort William.

**By bus.** Highland Omnibuses and Westerbus, both at Farraline Park, Inverness (tel. 33371) provide daily services to Ullapool, Gairloch, Aultbea and Kyle of Lochalsh and, in summer, they run many excursions and tours from Inverness, Dingwall and Fort William.

**By air.** Loganair fly between main airports and Orkney, Shetland and the Outer Hebrides.

**TOURIST INFORMATION.** Remember that throughout the western Highlands and islands Sunday is like a day of national mourning. The only tourist information centers open on Sundays (and then for only a few hours in the afternoon) are at Aviemore, Inverness, Kyle of Lochalsh, Thurso, Torridon, Ullapool and Wick. These centers are also open weekdays, usually 9–8 in summer and 9–6 in winter; as are Culloden, Dornoch, Fort William, Gairloch, Glenfinnan, Muir of Ord, Nairn, Portree (Skye) and Strathpeffer; and in the islands Kirkwall (Orkney).

Other information offices that keep shorter hours, usually weekdays 10–6, summer only, are: Ballachulish, Bettyhill, Bonar Bridge, Broadford (Skye), Carrbridge, Durness, Fort Augustus, Grantown-on-Spey, Helmsdale, Inverewe, John o' Groats, Kingussie, Kintail, Lairg, Lochinver, Mallaig, Newtonmore and Torridon; and in the islands, Castlebay (Barra), Lerwick (Shetland), Lochboisdale (South Uist), Lochmaddy (North Uist), Stornoway (Lewis), Stromness (Orkney) and Tarbert (Harris).

You can "book-a-bed-ahead" or arrange local accomodations at all these offices except Culloden and Inverness.

**FISHING.** Splendid game fishing is to be had on freshwater lochs and streams all over the Region. In Shetland alone there are 200 lochs. Sea trout are found in the bays and sounds of the islands and congregate round the outfalls of the rivers. Almost every Highland and Island hotel offers its guests fishing from a neighboring river bank or from a boat. If you apply to local tourist information offices they will readily organize temporary membership of an angling association with which you may fish several lochs for the whole season for a $5 or $6 membership fee.

There is scarcely any coarse fishing. Sea-angling (skate, whiting, mackerel, cod and other varieties) is popular in the islands and at the mainland resorts of Thurso, Dunnet, Brora, Dornoch, Fortrose and Nairn. Record catches of heavy skate are regularly reported from Shetland.

The Hydro-Electric Board's fish-lift at Torrachilty Dam near Marybank, A832 from Beauly, is open to the public.

**GOLF.** In many areas there is hardly enough level ground for a green, but most east-coast towns and villages have at least one golf course apiece. There is one in Shetland, three in Orkney, two in the Outer Hebrides and one on Skye. The best golf course in the Region, over 360 years old, is Royal

Dornoch (B9167, off A9). It offers full catering facilities, a practice area and a light-aircraft strip adjoining the course. Book a round in advance at about $8. Rather less expensive and exclusive are the fine courses at Nairn (A96), Fort William (A82) and Fortrose and Rosemarkie (A832). Speyside, south of Inverness, is good golfing country and at Newtonmore and Kingussie you will pay about $6 per day.

 **HISTORIC HOUSES AND GARDENS.** Setting aside the rambling fortresses of a few clan chiefs, the Highland and Islands Region is noted more for desolate ruins than civilized castles and country houses. The following attract many visitors:

**Bualadhubh,** Eochar, South Uist (off A865). Traditional "black" house appropriately furnished. Open May–Sept., weekdays, 10–5.

**Cawdor Castle,** Nairn (5 miles south on B9090). Handsomely-kept castle and park of 14th–17th centuries. "Upstairs Downstairs" insight into a building that is still very much a home. Open daily 10–5, May–Sept.

**Dunrobin Castle,** Golspie (A9). Parts date from 14th century, but most is flamboyant 19th century. Rich furnishings. Estate exhibits include steam fire engine and hunting trophies. Open mid-Jun.–Aug., daily, 10.30–5.30.

**Dunvegan Castle,** Isle of Skye (west coast, on A863). Impressive medieval pile stained with blood and alive with the stormy history of the MacLeod clan. Relics include Fairy Flag and Rory O'Mor's Horn. Open May–Sept., daily, 10.30–5; Apr. and Oct., weekdays only, 2–5.

**Fort George,** Ardesier, Inverness (off A96). Not a stately home but an 18th-century garrison headquarters with interesting exhibits of Seaforth, Cameron, and Queen's Own Highlanders regiments, from 1778 to present day. Open Apr.–Sept., Mon.–Fri., 10–6.30; Oct.–Mar., Mon.–Fri., 10–4. (Opening times may be changed, so check ahead.)

Cawdor and Dunvegan have beautiful formal gardens but the horticultural paradise of the Region is **Inverewe,** near Poolewe on the northwest coast (A832). First planted in 1862, it now has many exotica including magnolias, palmettos and tree ferns, all set in a magnificent landscape. It is open daily throughout the year, 9–9. A N.T.S. property.

Among gardens regularly open to the public between May and Sept. are **Kyle House,** Kyleakin, Skye (A850); the **Constabulary Garden,** Nairn (A96); and **Nead-an-Eoin,** Plockton, Loch Carron (unclassified road off A890 or A87). Gardens occasionally open—see local press and posters for details—are the **Castle of Mey,** the Queen Mother's Caithness retreat 7 miles west of John o' Groats (off A836); **Dundonnell** on Little Loch Broom (A832); **Langwell,** Berriedale (A9); and **House of Tongue** (north coast of Sutherland near Tongue, A836).

 **MUSEUMS.** Many isolated community centers have displays of children's work illustrating the old life in their districts. Geological material is collected in town museums, sometimes with costumes and memorabilia of local events. The following short list includes some museums of special character:

**Clan Museums.** These can be found at Kintail on the A87 (Clan MacLennan); at Newtonmore on the A9 (MacPherson); and at Armadale, Skye, on the A851 (Donald).

**Culloden Visitor Center,** Culloden Moor, Inverness (A9). (Actually 6 miles from Inverness on B6009.) Jacobite rebellion, Gaelic history, battle of 1746. Open Jun.–Aug., daily 9.30–8; mid-Apr.–May and Sept.–mid-Oct., daily, 9.30–6.

**Heritage Center,** Bank Row, Wick (A9). Life of old port displayed in a cluster of restored cottages. Opening times under revue.

**Heritage Museum,** Achtercairn, Gairloch (A832). History and folklore of western seaboard. Furnished croft house. Winner of Scottish Museum of the Year award in 1980. Open May–Sept., weekdays, 10–1 and 2–4.

**Highland Folk Museum,** Duke Street, Kingussie (A9). Senior Scottish folk museum, established 1934. Open-air exhibits include "black" house, mill, and turf-built kailyard. Open Apr.–Oct., weekdays 10–6, Sun. 2–6; Nov.–Mar., weekdays only, 10–3.

**Hugh Miller's Cottage,** Church Street, Cromarty (A832). Birthplace and fossil collection of famed writer and geologist (1802–56). Open May–Sept., weekdays, 10–12 and 1–5; also Sun. 2–5, Jun.–Sept. N.T.S.

**Landmark Center,** Carrbridge (A9). Life imaginatively evoked. Multivision show. Open Jun.–Sept., daily 9.30–9.30; Oct.–May, 9.30–5.

**Shetland Museum,** Lower Hillhead, Lerwick, Shetland (A970). Agriculture, fishing, marine biology. Spanish armada relics. Open Mon., Wed., Fri., 10–1, 2.30–5 and 6–8; Tues. 10–1 and 2.30–5; and Thurs. 10–1.

**Strathspey Railway,** The Station, Boat of Garten (A95). Locomotives, rolling stock, railroad history in the north. Steam trains operate between Boat of Garten and Aviemore, an 8-mile trip. Open May–Oct., Sat. and Sun., 9–6; and daily Jul. and Aug.

**Stromness Museum,** Alfred Street, Stromness, Orkney (A965). Whaling, fishing, bird life, naval history. Open weekdays 11–12.30 and 1.30–5, except Thurs. P.M. and month of Feb.

**West Highland Museum,** High Street, Fort William (A82). Relics of Lochaber history, old clan maps, wanderings of Bonnie Prince Charlie. Open mid-Jun.–mid-Sept., weekdays, 9.30–9; mid-Sept.–mid-Jun., 9.30–1 and 2–5.

# INDEX

**(The letter H indicates Hotels and other kinds of accommodations.)**
**(The letter R indicates Restaurants.)**

272

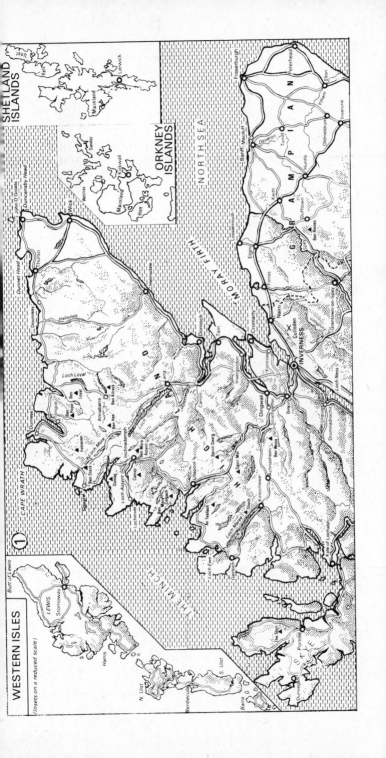

WESTERN ISLES
(insets on a reduced scale)

Butt of Lewis

LEWIS
Stornoway

Harris

N Uist

Benbecula

S Uist

Barra

THE MINCH

① CAPE WRATH

SHETLAND ISLANDS

Unst

Yell

Mainland

Lerwick

ORKNEY ISLANDS

Westray

Sanday

Mainland

Kirkwall

Hoy

John O'Groats
Duncansby Head
Wick

NORTH SEA

Dunnet Head
Thurso
Dounreay
Halladale

Durness
Kinlochbervie

Loch Loyal

Ben Klibreck

Altnaharra

Ben Hee

Ben Hope

Foinaven

Ben Stack

Loch More

Ben More Assynt

Quinag

Loch Assynt

Lochinver

Canisp

Suilven

Cul Mor

Ullapool

Helmsdale

Lairg

Dornoch

Tain
Invergordon

Cromarty

Nairn

Forres

Elgin
Lossiemouth

MORAY FIRTH

GRAMPIAN

Fraserburgh
Peterhead

Ellon

Inverurie
Oldmeldrum

Ythan

Turriff
Huntly

Banff Macduff

Deveron

Keith

Dufftown

Ben Rinnes

Spey

Grantown-on-Spey

Carron

An Teallach

Ben Dearg

Sgurr Mor

Ben Wyvis

Strathpeffer

Dingwall

Beauly

Drumnadrochit

Loch Ness

INVERNESS

Culloden ✕

Achnasheen

Lochcarron

Kyle of Lochalsh

Loch Maree

Loch Ewe

Gairloch

Slioch

Loch Carron

SKYE

The Storr

Portree

Dunvegan

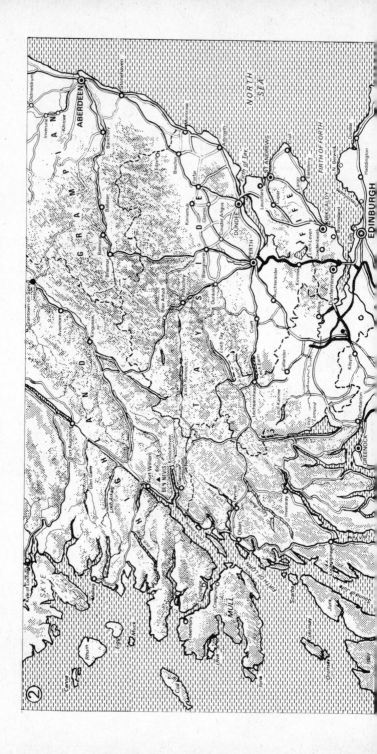

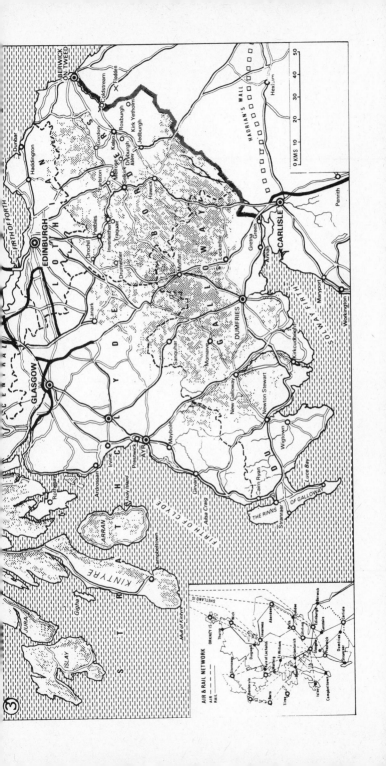

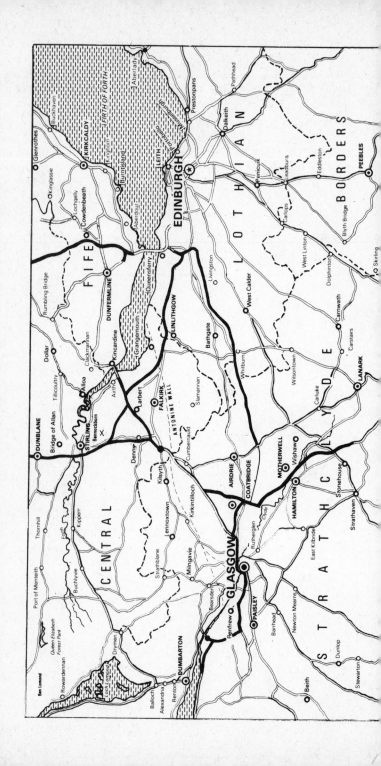